Best Places
to Stay in
New England

The Best Places to Stay Series

Best Places to Stay in America's Cities
Kenneth Hale-Wehmann, Editor

Best Places to Stay in Asia
Jerome E. Klein

Best Places to Stay in California
Marilyn McFarlane

Best Places to Stay in the Caribbean
Bill Jamison and Cheryl Alters Jamison

Best Places to Stay in Florida
Christine Davidson

Best Places to Stay in Hawaii
Bill Jamison and Cheryl Alters Jamison

Best Places to Stay in New England
Third Edition
Christina Tree and Kimberly Grant

Best Places to Stay in the Pacific Northwest
Marilyn McFarlane

Best Places to Stay in the Southwest
Gail Barber Rickey

Best Places to Stay in New England

THIRD EDITION

Christina Tree
and Kimberly Grant

Bruce Shaw, Editorial Director

Houghton Mifflin Company · Boston

For information about permission to reproduce selections
from this book, write to Permissions, Houghton Mifflin
Company, 2 Park Street, Boston, Massachusetts 02108.

ISSN: 1048-5449
ISBN: 0-395-54545-5

Printed in the United States of America

Illustrations by Chris Schuh
Maps by Charles Bahne
Design by Robert Overholtzer

This book was prepared in conjunction
with Harvard Common Press.

HAD 10 9 8 7 6 5 4 3 2 1

To Christopher John Davis
                    — C.T.

To L. M. Otero

                    — K.G.

We would like to thank Bruce Shaw
for his continuing interest and support.

Contents

Introduction

This isn't simply an inn book. We have looked at the full range of places to stay in New England, from grand old resorts to working farms, from spas to youth hostels, from some of the most expensive places to some of the best bargains. This book is for the enterprising traveler, willing to wander off the beaten path. Some of our suggestions are well known, but many are found in no other guidebook, the result of more than twenty years of scouring New England.

The book's organization is unorthodox. Places are grouped by their nature — Romantic Getaway, Family Find, or Beachside — rather than by their location. This approach was suggested by experience. Christina Tree has been writing about New England for the *Boston Globe* travel section for more than twenty years and she is frequently asked for advice on a place to "get away to." Usually the person isn't set on being in one specific spot but may wish to be on an island or by the sea. More often, the quest is for outstanding food or a romantic atmosphere or for a special place to go as a family.

To orient readers, we have also keyed the lodging places to state maps in the front of the book, so you can tell quickly what we cover on Cape Cod or around Tanglewood, in Boston or Bar Harbor.

Obviously our criteria differ when judging the "best" Farms and "best" City Stops. Our primary standards are cleanliness, the palpable presence of a host (be it manager or owner), and a conviction that we would like to stay in the place for more than one night. These entries are not, we should note, paid advertisements. *We ask the places included in this book for no fee of any kind, nor do we require them to buy or sell this book in order to be included.* In contrast to the practices of many of the guides on the market, we also personally visit each place, and if management changes while the book is in production, the entry is removed until we can recheck it.

In this edition of the book, we should also note that all the research has been done by the authors. Christina Tree, who has been the book's primary author since its inception, has also written four other New England guidebooks and still writes regularly for the *Globe*. She is also a contributing editor to *The Original New England Guide* and *New England Living*. Kimberly Grant, who is a professional photographer as well as a travel writer, comes to this edition as a co-author after contributing significantly to the first two editions.

We would like to point out that, had this book been written a decade ago, some of the categories would have been different. There would have been few Bed-and-Breakfasts or Resort Villages, for instance. And there would have been many more Family Finds. Even since 1985, when we did the research for the first edition of the book, there have been some changes. We began, for instance, by noting whether places offered all private baths or not. Now roughly 90% of the entries do and, except for the smaller places, we simply note those that don't.

Over the past few years many inns have been refurbished and have raised their prices. Innkeepers tell us that travelers want more and are willing to pay for it. Certainly there seem to be many more inns and B&Bs with wing chairs and four-poster beds, fluffy towels, and $80-$250 room rates. There are also a number of new condominium resorts that offer families the best of resort facilities on a per-unit (not per-person) basis.

On the other hand, a number of fine old resorts, large and small, are maintaining the same standards and traditions that have attracted generations of devotees. But very few now include all three meals in their rates. Just a few years ago, AP (American Plan) and FAP (Full American Plan) were seen in most resort brochures. Now the terms have become so rare that we have dropped them altogether, substituting "all meals included" where appropriate.

The terms that we do use to describe meals are MAP (Modified American Plan), which include breakfast and dinner, and occasionally EP (European Plan), an elegant way to say that no meals are included in the rates. B&B (Bed-and-Breakfast) means that breakfast is included.

There's more to the jargon of room rates, and we have tried our best to avoid it. We have indicated whether the price is per person or per couple and noted instances where the price of the room changes with the number of people in it (single or double occupancy).

When it comes to describing the form of payment, we assume that you know that your cash and traveler's checks are acceptable anywhere and your personal check, almost anywhere. We simply note "Major credit cards" to indicate that the basic ones—American Express, MasterCard, and Visa—are accepted. If American Express is not accepted, we note the cards that are. We have supplied fax numbers where possible because many places now accept deposits in the form of checks sent by fax.

There is also the little-noted detail of room and meals tax, which is inescapable. It varies from state to state and, in Massachusetts, within the state. In 1990 it goes like this: Connecticut, 7.5%; Massachusetts, 5.7%, but a 4% town tax is added in Boston, on Cape Cod, and on Nantucket and Martha's Vineyard; Maine, 7%; New Hampshire, 8%; Rhode Island, 11.6%; and Vermont, 7%. In addition, a number of places also add a service charge or a gratuity (tip), which can run as high as 15%. We have tried to note high gratuities wherever we found them, but it's been difficult to catch every instance.

We have done our very best to provide you with accurate and up-to-date information. As is true with any guidebook, certain information changes quickly. Please be sure to call and make reservations, if you can, at these places. And we suggest that you draw up a list of the four or five points that most concern you when you stay somewhere, and ask the person with whom you are making your reservation about them. If money is important, be sure that you know what your room rate will be. If noise bothers you, be sure that you ask for a quiet room. We have found over and over again that we get what we ask for.

We are proud of *Best Places to Stay in New England*. It's the most comprehensive list of outstanding lodging places in this region. Please let us know what you think.

We would like to thank Bruce Shaw for his role as the book's co-creator and as the publisher who has parlayed *Best Places* into a series that now includes nine books. We would also like to thank Luise Erdmann, our manuscript editor at Houghton Mifflin, for her patience and skill.

—C.T.
—K.G.

January 1990

Maps

Maine

Vermont

New Hampshire

Massachusetts

Connecticut

Rhode Island

Bulne '87

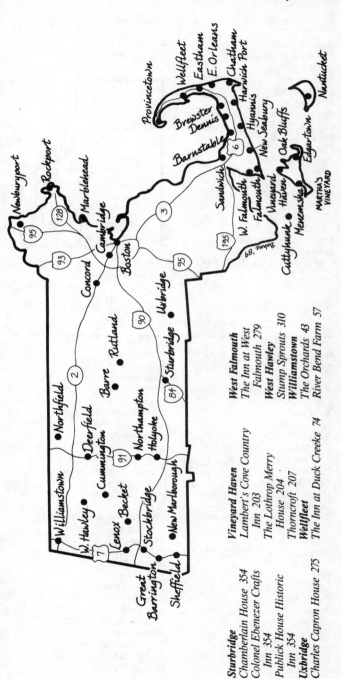

Sturbridge
Chamberlain House 354
Colonel Ebenezer Crafts
    Inn 354
Publick House Historic
    Inn 354
Uxbridge
Charles Capron House 275

Vineyard Haven
Lambert's Cove Country
    Inn 203
The Lothrop Merry
    House 204
Thorncroft 207
Wellfleet
The Inn at Duck Creeke 74

West Falmouth
The Inn at West
    Falmouth 279
West Hawley
Stump Sprouts 310
Williamstown
The Orchards 43
River Bend Farm 57

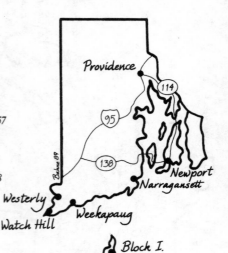

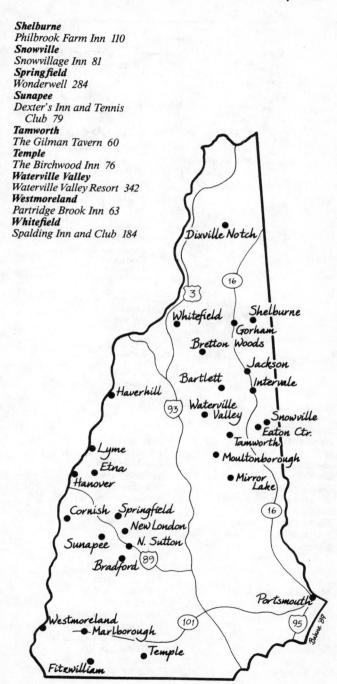

Vermont

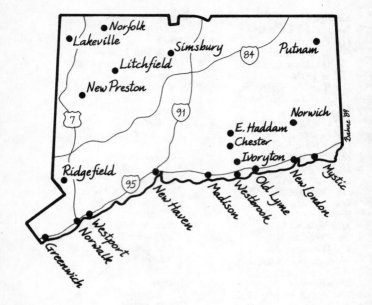

Connecticut

Beachside

These beach bum specials are either right on or within an easy sandal shuffle of sand.

Connecticut

Madison Beach Hotel
94 West Wharf Road
Exit 61 on I-95
Madison, Connecticut 06443
203-245-1404

Innkeepers: Mr. and Mrs. Henry M. Cooney, Mr. and Mrs. Roben P. Bagdasrian
35 rooms, 6 suites
$65-$120 per couple, $65-$105 single, $150-$195 suites; less off-season
All 3 meals served
Major credit cards
Children welcome
Open March through December

This is as close as you can stay to a beach anywhere in New England. The Madison Beach is a rare survivor among Connecticut's old wooden Sound-side hotels and it's a beauty, built around the turn of the century and totally, tastefully renovated. There are now only 35 spacious rooms (reduced from 52), each with a bath and a water view. In 1989 an annex was added, containing three Victorian-style rooms, all with water views, too.

The beach itself is more than just an amenity. It's not too large but it has character, curving to a rocky point and backed by beach grass. Like the broad expanse of Connecticut Sound, it seems to change with the hour and season. This particular strip belongs to the hotel, but a few steps away there is also the town's West Wharf, a favorite fishing place with its own small beach, overlooking a line of beachside cottages and the grand old Madison Beach Club.

At the Madison Beach you can play lord of your own beachside manor. While the most reasonably priced, first-floor rooms look onto the front porch (which runs the length of the hotel), the second-, third-, and fourth-floor rooms each have a private patch of the upper porch. Most rooms lack closets (there are corner racks instead) but otherwise offer all the atmosphere and comfort you could wish. The furnishings include refinished oak dressers from the old hotel, bamboo and wicker headboards and chairs, genuinely interesting artwork, desks, and brass bedside reading lights. Each has cable TV and air conditioning. The second rooms of the suites are small but inviting spaces with sinks, fridges, and tables (no stoves).

The wainscoted lobby is filled with white wicker; it's bright and comfortable enough to tempt you to sit a spell, watching the stream of beachgoers in summer or just looking out to sea in winter. The porch beyond is lined with rockers from the hotel's previous life.

The Wharf bar and restaurant is in a separate wing, apart from the guest rooms, a good thing since it has a strong local following. The luncheon menu ranges from BLTs to softshell crabs, the dinner menu, from fried seafood to lobster thermidor.

The town of Madison actually offers the lion's share of Connecticut beachfront. State-owned Hammonasset Beach is a great place to walk and bird-watch as well as swim, and there are fine town strands. But there are no other hotels. This is a low-key, private kind of resort town with a classic Colonial common, a Main Street line of stores, and a dozen blocks of summer mansions and cottages in an assortment of architectural styles, many with water views.

Water's Edge Inn & Resort

1525 Boston Post Road
Westbrook, Connecticut 06498
203-399-5901
800-222-5901
Fax 203-399-6172

Manager: Paul Cullen
136 units; 33 rooms and suites in the main house and library building; the others, 1- and 2-bedroom time-share condominium units
Rooms $140-$190, suites $160-$250, condominiums $200-$250; less with packages, much less in winter
All 3 meals served

Major credit cards
Children welcome; special rates and activities
No pets
Open year-round

In its previous life, from the 1920s through the '50s, this was Bill Hahn's, a modest stone building with large windows overlooking Long Island Sound. In those days it was patronized by and featured actors and entertainers, unknowns like Woody Allen, Art Carney, and Barbra Streisand to name a few.

The original building is now a small part of the many-windowed mansion that is now Water's Edge Inn & Resort, set on 15 landscaped acres that roll down to its private beach. There's a spacious, multitiered dining room in which all three meals are served. The à la carte dinner menu includes entrées such as brace of roasted quail with walnut rosemary mousse and roasted sweet garlic ($21.50).

The guest rooms are large, decorated in reproduction antiques, all with TVs and phones. The higher prices are for the water views. The condominium units have fireplaces and full kitchens, and many have water views.

The big attraction here is obviously the private beach, but there is also an outdoor pool and tennis courts. A new spa annex also includes an indoor pool and exercise facilities. Golf is available nearby.

Maine

The Dunes on the Waterfront
P.O. Box 917
Route 1
Ogunquit, Maine 03907
207-646-2612

Owners: The Perkins family
19 cottages, 17 motel units
$78-$100 for 2-4 persons in cottages; $60-$90 per couple in motel rooms
3-day minimum required during July, August, and holiday weeks; cottages available only by the week from mid-June to mid-September, with a 2-week minimum during July and August
No meals served; kitchens in cottages
MasterCard, Visa
Children welcome

No pets
Open mid-May through Columbus Day

The Dunes dates from the '30s, a period when hundreds of overnight cottage complexes—the forerunners of motels—were built along Route 1 in Maine. It has remained in the same family and has always been the finest of its kind, holding its own as most of the other cottages have disappeared. It is still one of the nicest places a family can find to stay in Ogunquit and one of the most popular of Maine's South Coast resorts.

To begin with, the location is unbeatable—right on the tidal Ogunquit River with a view of the high sand dunes beyond on Ogunquit Beach. You enter from busy Route 1, but the cottages are set well back amid 12 lawn-covered acres. There is a small "sitting" beach, a swimming dock, and rowboats. At high tide you can row across to the main beach, and at low tide it's an easy wade—a luxurious access to the 3-mile strand for which other people pay steep parking fees. Dunes guests, moreover, have access to the least populous part of this spectacular beach.

This is a great place for families. There is a shuffleboard court, a croquet ground, an outdoor swimming pool, and swings.

The cottages are a vanishing breed: white with green trim and pine walls inside. Some one- and two-bedroom units have a combination living room and bedroom with a fireplace; there is also electric heat, air conditioning, a kitchen, and a screened porch.

The motel units vary in size. Some have just two twin beds; others have two doubles. All have air conditioning and TV.

Massachusetts

Cliffside Beach Club
P.O. Box 449
Jefferson Avenue
Nantucket, Massachusetts 02554
508-228-0618

Manager: Robert Currie
22 rooms, 1 3-bedroom apartment, 4 studio units, suites, 1 cottage
In season (late June–Labor Day): Rooms, $220-$335; apartment and suites, $425-$525
Off-season: Rooms, $145-$195; apartment and suites: $280-$320

Room rates based on double occupancy; cottage and suites
based on 4, the apartment on 6; additional guest charge,
$20 per night; Continental breakfast included; multiday
minimum on summer weekends; add 9.7% tax and 3%
service charge
Lunch and dinner also served
No credit cards
Children welcome
No pets
Open late May through mid-October

Offering both hotel rooms and luxury housekeeping units, the
Cliffside is Nantucket's only hotel with exclusive accommodations directly on the beach while being just a 15-minute walk to
town. It is clearly a place for the beach lover, although tennis is
available only a 5-minute walk away, and a good French café,
right on the water, is part of the complex.

The Cliffside used to be a private club. The lobby, the former
clubhouse, has a vaulted ceiling with lovely quilts hanging from
it. Airy and bright, it looks out to a wooden veranda over the
beach and to the sea beyond. Guests are assigned their own
places on the beach so that there is no fear of overcrowding.

The rooms incorporate a traditional exterior design with a
contemporary interior. The building's cedar shingles, redwood
trim, and southern yellow pine decks blend magnificently with
the beach. The arrangement of the buildings—with the beach
as a focal point and brilliant green, yellow, and blue umbrellas
on the beach—is the stuff of a painting. The woodwork in each
of the rooms is outstanding; many have custom-milled cedar.
All the furnishings were designed by Nantucket craftspersons.
Sixty-year-old beaded hemlock was reclaimed from the old
Beach Club changing rooms, and heart pine from old South
Station in Boston was also used. The rooms are designed for
summer, decorated with very simple upholstery and quilts for
the beds. The cathedral ceilings give a feel of airiness, and
subtle lighting and local artists' prints contribute to a relaxed
feeling.

Hargood House
493 Commercial Street
Provincetown, Massachusetts 02657
508-487-1324

Owner: Hal Goodstein
19 apartments
$88-$160 per day; $595-$1,075 per week

1-week minimum in season; 2 nights off-season
No meals served; kitchens in apartments
Major credit cards
Children over 10 welcome in season only
Declawed cats and small dogs accepted with advance approval
Open year-round

Devoted guests know a good thing when they find it, and thus it's essential to book reservations well in advance (a season ahead, actually!) for the Hargood House. This unique apartment complex is literally on the water's edge, just a short walk to the bustling center of town, yet sufficiently far to avoid the noise at night. Since the longtime owner is with the Chamber of Commerce, you'll never want for information on what to see and do.

The complex consists of four restored Cape houses, beautifully landscaped with flowers and shrubs. Three are around a spacious green lawn, which backs a nice patch of sandy beach on the harbor; the fourth is across the street. Water views there are limited, but guests, of course, can use all the facilities on the ocean side.

The owners have certainly capitalized on the natural resources of sun and sea. All the one- and two-bedroom apartments use their space well, and each is furnished individually and somewhat eccentrically. Imaginative remodeling reigns supreme here. Spacious decks and large windows are the norm, and all are heated, utterly clean, and have a private entrance, tasteful furnishings, a complete kitchen with stemware, good china, and a dishwasher, and a modern bath. Some have alcove beds, beamed or cathedral ceilings, fireplaces, and eat-in kitchens. The rate card details the special features of each room accurately.

On the decks, lawn, and beach there are more than enough chairs and umbrellas to go around. It's a pleasure not to have to fight the crowds at the beach.

The Inn on Sea Street
358 Sea Street
Hyannis, Massachusetts 02601
508-775-8030

Innkeepers: Lois Nelson and J. B. Whitehead
6 rooms (3 with private bath)
$55-$80 per couple, including breakfast
Major credit cards

Children over 16 welcome
No pets
Open April to mid-November

On a street lined with guest houses of varying quality and services, the Inn on Sea Street stands above the crowd — everything inside is a delightful surprise. The amenities found here would easily cost much more elsewhere, but the innkeepers prefer to give guests plenty of reasons to return time after time. Young couples tend to be the steady clientele.

This small white Victorian inn exudes informality and the "stuff" of a bygone era. The most interesting guest room, to the left of the front door, was once a sun room. When Labor Day arrives and the nights grow cooler, it is not made available unless specifically requested. (It can get warm here in the summer, though.) The furnishings are light and airy; shades, of course, can be drawn over the panes of glass that make up the walls. One gets the feeling here of being young again, sleeping at Grandma's house in the country; the night feels closer and bigger.

Two spacious rooms upstairs in the front of the house are quite special. They share a bathroom that has an old-fashioned tub and a black-and-white-checked floor. The third guest room upstairs has a private bath, but you must walk down a private stairway to reach it — fanciful except, perhaps, in the middle of the night. As is common on the Cape, the floors of the rooms have been painted beige, blue, or white or left a natural color. Choice antique pieces have been placed carefully, and Oriental rugs are scattered throughout the house. Downstairs, toward the rear of the house, is a large guest room with a lovely lace bedspread and its own bath. The most private room, with a canopy bed and TV, has its own entrance at the back of the barn.

In the evening, the innkeepers will light a fire in the living room hearth and then leave, turning the TV, games, and books over to the guests. It's an extremely homey and comfortable room.

A breakfast of fruit, cheese, eggs, granola, and excellent coffee and tea is served at four small antique tables. Lace and muted wallpaper relax the senses. Outside, under a large tree, is a nice place to extend your morning coffee.

Hyannis is a hopping town, with shops, live theater, and plenty of good restaurants. The beach, of course, is quite close. Ferries to Martha's Vineyard and Nantucket leave from Hyannis, so you might plan a day trip to one of the islands.

Nauset House Inn
Box 774
Beach Road
East Orleans, Massachusetts 02643
508-255-2195

Innkeepers: Al and Diane Johnson
14 rooms (8 with private bath)
$35-$80 per couple, including breakfast
MasterCard, Visa
Children over 12 welcome
No pets
Open April through October

Country casual and hospitable best describe this inn, a family-owned and operated 1807 farmhouse. A total of three buildings provide a good deal of privacy. Nauset House also happens to be a 10-minute walk from spectacular Nauset Beach. The National Seashore isn't far; neither are walking paths and bike trails.

The large, comfy living room is a blend of styles. A handmade afghan is draped over the couch; a working fireplace roars in the off-season; the glass-topped coffee table displays beach memorabilia the hosts have picked up — sand, shells, and the like; a collection of blue glass graces one windowsill. There are lots of books, a game table, and another sitting area for relaxed conversation. It's the kind of room people aren't afraid to use. A glass of wine is complimentary in the evening.

Through the living room is a low-ceilinged dining room with a brick floor and dried flowers hanging over the fireplace. Served at two long tables, a Continental breakfast will run $2.50 and a full, $4.50. The BYOB bar is set up in here. A sliding glass door provides easy access to the sunny brick patio with lawn chairs. Guests can sit in the shade of an ancient apple tree and share the sun with a jar of steeping sun tea.

Through the breakfast room, a thick, arched doorway leads to a surprise. In 1907 a working conservatory was dismantled in Greenwich, Connecticut, and reassembled here piece by piece. Grapevines are threaded through trelliswork, and white wicker is set amid the almost tropical plantings and flowers. Stained glass panels, made by the hosts' daughter, make a dramatic statement.

The cozy guest rooms are comfortably furnished with a mix of antiques. The Rosebud Room, off the living room by itself, is our favorite. It has a small deck overlooking the back patio. Three rooms upstairs in the main house share one bath, as do the three rooms downstairs. The rooms in the carriage houses all have private baths. The ceiling borders, by the way, are hand-painted rather than stenciled.

Wauwinet

P.O. Box 2580
Nantucket, Massachusetts 02554
508-228-0145
800-426-8718

General manager: Russell Cleveland
40 rooms, 5 cottages
$250-$450 per couple per room, $450-$675 per cottage
  mid-June through Labor Day; $195-$390 per room,
  $375-$575 per cottage, spring and fall; $35 per extra person
  in room; Continental breakfast included
3-night minimum on July, August, and holiday weekends
All 3 meals served
Major credit cards
Children welcome
No pets
No smoking rooms and handicapped access rooms available
Open late April through October

The Wauwinet dates from the 1850s, but it underwent a multi-million-dollar transformation in the mid-1980s and is now one of the most expensive inns in the Northeast. What hasn't changed is its location, the most isolated and dramatic of any inn on Nantucket. It's at the end of the hardtop, as close as you can build to the narrow, northeastern tip of the island, facing the quiet, beach-rimmed bay and backed by the dune-lined open Atlantic. Only four-wheel drives can travel the 5-mile sandspit from here to Great Point, a haven for fishermen.

This was never a "grand hotel," and although it's three stories high, it gives the impression of a low-slung, low-key seaside retreat. The focal point of the public rooms is a broad, wicker-filled porch overlooking the lawn stretching to the beach. There is also a library and living room, both brightly decorated in flowered chintz with *trompe l'oeil* touches and masses of fresh flowers. Audubon prints, original paintings, and unusual antiques everywhere, even in the hallways. There isn't a dull or dusty corner in the place.

Frankly, we find dull corners soothing and the Wauwinet decor a shade too bright and busy. But, given the rates, guests may demand this sense of plenty.

Each room has an exceptional antique or two and any number of decorating touches. Superior rooms (from $340 per couple in summer) have water views, deluxe rooms (from $410) offer sitting areas as well. The cottage suites (from $450), across the road near the tennis courts, have no views at all but do accommodate from four to eight guests and come with kitchens and fireplaces. Of course, the bathrooms are magnificent, replete with thick towels and Crabtree & Evelyn accessories. The rates include a Continental breakfast served in the room. A full breakfast is also served at the inn's restaurant, Topper's.

Blessedly removed from the inn proper, Topper's is one of the most popular spots on Nantucket; guests are advised to reserve for dinner when they book a room. The decor is opulent and the menu is "nouveau American." You might begin with wild mushroom strudel with fresh herb beurre blanc and Nantucket Bay scallops bedded in ginger- and garlic-flavored vegetables. If it's available, try the prickly pear sorbet for dessert.

The Wauwinet offers a number of small luxuries, like secluded tennis courts, an intimate wine bar, sailing, fishing rods, bicycles, croquet and van service into town. It also has a staff of 120 to serve no more than 80 guests.

Wequassett Inn

Pleasant Bay
Chatham, Massachusetts 02633
508-432-5400
800-352-7169

Manager: Clive C. L. Chu
103 rooms
$150-$200 per couple, rooms; $275, suite, EP

All 3 meals served
Major credit cards
Children welcome
No pets
Open late May through mid-October

The Wequassett Inn is a complex of nineteen buildings with views of Pleasant Bay, Round Cove, and the woods. Tennis enthusiasts feel right at home, as do people who enjoy manicured lawns and luxury living. You can enjoy a moderate sense of privacy here, depending on where you stay.

There is a variety of accommodations. Cape cottages, scattered among groves of pine trees, have two, three, or four guest rooms each. Most are quite near the water and have picturesque views of the sailboat-dotted cove. Relaxing on the private wooden decks appears to be one of the most popular activities late in the afternoon. The decor is country Americana, with easy chairs and homey touches of dried flowers in baskets. There are also four long buildings of either two or three stories. The upper stories have private decks, while the lower floors have sliding doors opening onto the grassy lawn. Some overlook the five tennis courts and woods.

The renowned restaurant serves three New England and Continental meals daily in a lovely setting overlooking Pleasant Bay. Brunch is a very popular event. The restaurant and bar are in a historic Colonial house, named Square Top because of its roofline. Flagstone walks lined with colorful, abundant flower beds connect the public buildings.

A large heated swimming pool and a bar sit at the wide end of a strip of sand that reaches out to Clam Point. There's plenty of sand and space for everyone. Swim and sun on the beach along Pleasant Bay or take one of the launches across to the famed Nauset Beach. A walk out to the edge of the dock at sunset is a special treat. Novice and experienced sailors alike can join the sailing program.

Off the premises a few miles away, Chatham is teeming with things to do: famed restaurants, a few historic sights, a band concert on the green, shops, a fish pier, a lighthouse, or a trip to Monomoy Island for bird-watching.

White Horse Inn
500 Commercial Street
Provincetown, Massachusetts 02657
508-487-1790

Innkeeper: Frank Schaefer
12 rooms (2 with private bath), 6 studios
$50–$90 per couple, EP
3-night minimum for studios in season
No meals served
No credit cards
Children accepted
No pets
Open year-round

The White Horse Inn embodies the spirit of Provincetown: it's a bit bohemian, artistically aware, and very casual. In season, guests are active: sunning themselves, sipping coffee at outdoor cafés, and people-watching. In the off-season, guests tend more toward quiet moments and beachcombing. Through it all, the stable presence of Frank Schaefer (he's been here since 1963) helps keep things grounded.

This two-hundred-year-old captain's house, in the quiet East End, is crisp and white, with blue shutters and a yellow door, but the facade doesn't belie the eclectic interior. The living room is filled to the brim with original works of art (most by local artists), antiques, enormous jade trees, and a wood-burning stove.

The rooms in the main house, with low ceilings and shellacked floors, are rather simple. Ten of the rooms share three baths (some with those old-fashioned metal shower stalls).

The best accommodations are the studio apartments, in a separate wing, where you'll find things such things as Eugene O'Neill's stained glass windows, Isabella Rossellini's writing table, woodcarvings that have been used as wallboard or door moldings, and a slab of marble from the Bank of Boston that's now a writing table (perfectly placed, by the way, in front of a small window that peeks out onto the ocean). One studio has a sliding glass door that opens onto a private deck.

Frank doesn't offer breakfast because there are so many great little places in town. In the backyard is a garden, a hibachi for guests to use, and a bike rack. Directly across from the house is a path that leads right down to the water. This is quite a find.

■ *See also:* Chatham Bars Inn, Chatham, Massachusetts; Katama Shores, Edgartown, Massachusetts

Rhode Island

The Ocean House
Bluff Avenue
Watch Hill, Rhode Island 02891
401-348-8161

General manager: E. F. Brankert
59 rooms
$156-$188 per couple, MAP
2-night stay on weekends required
Lunch also served
MasterCard, Visa
Children over 3 welcome
No pets
Open late June through Labor Day

Here is a huge old resort set above a beautiful long, sandy beach in posh, residential Watch Hill. Although the Ocean House is not maintained as opulently as some of the few remaining grand old New England resorts, it is certainly a great place for kids, since they can simply walk down the lawn and onto the beach. The hotel has a lifeguard on its beach; bring your own towels.

Accommodations are in standard (more often than not with twin beds), clean, motel-like rooms. Be sure to ask for one with that gorgeous water view.

The best aspect of the inn, though, is the common rooms. The ceilings are extremely high, the furniture and decor connote another era, and Art Deco chandeliers hang in the lobby.

The dining room has spectacular ocean views, and there is an enormous wraparound glassed-in porch that gives you the impression of being on a huge ocean liner. Lunch is also served, so you'll never have to leave the hotel except to wander to and from the beach. Dress is informal at dinner, but jeans aren't acceptable.

Change of Pace

Pace rather than place is the key to what all four of these options offer. Whether under sail, on a bike, or on foot, these vacations set you in motion — slow motion.

All New England

American Youth Hostels
1020 Commonwealth Avenue
Boston, Massachusetts 02215
617-731-5430

29 hostels throughout New England
$6 (average) per person per night
Membership fee (yearly, mandatory): $26 single, $36 family,
$11 youth (age 17 and under)
3-night maximum stay (unless a hostel is not crowded)
Cooking facilities available
Cash only
Children welcome
Pets discouraged
Opening dates vary, but 13 are open year-round

In a nutshell, AYH offers simple, safe, supervised, inexpensive, and friendly accommodations in areas of scenic, cultural, or historic significance, and membership is open to people of all ages. The idea is that through hosteling, travelers from all over the world have an opportunity to exchange stories, ideas, and practical travel information.

Hostels can be found in castles, farms, old mansions, a Coast Guard station, or even a retired sailing vessel. They are generally closed during the day, even when the weather is bad. Though the standards and rules are fixed, individual hostels vary as much as the personalities of the resident volunteer managers.

Dormitories are segregated by sex and can have from 4 to 20 beds per room. Some hostels have "family rooms"; if so, this fact will be noted in the hostel directory. You must bring or rent a "sleep sack," which is basically a double-size sheet that has been folded in half and sewn around the bottom and three quarters of the way up. It should completely enclose you and have a place where a pillow can be attached. Hostelers are sometimes permitted to use two sheets and a pillowcase. If you don't want to make your own sleep sack, the Greater Boston Council sells a lightweight one.

It's generally expected that hostelers will contribute to the cleaning of the hostel. Assigned chores, rarely more than ten to fifteen minutes' worth, can be anything from sweeping floors to cleaning an oven to raking the lawn. This way, people tend to feel more of a sense of responsibility for their community.

Whether it's winter in the mountains or summer on Cape Cod, reservations are a good idea in high season.

In Massachusetts, there are hostels in Boston; Martha's Vineyard and Nantucket; Truro, Eastham, and Hyannis (Cape Cod); Fall River; and Littleton, Dudley, and Northfield in the central part of the state. The sole Rhode Island hostel is in Kingston. In northwestern-central Connecticut there are hostels in Lakeside, Windsor, and Bolton. There's one hostel in Bar Harbor, Maine, and three others in Maine's interior: Greenville Junction, Monson, and Carmel. Three more are scattered throughout New Hampshire: in Peterborough in the south, in Raymond (near Manchester), and up north in Randolph. Vermont's hostels are well situated: in Woodford and Stowe near the Appalachian Trail; in the capital, Montpelier; in the Northeast Kingdom in Craftsbury Common; in the college town of Burlington, near Lake Champlain; and in Ludlow, Rochester, and Underhill Center.

Membership is required before staying at the hostels. Once this fee is processed (it takes approximately two weeks) you are free to use hostels all over the U.S. and the world for one year. You will receive a handbook outlining the directions to and facilities of each hostel. A newsletter will list 200 or so inexpensive day, weekend, and extended outdoor trips suitable for people of all ages and physical development.

Elderhostel

Elderhostel National Headquarters
80 Boylston Street, Suite 400
Boston, Massachusetts 02116
617-426-8056

135 locations, thousands of programs
$225-$250 per 6-day program, including meals and lodging

No credit cards
Most programs in summer, some year-round
Minimum age: 60

You can stay in seaside estates or White Mountain lodges, in North Woods cabins or on New England's most famous campuses. Your morning classes can range from Shakespeare to American Painting to the Sociology of Gossip. The cost of your program, which includes three squares and extensive sports facilities, equals that for one day in an elegant country inn or Boston hotel. The only hitch is that you have to be age 60 or older.

One of the world's most successful travel concepts, the non-profit Elderhostel program was launched in the summer of 1975 with 200 students on five New Hampshire campuses. In 1989, more than 200,000 people were enrolled in 1,500 places around the world.

In New England alone there are now thousands of Elderhostel programs at 135 places. More than half are on prep school and college campuses, the remainder are in a variety of low-profile, highly rewarding places. There are art courses aboard coastal schooners, biology courses in backwoods cabins and pottery courses in quiet hill towns.

In Massachusetts, for instance, you can attend courses in Film Across Cultures and a Brief History of Time at Hampshire College in Amherst or Politics and Media at Emmanuel College in Boston, while in Maine you might want to check out the Hersey Retreat on Penobscot Bay, where the sell-out course is Writing a Life Story—Yours and Mine. Or visit Ferry Beach, a church-owned conference center near Kennebunkport, Maine, where the popular course is Exploring Southern Coast Lore.

The largest, most popular program is at the Episcopal Conference Center in Ivoryton, Connecticut, a 650-acre compound with its own lake and courses ranging from New Frontiers of the Mind to Discovering Nature from a Canoe.

The typical Elderhostel program offers three usually very different classes. Most participants rate the rewards of meeting other active, older people who are interested in learning and new experiences right up there with the beauty of the locations and joys of study.

If you are at least 50 and can't wait to be 60 to join, you can accompany someone 60 or older to an Elderhostel program.

Maine

Maine Windjammer Association
Box 317
Rockport, Maine 04856
800-624-6380

12 two-masted schooners

Schooner *Stephen Taber*
Windjammer Wharf
Rockland, Maine 04841
207-596-6528
800-999-7352

$425-$575 per person, including all meals for 6 days
3-day cruises also available
Sailings from Camden, Rockland, and Rockport Harbor,
  Maine
Children over 11 welcome on some vessels
No pets
Sailings from Memorial Day weekend to mid-October

The sting of a salt breeze and the warmth of the sun, the scent of pine trees and the aroma of blueberry pie from a woodstove. For windjammer passengers, Maine isn't seen through a windshield or from an inn's window. They taste, feel, smell, and savor the essence of coastal Maine.

Of course, it doesn't happen overnight. Passengers arrive on Sunday evening, nervously eyeing the two to three dozen strangers with whom they'll be sharing a week under sail.

But on Monday morning they cast off in more ways than one. Wearing old jeans and sneakers (the uniform of the windjammer fleet), they help haul a line, watch the tall sails fill, and feel the rhythmic pull of the schooner as it gets under way. They pick up a book but never get into it. There's too much to see — harbor sails to starboard and islands all around. They simply steep in life on Penobscot Bay. As the wind and sun drop, the schooner eases into a hidden harbor.

Supper is hearty Yankee fare, maybe fish chowder and beef stew with plenty of fresh cornbread, served on the shiny long tables of the galley. There is usually a clambake on a deserted island one evening, too. After supper, the vessel's yawl is available for a foray into a quiet village. As the moon rises there is singing and yarn-swapping back on board.

By Wednesday the days begin to blur. The sailors watch cormorants, spot a minke whale, and see eagles circling over island nests. The weather changes constantly, and occasional fog, even rain, is all part of the week's adventure.

On Saturday morning a sadness settles over the boat. Sunday's strangers are now friends. No one wants to leave.

Choosing a vessel is the most difficult part of a windjammer vacation. The twelve members of the association are all proud, trim vessels with their own followings. All share the distinction of being among the few dozen schooners currently plying a coast that once saw literally thousands of their prototypes. The *Stephen Taber*, listed separately, has a strong following of its own and so has withdrawn, after many years, from the association.

Some windjammers are actually new vessels, built along the lines of the old coastal schooners. Others, although substantially rebuilt over the years, date from the 19th century.

The *Stephen Taber* and the *Lewis R. French* were originally launched in 1871, and both the *Mattie* and the *Isaac H. Evans* date from the 1880s. The *J&E Riggin, Mercantile, Roseway, Adventure, American Eagle, Timberwind,* and *Nathaniel Bowditch* have all been sailing at least since the 1930s. The *Mary Day* was launched in 1962, the steel-hulled *Angelique* in 1980, and the *Heritage* in 1983.

Of course, each schooner is as individual as its history, and the captains are hardly interchangeable. Roughly half the vessels now offer hot showers and cabin sinks. Some disdain such amenities. All offer comfortable bunks and cozy, well-heated gathering spaces as well as wide, gleaming decks. They range in length from 64 to 121 feet and carry anywhere from 20 to 38 passengers. In a drizzle, an awning shelters the forward part of the deck, permitting plenty of space to sip coffee and play cards or Scrabble. Captains claim as many repeats from wet as dry weeks.

New Hampshire

Appalachian Mountain Club – Pinkham Notch Camp and Hut System
P.O. Box 298
Pinkham Notch Camp
Gorham, New Hampshire 03581
603-466-2727

Pinkham Notch Camp and 8 high huts; also Bascom Lodge
   (413-743-1591)
$36.50 per person, MAP, at full-service huts; $20 for children
   under 10, MAP; EP and backpacker rates available;
   discount for members
MasterCard, Visa
Children welcome
No pets
Pinkham Notch Camp open year-round; season for high huts
   varies

The Appalachian Mountain Club was founded in 1876 to blaze
and map hiking trails through the White Mountains. A few
decades later, when logging operations scarred these slopes,
outraged club members were instrumental in establishing the
White Mountain National Forest. In ensuing decades, the club's
scope widened to include feeding and sheltering hikers in a
chain of eight high huts — each a day's hike apart in the Presidential Range — as well as in its Pinkham Notch base camp.

   Huts in name only, the high-altitude hostelries are comfortable if Spartan. Our favorite is Mizpah Spring, at 3,800 feet, just
below treeline on the southern flank of Mount Clinton. You
reach it by hiking up from Crawford Notch; the next morning,
you can continue up to the summit of Mount Washington.

   The newest hut, Mizpah is nicely designed, with a wall of
windows overlooking Mount Jackson. Classic French railroad
posters brighten the walls, and books in the corner library date
from the 1890s. Its eight bunkrooms each accommodate at
least six hikers on tiered bunks. As in all the huts, there is one
lavatory per sex, and do bring a flashlight — there is no electricity.

   Lonesome Lake Hut, the southernmost in the chain, is a
popular family destination because it's just 1.7 miles up from
Franconia Notch and there is a lake here, good for swimming
and canoeing.

   Greenleaf Hut, at 4,200 feet, is just at treeline above Eagle
Lake. Galehead and Zealand huts are smaller, each accommodating just 36 people and conveying an off the beaten trail
feeling. Carter Notch lies in a divide between two high mountains and is easily reached; there is even a short cut via the
Wildcat Mountain Gondola, then an easy walk along a ridge
trail (another good one for young hikers). Madison Springs Hut,
the oldest, has the most rugged setting, nestled above the sheer
walls of Madison Gulf and below the stone face of Mount John
Quincy Adams. Lakes-of-the-Clouds Hut is the largest (hous-

ing up to 90), the highest, and frequently the noisiest. Well above treeline on Mount Washington, at 5,000 feet, it is popular with Boy Scout troops.

At all the huts, the atmosphere is friendly and the food plentiful. Hikers from throughout the country trade stories, play games, and participate in guided walks offered by resident naturalists.

Pinkham Notch Camp is a comfortable complex at the eastern base of Mount Washington. Guests dine family-style at long tables in the dining room or snack on the soups and warm drinks available in the common room. The rooms here feature two or more simple but comfortable bunks. Bathrooms are one to a hall.

Throughout the year, special interest programs are offered at Pinkham Notch. They include workshops on photography, nature drawing, bird-watching, botany, and history as well as camping and cross-country skiing.

Bascom Lodge is a handsome, rustic, wood and stone building constructed on the summit of Mount Greylock (the highest mountain in Massachusetts) in the 1930s by the Civilian Conservation Corps. It is now managed by the AMC and offers many of the programs available at Pinkham Notch Camp. It welcomes hikers and motorists alike (you can drive to this summit), offering dorm-style rooms and hearty meals in its high-ceilinged hall. It's open mid-May through October.

City Stops

New England's major cities all offer a far broader choice of lodging—from bed-and-breakfasts to new luxury hotels—than they did just a few years ago.

Connecticut

The Inn at Chapel West
1201 Chapel Street
New Haven, Connecticut 06511
203-777-1201

Innkeeper: Steven G. Schneider
10 rooms (all with private bath)
$125-$175 per couple, including breakfast
Major credit cards
Children welcome
Pets with advance notice
Open year-round

Dating from 1847, this green Victorian clapboard home is stately, elegant, and sophisticated. Though you're a short walk from the historic town green, the bustle of Yale University, and the rejuvenated city center, waking up here can be something like waking up in rural England. There is a very hushed feeling upon entering the house.

The parlor with its piped-in music has Queen Anne chairs, sea-foam green upholstery, hardwood floors, and 1840 bird's-eye maple woodwork. There is no kitchen, but light breakfasts are served, catered from a nearby restaurant.

The guest rooms are individually styled and look as though they're right out of a designer's notebook. One is pink and teal with custom draperies, brass fixtures, Victorian face masks, and wainscoting. Another has a gatekeeper's chair and a brass bed with onyx finials. In a feminine-looking room you'll sleep in a Bavarian canopy bed and enjoy the needlepoint chair and mahogany armoire.

The Poppy Room has a four-poster bed and French country furnishings. The Windsor Room is fitted with mahogany and a country quilt. Another has musical dolls, a French quarter daybed, and Oriental overtones. On the light and airy third floor is a room decorated in white with a white leather wing-back chair. A vivid mural of clouds enlivens the room. Each room has its own special items and amenities, such as padded hangers and bathrobes. All the rooms have down pillows and some have bed chests.

New Haven teems with life because of Yale University. There's the Yale Center for British Art, in addition to many other museums, and the Yale Repertory Theatre as well as numerous local companies offer entertainment. Even if the university weren't here, you could easily spend a weekend enjoying the chic restaurants, bookstore-cafés, or diversions like the West Rock Nature Center.

Maine

The Inn at Park Spring
135 Spring Street
Portland, Maine 04101
207-774-1059

Innkeeper: Wendy Wickstrom
7 rooms (all with private bath)
$80-$90 per couple, including breakfast
Major credit cards
Children over 4 welcome
No pets
Open year-round

This classy addition to Portland's lodgings is a symbol of the new vigor of Maine's principal city. Opened in December 1983, the inn is styled as a guesthouse cum executive lodging and is very capably managed by Wendy Wickstrom. Flexible and creative service is the key to the inn's success. Guests are not shooed away at a rigid check-out time, and they don't have to rush out of bed for their morning coffee, juice, and pastry. Many special provisions can be made for businesspeople, such as installing additional phone service, catering a lunch, and transforming the living room into a meeting room.

This town house, built in 1845, has been completely redone. The decor is sophisticated and eclectic, from the entrance hall with coral-colored walls and Oriental runners to the contemporary bath with cedar walls on the third floor. In the Park Room, guests can luxuriate in a four-poster bed and enjoy a marble fireplace and European-style bath. The Museum Room has a landing with chairs on the fire escape. One of the two rooms on the lower level has an enclosed brick patio with table and chairs. One third-floor bedroom has a skylight. The baths have luxurious toiletries and linens.

The inn can serve as a fine base for visiting Portland's West End and Old Port districts, the distinctive Portland Museum of Art, and all the shops and restaurants nearby.

Moonshell Inn
Island Avenue
Peaks Island, Maine 04108
207-766-2331

Innkeeper: Elinor (Bunny) Clark
6 rooms, including 2 that can form an efficiency unit (shared baths); 3 rooms next door
$60 per couple, including breakfast; off-season: $40
Breakfast not always served
No credit cards
Children welcome
No pets
Open year-round but occasionally closed off-season

A simple, unpretentious place, the Moonshell Inn is a convenient escape from the mainland but just a 15-minute ferry ride from Portland's Old Port neighborhood. The ferries (one carries cars, one doesn't) run regularly throughout the day. The inn is only about 5 minutes from the landing, to the left down Island Avenue.

This is a bit of a do-it-yourself hostelry because Bunny Clark, the innkeeper, is often not available to greet her guests. But her very friendly notes, which welcome guests and direct them to their rooms, fill the void. Perhaps in a more elegant B&B this casual approach would not work; here, it seems in keeping with the relaxed island atmosphere.

The gray and white clapboard inn offers six airy rooms with painted floors, straw rugs, baskets of shells, and white curtains and bedspreads. Bunny's neighbor, Ruth Sargeant, a well-known regional writer, provides three additional rooms that are perfectly adequate but not quite so appealing.

Breakfast is served on a glass-enclosed deck overlooking Portland and Casco Bay. Homemade breads, fresh fruit, juice, and coffee are offered. Be sure to return to the deck at day's end for a spectacular view of the sunset over Portland.

It's a good idea to bring your own bicycles (a few are available for rent), or plan to walk around this 1-square-mile island. Nature trails, beaches, and coves are on the far side. There are several restaurants and a grocery store for picnic supplies — all within a few minutes' walk of the inn. Guests may keep snacks in the refrigerator but may not use the stove. When breakfast is not served at the Moonshell, guests can find a good meal at the Cockeyed Gull, practically next door.

Pomegranate Inn
49 Neal Street
Portland, Maine 04102
207-772-1006
800-356-0408

Innkeepers: Alan and Isabel Smiles
6 rooms (all with private bath), 1 apartment
$95 per couple, including breakfast; apartment rented by the
    weekend and week
MasterCard, Visa
Children over 16 welcome
No pets
Open year-round

Visiting Portland's Museum of Art? You'd be well advised to stay at the Pomegranate Inn and surround yourself with art before and after museum hours. Isabel's artistic sensibilities come from her years as an interior designer and co-owner of an antiques business in Greenwich, Connecticut, and this Italianate house is quite a showpiece for her talents. With a double set of front doors, high ceilings, and lofty common rooms, the architecture provides just the right backdrop for the art.

For nine months before it opened, a friend's daughter lived at the house and painted (and signed) all the guest room walls. (No, look again; it really isn't wallpaper.) She also did all the faux marbling in the house, including that on the four columns in the living room. A gallery guide might well be in order, along with profiles of artists and periods.

As you head upstairs to the guest rooms, a landing is painted in checkerboard style. A series of oil paintings on the brash yellow and orange walls leads you on. Most of the guest rooms are off the long narrow hallway, with recessed lighting. Room 2 has fluffy down comforters and multiple pillows on twin beds and a small television on a graceful pedestal, posing as a piece of art itself. The walls in Room 3 have been painted with bouquets of large, wild burgundy flowers and complement the wine and mauve rug. Room 4 is large, accommodating bow windows and four-poster twin beds. Room 6 has rose striped wallpaper with coordinated bedding. The smaller Room 5 has water-colors hanging in the bathroom and little, delicate clusters of irises all over the walls. All the bathrooms have new tiling, porcelain sinks, and the like.

Upon their arrival, guests are offered Perrier or tea, which can be taken in the small, dark, and very cozy second-floor sitting room. Alan cooks breakfast, which often includes poached eggs, broiled tomatoes, or French toast.

In the quiet, western part of the city in a neighborhood of lovely, large homes, this mansion is easy to reach from the highway.

Portland Regency in the Old Port

20 Milk Street
Portland, Maine
207-774-4200
800-727-3436

Manager: Anne DeRepentigny
95 rooms
$100 per couple, $95 single occupancy in summer; $65-$95
 double, mid-October through May
Major credit cards
Children welcome
Pets by prior arrangement
Open year-round

The Regency provides the amenities of a first-class small hotel plus an unbeatable location. The charming restored area known as the Old Port is just outside the door, with intriguing shops, excellent restaurants, and the waterfront all a short walk away. The building itself is a century-old armory, its exterior intact. Inside, 95 rooms have created to take advantage of such special architectural features as arched, small-paned windows. Working within the constraints of an existing building has, in some cases, meant odd-shaped rooms, but all are pleasingly appointed with handsome Colonial reproductions and flow-ered chintz fabrics, honor bars, and telephones in the bath as well as the bedroom.

Two restaurants offer very different choices for dinner. The Atrium features elegant dining with a nouvelle American menu that highlights Maine seafood. The service is extremely atten-tive and swift. The decor is an odd combination of pink fake cinderblock walls with tall green tubes placed along them, a Greek marble floor, and lush greenery. There's an extremely vertical feeling to the room that is underscored by a high, plain ceiling and views of guests walking to their rooms on two upper levels.

A very different experience is offered by Ga's. A publike gathering spot for the neighborhood, it serves more casual food and often has live entertainment.

One of Portland's most extensive health clubs is at the Regency, and guests may use the Nautilus equipment, sauna, steam rooms, and whirlpool. There are aerobics classes, too. Throughout the hotel—in the hallways, the lobby, and the Atrium—classical music wafts from speakers.

The Regency offers valet parking, sparing guests the hassle of finding a parking place in this very popular part of Portland. Once you've given the attendant your keys, you're free to explore the city on foot. You might even walk the few blocks to the waterfront and take a ferry to one of Casco Bay's islands for a picnic.

Massachusetts

Boston Harbor Hotel at Rowes Wharf
70 Rowes Wharf
Boston, Massachusetts 02110
617-439-7000
800-752-7077
Fax 617-330-9450

Managing director: François-Laurent Nivaud
230 rooms and suites
$235-$295 per couple, $350-$975 suites, EP; weekend
    packages available
All 3 meals served
Major credit cards
Children welcome
Pets with approval
Open year-round

Boston's most impressive luxury hotel is part of a large office-condominium complex on the former site of Rowes Wharf, on the harbor. Built on a pierlike structure, the elegant architecture, with an 80-foot archway and copper-domed rotunda, was called a "triumph of urban design" by the *New York Times*. Come for the view.

No expense has been spared in the interior detailing, either. Marble floors, fabric-covered walls, museum-quality art, and small-scale public spaces create the feeling of an elegant private club, much like the small, great hotels of London. There is a high employee-guest ratio, resulting in excellent service.

The rooms have sweeping views of the harbor (and the vessels that ply the water and the airplanes — barely heard — that take off from Logan Airport) or the glittering city skyline. They are decorated with rich flowered fabrics and chintzes, crystal lamps, and Chippendale furniture. Fresh flowers, bathrobes, a mini-bar, a television, and three telephones in each room are standard. Neutrogena amenities are provided in the bathrooms.

The restaurant is very much like a smart Boston club; its two sections offer both a formal and an informal atmosphere with similar menus of regional American cuisine and seafood. The salad niçoise, with grilled fresh tuna, is a culinary masterpiece. The bar, which also has a separate entrance from the street, has become a meeting spot for financial district workers waiting for the commuter ferry. Afternoon tea, authentically set and served in the Harborview Lounge, is fast giving the other hotels in Boston a run for their money.

A health club and spa has a 60-foot lap pool, a whirlpool, sauna, steam room, and massage and treatment rooms. There's a marina for guests arriving in their own boat, even if it's a dinghy (this is the first public dinghy dock in Boston).

A comfortable and stress-free water taxi takes you directly from the airport to the hotel. If you arrive via South Station or the Southeast Expressway, the hotel couldn't be more conveniently located. The hotel is within easy walking distance of the Aquarium, Faneuil Hall Marketplace, the North End, and the Tea Party Ship Museum.

The Bostonian Hotel

Faneuil Hall Marketplace
Boston, Massachusetts 02109
617-523-3600
800-343-0922
Fax 617-523-2454

Managing director: Timothy P. Kirwan
153 rooms
$170-$550 per couple, EP; weekend packages available
All 3 meals served
Major credit cards
Children welcome
No pets
Open year-round

The Bostonian is an intimate, newer (1982) hotel that incorporates two historic buildings in a predominantly modern structure. Across from Faneuil Hall Marketplace, in Boston's oldest commercial district, the hotel has blended well with its neighbors. Businesspeople during the week and families on weekends love the festive atmosphere of the Haymarket, with its hawking vegetable vendors.

The red brick building has a porte cochere and a circular cobblestone driveway around a courtyard. The centerpiece of the courtyard is a fountain and a stainless steel sculpture, *The Spirit of Boston,* by David Lee Brown.

The lobby is designed only for guests, who are treated to solicitous service. Other visitors use a separate entrance to reach such public spaces as the bar and restaurant. Traditional and contemporary elements have been combined to create an intimate feeling found only in small private clubs and guesthouses. The registration desk and cashier are practically invisible. A roaring fire and bowls of apples welcome guests in the winter. The doormen wear distinctive uniforms with Russian fur hats. The luggage is taken directly to the guest rooms via a service elevator, never to the lobby.

An exposed glass elevator connects the public lobby with the nationally acclaimed Seasons restaurant on the rooftop. It is also enclosed in glass, with a lighted stainless steel ceiling arched with laminated wood beams, affords a broad view of Faneuil Hall Marketplace. The food is some of the best in Boston; the kitchen has seen Boston's best chefs, including Jasper White, Lydia Shire, and Gordon Hamersley. Bill Porier is now in charge; if history is to repeat itself, keep an eye out for him. The manager takes a personal interest in a rather extensive all-American wine cellar. (Room service, which is impressive, is 24 hours a day.)

Four different color schemes and two types of furnishings are used for the guest rooms. Those in the new sections of the hotel follow a contemporary style, while a more traditional approach (French country provincial furnishings) has been taken in the rooms in the historic sections. Hallways zigzag and corners aren't always right angles in this more interesting half. Room 734 has a beamed ceiling, a water view, and French reproduction furniture. Suite 735 has a two-story room with a fireplace and is decorated in warm brown colors.

The extensive bathroom amenities are unusual: small packets of Woolite, Roger et Gallet products, silk sachets, and, of course, terrycloth bathrobes.

Most of the rooms have French windows opening onto small balconies with wrought-iron railings and flower boxes filled with seasonal plantings year-round. Most suites have a Jacuzzi, many have oversize oval tubs; all have VCRs. A morning newspaper will be waiting at your door in the morning as well as your shined shoes (a complimentary service) if you left them out the night before. There isn't a health club on the premises, but a Nautilus facility is available.

The Atrium Lounge is a great place for people-watching, away from the hustle and bustle of Faneuil Hall Marketplace.

Copley Plaza Hotel

Copley Square
Boston, Massachusetts 02116
617-267-5300
800-826-7539
Fax 617-267-7668

General manager: Jan Chovanec
300 rooms, 50 suites
$190-$240 per couple, $170-$220 single occupancy, suites
$250-$400; weekends: $125-$150 per room; $20 for extra
person over 12 in same room; special package and
off-season rates available
All 3 meals served
Major credit cards
Children welcome
Small pets welcome
Open year-round

The Copley Plaza, one of Boston's "grandes dames," has just had a facelift. The magnificent building dates from 1912 and closely resembles New York's Plaza both physically and in atmosphere: a marble lobby with a frescoed blue sky ceiling; a Tea Court amid the marble and potted palms; Copley's, a book- and picture-lined dining room straight out of *The Bostonians*; and the Plaza Dining Room, one of the grandest rooms in the country where the public may dine. Beyond lies Copley Square, the centerpiece of the Back Bay, with its blocks of town houses and Boston's smartest galleries and shops.

The John Hancock, at 60 stories Boston's highest building (its rooftop Observatory is the best spot for a historical as well as geographic overview of the city), happens to be next door, and until 1987 it also owned the hotel. What's happened under new, local ownership is a total renovation of the guest rooms. All have superb vintage 1912 mirrored closets and wall detailing, but many were dingy by current standards until their recent overhaul—which includes tasteful carpeting and reproduction furniture, TVs hidden in armoires, and marble bathrooms.

With the exception of six central rooms on each floor, each room actually differs from its neighbor and many "superior" (medium-price) rooms are actually two-room suites, with day-beds that fold out to accommodate a couple of children. The hotel also supplies cribs complete with cuddly animals, television with special cable channels for children, and a special children's guide to museums, events, and restaurants. Guests, incidentally, have access to the Spa at the Heritage, Boston's newest and most elegant fitness center, a short walk up Boylston Street, by the Public Garden.

The public spaces in the Copley Plaza represent the true heart of the Back Bay. The Plaza Bar, richly paneled and dimly lit, with deep leather seats, evokes an exclusive Fifth Avenue men's club — until the evening entertainment begins and big-name performers bring patrons to the edge of their seats. The Copley Bar is altogether another scene: a central bar invites singles and couples alike to gather. The restaurant Copley's is moderately priced yet opulent. The Library Bar, with book-lined walls, is yet another special space, and the Plaza Dining Room rivals any restaurant in Boston, both in ambience and quality. Chef de cuisine Philippe Reininger is the magician behind appetizers like pumpkin and pink radish soup garnished with haddock ($6) and entrées like fillet of salmon with cèpes (mushrooms) and young leeks flavored with walnut oil ($28) and medallions of venison in *poivrade* sauce with celery root chips and onion compote ($31).

The Four Seasons
200 Boylston Street
Boston, Massachusetts 02116
617-338-4400
800-332-3442
Fax 617-423-0154

General manager: Robin Brown
288 rooms, roughly half with Boston Common views, 68
  "Four Seasons rooms" with sitting rooms, 11 rooms with
  wheelchair access, 12 suites
$245-$340 per couple midweek, $150-$235, weekends
All 3 meals served
Major credit cards
Children's program
Pets with advance approval
Open year-round

A shade gaudy (there's a crystal chandelier in the porte cochere, and the grand staircase would look more appropriate in Miami) and less formal than the Ritz, the Four Seasons is also more welcoming. With a warm assurance that he is happy you have come, the doorman whisks your luggage away. The bellhop carefully outlines all the hotel's facilities, which include a spectacular eighth-floor pool and a full spa, and services, such as 24-hour room service and an overnight shoeshine.

If you are going to stay here, do it right and book a room overlooking the Public Garden. A Four Seasons Room ($210 per couple on weekends) is as luxurious as you need go: a bedroom divided by French doors from an elegant little sitting room with a windowside table that's perfect for breakfast. Of course, there's a wet bar, cable TV, fresh flowers, bottled water, and a marble bathroom with a hair dryer, robe, soaps, creams, and shampoo.

For New Englanders who live in the suburbs or country, the Four Seasons actually makes a great "Gourmet Getaway." Its formal, second-floor dining room, Aujourd'hui, is one of the best restaurants in town. It's spacious, richly paneled, and decorated with beveled mirrors and old prints. Request a table with a view of the Public Garden. You might begin with a charlotte of Louisiana crab with bell peppers, followed by a peasant salad; the peppered Maine lobster with spring rolls is exquisite. The combination of ambience, food, and deft and personal service is difficult to beat. A less expensive menu is available, for both lunch and dinner, in the attractive Bristol Lounge, off the lobby.

The dining room aside, the hotel is comfortably informal. Even children feel welcome; babysitters are available and there are videotapes to amuse youngsters, who can eat in their rooms while their parents dine in style.

The Four Seasons is within walking distance of the major shops, both in Back Bay and downtown, and if you don't want to take the subway to a business appointment or the waterfront, a complementary limousine is provided.

Hotel Meridien
250 Franklin Street
Boston, Massachusetts 02110
617-451-1900
800-543-4300
Fax 617/423-2844

Manager: Hugues Jaquier
269 rooms, 57 suites
$200 per couple, $350-$800 suites, EP; weekend packages
   available
All 3 meals served

Major credit cards
Children welcome
Small animals accommodated
Open year-round

Without question, you come to the Meridien for the service, which is not to be outdone in New England, and the superb French cuisine.

This is Boston's former Federal Reserve Bank building, a 1920s Renaissance Revival structure of granite and limestone modeled on a Roman palazzo. When it reopened in 1981 as the Meridien Hotel, three stories and a glass mansard roof had been added, as well as other modern touches, like a six-story atrium and sloping glass walls in many guest rooms. Despite its size, it conveys the ambience of a small hotel.

The magnificent public spaces are on the floors above the vehicular entrance. There is the former "members' court," now the restaurant Julien, with its vaulted, gold leaf – edged ceiling. One has the sense of dining in a very elegant courtyard, one with upholstered wingback chairs. The food is a perfect mixture of nouvelle and traditional French fare, and you're likely to be waited on by four or five different service people.

On a level above the restaurant is the Julien Lounge, a truly luxurious bar with coffered ceilings and two N. C. Wyeth murals on paneled walls. Enjoy your morning croissants, Sunday brunch, or light dinner in the smaller Café Fleuri, in the soaring atrium.

The guest rooms, in contrast, are light and modern. Because most of them have been carved from former office space, they come in more than 150 different sizes and shapes. Hermès toiletries, roses in the bathroom, chocolate truffles, and tomorrow's weather forecast are among the small niceties that include live plants, mini-bars, sofas, radios, and bathroom scales and telephones.

Guests can enjoy Le Club Meridien, a third-floor sports facility with a 4-foot-deep lap pool, a Jacuzzi, aerobic exercise equipment, and a sauna.

The Meridien is in the heart of Boston's financial district; midweek, 95 percent of its guests are here on business. On weekends, when packages include free parking and breakfast in bed, tourists account for half the clientele.

The Meridien has an unusually large staff (326 for 326 rooms), and you can't help but notice. The French management is apparent from the moment you are greeted with "*bonjour.*" But there is nothing at all stuffy about the Meridien, and an unusually friendly atmosphere prevails.

The Ritz-Carlton Boston
15 Arlington Street
Boston, Massachusetts 02177
617-536-5700
800-241-3333
Fax 617-536-9340

General manager: Sigi Brauer
278 rooms, 47 suites
$265-$685 per couple, EP; weekend packages available
All 3 meals served
Major credit cards
Children welcome
Smaller pets welcome
Open year-round

"We are not merely surrounded by traditions, we have become one," says the Ritz's promotional material. It's true. Despite the flood of new luxury hotels, the Ritz remains *the* place to stay in Boston.

The 16-story hotel was built in 1927, and an addition, which includes 52 condominiums, was completed in 1981. From within the hotel, it is extremely difficult to distinguish between the two. The new rooms have the same careful detailing found in the old ones. The only visible difference is in the bathrooms; those in the new wing are roomier and modern; the old ones (newly refaced in Vermont marble) have porcelain fixtures from the 1920s.

The most handsome rooms are the suites, with elegant mirror-topped mantels (there are 42 working fireplaces) and fine antique breakfronts, desks, and sofas. All the rooms are large and have closets that lock and a safe. Some also have a refrigerator and honor bar. Most have fine views, either of the Public Garden or over the rooftops of Newbury Street. (And the windows open.)

The elevator is run by a white-gloved operator, and many of the hotel's 570 employees have been here for more than ten years (a few since the '40s). A room service kitchen on each floor, open 24 hours a day, provides superb service.

The second-floor Dining Room is very formal, with tall, mullioned windows overlooking the Public Garden and a menu offering Continental cuisine. The Lounge (no windows) is a gathering place rather like a drawing room and is popular for tea. Downstairs, on the entry floor, the Café is a less formal place for breakfast and lunch (with entrées such as grilled baby flounder with lemon butter and champagne by the glass). The

Ritz Bar, a popular meeting spot, has recently acquired the look of a richly paneled club, complete with a fireplace. A full range of health and fitness facilities, ice skates (to use on the pond across the street), jogging shoes for a run along the Esplanade, and a chauffeured limousine (to make morning appointments) round out the facilities of this full-service hotel.

Terrace Townehouse
60 Chandler Street
Boston, Massachusetts 02116
617-350-6520

Innkeepers: Bob and Gloria Belknap
4 rooms (all with private bath), 1 apartment
$115-$125 in season, $100-$125 off-season, apartment $650
　　per week including full breakfast and afternoon tea
MasterCard, Visa
Children over 12 welcome
No pets
Limited smoking areas
Open year-round

This elegant bed-and-breakfast is in a brick town house on a tree-lined street in Boston's South End, only a few blocks from Copley Square. The owners have meticulously restored the house to its original elegance. The small entrance is finished with a black and white marble floor, and there are wide hardwood floors throughout. The hall and stairwell are painted a striking peach color and accented with antique French prints, white woodwork, and brass sconces.

Among the guest rooms, the China Trade Room has an Asian motif, using Clarence House and Pierre Deux prints. The walls are a bright, cheery yellow and the furniture is antique wicker. Old botanical prints decorate the walls, while dhurries cover the hardwood floors. The room has the comforts of a luxury hotel and the cozy feeling of a private home.

Another, the Drawing Room, has the feeling of an English club, with dark brown woodwork and warm brown colors. It has a tented four-poster canopy bed in a blue toile and a love seat by the bay window.

On the first floor, in the original reception room, is the British Officer's Room, decorated in turn-of-the-century style, even to an 1897 issue of *Punch*. This room, which is smaller than the others, has a wall of books, a sink built into a bureau, and a tiny but well-planned bathroom. It's as if a British officer had left his possessions behind for guests to enjoy.

The choice room is the French Dining Room, which has a very comfortable king-size bed, a crystal chandelier, dark green lacquered walls, and French antiques. It looks down on a handkerchief-size garden with a fountain and flowering plants.

Each room has its own telephone line. The apartment, on the ground floor, has a fireplace and a small bedroom. There is a library on the third floor with over a thousand volumes where tea is served in the afternoons. A full breakfast is served on antique china in each room, along with the morning *Boston Globe*.

Gloria graduated from La Varenne in Paris and used to be a caterer in California, so the full breakfasts and afternoon teas are special.

■ *See also:* The Charles Hotel at Harvard Square, Cambridge, Massachusetts; Guest Quarters Suite Hotel, Boston, Massachusetts; The Midtown Motel, Boston, Massachusetts

---

New Hampshire

Sise Inn
40 Court Street
Portsmouth, New Hampshire 03801
603-433-1200

Innkeepers: Carl and Gisele Jensen
32 rooms and suites, carriage house
$78-$136 for rooms, $160 for suites, including Continental breakfast
Major credit cards
Children welcome
No pets
Open year-round

The Sise Inn is a lovely Queen Anne home that was built in 1881. A firm in nearby Hampton bought the large old building in 1984, had it restored by local artisans, and built an addition that beautifully duplicates the woodwork and decor of the original house. It's now owned by Someplaces Different, a chain of inns in Canada.

A well-run, comfortable place to stay, it's within walking distance of Portsmouth's many historic houses, outstanding restaurants, and waterside shops.

Midweek, it caters to businesspeople. All the rooms have telephones and, usually, writing desks. In three suites on the third floor, French doors separate the bedrooms from the large sitting rooms, which have good-size tables and four chairs for small conferences. On the ground floor, two function rooms have conference tables for larger meetings.

The guest rooms are luxuriously carpeted and decorated in period antiques. The sitting room on the first floor is just off the exquisite oak-paneled foyer. It has deep blue leather couches in front of the fireplace that are wonderful to sink into at the end of a long day.

The Danish-born innkeepers, Gisele and Carl Jensen, serve a generous Continental breakfast in a bright breakfast room that has an enclosed porch and deck. The kitchenette at one end of the room can be used by guests to store cold drinks or make a cup of tea or coffee late in the day.

Rhode Island

The Old Court
144 Benefit Street
Providence, Rhode Island 02903
401-751-2002, 401-351-0747

Manager: Carolyn Chabot
11 rooms (all with private bath)
$105-$130 per couple, including breakfast
Major credit cards
Children welcome
No pets
Open year-round

Built in 1863 as an Episcopal church rectory, the Old Court has been beautifully remodeled with Victorian styling. The three-story brick building is best described as baronial yet cozy. Twelve-foot ceilings and Italian architectural detailing coexist with such things as an electric percolator and room phones.

Burgundy carpets throughout the public spaces create a feeling of luxury and cushioned comfort. Mahogany balusters on the stair rail make the climb or descent a grand experience. The guest rooms have hardwood floors with Oriental carpets. They are well appointed with fine furnishings as well as televisions. The beds have blanket covers — an elegant touch. Antiques and decorations such as a Chippendale Roman clock are usually seen only in private homes, not public accommodations. Accessories in the modern and well-planned bathrooms are by Vidal Sassoon.

Across the street, for a higher price, is a first-floor apartment with two bedrooms, a kitchen, and a living room.

Breakfast is served at a large mahogany table or one of the smaller bistro tables. When we visited, a tray of croissants was piled high, and cappuccino and espresso were offered.

With free parking in back, the Old Court is in a quiet, historic neighborhood that's nice to stroll around in the evening. It's minutes from the Rhode Island School of Design and Brown University and just down the hill from the city's business and shopping district.

Omni Biltmore Hotel

Kennedy Plaza
Providence, Rhode Island 02903
401-421-0700
800-THE-OMNI
Fax 401-421-0210

Managing director: Robert Gary James
289 rooms and suites
$120-$280 per couple, EP
All 3 meals served
Major credit cards
Children welcome
No pets
Open year-round

Finally, Providence's grande dame of hotels has been properly remodeled and is being run competently. Omni has brought this full-service hotel back to life with style. The hotel's landmark exterior glass elevator, which has a panoramic view of the city's revitalized downtown, takes guests to their rooms.

The rooms have bright colors with chevron- and stripe-patterned, rose-colored wall-to-wall carpeting. The doorknob plates still have the Biltmore crest on them, from the hotel's inception in 1922. There are many added features, but they are better in the deluxe mini-suites, which are recommended. Many bathrooms have windows, a pleasant change from the usual claustrophobic feeling of many new luxury hotel bathrooms.

Standford's American Bar and Grille is bright and cheery, with black and white ceramic tiles, an open grill, rotisserie kitchen, and polite service. The cuisine is classic American and international, prepared in a contemporary manner; prime rib of beef and lobster are two specialties. An excellent selection of wine and bottled beers is available.

Overlooking the historic East Side, the hotel is also near the famous Arcade, the nation's oldest covered shopping mall.

College Stops

College or prep schools may be the reason you come, but these lodgings will make you want to stay.

Connecticut

The Queen Anne Inn and Antique Gallery
265 Williams Street
New London, Connecticut 06320
203-447-2600

Innkeeper: Captain Morgan Beatty
8 rooms and suites (all with private bath)
$45-$135
MasterCard, Visa
Children over 12 welcome
No pets
No smoking
Open year-round

The Queen Anne is an 1880 Victorian charmer on a hillside above New London, about as handy as you can be to both the U.S. Coast Guard Academy and Connecticut College.

The rooms are comfortable and imaginatively furnished. One is apricot and green with a fireplace, a four-poster brass bed, and clubby wooden panels for a masculine look. Another has a sunny porch and a four-poster bed. Each is individually decorated. You might choose the pink and white, the cranberry and rose, the green, or the rose and blue room. When we last visited, a third-floor luxury suite was in the making.

A full breakfast is served in the front parlor lined with bookshelves and warmed by a working fireplace. There are hot sweet rolls and coffee, served with sausage and eggs.

All the furnishings here are for sale, as are antique nautical charts and oil paintings and prints of local scenes.

The Queen Anne is just off I-95, a short drive from the Mystic Seaport and just across the river from the Nautilus Memorial and river tours of the submarine base. A nice bonus: guests can use the Waterford Health and Racquet Club.

■ *See also:* The Inn at Chapel West, New Haven, Connecticut

Massachusetts

The Charles Hotel at Harvard Square
One Bennett Street
Cambridge, Massachusetts 02138
617-864-1200
800-882-1818
Fax 617-864-5715

General manager: Alan Ireland
300 rooms and suites
$191-$1,200 per couple; weekend packages available
All 3 meals served
Major credit cards
Children welcome
Pets welcome
Open year-round

Built of brick to match Harvard's buildings and the sidewalks of Cambridge, the Charles fits in well. It has many large windows to permit views of the river, the university, and its own square, a brick plaza with a café, street vendors, and a cluster of shops. Inside, the walls are hung with paintings of Cambridge and exquisite quilts. The spare, modern lines of the public rooms set off New England antiques.

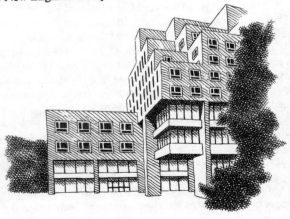

The guest rooms all feature down quilts and have three telephones and two cable TVs (one in the bathroom and one in a tasteful armoire that includes a desk and honor bar). The baths have terry bathrobes and scales. Some rooms are equipped with computer modems, and computers may be rented. An elaborate spa offers a pool, solarium, Jacuzzi, sauna, splash pool, exercise room, massage, and hair and skin salon.

Opened in 1985, the Charles caters largely to Harvard University's visiting alums, friends, and VIPs. Guests have easy access to Boston via the Harvard Square subway station. Cambridge shops, restaurants, sights, and street life are attractions in themselves. The hotel's two restaurants — the bright, informal Bennett Street Café with tables outside in warm weather and the very expensive Rarities, serving haute cuisine — have already earned a strong local following. The Regattabar, featuring top jazz groups from Tuesday through Saturday evenings, is also very popular.

Hotel Northampton
36 King Street
Northampton, Massachusetts 01060
413-584-3100
800-421-2134
Fax 413-585-0210

General manager: Rick Greilich
73 rooms
$85-$142 per couple, EP; special packages available
All 3 meals served
Major credit cards
Children welcome
Pets accepted
Open year-round

After years of restoration and renovation of this 1926 building, the classic Hotel Northampton can again take its place as the centerpiece of its lively city.

The lobby is grand, with plants, rich carpeting, and comfortable chairs in front of an ever-present crackling fire. The glassed-in porch, with yet more greenery and brick, is the perfect place for morning coffee and the newspaper, a snack, or quiet evening conversation. (Group functions are often held here, so you may find yourself sharing the lobby with a wedding party or reunion.)

Your dining choices are many. The new Coolidge Park Café is a lively meeting place for residents and students. There's often live entertainment on weekends as well as a generous shrimp platter for those who have stopped in for a drink. Prices are moderate, and light dishes include chicken teriyaki, a cold scallop salad, and lobster salad on a croissant. In warm months, under the shade of old trees, the café spills out onto the terrace.

Two elevators take you to the guest rooms and suites featuring Laura Ashley fabrics, wicker accents, and reproduction Chippendale, Federal, and Duncan Phyfe furnishings. King canopy, double, and twin beds are available. Many of the suites have Jacuzzis, and their balconies and terraces overlook King Street. All rooms have a telephone, radio, and television. There is ample free parking in back.

Northampton is in the Pioneer Valley, the home of four colleges (Smith, Mount Holyoke, Amherst, and Hampshire) and the bustling University of Massachusetts. A culturally rich and diverse area, it can be chic and country at the same time. Lovely hikes to the summit of Mount Holyoke, water sports on the Connecticut River, and skiing at Mount Tom are all within short drives. Guests also have privileges at the YMCA about a mile and a half away. Bradley Airport is 40 minutes away in Connecticut.

The Midtown Hotel

220 Huntington Avenue
Boston, Massachusetts 02115
617-262-1000
800-343-1177
Fax 617-262-8739

Manager: Peter Martino
161 rooms
$89–$119 per couple, EP; winter packages available
All 3 meals served
Major credit cards
Children welcome
Pets usually not accepted
Open year-round

The Midtown does not pretend to be what it isn't but plays up its prime attractions: spacious and clean lodgings, solid service, and a great location at a good price. Almost anyplace else this hotel would be quite ordinary, but on Huntington Avenue, within an easy walk of some of Boston's major tourist attractions, cultural institutions, and shopping areas, it is a gem.

The style of the place is '50s motel, but it has been renovated and updated so that everything looks new. All of the rooms have space to spread out—great for tourists or businesspeople spending the week. The few suites offer even more space. The rooms have a radio, TV, and good closets. Free parking, laundry service, a sauna and massage room, an outdoor swimming pool, meeting facilities, and a restaurant are among the amenities. Winter packages include breakfast and can be $20 less per room.

The Orchards

222 Adams Road
Williamstown, Massachusetts 01267
413-458-9611
800-231-2344 in Massachusetts
800-225-1517 elsewhere
Fax 413-458-3273

Resident manager: Henricus Bergmans
49 rooms and suites
$120-$180 per couple, EP; midweek packages available
All 3 meals served
Major credit cards
Children welcome
No pets
Open year-round

The Orchards' exterior, a salmon-colored concrete building right on busy Route 2, belies the gracious atmosphere within. The public rooms gleam with polished antique wood, and floors are covered with Oriental rugs. The guest rooms have been furnished with care and a sense of comfort. Above all, staff members are committed to making this a very special place.

To begin with, there is early morning coffee and danish, served in the living room for those who set out before 7:30 A.M. Breakfast itself is deliciously English, complete with silver teapots and strainers, rashers of crisp bacon, and breakfast meats.

The Orchards strives consciously to be an English country inn. Note the prints of British countryside and hunt scenes, the fine china and silver, and the observance of afternoon tea. Rather un-British is the fare in the dining room, such as strawberry bisque, moist poached salmon, crispy Cornish game hen with pecans and wild rice, and veal with seafood. This could be pretentious in some places, but it works in Williamstown, the ivy-clad home of Williams College and the Sterling and Francine Clark Art Institute, one of America's finest small museums.

The Orchards is a key part of this community, offering after-dinner theater in the big conference room and concerts on the vintage Steinway grand piano. The lobby is played down, with the focus instead on the living room, which has a cupola, glass chandeliers, a green marble fireplace with an old mantel, and elegant furniture.

The rooms have double sinks, separate dressing rooms, and built-in refrigerators. There are also ample closets, phones for the bath as well as bed, piles of thick towels, and a generous allotment of English bath soaps. Some rooms have four-poster beds and glass-faced fireplaces. Ask about the view when reserving and, if possible, choose a room on the leafy back or side streets rather than one overlooking the Grand Union across the street.

The Yankee Pedlar Inn
Holyoke, Massachusetts 01040
413-532-9494

Owners: The Banks family
47 rooms
$55-$75 per couple, including Continental breakfast
All 3 meals served
Major credit cards
Children accepted
No pets
No smoking rooms available
Open year-round

The Yankee Pedlar Inn, at the junction of Routes 202 and 5 just off I-91, is a cluster of buildings with a large, popular restaurant. Currier and Ives prints, historical photographs, blue onion china, and brass lamps predominate. The rooms have been furnished traditionally, with hooked rugs, antiques, canopy beds, and four-posters. Each one is different. Many have sitting rooms as well and are actually attractive small suites.

The Pedlar has long enjoyed a reputation for excellent food, which now can only be enhanced with the addition of chef Joseph Forjuno to the staff. Fresh seafoods and creative New England dishes like Pedlar lobster pie and sand dollar scallops are offered daily. An extensive wine list is also available. There are no doors in the kitchen, and guests are encouraged to watch their food being prepared.

The Oyster Bar, a pubby corner of the house, features oyster stew and creative sandwiches; here guests will find coffee and a Continental breakfast laid out in the morning. The Gilded

Cage Lounge, with paneling from Kenilworth Castle, features entertainment nightly.

The Yankee Pedlar is close to the Mount Tom Ski area, Quabbin Reservoir, Springfield, Mount Holyoke College, and Smith College. In nearby Amherst are Amherst and Hampshire colleges and the University of Massachusetts.

- *See also:* The Deerfield Inn, Deerfield, Massachusetts; Northfield Country House, Northfield, Massachusetts; River Bend Farm, Williamstown, Massachusetts

---

New Hampshire

The Hanover Inn
Hanover, New Hampshire 03755
603-643-4300

General manager: Matthew Marshall
92 rooms
$119-$130 per room, $159-$179 junior suites
All 3 meals served
Major credit cards
Children welcome
Small pets welcome
No smoking rooms available
Open year-round

This four-story landmark is an extension of Dartmouth College. It faces the college's oldest buildings across a magnificent green and is right next to Hopkins Center, a modern arts complex where concerts, plays, art films, lectures, and art exhibitions are always being held.

On a sunny summer day, the front terrace is crowded with visitors and residents enjoying a light lunch or late afternoon beer. The white rockers on the long porch are usually occupied. In cooler weather, a sitting room with claw-foot sofas and floral-patterned armchairs invite lounging by the fireside. Gilt-edged mirrors and delicate brass wall lamps ornament the rooms, and a grandfather clock chimes. Leatherbound books line the shelves of secretaries stocked with hotel stationery.

Each of the guest rooms is individually decorated, painted in pastel colors or papered with flowers. Some have canopy beds with eiderdown quilts and armchairs; others have large antique desks. The larger rooms have vanities.

Dining options range from the casual, contemporary Ivy

Grill, offering American cuisine cooked over an open flame, to the formal Edwardian decor of the Daniel Webster Room, where more traditional New England and classical cuisine is featured. There's also a pine-paneled tavern decorated with historic photographs and trophies.

Guests can use the college's indoor pool, tennis courts, and golf club. Some of the inn's patrons are affiliated with Dartmouth; others are exploring the upper Connecticut River valley.

Vermont

The Middlebury Inn
14 Court House Square
Middlebury, Vermont 05753
802-388-4961
800-842-4666

Innkeepers: Frank and Jane Emanuel
55 rooms, 20 motel units
$86-$122 per couple, EP
All 3 meals served
Major credit cards
Children welcome
Pets in motel only
Open year-round

Right on busy Court House Square and overlooking the village green and bandstand, the 1827 Middlebury Inn and its 1825 Porter House annex-mansion have always been at the heart of this old college town. But many tour groups also stop here.

The top floors of the imposing three-story inn contain a maze of rooms, wide halls, and high ceilings. (A tiny old elevator still works.) Cozy little libraries and sitting areas with wood or wicker couches or chairs, magazines, and antique library shelves pop up in unexpected places. Drawings, ornately framed paintings, and photographs line the passageways, which drop two or three steps here and add two or three steps there. Of different sizes and shapes (some can accommodate five people), the most private rooms are tucked away in dead-end alcoves. (Be sure to ask for a quiet room.) Unexpected surprises include wallpapered sprinkler pipes, hand-cut lampshades, and antique beds of maple and cherry.

The mansion next door has only five rooms, and a spiral staircase leads to the second floor. The truly stately feeling here is carried over from the inn and magnified. The large rooms, with TVs and a sitting area and phone, are each decorated in traditional Victorian fashion.

The main floor of the inn houses a nondescript bar, a gift and antiques shop, two elegantly appointed blue dining rooms, and lots of wooden tables and chairs. Various porches allow warm-weather dining outside. Lunch is taken on the indoor porch next to the gift shop, while breakfast buffets and Continental dinners are offered in a larger room with three bay windows or in a smaller room with walls of books.

The Emanuels were awarded a grant by Vermont's Division of Historic Preservation in 1977; their visible work includes the painting and papering of the guest rooms and public areas. Not so visible is the extensive rewiring and updating of plumbing and heating facilities.

Country B&Bs

Many of these bed-and-breakfasts are every bit as handsome as the places we describe under inns. The hosts, however, tend to sit down to breakfast and make a point of talking with their guests; dinner, although available in some cases, is not routinely served.

Connecticut

Felshaw Tavern
Five Mile River Road
Putnam, Connecticut 06260
203-928-3467

Innkeepers: Terry and Herb Kinsman
2 or 3 rooms (2 with private bath)
$70
No credit cards
Children welcome
No pets
Open year-round

Putnam is a little dot of a place that was probably better known in the 1700s than it is today. The Felshaw Tavern, however, is as famous now as it was then; it takes its name from the original tavern of 1742. General Israel Putnam (of Bunker Hill fame) was one famous soldier who stayed here. Terry and Herb Kinsman bought the place about ten years ago and brought it back to life.

The inn sits on a little more than 3 acres and is set back from the road behind a low stone wall. It has been carefully refitted with many fine pieces built by Herb. Though cabinetry isn't his livelihood, it could have been. He made the black walnut grandfather's clock in the formal dining room as well as the handsome front door.

If you come through the back door, you'll enter by the sunroom, where breakfast is usually served. In the kitchen hang muffin irons still used by Terry for her bran muffins. She keeps china and crystal in a Dutch *kas* made of Netherlands oak that dates from 1670. In the winter, the dining room is warmed by a fireplace.

A parlor provides musical enjoyment with a sophisticated sound system. Listen to your favorite compact disc here amid fine woods and a beamed ceiling. An adjacent TV room has another fireplace, a Winthrop desk made by Herb, and lots of books. The ceiling here is all wood.

Upstairs are the guests' quarters. Both rooms are spacious and charming and have private baths, four-poster beds, antique furnishings, and fireplaces. You can watch TV or read in the cozy, oak-paneled study upstairs.

The Felshaw Tavern is off Route 395 and U.S. Route 44. Putnam is near Pomfret, with its prep schools and lovely stone and brick churches. You can visit the Most Holy Trinity Church and the Rectory School.

Manor House
P.O. Box 447
Maple Avenue
Norfolk, Connecticut 06058
203-542-5690

Innkeepers: Diane and Henry Tremblay
8 rooms (6 with private bath)
$65-$145 per couple
Major credit cards
Children over 12 welcome
No pets
Open year-round

You'll be warmly received at the appropriately named Manor House in the quiet town that Yale musicians call their summer home. Encircled by a handsome stone wall and dominated by a big stone entrance, the house sits on 5½ acres of well-tended fields, lawn, and gardens.

This gray stucco Tudor home with heavy English overtones was built by Charles Spofford, the same fellow who designed the London subway system. The grand, open entryway is filled with dark, rough wood; the beautiful stained glass was a gift from Louis Tiffany. The colors and texture of Moroccan rugs throughout the house add to the sense of warmth.

The rooms have been individually decorated. One has a cherry headboard that came from a hearth on a Maine fireplace, another has an antique iron and brass bed, while yet another has a sleigh bed. The Morgan Room has a private antique elevator that still works and a balcony overlooking the lawn. The master bedroom, the Spofford Room, has a fireplace and a king-size canopy bed with ornately carved canopy rails from an old ship.

The sun room is one of the designer's most pleasant accomplishments. The informal bar has a small refrigerator where guests can stock their favorite libation. If the compact discs don't catch your eye, you can sift through the extensive collection of 78 rpm records here. The Tremblays also have a collection of old books by Connecticut publishers.

At the back of the house you may spot deer eating the tops off the tomato plants or you can pick your own raspberries. Henry's beehives, which yield the honey that guests use on their morning toast, are here as well. Breakfasts are quiet full — special waffles or an egg dish served in the elegant dining room or on the porch or lawn.

In the summer Norfolk has music, in the fall the foliage, and in the winter cross-country skiing and its own music series.

Maine

The Bagley House
R.R. 3, Box 269C
Freeport, Maine 04032
207-865-6566

Innkeeper: Sigurd Knudsen
5 rooms (3 with private bath)
$60-$80 per couple
Major credit cards
Children welcome
No pets
Open year-round

Just 10 minutes from the hustle and bustle of outlet shopping in Freeport, the Bagley House is a world apart on its 6 acres of field and forest. The Colonial house (1772), the oldest in the town, was originally a school, a worship place, and an inn. Today, travelers immediately feel a sense of belonging as they enter the seemingly unobtrusive home that has been restored with meticulous attention to detail.

A beautifully preserved house isn't enough to make a great bed-and-breakfast, though. That's where Sig's personality comes into play. Sig has been in the business of nurturing people since he began his social service career in 1965. His experience among Alaskan Eskimos for ten years also taught him the importance of making people feel at home.

The most magnificent part of the house is the country kitchen, with a dominating fireplace, a collection of hanging baskets, wide pine floors, hand-hewn beams, and a beehive oven. Despite all this wood, it has a remarkably light feel to it. For breakfast, guests gather around the long baker's table, where Sig serves a hearty, beautifully presented meal. Maine blueberry pancakes, French toast made with a croissant with Cointreau, and roast beef hash are some of his specialties.

Each immaculate guest room uses one of Sig's sister's hand-sewn quilts as well as antique furniture, flowers, and an electric blanket. One room has a queen-size bed and working fireplace; others have double beds, two of which have an extra single bed. You may be lucky enough to sleep in one of the special beds that a Maine craftsman designed for Sig. The quietest room is the Cozy Nook. Two double beds are tucked under the sloping, beamed ceiling. Wall-to-wall carpeting and an exposed brick wall insulate you further from the world. The bath for this room is private but off the landing. The shared bathroom has a lovely pedestal sink.

The small living room has a working fireplace, and the library is stocked with books and magazines. Sig's collection of Alaskan folk art, artifacts, and carvings is displayed throughout the common rooms. Two-night Folk Art Retreats are occasionally offered; they include lessons by day and a lobster dinner by night. Sig's sister, who also fills in for Sig as innkeeper, is the teacher.

Within a 30-minute drive are numerous distractions: Portland, Bates, and Bowdoin colleges, lighthouses, state parks, and a ship launching at the Bath Iron Works. On foot you can go berry picking (out the back door) or cross-country skiing on private trails. This is one of the best values in Maine.

Blue Hill Farm Country Inn
Box 437
Blue Hill, Maine 04614
207-374-5126

Innkeepers: Jim and Marcia Schatz
14 rooms (7 with private bath)
$58-$68 per couple, $10 less for single
No credit cards
Limited accommodations for children under 12

No smoking
Open year-round

Off on a country road with 48 acres of its own woods and brooks, this pleasant B&B is well placed for exploring much of Maine's most interesting coastline, from Castine to Bar Harbor. It's 2 miles from the village of Blue Hill, 11 miles off Route 1.

Jim and Marcia Schatz have done some amazing things with the property. They've transformed the barn into an unusually welcoming space: a large, open combination sitting and breakfast room with seven guest rooms upstairs. Each of these new rooms is small but nicely decorated with iron beds and interesting art, and each has a modern bath.

The atmosphere in the farmhouse, which rambles off the large kitchen, is very different: downstairs there are small sitting rooms with sofas, one with a woodstove. The seven rooms upstairs, which include one appealing single, are old-fashioned, with shared baths.

The Schatzes are obviously attuned to the unusual wealth of the Blue Hill area's art, music, and crafts. In the summer there are frequent chamber music concerts in the barn, and the check-in desk is lined with local products; walls throughout display the work of area artists.

Londonderry Inn

Belmont Avenue (Route 3)
Belfast, Maine 04915
207-338-3988

Innkeepers: Suzanne and Buzz Smedley
7 rooms (shared baths)
$45-$50 per couple
No credit cards
Children over 12 welcome
No pets
Open Memorial Day through October

Bright and airy comfortable rooms, breakfasts served in the big country kitchen or out on the sunporch, and hiking on 51 private acres are some of the pleasures of the Londonderry Inn. The Smedleys encourage guests to relax and play board games or read in the two sitting rooms and library, and they are delighted to help plan your activities in the Belfast area.

The old clunker of a piano is yours to play, and Suzanne will be glad to give you a quart container if you'd like to pick raspberries while they're in season. They grow in such abundance (the property used to be a working farm) that the Smedleys have enough to sell to nearby stores as well as to feature them as a summer breakfast treat. Whatever the season, you'll be served a full breakfast with homemade muffins or perhaps a granola and yogurt parfait.

The house itself has a bittersweet history. It was built in 1803 by a sea captain, but he and his wife were lost at sea before they moved in. The guest rooms are furnished with family antiques, and each is named for someone who has lived here and contributed to the house's history. There are two and a half shared baths.

Belfast, about 20 minutes north of Camden on Route 1, lacks the trendy bustle of the latter town. Instead, you'll find a community of handsome ship's captains' homes and a 19th-century Main Street where interesting restaurants and shops have begun to sprout. At the town landing, you can climb aboard several different boats for a day's cruise of Penobscot Bay.

Mill Pond Inn

R.F.D. 1, Box 245
Route 215
Damariscotta Mills, Maine
207-563-8014

Innkeepers: Bobby and Sherry Whear
9 rooms, 1 with small adjoining room with twin beds (all with private bath)
$55-$65 per couple, $95 for the suite
No credit cards
Children over 5 welcome
No pets
Open year-round

A bit off the beaten track, the Mill Pond Inn is nestled by a quiet pond in a small village that hasn't changed much since the days when the mills were the major source of income for the community. This 1780 gray clapboard house with a distinctive red door offers four double rooms, all with private baths. One room has a small adjoining room with twin beds, making it ideal for families. Each of the bedrooms also has a working fireplace! The view of the pond from the third-floor bedroom is glorious.

The country and antique furnishings are wonderfully appealing in both the bedrooms and the common rooms downstairs. These latter include a living room, dining room, and publike gathering room with a large-screen color television and games.

At breakfast time, Bobby—a professional chef—is likely to simply ask you what your favorite breakfast is. Among his specialties are pancakes with fresh blueberries and omelettes with crabmeat and vegetables from the inn's garden. Bobby also cooks dinner for guests who make reservations; his baked stuffed lobster is an all-time winner. Both Bobby and Sherry enjoy doing extra things for people, sensing what might make them feel particularly at home—breakfast in bed or perhaps cookies and milk in the evening.

Nature lovers will find plenty to do here. There are forty-six species of wildlife on the mill pond and Damariscotta Lake, across the road. There's even a resident family of bald eagles a few minutes' drive or canoe paddle away. In the spring, the pond jumps with alewives that have come to spawn. In the winter, you can pack a picnic lunch and skate across the lake to a tiny island; in summer, ask Bobby for a ride in the 16-foot motorboat. Canoes are also available for use on the lake, and there is both fishing and swimming, right from the backyard.

Wooden Goose Inn
Route 1
Cape Neddick, Maine 03902
207-363-5673

Innkeepers: Jerry Rippetoe and Tony Sienicki
6 rooms (all with private bath)
$95 per couple
2-night minimum on weekends
No credit cards
Children over 12 welcome
No pets
Closed in January

This jewel of a B&B might well be more aptly named the Gilded Goose. Few, if any, accommodations along the Maine coast are as lavish. Jerry and Tony are dedicated to leaving no special touch undone. For real pampering, this is the place.

The four rooms in the inn and two additional ones in the ell are meticulously and extravagantly decorated with handsome fabrics, elegant beds (one with a canopy), and private baths in which you could take up residence. One even has a painting on an easel for bathers to contemplate from the claw-foot tub in the middle of the carpeted room. All the lushness is underscored by thick carpeting throughout, elaborate draperies, air conditioners in all rooms, love seats, ruffled pillows, and restful, shaded sunlight during the day and candlelight in the evening.

You awaken (if you wish) to a gentle knock heralding the arrival of a silver tray bearing coffee or tea. (By the time you open the door, the deliverer has disappeared, leaving the tray discreetly by the door.) Breakfast follows at a 9:00 or 10:00 A.M. seating. A typical meal may include fresh juice, date bread, cinnamon muffins, strawberries Romanoff, potato pancakes topped with a poached egg and Hollandaise sauce, or pepper and onion sausage and steamed broccoli. Everything is home-made.

A selection of tarts, also homemade, is served at tea, between four and six every afternoon. There might also be a flourless chocolate torte or a savory pâté. Both breakfast and tea are served with handsome china and cutlery.

An oasis in the midst of the bustling southern Maine coast, the Wooden Goose is right on Route 1 not far from Ogunquit, with its many shops, galleries, restaurants, and summer theater. Jerry and Tony report they're often booked for weekends several months in advance.

Massachusetts

Canterbury Farm Bed and Breakfast
Fred Snow Road
Becket, Massachusetts 01223
413-623-8765

Innkeepers: Linda and David Bacon
5 rooms (1 with private bath)
$45–$70 per couple
MasterCard, Visa
Children welcome
No pets
Open year-round

Canterbury Farm is a special place to stay for three reasons: its location, its feeling of country comfort and informality, and its winter appeal as a cross-country ski lodge, offering its own groomed and tracked trails, rentals, and lessons.

Although it's near all the attractions of the Berkshires (especially Jacob's Pillow, summer camps, lakes, woods, and hills), it really feels off the beaten track. High in the Berkshire Hills, off a dirt road on its own 200 acres of gardens, fields, and woodland ski trails, this country bed-and-breakfast offers peace and tranquillity and the beauty of nature during all four seasons.

The house itself, which dates from 1780, is a mixture of

Colonial and Federal styles, now authentically restored and furnished with antiques, country accessories, and modern conveniences. There are four guest rooms on the second floor (one with a fireplace) that share two baths, and one guest room on the first floor with its own bath. Also on the first floor is a sitting room, more like an informal family room, with a TV, a piano, games, and books. Everyone is provided with a full country breakfast.

Linda and Dave Bacon have had their B&B since 1983, although the home has been in Linda's family since about 1940. Dave, who is a landscape specialist and operates a tree farm on the property, has cut 11 miles of cross-country ski trails through the woods and hills, paying careful attention to conservation principles and natural aesthetics. He plans to cut more trails in the near future.

Another special feature of this place is that, with young children of their own, the Bacons welcome other children as their guests.

The General Rufus Putnam House
344 Main Street
Rutland, Massachusetts 01543
508-886-4256

Innkeepers: Marcia and Gordon Hickory
3 rooms (1 with private bath)
$75-$105 per couple
Cash only
Infants and teenagers welcome
Kennel on premises
Open year-round

This 1750 Colonial house has an interesting history, which you will no doubt hear should you visit. General Putnam, a soldier in the French War of 1754, was an engineer involved in the fortifications of West Point; he had a hand in compelling the British army to evacuate Boston and was also the founder of Ohio. Until 1950, the house was a museum of his life. Then the treasurer ran off with the funds and the house was sold privately. Since the Hickorys purchased it in 1981, they've restored it authentically.

You'll be greeted by a woman in a floor-length skirt, apron, and white ruffled bonnet. Afternoon tea is served in all four common rooms; one is a lovely little library with wing chairs, while one feels more like a den. There are eight fireplaces in the house, and a few are often going at once.

Thoughtful touches abound in all the guest rooms: home-made sewing kits, baskets of potpourri and fresh fruit, writing tables with paper and pen, and a folder with colonial recipes. One room is extremely well suited for a couple with an infant. It has a connecting oversize closet that has been converted into a nursery. In the shared bathroom down the hall is a basket full of toiletries you may have forgotten.

An hour before breakfast, a fresh pot of coffee will be waiting outside your door. Breakfast, at 8:30 A.M., is served in the "keeping room" by candlelight at a long trestle table. In keeping with tradition, you'll partake in a hearty colonial meal, perhaps of crusty baked macaroni and cheese, welsh rabbit, egg pie, pound cake, a crock of baked beans, and apple pie. By the way, the night before you'll be given a card on which to mark your breakfast selection; no one is forced to eat macaroni and cheese for breakfast.

Out the back door are 7 acres of an old herb garden, rolling meadows, maples and pines, stone fences, a well-hidden swimming pool, and some domestic animals. A large packet of information about things to do in the area is in each guest room.

River Bend Farm
643 Simonds Road
Williamstown, Massachusetts 01267
413-458-5504, 413-458-3121

Innkeepers: Dave and Judy Loomis
5 rooms (all share 2 baths)
$50 per couple
No credit cards
Children welcome
No pets
Open year-round

The Loomises have been caretakers of this Trustees of Reservations property since the early 1980s. A real historical timepiece, the authentic 1770 Georgian home is the embodiment of colonial life, and a foot in the door takes you a giant leap back through centuries. The town's history unfolded under its roof.

The most intriguing and dominant feature of this house is the central chimney, which serves five fireplaces, two bake ovens (it's said that bread for Revolutionary War soldiers at the battle of Bennington was baked here), a smoking chamber in the attic, and an ash pit in the basement. The chimney, 13 feet thick at its base, narrows considerably as it goes through the roof. You can see it from practically everywhere inside; it's as though the house were built around it.

A substantial Continental breakfast is served in front of this hearth. Dried flowers and herbs hanging from the mantel, a functional copper-and-tin-lined sink, and 14-inch-wide floorboards confound your sense of time. Even the granola is ladled out of a big crock into spackled tin dishes. It's dreamy to sit in front of the fire, rocking in one of the two rockers.

Each guest room reflects careful, scholarly restoration. The bed in the first-floor room has blocks underneath to level it, necessitated by incredibly uneven floorboards. The bulging and slanting walls, which follow the line of the fireplace, are most noticeable in this room. The smallest room is small indeed, with a short double rope bed of solid maple. Old-fashioned lighting fixtures, latch doors, low ceilings, and exposed original wallpaper lend authenticity to the experience. Of the two baths, one has an antique claw-foot tub, while the other, downstairs, has a shower and shelves filled with old glass bottles, antique pottery, and jugs.

The very comfortable living room, once a tavern, now displays a collection of pewter and old muskets. If you look hard enough you may find a 16-inch floorboard or two. The law in those days was that all 16-inchers had to go to the king to help build ships, but a few snuck in as testament to the solid construction by Colonel Benjimin Simonds. The front of the house, by the way, is covered with plaster, which was more expensive and more prestigious, while the sides and rear of the house are of mere planks.

The Loomises continue to operate the house as a bed-and-breakfast to support the restoration, but they believe in keeping prices reasonable. Sometimes the entire house is available for one group of people (10 maximum), who can rent it for $300 a night. It's a wonderful private retreat for family and college reunions.

Windfields Farm
R.R. 1, Box 170
Windsor Bush Road
Cummington, Massachusetts 01026
413-684-3786

Hosts: Arnold and Carolyn Westwood
2 doubles (with shared bath)
$50 per couple, $40 single, $15 per extra person
Special winter weekends: both rooms (4 people) plus kitchen
   $220, $330 for 3-day weekends

No credit cards
Children over 12 welcome
No pets
Open May through February

Windfields offers many of life's true luxuries: a spring-fed pond in summer, cross-country skiing in winter, and bountiful breakfasts of eggs, maple syrup, jams, and berries, all produced on the premises.

Although the farmhouse was built in 1860, it is a classic Federal design with two large, 15-by-15-foot upstairs bedrooms. The rooms are homey, with flowery wallpaper, wide-boarded floors, and hooked rugs. One has a fine four-poster bed and antiques; the other is plainer. The living room, low-beamed with a stone hearth, is lined with books. Meals are served in a cheery dining room, graced with original art.

The house is up a dirt road, not far from West Cummington, a village in the Hampshire hill. West of the Connecticut River valley but east of the Berkshires, this is high, rolling countryside, webbed with back roads leading to orchards, craft studios, and maple producers.

In 1961 the Westwoods bought Windfields as a summer home. Over the years they have planted a sizable organic garden, built a sugar shack, added a solar wing to the house, and turned the pond into a sand-edged oasis.

In the winter they open up an extra kitchen for guests to use and offer "winter weekends" to a minimum of four people, friends or a family who tend to cook their own lunch and dinner. Cross-country ski rentals and an unusual assortment of trails are all up the road. Windfields itself includes 200 eminently explorable acres and adjoins the Audubon Society's 1,500-acre West Mountain Wildlife Sanctuary.

- *See also:* Elling's Guest House, Great Barrington, Massachusetts

---

New Hampshire

Amos A. Parker House
Route 119, Box 202
Fitzwilliam, New Hampshire 03447
603-585-6540

Innkeeper: Freda B. Houpt
5 rooms (all with private bath)

$55-$80
No credit cards
Children over 9 welcome
Pets welcome with advance approval
Open year-round

This white clapboard, 18th-century home is a mix of formal elegance and homey comfort. The house sits squarely on Route 119, a major country road but one that gets little traffic after dark. Its back rooms overlook a deep, nicely maintained garden stretching off toward the wooded hills.

Freda Houpt is an enthusiastic transplant from the Midwest, where she lived on a farm as well as in Chicago. She can't say enough about the way New Hampshire's Monadnock Region manages to combine genuine country with urban amenities — fine art, music, and theater.

The formal rooms in the Amos Parker House retain their original paneling and hearths. The dining room is especially gracious, and it's here that you feast on breakfast creations so special that Freda refuses to divulge their recipes, even when *Yankee* magazine begs.

There is plenty of space to relax here. Besides the parlor, there's a friendly little room with a deck overlooking the garden and an inviting, open-beamed barn room with a deep couch and ample reading material.

The downstairs guest room is a romantic little suite with its own fireplace, bath, and kitchenette. Upstairs you can choose from canopy and four-poster beds, with or without bath or fireplace. Each room is decorated with flair as well as care.

Fitzwilliam itself is a picture-perfect New England town, complete with classic common, band concerts, steepled church, and town hall. It is known for its many antiques shops and for the Rhododendron State Forest, a preserve with rare wild rhododendrons growing to unusual heights which bloom early in July.

There is also swimming in Laurel Lake and cross-country skiing on an extensive network of trails. Mount Monadnock, one of New England's most popular hiking mountains, is just down the road. The Fitzwilliam Inn in the center of the village is a dependable, moderately priced dining option.

The Gilman Tavern
Main Street
Tamworth, New Hampshire 03886
603-323-8940

Innkeepers: Sue and Bill McCarthy
4 rooms (1 with private bath)
$60-$85 per couple
No credit cards
Children welcome, but ask ahead
No pets
Open year-round, but do call to check

The village of Tamworth embodies all the quaintness of a typical New England village but at the same time is friendly and open. The owners of this delightful bed-and-breakfast have imbued the tavern with these same qualities.

Sue and Bill McCarthy have an impressive collection of Shaker furniture, high-poster beds, antique clothing and baskets, and Early American bric-a-brac. The inn has old maple floors, stenciled walls, and large, warm common rooms.

The guest rooms are each decorated with a particular theme and have wonderful views. The Village Room has an amazing pickled and stenciled floor. Old toys and dolls, grain-painted furniture, and antique clothing on wall hangers abound.

Sue and Bill, who own a restaurant nearby, serve a hearty breakfast with many homemade specialties. They also serve refreshments at 4:00 P.M., such as mulled cider, hot cocoa, or tea in the winter in front of the fireplace, cold lemonade in the summer. The brick courtyard, where guests eat in warm weather, is overflowing with flowers and bordered by a picket fence. It's a quiet place to spend the afternoon.

Though the Gilman Tavern is tucked away in a village that seems remote, it's close to Lakes Ossipee and Winnipesaukee, putting water sports and fishing within driving distance. There is also mountain climbing, hiking, and, of course, antiquing. In the summer, the Barnstormers Theatre comes alive, just a short walk down Main Street.

Haverhill Inn
Dartmouth College Highway
Haverhill, New Hampshire 03765
603-989-5961

Innkeeper: Stephen Campbell
4 rooms (all with private bath)
$65 per couple, less single, midweek, off-season
No credit cards
Children over 8 welcome
No pets

No smoking
Open year-round

Haverhill has a covered bridge—the oldest in New England—
and two commons, where all-day flea markets are held on the
last Sunday of the month.

The Haverhill Inn is a gem, a classic 1810 Federal house with
canopy beds, fireplaces in every room, and plenty to read about
its surroundings, past and present.

Stephen Campbell, a computer systems manager at Dartmouth College, has a keen interest in the history of this upper
reach of the Connecticut River's Upper Valley. The walls of the
inn are decorated with old maps, and regional histories are
within reach of the comfortable chairs and sofas in the sitting
room. There is also a full complement of menus from nearby
restaurants, which Campbell is delighted to discuss.

A full breakfast is served at the long table in the dining room,
in front of the huge old hearth. Hiking and, in winter, cross-
country ski trails begin at the back door; in warm weather, this
is also the departure point for a three-day inn-to-inn canoe trip.

Olde Orchard Inn
R.R. Box 256
Lee Road
Moultonborough, New Hampshire 03254
603-476-5004

Innkeepers: Jim and Pat Knoche
5 rooms (all with private bath)
$60-$70 per couple
American Express
Children welcome, but confirm
No pets
Open year-round

The Olde Orchard Inn is an unexpected treat amid secluded
meadows and woods and, yes, old orchards. It's all quite idyllic,
to say the least. The two-hundred-year-old house is really two
houses joined together, one red brick and the other white clapboard.

Both guest and common rooms have whitewashed walls with
chair rails and moldings painted in rich colonial colors. Each
bedroom is referred to by its particular color scheme. The Gray
Room, on the first floor, is especially nice with its own fireplace. There are handmade quilts on the beds, nice linens, and
some fine stencilwork. Yet, unlike many country B&Bs, the

place is not cluttered with Early American crafts hanging from every wall.

The sitting room with camelback sofas is inviting on a frosty day. The dining room, where you'll get a large country breakfast, is equally warm.

After a hearty breakfast, you will be ready to tackle the cross-country ski trails on the property or swim in the pond. There are also many recreational opportunities at nearby Winnipesaukee and Squam lakes.

Partridge Brook Inn

P.O. Box 151
Hatt Road
Westmoreland, New Hampshire 03462
603-399-4994

Innkeepers: Don and Renee Strong
5 rooms (all with private bath)
$55-$65
MasterCard, Visa
Well-behaved children welcome
No pets
Open year-round

When Abiathar Shaw, a wealthy nailmaker, built this house in 1790, he was determined that it would be the finest in the county. He certainly succeeded, and Renee and Don Strong have carried on the goal of excellence and beauty. When the Strongs, an active, retired (well, semiretired) couple from Connecticut, bought the place in 1985, the house had been a victim of benign neglect. Fortunately, none of the beautiful woodwork, the center chimney, or wide pine floors had been destroyed.

The house, now fully restored, is one of the finest examples of Federal architecture and interior design in all of New England. The parlor bedroom is particularly beautiful. The mantel and moldings were intricately carved by a woodcarving artist, Theophilus Hoyt, in 1811. By the time he had finished his work here, a hundred days later, he had won the hand of Shaw's daughter, Sabrana. Perhaps he worked particularly hard and long to impress her, for the carvings are exquisite. The old pine floor, delicately stenciled in black, circular patterns, is also unusual and beautiful.

Renee has completed the decor with a white-on-white flowered wallpaper and a quilted white spread on the brass bed. All the beds are king- or queen-size and there are working fireplaces and modern bathrooms in the guest rooms. Those wor-

ried about the chill in some old inns in the winter will appreciate the individual thermostat in each room. All the modern
amenities are here, along with the elegance and grace of another
era.

Best of all, however, is the warmth of Don and Renee, who
make you feel as if you are truly a guest in their beloved home.
Renee cooks a wonderful breakfast, including apple pie, which
she insists is a perfectly respectable breakfast dish. If you're here
during blueberry season, you may also be treated to pancakes
made with blueberries from the garden.

Renee loves to talk about the history of the house, which at
one time was a stop on the Underground Railroad. Next to the
chimney behind a door is a narrow hiding place where slaves
were hidden. If you have a particular interest in the ordinary
lives of the previous inhabitants, Renee will point out the three-
holer — one for Mama, one for Papa, and a little one for baby
— from the old outhouse.

Partridge Brook Inn is quite pastoral, with two sheep, a brook
ideal for trout fishing, and acres of pasture and woods to explore. There is also the small city of Keene nearby, with craft
and antiques shops to poke around in as well as a state college
offering concerts and other cultural events. And Spofford Lake
will serve swimming and boating enthusiasts.

Thatcher Hill Inn

Thatcher Hill Road
Marlborough, New Hampshire 03455
603-876-3361

Innkeepers: Marge and Cal Gage
7 rooms (all with private bath)
$60-$150 per couple
MasterCard, Visa
Children over 6 welcome
No pets
Open year-round, but do call to be sure

Thatcher Hill Inn is on a back road atop, not surprisingly,
Thatcher Hill. The guest rooms are freshly painted, stenciled,
and papered, with wide pine floors, handwoven rugs, and
working fireplaces. Marge Gage spent two years creating the
quilts on the brass and wooden beds. According to her, these
have served as "the inspiration" for the decor and color schemes
of the very individual rooms. On each door is a hand-painted
slate sign, made from pieces of the roof that fell to the ground
while the renovation work was being done. The bathrooms have

old-fashioned claw-foot tubs and heated towel bars but are otherwise very modern. One nice bonus is a lovely room on the first floor that can be handled by a wheelchair all the way to the bathroom.

The common rooms, with tin ceilings and attractive antiques, also house Cal's charming collection of music boxes. The large keeping room has deep, comfortable couches, an exquisite quilt on the wall, and a big fireplace.

The granite patio is just as restful, with white lawn furniture and a view of meadows, woods, and the hills and mountains beyond. A few yards away is the Gages' fine old barn, with a cupola, from which there are spectacular views.

For more vigorous activity, there is hiking and cross-country skiing on their 60 acres as well as nearby downhill skiing, boating, swimming, and canoeing. Four or five times a year the inn is the site of dressage competitions for the Monadnock Equestrian Center.

Vermont

Hickory Ridge House
R.F.D. 3, Box 1410
Hickory Ridge Road
Putney, Vermont 05346
802-387-5709

Innkeepers: Jacquie Walker and Steve Anderson
7 rooms
$42-$75 per couple
MasterCard, Visa
Children welcome
Handicapped access
No pets
No smoking
Open year-round

A brick manse built on a southern Vermont hillrise in 1808, Hickory Ridge is a rare beauty. The ceilings are high and the old paned windows fill the rooms—painted pumpkin, rose, blue, and other authentic old colors with bright light.

The house is set off by itself in 12 acres of rolling meadow, near the village of Putney, a community known for its private school and college as well as a crafts, summer music, and drama center. It's an interesting place.

Steve Anderson can greet you in German, Russian, or

French. Between them, Jacquie and Steve have some surprising skills, from college teaching to chimney sweeping. The house is well stocked with books, its walls hung with original art.

One ground-floor room offers easy access and a bathroom designed for disabled guests. The upstairs rooms are airy and comfortable, furnished with carefully chosen antiques, including a sleigh bed. The original Federal bedrooms are large, with Rumford fireplaces. The smaller rooms are in a relatively new back wing, beyond an inviting upstairs sitting room.

This house is not cluttered. There are just enough pieces of furniture, just enough special touches, to give it unusual charm.

Breakfast features homemade muffins and breads, and dinner is offered by prior arrangement, a welcome amenity in winter. Two of Vermont's most highly rated restaurants are a short and scenic drive away, just over the hill in Newfane. You can also dine at the Putney Inn, down the road, or in Brattleboro, also nearby.

It's an easy walk to the swimming hole, and there is fishing and canoeing in the Connecticut River. In the winter, there are miles of cross-country ski trails.

The Inn at the Round Barn

R.R. Box 247
East Warren Road
Waitsfield, Vermont 05673
802-496-2276

Innkeepers: Doreen, Jack, and Annemarie Simko
6 double rooms (all with private bath)
$80-$120
Major credit cards
Children over 10 welcome
No pets
Open year-round

The Joslin Round Barn is one of only a dozen round barns left in Vermont, and it's always been something visitors have stopped their cars to admire. It sits on the East Warren Road on the quiet side of the Mad River Valley, away from the ski area and Route 100 traffic, set in 85 acres, mostly fields that stretch back into the hills.

Jack and Doreen Simko have painstakingly restored both the barn and the farmhouse, now a B&B. The downstairs rooms are unusually gracious without being stuffy. There's a living room with books, a fireplace, and music and a bright, wicker-filled sunporch, the scene of elegant breakfasts that guests tend to linger over. Some guest rooms have canopy beds and Jacuzzis, while others simply have spool or Victorian beds and standard bathrooms.

The Simkos' previous life (which their two sons carry on) was the flower business, and the house is filled with buds and greenery. There's a greenhouse now behind the barn, and you can swim into it from the 5-foot lap pool that's been created in the bottom of the barn itself. The upper two floors of the barn are now used for concerts, plays, and receptions.

Outside there are manmade ponds, one 15 feet deep for swimming. There are also informal trails, good for snowshoeing and cross-country skiing. There are also formal ski touring centers and three major ski mountains, Sugarbush, Mount Ellen, and Mad River Glen. In the summer, there is a choice of summer theater, tennis, and golf, not to mention soaring and horseback riding.

The Shoreham Inn and Country Store
Shoreham, Vermont 05770
802-897-5081

Innkeepers: Cleo and Fred Alter
11 rooms (all with shared bath)
$70 per couple
Dinner by reservation only
No credit cards
Children welcome
No pets
Open year-round

From the exterior, this three-story farmhouse is unremarkable (except for the fifty or so windows!), but inside lies one of the true hidden gems of Vermont. The masterminds of the whole marvelous place are Cleo and Fred, innkeepers since 1973 and two of the friendliest, most down-to-earth people to be found.

Upon entering, one's senses are bombarded—the place is chock full of country auction antiques, potpourri in every corner, maybe some classical music, the aroma of coffee beans. The stairway, with a balustrade from an old church in town, leads to the comfortable guest rooms that share seven bathrooms. The bedrooms are quite large, with simple and sparse furnishings. Often they have twin beds to accommodate the cyclists who ride through. Most have old-fashioned creaking floors, and each has been named after a famous local personality.

If guests have made reservations, they are greeted with a

demiliter of Korbel and something to nibble on. Downstairs is an "antiques room," where guests may try on turn-of-the-century clothing or just soak up the ambience of the 1800s. Once a month, on Sunday afternoons, an art exhibition is held in the living room (refreshingly, nothing is for sale). Sunday tea is served is served January through March.

The dining room contains five beautiful tables, a fireplace, and a big antique hutch with many different sets of old china and tableware. Breakfast consists of fresh fruit, pitchers of juice, preserves, fabulous imported granola, croissants, breads and muffins, cottage cheese, light yogurt, eggs, French toast, quiche, tea, and coffee.

The inn and the Country Store next door (built in 1799 and 1828, respectively) are a great combination. The take-out kitchen in the rear of the store provides travelers with picnic lunches. It also has a wonderful selection of gifts, crafts, cheeses, and beverages. Picnic tables in front of the inn are for all to use. Cleo and Fred also strive to acquaint visitors with the area's points of interest.

Country Inns

We used several criteria to select these inns: the innkeeper (not a general manager) is there when needed, the service is excellent, and the atmosphere, memorable.

Connecticut

Tollgate Hill Inn and Restaurant
Route 202
Litchfield, Connecticut 06759
203-567-4545

Innkeeper: Frederick J. Zivic
10 rooms and suites (all with private bath)
$90-$130 per couple, including breakfast
2-night minimum stay on weekends
Lunch and dinner also served
Major credit cards
Children welcome
Pets welcome
Open year-round

Litchfield looks like a Norman Rockwell painting: it's filled with brilliant red leaves in autumn and dressed like a winter palace at Christmastime. When you go to Litchfield, plan on staying at the Tollgate Hill Inn and Restaurant. It's been a waystation for travelers since 1745, when it was a popular stop between Hartford and Albany.

The red clapboard gambrel house sits far enough back from the road so that noise isn't a problem. An old English phone booth and a schoolhouse are in the back. The six rooms in the inn may have a fireplace, sitting area, and a love seat or sofabed. Those on the third floor have handsome cathedral ceilings, are nicely decorated, and cost the least. The walls are painted with cozy colors: apricot, duckling yellow, and red and white.

The schoolhouse was moved to its present site in 1923 from

Berlin, Connecticut. Its two rooms and two suites provide homey inn decor without sacrificing the necessities many travelers would not want to be without: a cable TV and a direct-dial phone. Both suites are large, have sitting areas, and are decorated with matching fabrics. In one, an old blackboard has been covered in designer material. The other has a four-poster bed, matching wingback chair and love seat, and a fireplace.

The main inn has two delightfully romantic dining rooms that serve lunch and dinner to the public. On the menu is smoked salmon, roast duck, oysters on the half shell, and poached sea scallops. Choose from among 100 vintage wines to accompany your meal. Little wonder the restaurant gets as much attention as the inn.

Adjoining one dining room is a bar, open until 11:00 P.M. or until people finally wander home. It's an attractive place, with cane bar stools, paneling, and a fireplace. Out back is a Federal ballroom with a fiddler's loft (and piano) that's open on Saturday nights and is sometimes used for dinner or meetings.

Wake Robin Inn
Route 41
Lakeville, Connecticut 06039
203-435-2515

Innkeeper: Henri J. P. Manassero
25 inn rooms; 15 rooms in annex
$90-$200 per couple, EP
Dinner served
Major credit cards
Children welcome
Pets welcome in annex
Open year-round

The small, relaxed town of Lakeville, the home of the Hotchkiss School, is filled with elegant old properties, and the restored Wake Robin Inn is counted among them. This three-story white clapboard structure, formerly the Taconic School for Girls, exudes a grand old resort ambience.

The foyer has a white brick fireplace, Oriental carpets, hardwood floors, a hotel-style reception desk, and wingback chairs, giving it a formal and sophisticated yet relaxed feeling. The breakfast room also has a fireplace, and plans call for one end of it to become a library.

The front rooms upstairs provide outstanding views of the Berkshire foliage. One room has a sleigh bed; Room 24 has a private balcony; most have a double and a twin or two twin beds. The color schemes of the complementary wallpaper and drapes are country chic. The third-floor rooms have unusual angles because of the roofline, with wallpaper wrapping around the ceiling. If the inn itself is full, stay somewhere else —the nearby single-story motel annex houses primarily race-track workers.

The inn's restaurant is in the extended parlor room, where a deck has been added for terrace dining. Served on Wedgwood china by candlelight, the French dishes include medallions of veal, chicken breast with wild mushrooms in a light cream sauce, and a medley of shrimp, lobster, and salmon. The forest green, knotty-pine bar offers lawn views as well as a deck.

Maine

Country Club Inn
Box 680
Rangeley, Maine 04970
207-864-3831

Innkeeper: Sue Crory
20 rooms (all with private bath)
$63-$72 per person, MAP; $79 per couple, B&B, off-season
Major credit cards
Children welcome
Pets welcome for a fee
Open mid-May to mid-October, late December to late March

Crowning a hill in the Rangeley Lakes district of Maine, the Country Club Inn boasts spectacular views—in fact, some of the best in New England—of lakes, mountains, and valleys, whether from the guest rooms, the golf course, the pool, or the deck. The main lodge has an open, beamed living room, a dining room that serves good, reasonably priced meals, and a small cocktail lounge. Guests stay in sunny, motel-style rooms.

With a floor-to-ceiling fieldstone fireplace, comfortable sofas, and a selection of magazines, the large living room is the focal point of this friendly inn—except on summer evenings, when guests frequently wander out to the deck to soak up the country air.

One wall of the pleasant dining room is a large picture window. Sun floods the room, complementing the pastel table-cloths and bright flower arrangements. Those on special diets can choose from chicken, broiled swordfish, scallops, and a stir-fry vegetarian dish. Soups, salads, fresh bread, and homemade cakes, pies, and fruit salad complete a healthy, satisfying meal.

The clean, boxy guest rooms, on the ground floor of the main lodge and in a separate one-story building, are comfortably furnished with twin beds, a table, chair, and bureau; all have private baths.

The lodge is next to an 18-hole golf course, with carts and professional instruction. There is also an outdoor swimming pool. Guests can also take advantage of the myriad sporting opportunities offered by the Rangeley Lakes.

The Crocker House Country Inn
Hancock Point Road
Hancock, Maine 04640
207-422-6806

Innkeepers: Richard and Elizabeth Malaby
10 rooms (all with private bath)
$68-$75 including full breakfast, from $50 off-season
Dinner served to the public
Major credit cards
Well-mannered children welcome
Well-mannered pets welcome
Open late April to New Year's Eve

Just a half hour's drive north of Bar Harbor, Hancock Point has a different feel entirely. It is very quiet and private, an old summer community with an octagonal library, a summer chapel, the second smallest post office in the United States (we'd like to see the smallest!), and four clay tennis courts. The nearby dock is maintained by the Hancock Point Village Improvement Society.

The Crocker House was built in 1884 as an annex to one of the large hotels, of which there were once a number on the point. It's been beautifully refurbished inside and out, its gray shingles and white trim painted and baths, upgraded or added, nicely done with natural woods. The guest rooms are tastefully furnished, and there are nice touches like soap and shampoo in the baths, chocolates by the bed.

Dining is important here. A full breakfast is served from 8:00 to 10:00 A.M., and dinner is a several-course affair. Appetizers might include cream of mussel soup or pâté mousse truffe, entrées: poached salmon Florentine, Crocker House scallops, gray sole meunière or veal Monterey. Sunday brunch is a production, featuring brandied French toast, steak and eggs, and a Cromlet (Crocker House omelette).

Richard and Elizabeth Malaby have established a strong local reputation for their restaurant as well as a following among guests who have visited since 1980. There is plenty to see and do around here, but the Crocker House is the kind of place where you want to simply stay within walking and bicycling (bikes cost $5 per day) distance. It's also possible to come by sea; request a mooring.

Surry Inn

P.O. Box 25
Surry, Maine 04684
207-667-5091

Innkeeper: Peter Krinsky
13 rooms (11 with private bath)
In season (June-October): $52-$62 per couple, including full breakfast; $12 for each extra person; less off-season
Dinner also served
MasterCard, Visa
Children over 5 welcome
No pets
Open year-round

The Surry Inn is a warm and friendly place with five common rooms. Games, good books, and fireplaces abound. The furniture is comfortable and inviting. A 60-foot porch that runs the entire length of the inn has wicker furniture and is bathed in the afternoon sun. There are lovely views of Contention Cove, the lawn sloping down to it, and the sunset.

Many of the bedrooms have been decorated with stencils. All of them have white or light-colored walls that give them a clean and airy feeling. Many of the rooms have views to the cove.

A full breakfast is served, and there is a choice of six to eight entrées each night. The food is excellent and reasonably priced. For the cost of an entrée elsewhere, diners have a choice of soup, a green salad, hot homemade bread, medallions of pork sautéed with apples, onions, and herbs, and a choice of desserts (probably homemade), such as lemon mousse with fresh blueberries and cream. Other entrées could be veal scallops in an herbed mustard and cream sauce, fresh scallops sautéed in garlic butter with tomatoes and ripe olives, or broiled fresh halibut with sour cream and fresh fines herbes. A good, inexpensive house wine is available.

To work off such fine meals, there is canoeing, rowing, croquet, and horseshoes. The water in the inn's cove is unusually warm for Maine, usually between 60 and 70 degrees. This may well be one of the few places in Maine where you will want to swim!

Massachusetts

The Inn at Duck Creeke
P.O. Box 364
Wellfleet, Massachusetts 02667
508-349-9333

Innkeepers: Judith Pihl and Robert Morrill
23 rooms (some with private bath), 4 cottages
$55-$80 per couple, including breakfast
Major credit cards
Children welcome
No pets
Open May through Columbus Day

Wellfleet is a small, quiet town on the northern, bay side of the Cape. While it's hardly in the country, it does have that country feeling to it. To enjoy Wellfleet's relaxed and easy pace, you'll want to stay at the Inn at Duck Creeke. While it's a bit out of the center, on the road into town, it will also give you that lazy, summer vacation feeling.

Originally a sea captain's home built in the mid-19th century, the building was converted into an inn more than fifty years ago. The reception desk is high and formal, almost like a hotel's, and the foyer is spacious, with a few comfortable wing chairs should you be waiting for someone. The wallpaper is dark blue with little white flowers for relief; the floors are knotty pine and hardwood. The complimentary Continental breakfast is served from 8:00 to 10:00 A.M. in a dining room; you bus your own dishes.

The upstairs rooms are furnished simply—country comfortable and utilitarian. The halls are narrow and turn frequently; you step up or down here and there to get to your room. The third floor tends to be a bit warm in the summer, so the rooms have air conditioning. They also look much more rustic looking and have wall-to-wall carpeting and more angled ceilings. The bathrooms are bright and shiny, whether shared or private. Behind the inn, on the edge of the woods, are two guest houses: Saltworks, a saltbox Cape building with five rooms; and the Carriage House, with two rooms, exposed barnboard, and a cathedral ceiling.

A fish dinner at one of the inn's restaurants is a treat. The

Tavern Room dates from the early 1800s; during the summer there is occasional live entertainment here. Choose from an assortment of appetizers: chili, hummus, Cajun chicken wings, nachos, or shrimp. Entrées run $11-$15 for various seafood dishes: mussels, scallops, lobster, shrimp, or a seafood gumbo. For more elegant dining overlooking a duck pond, Sweet Seasons, next door, has Continental dishes.

Wellfleet's summer crowd is mostly permanent, but don't let that deter you from wandering around the town and driving its back roads. First head down to the dock, then to White Crest Beach, Cahoon's Hollow Beach, or over to the National Seashore and Marconi Beach. The Audubon Society also operates a wildlife sanctuary nearby.

The Old Inn on the Green
New Marlborough, Massachusetts 01230
413-229-7924

Innkeepers: Leslie Miller and Bradford Wagstaff
6 rooms (5 with shared bath), 8 suites (all with private bath)
$75-$110 per couple, including breakfast
Dinner also served on weekends, Sundays in season
No credit cards
Children welcome
No pets
Open year-round except March

A classic, double-porch tavern that was built in about 1760, this building served as a village inn right through the 1920s, then slipped (along with New Marlborough itself) from public notice, slumbering through the country inn revival.

It was only a matter of time, however. New Marlborough itself is a gem of an old town, and the inn, which overlooks the green, has been deftly restored. Authenticity is the unspoken but proud buzzword here—minimalist period furniture, a harvest table that seats sixteen, flickering lamps on the dining room walls. The floors are made of wide unfinished planks, with an occasional throw rug. The walls are very simple white plaster with pastel blue trim and stenciling. Large flower arrangements and curtain material from Old Sturbridge Village, transformed into functional and pretty window dressings, add a warm touch to the first floor.

The bedrooms are large and furnished with antiques. The large corner room has a double and twin bed with a private bath. One room has an iron and brass bed with a giant wood and tile shower in the hall. Two front rooms have old doors that fold back on themselves, transforming them into one huge one. In the early days, when the inn was a stagecoach stop, it functioned as a ballroom, and late at night it turned into a bunkroom for the people who couldn't afford a private room. (Bedrolls fell wherever there was open space.) The front rooms have access to the balcony, with its views of the mountains beyond the village. It's a bit too easy to while away the afternoon, watching the comings and goings of the quiet town in one of the rocking chairs. Complimentary wine is offered in the afternoon.

Breakfast is bigger than Continental but not exactly "full." Since the inn is small enough, Leslie Miller will make eggs on request. The prix fixe menu changes daily and seasonally. One possibility is spring watercress soup, prime rib of beef in beer and horseradish, with oven-browned potatoes and wild mushrooms, topped off with strawberry shortcake or chocolate rum cake. This is the kind of place people drive two hours to for a special dinner, dine for three hours, and drive the two hours home (if they can't get a room.) Dinner reservations are required; don't wait until the last minute.

At our last visit, Bradford was busy carving eight "comfortable but not plush" suites from an old working barn just a hop, skip, and a jump down the road. The interior architectural design just may win some kind of award from *Architecture Digest*. Though designed for business meetings, it is available for travelers.

New Hampshire

The Birchwood Inn
Route 45
Temple, New Hampshire 03084
603-878-3285

Innkeepers: Bill and Judy Wolfe
7 rooms (5 with private bath)
$60-$70 per couple, including breakfast
Dinner also served
No credit cards
Children over 10 welcome
No pets
Open year-round except 2 weeks in April

Built as an inn in around 1800, this brick building with a wooden addition sits in the center of a picture-perfect village in

New Hampshire's Monadnock region. Late afternoon birds chirping, front porch rockers, lilac trees, and birches all contribute to the serenity of this quiet corner of a quiet town green. Inside, lovers of country inns will not be disappointed, but this is not the place for those who require a private bath and color TV.

Judy and Bill Wolfe, who have owned the inn since 1980, are enthusiastic hosts. They've restored the fine 1825 Rufus Porter murals on the dining room wall. There's a cheery tavern room (with a BYOB bar) with a stenciled floor, red glass, local crafts, toy trains, a gumball machine, and tables set up for checkers and chess. A square Steinway grand piano from 1878, many other antique instruments hanging on the walls, and a modern television occupy the parlor.

Each of the eight rooms has its own theme (the Seashore Room, Music Studio, Bottle Shoppe, Editorial Room), carried out in wallpaper and antique furnishings. Braided oval rugs lay on wide floorboards. All rooms are on the second floor except one room accessible by a wheelchair. Room 5, with lots of books, is small; single travelers are put there.

Entrées, posted on the blackboard, might include filet mignon, lamb chops, roast duckling, or fresh fish. Bill is the entrée chef and Judy bakes the breads and desserts. In addition to the main intimate dining room, there is a smaller dining room that can accommodate up to twelve people for a private party.

Temple Mount, a fine family ski area with extensive snow-making and a cross-country ski network, is just 3 miles up the road. In the summer, this is great country for aimless touring, music, hiking, antiques, and shopping.

The Chase House
R.R. 2, Box 909
Cornish, New Hampshire 03745
603-675-5391

Innkeepers: Marilyn and Hal Wallace
5 rooms, suite available (all with private bath)
$75-$95, including breakfast; $15 more in foliage season
MasterCard, Visa
Well-behaved children welcome; infants by prior arrangement
No pets
No smoking
Open year-round

It is easy to understand why the Chase House is a National Historic Landmark. The birthplace and home of Lincoln's secretary of the treasury, Salmon Portland Chase, this once-neglected Federal home was given new life by its present owner, Peter Burling, and two professional restorers in 1985. Peter's wife and her decorator chose furniture and colors that completed their work. The house is elegant, authentic, perfect. There are beautiful period wallpapers in the sitting rooms and guest rooms, with richly draped swags at the windows. The upstairs hallway has maple floors with a stenciled border that Peter unearthed beneath layers of linoleum.

For all its elegance and beauty, the Chase House is a friendly, pleasant place to stay, largely due to the unpretentiousness and cordiality of Marilyn and Hal Wallace. They have great respect for the historic house they live in as well as their guests, and they do everything they can to make a stay memorable. Marilyn's breakfast is, as Hal says, a knockout — fresh fruit compote with grenadine sauce, several kinds of eggs, homemade breads, a variety of breakfast meats, and blueberry pancakes or French toast. Guests eat in the cheerful breakfast room or out on the deck, overlooking the flower and vegetable garden. The views from the deck and the sunny guest rooms are of meadows and woods. Across the road is a river where guests can fish or walk along the riverbank. Throughout the area, there are trails for skiing and hiking, including 3½ miles of groomed trails on Chase House land.

Cornish is a picturesque New England town. It has the longest covered bridge in the United States, linking it to Windsor, Vermont, and some smaller covered bridges as well. Other special places are the Saint-Gaudens National Historical Site and some fine historic homes in the area; many of them once belong to famous artists and writers.

Christmas Farm Inn

Jackson Village, New Hampshire 03846
603-383-4313

Owners/hosts: Sydna and Bill Zeliff
37 rooms and suites (all with private bath)
$136-$180 per couple, MAP
Major credit cards
Children welcome
No pets
Open year-round

There's a real all-in-the-family feeling here, one like that of an inn-siders club. One of the best things about this inn is that it has such a variety of accommodations. The food is also note-worthy.

The main inn has Colonial rooms, two with a luxurious Jacuzzi and sitting area. More modern rooms, with carpeting and individual thermostats, are next door in the Salt Box. There are a few more private two-bedroom cottages with porches, a refrigerator, television, and fireplace. An authentic sugaring house has been converted into a two-room suite. As in many of the cottages, the log cabin, made from trees on the property, requires a minimum of four adults.

The dining room is country elegant, with meals served by candlelight. Start with escargot or crab ravioli and move onto the main dishes, which might include sautéed veal, chicken saltimbocca, and seafood Alfredo.

The inn sometimes has a commercial feeling, since the function center, a renovated barn, accommodates weddings, small business gatherings, and the like. But this building also houses a bar, games, four large suites, a massive fieldstone fireplace, and a sauna.

Across the street is a great swimming pool, putting green, wax room for skiing, and a playground. Quite a few special events and packages are planned throughout the year. As you might expect, Christmas is a special time here.

Jackson, a typically quaint village in the heart of the White Mountains, is full of things to do in every season, for this is hiking and skiing country. Downhill skiing is available nearby at Attitash, Wildcat, and Cranmore mountains. The Jackson Ski Touring Association has 125 kilometers of well-maintained cross-country trails. Route 16 north to Pinkham Notch and Tuckerman's Ravine, the Mount Washington Auto Road to the summit, and the Kancamagus Highway to the east are a few of the most scenic drives in all New England. And there's always shopping in North Conway.

Dexter's Inn and Tennis Club
Stagecoach Road
Sunapee, New Hampshire 03782
603-763-5571
800-232-5571

Innkeepers: Michael and Holly Durfor
18 rooms (all with private bath)
$115-$155 per couple, MAP; off-season B&B rates
MasterCard, Visa
Children welcome

Pets permitted in Annex rooms ($10 daily charge)
Open May through October

Dexter's is a standout. The big yellow clapboard house sits atop a steep back road, commanding a sweeping view of the lake and the mountains. It is shaded by mature trees and backed by a stretch of flowers and lawn. There is a fine pool, nicely hedged (thus meeting the legal requirement for a fence), and the three tennis courts are the stuff of tournaments.

A formal living room has upholstered chairs and sofas around the hearth and some five hundred books. The "cocktail lounge" is the other gathering space: large and pine-paneled, with tables and plenty of games. The present dining room is a small, sunny room on the other side of the house, with a view over the lake.

Many rooms are large and have floral wallpaper, modern furniture, and some antiques. The rooms are oddly shaped, and the halls zigzag to conform with the building. Room 12, in the Annex across the road, is a favorite, with a four-poster bed and a view. A small breakfast can be served in your room, if requested.

The main house was built in 1801 and restored in the 1930s by an adviser to Herbert Hoover. Since 1974, Frank and Shirley Simpson have added to and renovated the house; now they've passed the property on to their son-in-law, so things are sure to continue in the same tradition.

The Mount Sunapee area offers summer theater, boating, hiking and shopping, but this place should appeal particularly to tennis players. In bad weather, guests can use indoor courts in nearby New London.

Riverside Inn
Route 16A
Intervale, New Hampshire 03845
603-356-9060

Innkeepers: Anne and Geoff Cotter
7 rooms (3 with private bath)
$55-$95 per couple, including breakfast
Dinner also served
Major credit cards
Children welcome
Pets accepted with prior arrangement
Open year-round

The Riverside Inn is on the Intervale Resort Loop, just beyond the outlet malls and noise of North Conway. But once you turn into the circular drive of this turn-of-the-century country home, you will feel worlds away. Anne and Geoff Cotter make a special effort to make you feel at home.

A glassed-in porch along the front of the house has comfortable chairs, small tables to rest a book on, and a soothing fountain trickling in the corner. The sitting room inside is attractively furnished with a velvet settee and other Victorian antiques. There is also a well-stocked porchside bar and an elegant rose and green dining room.

The food served in this lovely dining room draws many guests as well as the public to the Riverside. Anne and Geoff once owned a restaurant and now serve superb international cuisine. If the sweet basil or vegetables taste especially fresh, that's because they are — straight from the Cotters' garden. Entrées may include a lightly curried shrimp with candied ginger or a more traditional veal fillet with herb batter, sautéed in butter.

The Riverside Inn is the former summer home of Geoff's family, and the guest rooms are named after various relatives as well as the family chauffeur and governess. All the rooms have coordinated drapes and bedspreads, and the bathrooms are modern and attractive. The entire inn has a lush, forest-green carpet. Up the stairway is a built-in bookcase from which guests can borrow books to read in their rooms.

Most people staying at the Riverside are happy to simply relax in the inn, lie in the hammock, or walk beside the meandering river along the property. For those who want more excitement, the Mount Washington Valley is just minutes away.

Snowvillage Inn
Snowville, New Hampshire 03849
603-447-2818

Innkeepers: Peter, Trudy, and Frank Cutrone
19 rooms (all with private bath)
$80-$120 per couple, including breakfast
Dinner also served
Major credit cards
Children over 8 welcome
No pets
Open year-round except April

The red shingle house sits up a back road, near the picturesque lakeside village of Eaton Center. Although it's just a short drive from Mount Washington Valley, both village and inn feel away from it all. The inn consists of three buildings, with seven rooms in the main house, eight in the Barn, and four in the newly added Chimney house.

Visitors are greeted gently by Boris, a huge white Samoyed, and some of the inn's four cats—or by one of the Cutrones, who have given up successful professional careers to be at Snowvillage, which was, they will tell you, "home at first sight."

If you don't like informal, cluttered, friendly places, don't come here. If you do, there's much to recommend Snowvillage. The views of the Presidential Range are spectacular and the gardens have won awards. The view from the bed in Room 13 doesn't get any better. The two rooms above the dining room are like a Swiss chalet. The barn rooms on the north side are larger, mostly with two double beds. The four rooms in the Chimney house have fireplaces, New England country decor, and a handsome common area with a fireplace.

The chalet-style dining room (light wood, ceiling fans, and picture windows, open to the public) is known for its whole-some and tasty dinners. They begin with homemade breads and home-grown greens, proceed to imaginative soups and such entrées as dill baked haddock or a Viennese beef tender-loin with a wine sauce, and are followed by French silk pie or "Salzburger nocker" (Trudy is Austrian). Vegetarian meals are also available.

Guests tend to take cocktails on the screened porch in sum-mer and by the fire in the beamed living room in winter. There is cross-country skiing on the property (13 kilometers of groomed trails) and skating on the lake. Rentals, lessons, and guided tours are available right at the inn. Alpine skiing is just down the road at King Pine. Some of New Hampshire's most famous ski mountains—Wildcat, Attitash, and Mount Cranmore—are a half-hour drive away. In summer there is swimming in Crystal Lake (just down the road) or in mountain streams. An abundance of books and places to read them, a variety of lawn games, a clay tennis court, and trails through the woods round out the inn's activities.

Rhode Island

Shelter Harbor Inn
Route 1
Westerly, Rhode Island 02891
401-322-8883

Innkeepers: Debbye and Jim Dey
24 rooms (all with private bath)
$78-$96 per couple, including breakfast

Lunch and dinner also served
Major credit cards
Children welcome
No pets
Open year-round

A country inn off Route 1? Well, technically it isn't in the country, but it does have that country feel about it. It's actually a mile from beautiful sandy beaches, stone walls, and saltwater ponds. If you haven't discovered this part of Rhode Island, you're in for an unexpected treat.

The main inn was built as a farmhouse in the early 1800s. As is true of many country inns, things aren't picture perfect here: the carpet on the stairs is slightly worn and the paint is chipping around a few doors. But there's a comfortable, warm feeling and a good choice of rooms. Most rooms have air conditioning; some have fireplaces and private decks. Next door, in the converted barn, are ten more rooms sharing a spacious living room, which opens onto an even more spacious deck. The only real area for guests in the main inn, besides the secluded terrace out back, is a small library. A long, third-floor porch provides views of Block Island on a clear day.

There are three dining rooms; one, a glass-enclosed terrace, has lovely table settings. The dinner entrées around $15 and include specialties such as fresh seafood pot pie.

On the grounds are paddle tennis courts, a hot tub (with shower and changing rooms), and a well-maintained croquet court. Nearby are Mystic Seaport, diversions at Misquamicut for the kids, the fishing village cum antiquing haven of Stonington, and the ferry to Block Island.

Vermont

Birch Hill Inn
P.O. Box 346
Manchester, Vermont 05254
802-362-2761

Innkeepers: Jim and Pat Lee
5 rooms, 1 cottage
$48-$53 per person double occupancy, including breakfast
Dinner served Monday, Tuesday, Saturday, Sunday
Personal check preferred; MasterCard, Visa
Children over 6 welcome
No pets
Open late December to early April, mid-May to late October

For 190 years this inn was a family home, and since 1917 Pat Lee's family has lived here. In 1981 Pat and Jim transformed this home into an elegant country inn, set in the midst of 140 acres crossed by stone walls and split-rail fences. Its accessible and tranquil location makes it an ideal spot; birch trees, pastures, and green rolling hills induce calm and romance.

The spacious entrance hall is bright and furnished with country antiques, such as a spinning wheel. The Federal doorway opens onto a graceful staircase that leads to the bedrooms upstairs.

The two largest bedrooms are in the front of the house, one decorated in pink, one in blue. The East Room, with two twin beds, has the most magnificent view. In the large master bedroom are exposed beams and a working fireplace. The furnishings include country wallpaper, French or hunting prints, and restored family antiques. The views reveal mountains, gardens, and the private trout pond (for fishing as well as reflecting).

The huge pine-paneled living room, with its well-stocked library and fireplace, opens onto a marble terrace. The cottage is off to the right (near the kidney-shaped pool) and includes a bedroom, sitting room, bath, and pantry with refrigerator. A single dinner seating at 7:30 P.M. serves the same menu, family style, to everyone at a long polished table that seats fourteen. At the cocktail hour, guests find savory hors d'oeuvres and a setup for their own libations.

The Southern Vermont Art Center is a half mile down the road, and Manchester is teeming with life. Other activities include strolling or cross-country skiing on the inn's paths and trails that begin at the front door.

Inwood Manor

East Barnet, Vermont 05821
802-633-4047

Innkeepers: Peter Embarrato and Ron Kaczor
9 rooms (with shared baths)
Doubles $65, singles $60 ($10 more in foliage season),
    including full breakfast
Dinner also served ($19.50)
5% charge for credit cards
Children not appropriate
No pets
Open year-round

Inwood Manor is a large yellow house on a plateau above the Passumpsic River near its junction with the Connecticut. Creature comforts like excellent ethnic dinners and sunny guest rooms complement days spent floating downstream in a canoe, exploring the woods on skis or foot, or sunbathing on a deck overlooking the river. Friendly, stress free, and isolated from commerce, the inn provides a thoughtful and restful retreat.

Ron Kaczor and Peter Embarrato have diverse talents, including cooking, decorating, and building. The house itself, once the main lodging for a large croquet factory, has been charmingly renovated. The 2½-acre pond behind the inn is stocked with trout, but it's also good for swimming.

The ground floor of the inn has several public rooms: the living room, with its Queen Anne sofas, thick carpets, and woodstove; the library, with an upright piano and a poker table, an overhead fan, and a good selection of books and games; and a sunny porch filled with plants, which is a cheerful place for breakfast.

Upstairs, the guest rooms open off a wide hallway and are decorated with items collected by Ron and Peter on frequent trips to Mexico, such as colorful wall hangings and ceramic pots. The rooms share four spacious hall baths, decorated with numerous religious pictures and leafy plants.

Both the innkeepers like to cook, and they travel far to collect spices and special ingredients. Soup-to-nuts dinners frequently feature regional Italian dishes with homemade pasta or Mexican specialties; fresh local produce is used. Dinner, served at one seating around a long table in a candlelit dining room, has the atmosphere of a private party in a friend's home. As Ron says, "We don't get many guests who come here to be by themselves. Our guests talk about travel, politics, food, cities."

Guests might visit the nearby White Mountains or walk to the waterfalls in the area. Twenty acres of woods and fields provide ample cross-country ski and hiking trails. Inwood Manor caters to canoeists and bikers all summer. Ron and Peter launch canoeing guests with a film of previous trips (there's also a canoe by the pond for practicing strokes). Guests paddle a scenic reach to Newbury, spend the night at a B&B (luggage is transferred), and continue down to Orford or Bradford, where they are picked up and shuttled back to the inn. This trip costs $95 per person per day, including meals and lodging; canoes cost $35 for two days.

Kedron Valley Inn
Route 106
South Woodstock, Vermont 05071
802-457-1473

Innkeepers: Max and Merrily Comins
30 rooms; 15 in the main house, 7 in the Tavern, others in
 the "log cabin"
$78-$169 per couple B&B, $118-$209, MAP; $10 per extra
 person in the room, plus meals; add 15% gratuity
2-night minimum on most weekends
Major credit cards
Children welcome; crib and cot charge
Pets permitted
Closed 3 weeks in April, 1 week in November

This brick inn and adjacent tavern have formed the center of
South Woodstock, one of Vermont's most affluent and picturesque villages, since the 1820s. Horses actually outnumber cars
in South Woodstock, and the surrounding hills are webbed
with trails — to which inn guests have access on mounts available from the Kedron Valley Stables, next to the inn.

The inn itself stands on its own merit as a luxurious retreat.
The rooms have all been carefully decorated; most have antique
quilts and seven have working fireplaces, seven more, wood-
stoves. The most splendid and spacious rooms are in the old
Tavern, but those in the main house, while varying in size, have
their own charm. The "log cabin" was built by the previous
owners as a motel annex, but even here the rooms are large and
furnished with antiques.

There is a large, pubby bar and an equally spacious dining
room with an ambitious menu (grilled fresh game hen, roast
Vermont lamb rack), which it rises to admirably. In the summer,
guests can swim in the large pond out back, and in the winter
there is downhill skiing at Killington or Suicide Six and plenty
of cross-country trails.

The riding offered by Kedron Valley Stables is outstanding.
This is the place for neophytes or stale riders to hone their skills
with weekend clinics, trail rides, or inn-to-inn treks.

The October Country Inn
Box 66, Upper Road
Bridgewater Corners, Vermont 05035
802-672-3412

Innkeepers: Richard Sims and Patrick Runkel
10 rooms (8 with private bath)
$100-$130 per couple, MAP, $170-$230 per weekend; $54 for
 each extra person in room, $25 per child 5-12; single rate,
 20% less; ask for 5-day rates; add 10% gratuity
No credit cards

Children welcome
No pets
No smoking
Open year-round except early November and early April

Just off busy Route 4 at one of its busiest junctions (Route 100 South), the October Country Inn is sequestered up a back road, seemingly a million miles from anywhere. Walk out the back door and up the terraced hill, up through the gardens and past the swimming pool, up and up for a sweeping view of steep valleys and the Green Mountains.

Painted oxblood red and retaining its plain farmhouse lines, the old house has been opened up inside to create both airy spaces and cozy corners. In the living room there are inviting books, magazines, games, and places to sit around the hearth and potbelly stove as well as at the big round table in the dining room. In yet another large, cheery dining room, guests gather at long tables for memorable meals—which can be Greek, Hungarian, Chinese, Mexican, Italian, or, occasionally, American. Candlelit dinners include homemade breads, cakes, home-grown vegetables, and herbs and wine.

Breakfasts are equally ambitious, geared to fuel the bikers who frequent the inn when the skiers aren't here (Killington's Northwest Passage lifts are just 5 miles away).

The guest rooms vary in size and decor but not in the care with which they are decorated.

More than the decor, even more than the food, what guests remember about this place is the warmth of its hosts. Richard and Patrick do their utmost to introduce you to the full beauty and possibilities of the area. Woodstock, with its many restaurants and shops, is 8 miles to the east, Killington's gondola is little more the other way, and the Calvin Coolidge Homestead is just down Route 100—which continues on through Ludlow to Weston. You might consider the five-day midweek rates because this inn is ideally situated for exploring much of what's most beautiful in central and southern Vermont.

The Rabbit Hill Inn
Pucker Street (Route 18)
Lower Waterford, Vermont 05848
802-748-5168

Innkeepers: John and Maureen Magee
18 rooms and suites
$60-$90 per person double occupancy, MAP; $55-$80,
    off-season

MasterCard, Visa
Children over 12 welcome
No pets
Open May through October, November 15 through March

Above a Connecticut River village with a view of the distant White Mountains, the Rabbit Hill Inn is both a peaceful retreat and a convenient base for exploring northern Vermont and New Hampshire — on skis or foot, in a canoe, by bicycle, or in a car. Formerly a popular stop on the stagecoach route between Portland and the New England interior, the inn now serves five-course, candlelit meals. (Although we have never eaten here, we have read rave reviews.) The inn maintains its own cross-country trails.

Maureen Magee views innkeeping as a theatrical event. She wants each guest's visit to be a special production, but she wants the guest to do the acting; she and her husband simply provide the stage and the right atmosphere, music, and food.

The main inn is a pillared Greek Revival building with an attached carriage house that also has a fine upstairs porch, topped by a gabled roof. The public rooms include a parlor with Federal decor where afternoon tea is served, a pub with a complete bar, and the Brick Bottom, an informal lounge with a woodstove and cracker barrel complete with checkers, a TV, and a VCR. There is also a greenhouse that supplies flowers — including edible flowers like nasturtiums and violets for salads and garnishes — year-round.

Each room is carefully furnished around a theme, such as the Victorian room. There is a diary in each room in which guests write their thoughts and see what others have thought before. Five rooms have fireplaces, and there are sweet touches, like homemade candy. The dining room is very elegant but small, with eleven tables. It is open to the public by reservation.

Maureen is a flutist and sometimes plays in the parlor. There is live guitar music in the dining room six nights a week.

Outdoor activities and unspoiled countryside are the inn's main diversions. In the winter the touring trails wind past brooks, pastures, and hemlock thickets. Downhill skiing, at Burke and Cannon mountains, is just 25 miles away. Warm weather offers canoeing, hiking in the White Mountains, nature walks, and bicycling. There is also swimming and fishing in a freshwater pond. A stroll through this village of nine homes reveals a 150-year-old post office and a library that still operates on the honor system.

Rowell's Inn

Simonsville
R.F.D. 1, Box 269
Chester, Vermont 05143
802-875-3658

Innkeepers: Beth and Lee Davis
6 rooms (all with private bath)
$120-$140 per couple, MAP; B&B rates midweek November-
   March; add 15% gratuity
No credit cards
Children over 12 welcome
No pets
Open year-round except April

Simonsville, a cluster of homes between Weston and Chester, is the unlikely site of Rowell's Inn. This distinguished red brick building has a third-floor porch with an arched ceiling and a gabled roof, features of its Federal heritage. A plaque to the left of the solid wooden door announces the inn's place on the National Register of Historic Places.

Built in 1820 as a stagecoach stop by Major Edward Simon, the inn has always been a place of rest and refreshment, although it has also served as a post office and general store during its colorful history.

A Mr. Rowell procured the inn in 1900 and completed the renovations that currently distinguish it, including the elegant tin ceiling in the sitting room and the cherry and maple floorboards. The dining rooms, the tavern, and the porch of the inn were lively luncheon spots for those making the overland trip to Manchester.

Beth and Lee Davis have restored the inn to its former eminence. An atmosphere of understated elegance prevails. The sitting rooms, richly furnished with upholstered sofas and antique tables, are warmed by fireplaces and potted plants. There's also a stained glass–backed bar with Vermont-brewed Catamount on tap and gaming tables.

Although each bedrooms is different, the corner room, with a brass double bed and stone fireplace, is particularly pleasing. The rooms have sinks, thick quilts, and hooked rugs. The two upstairs rooms that have been carved out of the old ballroom are also very grand.

A five-course dinner (appetizer, soup, salad, entrée, and dessert) is served at one seating in the intimate dining room. Guests will find the Davises likable and helpful hosts.

Ten Acres Lodge
R.R. 3, Box 3220
Luce Hill Road
Stowe, Vermont 05672
802-253-7638
800-327-7357

Innkeepers: David and Libby Helprin
10 rooms (8 with private bath), Hill House (8 rooms), 2 cottages
$60-$150 per couple in winter; $50-$120 in summer; $75-$150
in fall; cottages: $180-$250
Major credit cards
Children welcome
Pets in cottages only
Open year-round except 2 weeks in mid-April

On a quiet hillside above crowded Stowe village, this red clapboard inn (actually on 43 acres, not 10) looks across the street to cows grazing or a vast blanket of snow that's perfect for cross-country skiing. Here is country elegance without pretension or stiffness.

Amid many additions and a surprising amount of space, two living rooms connected by a fireplace set the tone of the inn. Comfortable and filled with books, they are the showplace for an antique desk, Oriental rugs, velvet couches, floral-print overstuffed couches piled high with pillows, beamed ceilings, and plank floors. To the left is the cozy bar, with antique wood chairs, wing chairs, and rich carpeting.

The dining room is spacious, but candlelight and small tables create an intimate atmosphere. Each specialty, including breads, soups, and pastries, is homemade, and the herb garden in the greenhouse ensures fresh spices year-round. The Continental menu includes tournedos with green peppercorns, Spanish red shrimp with grilled vegetables, and butterflied leg of lamb in a black currant sauce. A tremendous special salad should also be sampled. Happily, the quality of the wine cellar matches that of the cuisine. A children's menu is always available, and with prior notice, vegetarians and those on other special diets can be accommodated.

Each guest room has a charm and character of its own. A few are rather small. Room 3 has a brass bed; Room 12 has chairs made of snowshoes; the two largest rooms, 11 and 12, are also the nicest. Just a few yards from the inn, by the pool and tennis courts, are two renovated and more modestly furnished cottages — each with a kitchen, fireplace, and view.

Three Mountain Inn

Jamaica, Vermont 05343
802-874-4140

Innkeepers: Charles and Elaine Murray
10 rooms in the main house, 6 in Robinson House; 2-bedroom cottage
$75-$90 per person double occupancy, MAP; midweek and 5-day ski packages available
No credit cards
Children over 12 welcome
No pets
Open Thanksgiving through March, mid-June through October

This inn on Route 30 in the middle of a wooden village conveys a sense of age: the living room has wide-planked pine floors, the large hearth has an original Dutch beehive oven, and the ceilings are low. The two dining rooms, one of which doubles as a library, are small, and it's easy to imagine, especially by candlelight, that you are in an 18th-century tavern. The menus change frequently and feature Elaine Murray's soups, breads, and desserts. A house specialty is veal sautéed with shallots, with a dry white wine and cream sauce, served on rösti potatoes. Breakfast can be homemade doughnuts or muffins or something heartier.

The guest rooms have been individually decorated. One has a king-size four-poster bed, another, a private balcony overlooking the unusual stone swimming pool and colorful gardens.

Post-and-beam ceilings are exposed, made from the inn's former stable. Elaine stenciled the bedrooms, which are filled with framed needlework, locally made country furniture, candlewick spreads, and contrasting floral and striped wallpaper.

A small country house across the road is available for longer rentals, and still another house serves as a meeting space. For downhill skiing, Stratton, Magic, and Mount Snow are all 10 to 25 minutes away. Antique hunting, hiking, and fishing are summer pastimes. Best of all is Jamaica State Park, just a mile down the road. Skiers use the park's old railroad bed in winter. In addition to the inn's nicely landscaped pool, swimmers frequent Salmon Hole or walk the mile and a half to Hamilton Falls, where water cascades through three distinct pools.

Tulip Tree Inn
Chittenden Dam Road
Chittenden, Vermont 05737
802-483-6213

Innkeepers: Ed and Rosemary McDowell
8 rooms (all with private bath)
$75-$95 per person, MAP; 3-, 5-, and 7-day packages
2-day minimum on weekends, 3 on holidays
MasterCard, Visa
No children
No smoking
Closed April and most of May

This luxurious home in the woods was built by William S. Barstow, a businessman who was one of Edison's collaborators and who was canny enough to sell his holdings for $40 million and retire here right before the Great Crash of 1929.

It's the kind of place you feel pretty savvy yourself about finding. Although not far from Killington, it is definitely in its own hilltown world and caters more to cross-country skiers in winter. In the summer there is swimming, canoeing, and fishing in Chittenden Reservoir, just down the road.

All of the rooms are attractive, but you might request one with a Jacuzzi. You can also steep in a hot tub before cocktails in the library/tap room, then settle down to a four-course, candlelit dinner.

Vermont Marble Inn
12 West Park Place
Fair Haven, Vermont 05743
802-265-8383

Innkeepers: Bea and Richy Taube and Shirley Stein
13 rooms (all with private bath)
$65-$98 per couple, including breakfast
Dinner also served
Major credit cards
Children welcome
No pets
Open year-round

In the sleepy town of Fair Haven, on the New York border, is a marble mansion run by three old friends who obviously take delight in their new calling. They are as flamboyant and individual as the furnishings, as sincere as the house is Victorian.

The house was built in 1867 by Ira C. Allen, who wanted to show the townspeople that his marble business was doing well. A quick glance at the facade suggests that it was doing quite well indeed. The porch is a rather bright pink, but when it reflects onto the marble there is a nice fiery glow.

Inside are chandeliers, hand-carved marble fireplaces, and 12-foot ceilings with elaborate moldings and medallions of papier-maché and plaster. Soft Victorian colors prevail throughout the house. Many of the antiques and Victorian knickknacks in the long, formal parlor were brought from the innkeepers' homes on Staten Island. A smaller, less formal sitting room has a television and game table.

A long, broad staircase leads to the guest rooms on the second and third floors (the third-floor rooms are a bit smaller). All are named after English authors, and the decorations reflect their periods. The Byron Room, for instance, has a brass bed with a documented history. The Elizabeth Barrett Browning and Shakespeare rooms have canopy beds. Imagine the T. S. Eliot and George Bernard Shaw rooms in the Art Deco addition of the 1920s. The fixtures and tilework in Shaw's bathroom are completely black. The addition was built to serve as a play area for the Allen children, which explains the back staircase and the alcove at the top of the stairs, once used for overnight guests.

In the morning, Richy (your bartender in the evening) serves the breakfast prepared by Shirley—warm, crystalized grapefruit, granola, pancakes, and muffins or coffee cake. Dinner is relaxed; a menu might include asparagus and curry soup followed by scallops and shrimp flambé.

The relatively unknown Four Lakes region offers boating, ice skating, ice fishing, maple sugaring, and antiquing. For the less adventurous, there are wicker chairs on the front porch, and the town green is across the street.

The Village Inn

R.F.D. Box 215
Landgrove
Londonderry, Vermont 05148
802-824-6673

Innkeepers: Else and Don Snyder
20 rooms (15 with private bath)
$45-$68 per couple in summer, $45-$65 per person, MAP, in
  winter
MasterCard, Visa
Children welcome
No pets
Open December 15 through March, Memorial Day through
  October 20

The red, mostly clapboard inn is down a birch-lined dirt road in
the Green Mountain National Forest. The building rambles on
and on, back and around, beginning with the original 1810
house and ending with the latest addition, from 1976. The low,
connected buildings have been a family operation since the
early 1960s, and families will feel very much at home here.

Billed as a country resort, the facilities include all-weather
tennis courts, a heated pool, a three-hole pitch 'n' putt golf
course, and lawn games. During the winter, you can enjoy the
10-mile cross-country trail system from the inn into the national forest; sleigh rides are also available. Alpine skiing is a
short ride away at Bromley, Stratton, and Magic; skating and
snowshoeing are just outside; afterward, try a whirlpool at the
inn. Behind barn doors lies the heart of the inn: the huge,
timbered Rafter Room lounge (with a full bar), where you must
experience the supine couch near the hearth, which seats
twelve. Games and books can be found in the bar.

Eight guest rooms are in the old homestead and furnished
traditionally; the rest are contemporary. Meals are imaginative
and well executed.

West River Lodge

R.R. 1, Box 693
Newfane, Vermont 05345
802-365-7745

Innkeepers: Gill and Jack Winner
5 rooms (2 connecting, 2 with private bath)
$65-$75 per couple, including breakfast, $100-$110 per
  couple, MAP; ask for single and triple rates, off-season
  midweek rates

Lunch served on request
No credit cards
Children welcome
No pets
Open year-round

West River Lodge is a white farmhouse next to a big red barn, surrounded by farmland and circled by hills. In the 1930s it was a well-known riding school and since then has catered to horse lovers, doing so exclusively through the '70s until Gill (pronounced Jill, short for Gillian) and Jack Winner, former college professors, bought it in 1984.

Riding is still a big draw. The trails are extensive and you can bring your own mount (horses are boarded), take a lesson, or join one of the occasional all-day rides. Carriage driving is another option.

Nonriders, too, can enjoy the isolation of this place, actually just a mile or two off busy Route 30. There is a swimming hole in the river and, in winter, the surrounding fields and bridle trails invite cross-country skiing.

The rooms are cheerful, unpretentious, and country comfortable. The meals are what Gill describes as country cooking with a Welsh accent, to match her own. Guests dine around a large table in the low-beamed dining room and relax in the friendly, old-fashioned parlor. Special weekends range from art workshops to "centered riding."

The Whetstone Inn
Marlboro, Vermont 05344
802-254-2500

Innkeepers: Harry and Jean Boardman
10 rooms
$55-$70 per couple, $25-$60 single
Breakfast served daily, dinner on weekends
No credit cards
Children welcome
Pets welcome
Open year-round

A half mile from busy Route 9, the tiny hamlet of Marlboro remains much as it was two hundred years ago, unhurried and beautiful. One of just three buildings in the village, the Whetstone is a classic and charming country inn. Like the Boardmans, its unpretentious owners, it radiates character and hospitality.

Built in 1787, the inn was a tavern before it opened its doors to the stagecoach traveler. Like many inns of the day, it also served as a post office and general store—the original tavern bar with pigeonholes for mail remains just off the living room. Period furniture, open fires, wide floorboards, rockers, and jug lamps create a colonial ambience. Upstairs, each of the spacious guest rooms has a pleasing view of meadows and forests, the steepled church, and the backyard pond.

After learning guests' preferences, Jean serves a bountiful breakfast. It could be bacon and eggs, pancakes or waffles with maple syrup, homemade muffins and popovers, and seasonal fresh fruits. On weekends and occasional weekdays she prepares an equally ample and delicious dinner, a companionable affair served in a dining room that was the original kitchen.

Although there are many activities in the area, a good book, long walks, skating on the pond, cross-country skiing, conversation, or simply doing nothing are what lure many visitors back year after year. Reserve early, especially during the extremely popular Marlboro Music Festival (in July and August), which is within walking distance.

Windham Hill Inn
West Townshend, Vermont 05359
802-874-4080, 802-874-4976

Innkeepers: Ken and Linda Busteed
15 rooms (all with private bath)
$75-$85 per person double occupancy, $105-$115 single
    occupancy, MAP
Major credit cards
Children not appropriate
No pets
Open year-round except April

At the end of a dirt road amid a secluded 150 acres, this inn gives guests a feeling of serenity and intimacy. From every window, this carefully restored 1825 brick farmhouse, on the edge of a steep hill, looks down the West River valley.

The bedchambers and airy common rooms are filled with antiques, Oriental rugs, handsome quilts, and old photographs. One of the three living rooms is furnished with Victorian white wicker and has a woodstove and deck. The sunny bedrooms have distinctive furnishings and are charming and comfortable. In the restored barn, a stone's throw away, two rooms with private porches are especially inviting: the Matilda Room, with a low ceiling and a view of the open barn, and William's Room, with a wonderfully high ceiling. Each room in the inn, too, is named rather than numbered. Complimentary sherry and mints are found in the rooms.

Days begin with a hearty country breakfast and end with a superb candlelit dinner. Guests can be served at two large oval tables or, for a more intimate mood, at one of the four tables in the smaller dining room. Linda Busteed makes her own soups, appetizers, breads, and desserts. There is wine with dinner as well as a fully stocked bar.

The surrounding countryside permits many winter and summer activities, from skating on the pond to cross-country skiing, from hiking to summer jazz and chamber music. Skiing at Stratton is a half hour's drive.

Family Finds

Families are warmly welcomed at all of these places. They include motels, condominium complexes, and some outstanding country inns.

Maine

Bear Spring Camps
Route 2, Box 1900
Oakland, Maine 04963
207-397-2341

Managers: Ron and Peg Churchill
32 cottages for 140-150 guests
$365 (for 2 people) to $1,045 (for 7) per week, plus $100 per extra adult, $65 per child under 8, $25 per child under 3; less in May, June, and September; all meals included
No credit cards
Children welcome
No pets
Open mid-May through September

The Belgrade Lakes are just north of Augusta, in the rolling farm country generally known as mid-Maine. It's an area that doesn't promote itself much because it doesn't have to. Most visitors have been coming for generations.

This gem of a family resort has 80 to 90 percent repeat business. Each cottage is right on Great Lake and has its own boat ready for new arrivals. This is because, as the brochure notes, "We know that many of our guests want to go fishing as soon as they arrive."

Serious fishermen come in May for trout and salmon and in July there is still bass. In the summer, most fishermen bring their families, who play tennis or lawn games and, of course, swim (the lake bottom is sandy). Sailboat rentals are also available.

The cabins have niceties like fireplaces and hammocks on

the porch as well as full baths and electric heat. (Even in sunny weather, that extra blanket on the bed comes in handy.) It's the kind of place where, if something's missing, the cabin boy will fetch it in a jiffy, and there is daily maid service.

The main lodge is an overgrown farmhouse and the feeling, in contrast to that of most Maine camps, is very open, with many acres of clipped lawn. All meals are served in the spacious dining room, a box lunch is always available for those who want to go on an expedition. There are plenty of books and games in the main lodge for rainy days.

Goose Cove Lodge

Deer Isle
Sunset, Maine 04683
207-348-2508, 207-767-3003 in winter

Innkeepers: Eleanor and George Pavloff
11 cottages, 2 suites, 9 rooms (all with private bath)
August: per person weekly, MAP: cottages, $460-$600; suites, $450-$500; rooms, $385-$500; less June through July and early September; much less when only breakfast is served, mid-September to mid-October; add 10% service charge
1-week minimum, July and August, 2-day minimum in shoulder months
No credit cards
Children welcome at special rates
No pets
Open mid-June to mid-October

Goose Cove Lodge, on a very secluded cove, is particularly popular with hikers, naturalists, bird watchers, and families. The innkeepers put great emphasis on all of the guests getting to know one another. Dinner is served early, at 6:30 P.M., after guests have been encouraged to get together in the main lodge, around 5:30 P.M., for hors d'oeuvres.

Dinner is served family style (as is breakfast) in the attractive dining room that wraps around the lodge. After dinner there is usually some form of entertainment — perhaps a movie, music, lecture, or slide show — which is often put on by guests. All age groups are welcome and represented at Goose Cove.

The rooms are in cabins and two annexes to the main lodge. They are all quite different, but generally simple and rustic. Most have refrigerators. Wine, soft drinks, and snacks can be purchased — on the honor system — from the gift store. Activities include swimming in the cove of a sand beach if the tide is in or hiking on the many trails that wind through the property.

At low tide, the shore trail leads across a wide sandbar to Barred Island, a nature conservancy. Sailboat rentals and golf are nearby, and the scenic roads on Deer Isle lead to an unusual number of crafts shops and galleries.

The Green Shutters Inn and Cottages
Bay Street
Boothbay Harbor, Maine 04538
207-633-2646

Innkeepers: Clayton and Kay Pinkham
15 rooms (all with private bath), 7 cottages
$34 per person double occupancy, MAP, $17 per child 12 and under, $23 per extra adult; weekly cottage rates, $195-$230
MasterCard, Visa
Children welcome
No pets
Open Memorial Day through September

The Green Shutters is a friendly, informal resort of a breed that is fading fast. The large dining room in the lodge has open timbers and red-checked tablecloths, the cottage walls are knotty pine, and the wicker chairs, original. The cottages accommodate from two to fourteen people. Some have living rooms with working fireplaces; the others have electric heaters. The four with kitchens are available at very reasonable rates in the shoulder seasons. Some of the rooms have views of Linekin Bay — be sure to request them. The main inn and two lodges have porches with views of the bay.

Most guests prefer the modified American plan because the food at the inn is so good. All the bread, pies, cakes, and cookies are homemade. The specialties are, of course, fresh fish and Maine lobster, but a great variety of meat courses is offered as well. An elegant buffet is featured every Sunday night, and delicious picnic lunches are available. With very reasonable room rates, Green Shutters is a bargain.

The High Tide Inn on the Ocean
U.S. Route 1
Camden, Maine 04843
207-236-3724

Innkeepers: Frances and Hendrick Conover
3 cottages (2 are housekeeping), 22 motel units (all with bath); 5 rooms (4 shared baths)
In season (*per couple*): Cottages $80-$90, motel units $90-$115, rooms $55-$75

Off-season (*per couple*): Cottages $70-$80, motel units
   $75-$95, rooms $50-$70
Continental breakfast served
MasterCard, Visa
Children welcome
No pets
Open late May to mid-October

Once a private estate, this inn is on a lovely hillside that slopes to
the ocean. Other, motel accommodations have been built on
the property, but they have been placed in such a way that the
magnificent view has not been obstructed. All the buildings are
far enough from the main road that street noise is not a problem, as it can be in the Camden area. Small flower gardens are
planted along the rolling lawn from the inn to the ocean.

Lounge chairs and tables with umbrellas are placed for good
views of the water. A wooden staircase leads down to a pebble
beach, where rockhounds and shell fanciers may have a field
day.

The inn itself has five guest rooms, three with beautiful ocean
views. There are two modern motel buildings. The Oceanview
overlooks the lawn; the Oceanfront, the beach. There are views
of the mountains as well. It would be hard to find accommodations much closer to the water. The Oceanview Duplex is another motel unit with some water views. The very clean rooms
are all above standard motel units, and many have outside sitting areas.

Breakfast is served on the main inn's glass-enclosed porch,
which has a great view down to the water. The living room has
this same view. The porch, the living room, and a small bar all
have a fireplace. The porch is attractively decorated in white
and Williamsburg green. However, it's the landscaping and
water views that make the inn a good value. A path leads down
to the beach and harbor.

Hiram Blake Camp
Harborside P.O. Box 59
Blake's Point
Cape Rosier, Maine 04642
207-326-4951

Manager: Sandra Venno
15 cottages
July-August: $330-$660 per week, $88 extra per adult, $44
   per child, $275 per week for single room with bathroom,
   MAP
Off-season: $200-$500 per week, EP

No credit cards
Children very welcome
Restrained pets welcome
Open June through September

Hiram Blake Camp isn't for everybody. It's well off the beaten track at the tip of a peninsula that's mostly a wildlife sanctuary. The weathered cottages, squirreled away in a quiet cove in the upper reaches of Penobscot Bay, are a place where guests stay put. This is an old-fashioned family camp, run by the children, grandchildren, and great-grandchildren of Captain Hiram Blake, who founded it in 1916.

All the cottages are within 200 feet of the bay, washed with the special light and smell of the sea. There are six one-bedroom cottages, five with two bedrooms, three with three, and one single-person unit. Each has a living room with a wood-burning stove, and some have fireplaces, too. Each has a bath, a porch, and a kitchen where guests can prepare lunch. Dinners, which include soup, juice, salad, and dessert, are in the tradition of homemade Down East fare; lobster is available at any meal.

There are island picnics once a week (varying with the weather); guests are ferried over and given a lunch, which always includes chocolate cake and watermelon.

A pebble beach on the property is fine for swimming, and there are small sailboats and rowboats to use. Hiking trails have been marked on the camp's 100 acres, and there are more trails in nearby Holbrook Island Sanctuary. For rainy days, there is a recreation room with a Ping-Pong table, books, and puzzles.

Although the camp is open from June through September, meals are served only in July and August; a two-bedroom housekeeping cottage costs just $350 a week in the pleasant shoulder months. Reunions and small, informal conferences are welcome in the off-season.

Linekin Bay Resort
Boothbay Harbor, Maine 04538
207-633-2494

Innkeepers: Bob and Ida Branch
33 cabins, 37 lodge rooms (all except 3 with private bath)
$35-$55 for cabins, $40-$55 for rooms, all meals included
No credit cards
Children over 4 welcome
No pets
Open mid-June to September

This resort used to be called Linekin Bay Camp, and this goes a long way toward explaining its ambience. The name was changed to disabuse prospective guests of the notion that they would have to sleep in tents, not to convey the idea that it is in any way pretentious. In fact, the Branches, whose family has run the establishment for over fifty years, like to think of it as an adult camp. Everybody is on a first-name basis in this casual and informal setting. Although there are no required activities as such, meals are structured to introduce guests to one another. Linekin appeals to outdoors people seeking relaxation and an informal holiday. And the best part is that a stay here is a great value, with everything included in the price of the room.

In 1938, Linekin was converted from a girls' camp and the original ten cabins remodeled. Twenty-three cabins have since been added, the last three in 1984. They have 45 rooms altogether, and five spacious lodges hold another 37 rooms. Most of the rooms are rustic and a bit tatty, but they all have electric heat. All but three have water views, but many of the views are obscured by trees; be sure to ask for an clear view. Some of the cabins sit right on the water.

There are three common rooms in the main lodge, all pleasantly shabby. The largest room, 30 by 50 feet, is dominated by a huge fieldstone fireplace. Adjacent is a television room and upstairs, a card room. All three rooms have water views. The grounds are in a natural, ungroomed state, shaded by pine trees.

Good, homemade food and ample activities are what count at Linekin. Guests eat at the same table throughout their stay. The dining room, with the best views on the property, offers a selection of seafood daily. Lobster is available at least three times a week. On Tuesdays, a lunchtime cookout features lobster, steamed clams, and corn on the cob, and Friday lunch features a whole lobster. There are usually two entrées at lunch and always three at dinner. Every Sunday evening there is a smorgasbord so that guests can become acquainted with others besides their tablemates. There is no bar on the premises, and wine is not served at dinner.

Linekin's strong point is sailing. The largest resort sailing fleet in New England — 15 Rhodes 19s and five Lightnings — is made available to guests at no extra cost, and six instructors provide direction. A large saltwater swimming pool, heated to 80 degrees, is on a small piece of land that juts out into the bay, offering a special view from just about any lounge chair. Guests can also indulge in tennis on clay or all-weather courts, canoeing, water skiing (instruction provided), shuffleboard on courts overlooking the bay, fishing from the docks or boats, table tennis, or exploring the trails in nearby woods. Linekin is only a mile from Boothbay Harbor and its attractions, and guests can take the ferry from the resort's own dock to the center of town.

Because Linekin offers three meals a day at better rates than most resorts offering two, and because sailboats as large as the ones Linekin provides gratis usually rent for $45 a day, it's easy to believe that 80 percent of the business here is repeat.

Oakland House

Herricks
Sargentville, Maine 04673
207-359-8521

Innkeepers: Jim and Sylvia Littlefield
16 cottages, 17 rooms (7 with private bath)
In season, MAP: cottages, $50-$79 per person; rooms with
  private bath, $38-$57 per person, rooms with shared bath,
  $26-$44 per person
Off-season, EP: $40-$85 per cottage, $175 for a guest house
  with 10 bedrooms
No credit cards
Children welcome
Pets welcome in most cottages
Open May through late October (only cottages off-season:
  May and June, September and October)

Oakland House opened its doors in 1889 and has been managed by the same family ever since. Three-quarters of the business is repeat. The complex now includes not only the farmhouse but also ten cabins (all quite different and built in different periods) and a ten-room guest house, which used to be a summer house.

This resort caters to families with children. Saltwater bathing and activities on the lake's beach are particularly popular. There's badminton, croquet, and many scenic trails for hiking. The inn will also arrange for sailing and deep-sea fishing.

Liquor is not allowed in the dining room at any time, and dinner begins anytime between six and seven. There is a special dining room just for families with young children.

The cottages, which are scarcely visible to one another, are sited to take advantage of the water views and beyond to Egge-moggin Reach. They all have living rooms with fireplaces, a small utility room with an electric hot plate, an electric water heater, a sink, and a refrigerator. Hideaway, on the edge of a wide field and with a large porch, is ideal for families with children. Boat House has knotty pine walls, oak floors, and is right on the water. Birches, Ledges, and Oak Grove each have one bedroom with twin beds. Homestead is right on the water, and each side has a bedroom and a living room, all with spectacular views. Grindstone is log-style and secluded deep in the woods. Lone Pine is high on a hill with a fine view, and Westerly is 75 feet from a bathing beach.

There are three dining rooms in the main house. The tables have white tablecloths, and the ambience is old-fashioned and wholesome. All three meals are huge. Breakfast includes fresh doughnuts and muffins along with cereals, eggs, bacon, ham, sausage, and pancakes. Lunch is a choice of two entrées (anything from a club sandwich to seafood Newburg), salad, and dessert. Wednesday's buffet luncheon offers crabmeat salad and many other dishes. At dinner, there is a choice of two entrées, one of which is usually fish. Other weekly treats are a hot buffet on Fridays, a roast beef dinner on Saturdays, turkey dinner on Sundays, and a lobster picnic (inside or out) on Thursdays. Those going away for the day can ask for a picnic lunch.

The peace and quiet, great food, active tempo, and relatively small size (Oakland House can hold a maximum of seventy guests) make this a perfect resort for families.

- *See also:* The Dunes on the Waterfront, Ogunquit, Maine

Massachusetts

Captain Gosnold Village – Cottages and Motel
230 Gosnold Street
Hyannis, Massachusetts 02601
508-775-9111

Manager: Jill Golden
51 units, most with cooking facilities
$60-$75 per couple, EP
MasterCard, Visa
Children welcome
No pets
Open May through October

Between Main Street and Sea Street Beach (they are a 10-minute walk in opposite directions), the gray shingle Captain Gosnold Village is a well-shaded complex—a great place for both kids and those seeking privacy. And because you can cook for yourself, when you do eat out it will be a pleasure rather than a necessity.

Motel rooms are in two small buildings; they are paneled, with full indoor/outdoor carpeting, a refrigerator, cable TV, and coffee in the room. Each room has either one double bed or a double and a twin.

The cottages and efficiencies have either a private porch or a picnic table with an umbrella. None is of the cracker-box variety that line the highways of Cape Cod; these are quite spacious by comparison. The knotty pine–paneled rooms have cottage-colonial furnishings. Functional and tidy are the key words here. It's the kind of place where the inevitable grains of sand tracked in from the beach won't hurt.

All the units, except the one-room efficiencies, will comfortably accommodate extra persons for $15 a day. And for those chilly evenings at the beginning and end of the season, all units have heat. The newer cottages have as many as three bedrooms and can sleep fourteen people. With that in mind, the owners have installed three full baths and supplied three television sets.

The kitchens are completely equipped. Linens, towels, and blankets are provided; beach towels are not. There is daily maid service except on Sundays. Grassy, sandy lawns with scrub pines for protection make a nice barbecue or picnic setting. In the larger units, the kitchen is separate from the living quarters.

On the grounds there is a safe swimming pool, horseshoes, badminton, basketball, shuffleboard, charcoal grills, and a playground; baby-sitters can be arranged. Hyannis is a metropolis by Cape Cod standards. There is an airport, department stores, nightlife, and the Cape Cod Melody Tent, which features big-name stars.

Guest Quarters Suite Hotel

400 Soldiers Field Road
Boston, Massachusetts 02134
617-783-0090
800-424-2900
Fax 617-783-0897

Manager: Mark Fallen
310 suites
$119-$350, including full breakfast and private cocktail
    reception on weekends; $180-$285 weekdays
Lunch and dinner served
Major credit cards
Children welcome
No pets
Open year-round

This is one in a national chain of hotels geared — on weekends, anyway — to families. All the rooms are suites: one room doubles as a living/dining room by day, separated by a small hall with a built-in sink and fridge from a standard bedroom. At night, the first room becomes a second, ample bedroom (there's room for a cot as well as the fold-out sofa) where the kids can watch a movie (the TV is artfully concealed by day) while parents take in the jazz show or cabaret downstairs at Scullers.

A beautiful long scull is suspended upside down above the multistory lobby, a reminder of the annual Head of the Charles Regatta, which pits college teams from all over the country against one another, all within view of this riverside hotel.

Admittedly, the Guest Quarters is on the "wrong" side of the Charles River; it's technically in Brighton, but in fact it's nowhere — between the Mass. Turnpike and Storrow Drive. But for those who hate to drive in Boston, this location has its advantages. You get off the Pike, drive into the hotel garage, and use the shuttle service to get around. Every hour a bus makes a nine-stop circuit that includes Harvard Square, the Aquarium and Children's Museum downtown, Rowes Wharf, and Kenmore Square — for baseball fans.

For families, this is a great base. There is a small but serviceable indoor pool, a dramatic atrium lobby with a glass elevator to convey a sense of adventure, and reasonably priced dining options. You can walk out the door and across the bridge into Cambridge, but it's a ways to Harvard Square. After rush hour, however, it's just a 10-minute drive.

The hotel is on a bend of the river, so some rooms have an interesting view of both Cambridge and Boston. Several top-floor suites are on two levels, with the bedroom overlooking the living room. These are actually too romantic to waste on a family outing, but you might check them out and return sometime without the kids.

Harbor Breeze and Captain's Quarters

376 Lower County Road
Harwich Port, Massachusetts 02646
508-432-0337
800-992-6550

Innkeepers: David and Kathleen Van Gelder
14 rooms (all with private bath), 1 cottage
$65-$120 per couple in rooms, including breakfast; $650 per
  week in the cottage
Major credit cards
Children welcome
No pets
Open year-round

In a residential neighborhood, this spot is one of the few places on the Cape that is attuned to the needs and interests of families.

Harbor Breeze is on a lovely piece of property, with split-rail fences, pine trees, a garden courtyard, and walks lined with flowers. There are nine rooms all in a row to the side of the main house. Some of them connect to give families and friends proximity and accessibility to each other. Furnishings are traditional Cape Cod cottage style, simple and unpretentious, neat and tidy. Separate outside entrances, modern baths, and TVs are standard in each room.

About a mile away is the 1850s Victorian inn, Captain's Quarters, with period furnishings and homey touches in the five bedrooms. At both properties, you help yourself to a buffet breakfast of juice, fruit, cereal, and homemade sweet breads.

A separate cottage has a fully equipped kitchen, a combination living-dining room, and a bedroom on each floor; use of the pool is included. Special off-season packages are available.

In addition to lounging around the pool, you can find places in the yard to sit and relax. Or you can fish off the dock at Allen Harbor across the street, feed the ducks, walk 10 minutes to the beach, or take any of the bike trails. David Van Gelder will take you (for a fee) to nearby Monomoy Island, where you can snorkel, watch tidepools, and explore the dunes.

■ *See also:* Katama Shores, Edgartown, Massachusetts; Seaward, Rockport, Massachusetts

New Hampshire

Loch Lyme Lodge and Cottages
Route 10, R.F.D. 278
Lyme, New Hampshire 03768
603-795-2141

Innkeepers: Judy and Paul Barker
4 rooms (shared baths), 26 cabins (1-4 bedrooms)
Rooms $27; cabins $35 per person per night, $175-$475 per
  week; special rates for children; MAP available in summer;
  off-season: $24 per room; all rates include breakfast
Picnic lunches available in summer
No credit cards
Children welcome
Well-behaved pets permitted in cabins
Main lodge open year-round; cabins, Memorial Day to
  Labor Day

On a hillside opposite a sparkling lake in the Connecticut River
valley, Loch Lyme Lodge and Cottages offers moderately
priced accommodations in the lodge or private cabins, with or
without cooking facilities, and a wide range of activities. Children will find plenty to do — hills to roll down, fields to play in,
swimming, tennis, and games. Baby-sitting services are available so that parents can enjoy the peaceful atmosphere. Loch
Lyme is a friendly, family-oriented place, with cabins designed
to be lived in and hearty, nutritious meals, making it a good
choice for families and groups.

One of the lodge's main attractions is the private lakefront
beach, with large white wooden lawn chairs, a sandy swimming
area, a float, and a squadron of rowboats and canoes. Two clay
tennis courts and a recreation cabin, with croquet, badminton,
volleyball, and other sporting equipment, provide a variety of
diversions. Guests can bring bicycles; the relatively flat road
running up the valley is perfect for cycling. Just 10 miles from
Hanover and Dartmouth College and near many small towns,
the inn is close to many diversions, from cultural events to
hiking to church suppers.

The brown shingle cabins with green roofs are spread out
over a hillside and are pleasantly private. Families who want to
make their own meals can choose a housekeeping cabin, which
has from one to four bedrooms, a bath, a living room with a
fireplace, a kitchen or kitchenette, and a porch. The modified
American plan includes accommodation in cabins with one or
two bedrooms, a living room, porch, and bath and housekeep-

ing service. There are also four guest rooms in the main lodge, available year-round, but the cabins are more enjoyable in summer. The bed-and-breakfast rate includes a full breakfast until nine o'clock, then self-service until 11:30 A.M. The recreational facilities are available to all guests.

Hearty New England meals, emphasizing fresh fruit and vegetables, are served in the main lodge except on Sunday evenings, when there is a popular lakefront buffet — casseroles, cold meats and cheeses, and fruit. Visitors will find Paul and Judy Barker and their children — the latest generation of the family to run this lodge, which has been in operation since the '40s — friendly and helpful.

A variety of discounts is available; inquire for details. Children visiting on their birthdays will be the lodge's guests.

Philbrook Farm Inn
North Road
Shelburne, New Hampshire 03581
603-466-3831

Innkeepers: The Philbrook family
5 cottages (summer only), 19 rooms
$77-$92 per couple, MAP
Lunch also served
No credit cards
Children welcome
Pets in cottages only
Open May through October, December 26 through March

A framed child's drawing in a hall reads: "Only generations can come here. We are the fifth generation." Owned by the same family since 1861, Philbrook Farm is an imposing white presence high above the flood of the Androscoggin River.

Inside, the rooms meander on and on. Downstairs, you wander from the cozy game room through spacious summer parlors. One entire closet is stocked with jigsaw puzzles cut by Great-grandfather Augustus. The pine-paneled dining room is hung with watercolors by past guests. The guest rooms are furnished with the kind of hand-me-downs for which most innkeepers must scour antique stores and auctions. The Victorian cottages are big enough to hold several generations of most families.

Actually, Philbrook Farm welcomes newcomers as warmly as old regulars. Slightly off the beaten path, it caters to cross-country skiers in winter (downhill skiers also find it close to both Wildcat Mountain and Sunday River) and hikers in summer. Its own isolated 1,000-acre world includes many miles of trails. Just 2 miles from the Maine border, it is on the eastern verge of the White Mountains.

- *See also:* Pick Point Lodge, Mirror Lake, New Hampshire; Whitney's Inn at Jackson, Jackson, New Hampshire

---

Vermont

The Battleground
R.R. 1, Box 89
Route 17
Waitsfield, Vermont 05673
802-496-2288

General manager: Michael Lorraine
63 units (2 to 4 bedrooms)
Summer: $615-$850 per week; *winter:* $985-$1,360 per week;
   less off-season; rates for shorter and longer stays available
No meals served
Major credit cards
Children welcome
No pets
Open year-round

The Battleground's unusually attractive clusters of condominiums stand on only 20 of the complex's 60 acres, so most of the wooded and scenic acres here are left for walking or cross-country skiing. Since this is the other side of Sugarbush Access Road, this half of the valley is a quiet, private place well suited for families. All the condos, though close to several others, have secluded decks, and all the units are at the same altitude, so they do not look down on one another. The homes all face greenery and are within 75 feet of one of the three brooks that cross the property. In fact, the Battleground has its own covered bridge spanning the widest stream.

The condominiums are fully equipped, and most have been quite luxuriously decorated by the owners. All have cable TV and a huge fieldstone fireplace; some sleep as many as ten people and some have lofts. There is 24-hour security.

Summertime activities include a playground, a lighted and secluded pool, tennis courts, and a beaver pond. In the winter, guests can enjoy Mad River Glen, a mile up the road. Sugarbush is 3 miles the other way, and a cross-country ski trail runs right through the property.

The Colonial House
Box 138 R.B.
Weston, Vermont 05161
802-824-6286

Innkeepers: John and Betty Nunnikhoven
15 rooms (9 with private bath)
$24-$33 per person including breakfast; $8 per child ages
    4-12; younger children free; 10% less for senior citizens and
    3-day stay (weekends excluded); 15% less for 5-day stay
    (weekends excluded)
MasterCard, Visa
Children welcome
No pets
Open year-round

"Families should have a nice place to come to," observes John Nunnikhoven. His Colonial House is a long, red building—an old inn with a dining room wing and motel units rambling off behind—all looking as natural as the connected farmhouses and barns for which Vermont is famous.

John and Betty are from Iowa, but one day, many years ago now, they drove east, looking for the source of a special tobacco that had found its way to the family from the Vermont Country Store in Weston. They camped that night at Hapgood Pond and vowed to move to Vermont. It took a dozen years, but the Nunnikhovens have now been in Weston long enough to build up a strong following.

The check-in counter here is at the door of the kitchen, because that's where you will usually find Betty, baking bread for supper or breakfast, goodies for afternoon tea. Given the smells from the kitchen and the atmosphere in the common room, you will want to sit right down and relax. The room is walled in barnboard. There are dried flowers hanging from the rafters, and a comfortable sofa and chairs around the woodstove and in the new, greenhouse-like sunroom.

The guest rooms are clean, tidy, and comfortable, varying in size and shape depending on whether they are in the inn or motel wing. Off by itself is a recreation room with a Ping-Pong table, games, and books.

Breakfast is important here. In the morning John presides over the cheery dining room, whipping up pancakes (a different kind every day) and omelets (cheddar, jalapeño, salsa, Dijon—whatever) served with fresh breads, and coffee cakes. Betty is the wizard behind dinner: hearty down-home fare that might turn out to be a choice of honey-cured ham, chicken sesame, or broiled scrod served with a hearty soup or quiche, fresh vegetables and breads and desserts like peanut butter ice cream pie or fresh fruit shortcake (bring your own wine).

In the winter you can step right out the back door onto cross-country ski trails that stretch for 150 miles. Alpine skiers can choose from nearby Magic, Bromley, and Stratton mountains. In the summer you can walk the mile-plus into Weston, known for its summer theater and shops. Or you can take to the hills in a variety of directions. The best swimming is still in Hapgood Pond.

The Londonderry Inn
Route 100
South Londonderry, Vermont 05155
802-824-5226

Innkeepers: Jim and Jean Cavanagh
25 rooms (20 with private bath, some that can combine with a bath to form suites)
$60-$75 per couple on winter weekends and during holiday periods, $45-$60 winter weekdays and all summer, $31-$37 in spring and late fall; single rates in summer and off-season; buffet breakfast included
No credit cards
No pets
Children welcome
Open year-round

This rambling, 150-year-old clapboard homestead became a summer hotel in the 1940s, then went year-round when it found itself handy to Stratton, Bromley and Magic.

The paneled living room is huge; not exactly fancy, it's the kind of place where you want to linger because it seems full of possibilities: books, magazines, reading nooks, and space to simply breathe. There is also a full-service tavern and a game room with Ping-Pong, billiards tables, puzzles, and board games. There is also a nicely landscaped outdoor pool.

The guest rooms come big and small; some share a bath (at a special rate) to form suites accommodating four to six people. All are comfortable and cheery.

The dining room is open to the public, a pleasant place to dine by candlelight on baked Brie followed by duckling soup, then maybe bouillabaisse or veal Marsala, topped off by chocolate walnut pie.

Jim and Jean Cavanagh delight in helping guests plan their days. In summer there are antiques shops, back roads, swimming holes, and summer theater; in winter there are a number of skiing options, both cross-country and downhill. South Londonderry is well positioned for exploring much of southern Vermont.

The Mountain Meadows Lodge

R.R. 1, Box 3
Thundering Brook Road
Killington, Vermont 05751
802-775-1010

Innkeepers: The Stevens family
19 rooms (14 with private bath)
Winter: $48-58 per person, MAP
Summer: $43-58 per person, MAP, extra person in room:
$24, extra child under 6 is $5; special rates for children and groups
Lunch served in winter only
MasterCard, Visa
Children welcome
Pets welcome only in summer
Open Thanksgiving to mid-April, June to October 15

On the shore of an isolated mountain lake, yet minutes from Killington Mountain, this traditional family lodge is a perfect choice for people who prefer homemade meals and a friendly atmosphere to Killington's jazzy motels. Activity oriented, Mountain Meadows is designed for people who come to ski (cross-country or downhill) in the winter, to hike, bike, and swim in the summer.

Comfort and practicality define the decor of this large, rambling farmhouse. Glass walls in the spacious living room give an expansive view of the mountains and valley. A fireplace, plenty of comfortable sofas and chairs, and a variety of magazines and books make this room a popular gathering place both before and after dinner.

The large, cheerful, beamed dining room is the other popular meeting place. Two meals made with farm-fresh ingredients — an enormous breakfast of cereal, eggs, pancakes, or French toast, juice, milk, coffee and tea, and a dinner of soup, main course with fresh vegetables or salad, bread, and dessert — are served at a dozen tables. Between meals, guests can wander into the dining room and help themselves to coffee, tea, and hot chocolate. They can also keep snacks, wine, and beer in a refrigerator.

The carpeted guest rooms vary in size, ranging from private rooms for two to dorms with bunk beds. All have clean, modern bathrooms, plenty of blankets, soft pillows, crisp sheets, night tables with reading lamps, and dressers. A separate carriage house next door has seven bedrooms, with baths and common rooms downstairs.

In the winter, the lodge runs the largest cross-country touring center in the area, with miles of groomed trails, rentals, and professional instruction. In summer and fall, visitors can hike on the nearby Appalachian and Long trails, bike through the scenic valley, stopping at picturesque villages along the way, or canoe and fish in the lake (the lodge has canoes and rowboats). After a day of hiking or biking, the pool, on a hillside overlooking the valley, is particularly pleasant. Children will enjoy playing on the gently rolling fields around the inn.

The inn is well stocked with recreational facilities and board games; a shed houses pool toys, paddles, a volleyball, and lawn games.

Rutledge Inn & Cottages
Lake Morey
Fairlee, Vermont 05045
802-333-9722

Innkeepers: Nancy and Robert Stone
5 rooms in inn, 34 cottage units, 2 efficiencies
$51-$65 per person, all meals included; EP available
All 3 meals served
No credit cards
Children welcome
No pets
Open May through Labor Day

On Lake Morey, this old-fashioned lodge is popular with couples and families. Guests stay in cottages that line the lakeshore and cluster behind the main lodge. The cottages, in various sizes, are heated and comfortably furnished and have full baths; most have screened porches and fireplaces. Activities include water skiing, horseshoes, team games, and water sports. Rowboats, canoes, and sailboats are available free; other facilities include table tennis, shuffleboard, tennis, and a private beach.

Bountiful meals offer a wide selection and generous portions. The Rutledge is particularly famous for its desserts: more than fifty tempting ones are offered nightly. After dinner, some guests gather in the lounge to play bingo and cards, or read in the library, while others congregate on the porch. The Stone family, which has been operating the inn for eighteen years, and the energetic young staff are always ready to assist guests. The high percentage of return business attests to their success.

Silver Maple Lodge
R.R. 1, Box 8
South Main Street
Fairlee, Vermont 05045
802-333-4326

Innkeepers: Scott and Sharon Wright
8 rooms (6 with private bath), 6 cottages
$38-$50 per couple, light breakfast included; $5 per extra
    person in the room, third day free off-season
Major credit cards
Children welcome
Pets in cottage rooms
Open year-round

This distinctive 1880 Vermont house has steep gables and a big, screened, wraparound porch. It was in the 1920s that its previous owners, Elmer and Della Batchelder, began taking in overnight guests who tended to stop in Fairlee, a Connecticut River town with two large lakes. Eventually they added a few cottages.

Scott and Sharon Wright are an energetic, friendly young couple who obviously enjoy their guests. Over the past few years they have renovated the house bit by bit, adding a fireplace here and exposing beams there, adding bathrooms everywhere.

Still, they don't want to fancy the old place up too much. Scott grew up on a farm in nearby Tunbridge, and he knows the kind of Vermont hospitality he wants to extend. He prides himself on offering spotlessly clean, comfortable rooms and Sharon's baking at reasonable prices. The couple is also happy to share their love and knowledge of the Upper Valley with guests.

The one drawback to this place is something the Wrights can do nothing about—I-95 slices through a nearby meadow. But the house is set back from traffic noises on Route 5 and is far enough from the highway to be out of earshot.

Guests are welcome to use a couple of bikes and both rental 10-speeds and canoes are available for inn-to-inn expeditions, which the Wrights will gladly expedite. They also offer a bal-looning package: two days of lodging, breakfast, and a champagne hot-air balloon flight from the nearby Post Mills Airport for $200 per person.

Tennis Village
P.O. Box 623
West Dover, Vermont 05356
802-464-5773

Owners: Jack and Margit Ridgway
7 custom homes, 3 condominium units
$650-$1,050 weekly (summer) for 4-bedroom occupancy;
    $225-$300 weekends; winter rates about double
No credit cards
Children welcome
Pets reluctantly accepted with additional charge
Open year-round

If you're a tennis buff or a ski fanatic, or if you just want to get away with a group of friends or family, then you should know about Tennis Village, a special cluster of accommodations in the Mount Snow resort area. Despite the hefty price tag, you get a lot of facility and space for your dollar.

Rent a one- to three-bedroom condominium unit or an entire four- to ten-bedroom house. Each is fully equipped (everything except towels and sheets is there, and even those can be provided for a small charge) and has been designed for privacy and entertaining. The common space on the first floor has a TV, VCR, stereo, dining area, bar stools around the kitchen counter, a comfy couch configuration, and even a billiard table in the solarium. Many houses have screened-in porches, sky-lights, decks, wood-fired saunas; one resembles a log cabin, another a Swiss chalet.

The largest unit is Chateaux Snow and Clay, with over 5,000 square feet of living space. Its recreation room is 50 by 30 feet and has a dance floor that can be raised to reveal a swimming pool and Jacuzzi. A separate solarium has a shuffleboard court; there's also a sauna, table tennis, and a bar downstairs in the pool area. Four bedrooms (nothing to write home about but fine enough) are on the second floor; the master bedroom is on the third floor by itself. This house (others have similar designs and features) is a great choice for a family reunion. This is technically a ten-bedroom house and can be, in the shoulder seasons, rented to two separate parties. Each side is self-contained, though, and only the pool area is shared in this circumstance. Be warned that the other party may have its own idea of how loud to play the stereo.

For tennis buffs, each house comes with its own court. If you choose one of the condo units, two courts are available for the units to share. All the courts are fast-drying red clay; some are lit for night play. A ball machine on each court is standard, and a pro is available for lessons. Monday nights see a social round robin and cookout; various informal tournaments are arranged all the time.

Even if you're not a tennis player, these completely contained chalets are still a bargain if you want to base yourself here for a weekend or week of exploring. Just bring the groceries and some friends.

Jack Ridgway, by the way, designed and built all these houses, right down to the paper towel dispenser. He's in the process of constructing another six houses down the road in a new complex called Tennis Heaven.

The Tyler Place on Lake Champlain
Box 100
Highgate Springs, Vermont 05460
802-868-3301

Owners: The Tyler family
27 cottages and 23 studio suites and apartments
$140-$240 per couple, $40-60 per child, all meals included
No credit cards
Children welcome
Pets in cottages only
Open May through October

This 165-acre lakeshore spread is the definition of a real family vacation. Kids lead wonderful lives of their own while parents can enjoy numerous activities or just relax and still have afternoons with the children.

Tennis, sailing, windsurfing, canoeing, biking, boating, fishing, swimming in the heated pool, and many other sports are included in the packages. There are children's programs for six age groups, from infants to teens, under capable leadership. Intriguing sports activities, instruction, and entertainment are offered from breakfast through lunch and again at suppertime.

If you are not a parent or don't want to be around children on vacation, it is best to come here before or after July and August. The capacity is about 50 families and couples (or 200 guests of all ages).

Tyler Place has the look of a very upgraded summer camp. Cottages are fairly close together, to increase the chances for neighbors to get together if they wish. The cheerful, simple, but hardly rustic cottages are on or near the lake, and each has a fireplace in the living room. Cottages have three to six rooms; doubles, suites, and studios are in the main house. All accommodations feature separate air-conditioned rooms for parents.

Dining and leisurely cocktails (at the inn, with glimpses of the lake) can be with other couples at large tables or alone. Low-key entertainment takes the form of DJs, square dances, Monte Carlo nights, and specialty parties. Informal daytime activities include weekly get-acquainted punch parties, tennis round robins, cookouts, regattas, and guest-staff volleyball and softball games. By the way, there's a no-tipping policy.

Children of different ages cost different amounts. Reservations are on a weekly, Saturday-to-Saturday basis during the peak season, while "special week" rates run 15% to 40% less. Packages include breakfast, dinner, and a light lunch; box lunches are available for the day of departure. A wide variety of food is served to meet the tastes of all ages.

Wildflower Inn
Darling Hill Road
Lyndonville, Vermont 05851
802-626-8310

Innkeepers: Jim and Mary O'Reilly
4 rooms in main house (2 with private bath), 11 rooms in
   annex (all with bath), 4 suites, and 1 honeymoon cottage
$65-$130 per couple, including full breakfast; slightly higher
   during holidays; add 10% tax
MasterCard, Visa
Children welcome ($5 charge for 6-to-11-year-olds)
No pets
No smoking
Open year-round

Sitting up in bed in one of the large, sunny rooms upstairs, you notice a number of nice touches: fresh flowers in a pottery vase on the oak desk, framed prints of wildflowers on the flowery wallpaper, and a bouquet of dried flowers in the basket on the dresser. The wide floorboards are painted, spotted with bright rag rugs, and there is a handsome Shaker rocker next to the window, overlooking the meadow. Some rooms are downright romantic, with tasteful oak antiques and canopy beds.

This farmhouse dates from 1796 and, like all the other homesteads along this dramatic ridge, it was absorbed into a gentleman's estate around the turn of the century.

Jim and Mary O'Reilly have four young boys and a little girl, and children are particularly welcome here. There are plenty of animals—horses, chickens, peacocks, a donkey, a pony, kittens, and a dog. And there is a special children's corner, stocked with dress-up clothes and toys.

But the Wildflower Inn manages to be many things to many people. While some rooms in the carriage house are just right for families (with bunk beds and private baths). There is also a sauna and spa room.

Breakfast is a splendid event. The preferred tables are out on the sun porch, overlooking Burke Hollow. You help yourself to coffee or tea, granola, cereals, and fruit. Then comes a hot dish: fresh eggs, bacon, muffins, and pancakes.

Dinner was been added only recently, but already its fame has spread through the Northeast Kingdom. The chef is George Willy, formerly of Willy's (for many years the area's most popular restaurant), and he is now preparing five-course dinners. Each night he features a particular wine to complement the choice of entrées. In the summer, after ordering you can stroll about the lovely gardens, savoring the wine while waiting for the first course.

There are a choice of public spaces: an attractive parlor and a library stocked with games and the kind of books you really want to read. Off by itself there is also a friendly TV room.

Tea, served every afternoon, features cheese made in nearby Cabot and homemade snacks. Jim and Mary are delighted to help you explore this corner of Vermont, the least populated corner of the state.

Burke Mountain, in East Burke, is a major ski area in winter and offers an unusual toll road to its summit in the warm months. The view is off across Willoughby Lake, a narrow sheet of water walled by two abrupt mountains. Willoughby is beloved by windsurfers and sailors (there's always a breeze) and surrounded by public forest, webbed with trails.

In the winter, cross-country skiers can take advantage of the extensive touring network at Darion Ski Touring Center, just down the road. In any season this is beautiful biking and general exploring country. And at the end of the day, you can enjoy a beautifully landscaped pool with an incredible view.

Farms

In the past, hundreds of New England farms welcomed guests in the summer for weeks at a time. These choices are the best of those that still do. Most of them cater to families who ski as well as those who enjoy the informality and simple pleasures of farm life.

Maine

Seal Cove Farm
Box 75
Star Route 304
Mount Desert, Maine 04660
207-244-7781

Hosts: Floss and Barbara Brooks
3 rooms (1 with private bath)
$50-$55 per couple, including breakfast
MasterCard, Visa
Children welcome
No pets in the house
Open year-round

You won't be plowing fields here, and you probably won't even be milking cows, but Seal Cove is still a nice place for children to get a taste of a small working farm and for citified adults to unwind in natural surroundings.

Seal Cove is a diversified farm, with a herd of prize-winning dairy goats that produce milk for a classic chèvre and outstanding aged cheeses (made on the premises). Other animals include turkeys, chickens, pigs, sheep, and a horse.

You begin the day (at 7:30 A.M.) with strong coffee or tea and breakfast in the informal dining room with a fireplace. The hearty and important first meal of the day includes fresh fruit, bacon, sausage or ham, and some major dish. After breakfast the Flosses do their chores — milking and feeding the goats, collecting eggs, tending the sheep, and cultivating the organic gardens. Older children can help collect eggs, and Gardner, the Flosses' young son, will give you a tour around the property with knowledgeable explanations and unusual charm.

The living room has a warm, family feeling to it, with an open toy box, simple country furniture, and a cushy, worn couch. The guest rooms on the second floor, which offer good views of Western Mountain and Seal Cove Pond, are lovely. The beds have down comforters, and an extra mattress or cot can be brought in for families.

Just 30 miles away from this unhurried lifestyle is bustling and touristed Bar Harbor. A variety of outdoor pursuits in Acadia National Park is within minutes.

Massachusetts

Cumworth Farm
Route 112
Cummington, Massachusetts 01026
413-634-5529

Hosts: Ed and Mary McColgan
6 rooms (all with shared bath)
$50 per couple, including breakfast
No credit cards
Children welcome
No pets
Open year-round

Ed and Mary McColgan are not your average hilltown farmers. Ed has served as a state representative, and he headed the Massachusetts Bicentennial Commission. (But in the early spring, Ed does tap about 600 gallons of maple syrup. He also raises vegetables and sheep.) Mary still works several days a week as a congregate housing coordinator. But now that their seven children are grown, the fine, hip-roofed farmhouse has space to spare. Guests feel very welcome here—to settle down in an armchair in the spacious living room, to play with the barn cats, to wander out through the beautifully landscaped grounds to claim a lounge chair, or head into the meadows to see the sheep.

The bedrooms are furnished with antiques, and some have stenciling. The core of the house is a big kitchen, where baskets hang from the ceiling. Here guests have breakfast, which may include fresh eggs or pancakes with jams and syrup, both produced on the farm.

The surrounding area offers plenty in the way of antiques

shopping, summer hiking, berry picking, swimming, and skiing, both cross-country and downhill. William Cullen Bryant's interesting homestead, open to the public, is just up the road.

The one hitch here is a lack of nearby dining facilities. There are some fine restaurants in these Hampshire hills, but the better ones are a half-hour drive away — a lovely drive, one might add.

New Hampshire

Rockhouse Mountain Farm Inn
Eaton Center, New Hampshire 03832
603-447-2880

Innkeepers: The Edge family
15 rooms, 3 bunkrooms for children
$46-$52 per person, MAP; children to age 6, $22; 6-11, $28;
   12 and older, $32 in bunkroom, adult rate in separate room
No credit cards
Children welcome
Pets not encouraged, but exceptions are made
Open mid-June through October 25

The Rockhouse Mountain Farm is definitely a family place. There are hayrides, canoe trips, and barbecues. But there is also plenty of time and space to simply wander: through the old barn, along the private beach, or through the woods and meadows on this 450-acre farm. Though children are important here and can play with the animals and help out in the barn, there is also an effort to let parents have some time to themselves. Kids eat dinner in a separate dining room and can sleep in the girls' or boys' bunkrooms.

Edge family members have been operating the farm as an inn since 1946 and see many of the same families return year after year. The staff consists mostly of family friends and college students, some of whom are former guests. Everybody inn seems to be having a great time, and they go out of their way to make sure guests do, too. The informal atmosphere puts parents and kids at ease immediately.

Meals are hearty and homemade. Served family-style by candlelight, they are designed to help guests make friends. Breakfast is very casual, with grownups and children coming down to eat whenever they are ready.

The rooms are clean and comfortable. Surprisingly, there are fine paintings and antiques throughout this informal farmhouse. Some of the furniture was brought from Wales years ago by the Edge family.

Be sure to make reservations, for the Edges have a lot of repeat business. Family reunions are a specialty.

Vermont

Berkson Farms
Enosburg Falls, Vermont 05450
802-933-2522

Innkeepers: Richard and Joanne Keesler
4 rooms (1 with private bath)
$45-$50 per couple, including breakfast
No credit cards
Children welcome
Pets welcome
Open year-round

On 600 spectacular acres in the Missisquoi River valley, this working farm offers true country living and enjoyment. Come to Berkson Farms to get into the beauty of the place and rhythms of a farm.

The bedrooms in the beautifully remodeled century-old farmhouse offer panoramic views of the Vermont farmland. The honeymoon suite has a tall antique bedstead. The spacious living room and library, as well as the comfortable family and game room, are for the guests and host family alike. Meals are served at a round table that seats twelve. Breakfast, with food raised or grown on the farm, starts at 7:30 A.M. and ends whenever it's over. A buffet inside or out on the picnic tables starts at 1:00 P.M. sharp unless guests prefer to pack a picnic lunch to take on a nature walk or bird-watching excursion. Dinner, consisting of five to seven courses, begins at 6:30 P.M.

Guests and their children are welcome to help to milk more than two hundred dairy cows, collect eggs from the henhouse, plant the garden, or bring in the hay. During spring sugaring season, guests may carry in buckets of sap and boil it down to make maple syrup. Sheep, horses, pigs, geese, ducks, pigeons, and rabbits all make their home here.

To complete the picture, there are children's play areas, hayrides, swimming holes, cross-country skiing, and running trails. A short walk up the road leads to golf, ice skating, and shopping. Tennis, horseback riding, and summer theater are also in the area.

Harvey's Mountain View Inn
Rochester, Vermont 05767
802-767-4273

Innkeepers: Don and Maggie Harvey
9 rooms, 1 cottage
$42-$52 per person double occupancy, MAP; $55 single;
　family rate available
Picnic lunches available
No credit cards
Children welcome
Pets welcome in the cottage
Open year-round

Harvey's is a traditional white mountaintop farmhouse that has been operating as a farm for generations and as a country getaway for families since the early '60s. Animals outnumber humans here by a long shot, but there are some resort amenities, including a heated pool with a superb view, pony rides for children, and fishing in the pond.

　　Guests enjoy a full breakfast from 8:00 to 9:00 A.M., then generally set out on day trips to prowl the back roads off Route 100, here a corridor between high mountains. Rochester itself is well positioned for striking off in any direction, from the Champlain Valley to Sugarbush and Stowe.
　　The farm itself features a large maple-sugaring house that supplies breakfast tables far and wide and a collection of old farm implements. Dinner is served only to groups by prior request. In the evening, the house is generally pretty quiet, with guests reading, playing games, or recounting the day's adventures around the large, open hearth. There is peace of mind at Harvey's.

Knoll Farm Country Inn
Box 179
Bragg Hill Road
Waitsfield, Vermont 05673
802-496-3939

Innkeeper: Ann Day
4 rooms (all with shared bath)
$40-$55 per person double occupancy weekdays, $75-$95 per
    person per weekend, MAP; 5- and 7-day rates; for 1-night
    stay, add $5
No credit cards
Children over 6 welcome
No pets
Open May through October and January through March

High above the valley on 150 acres of pasture and woods, the
converted farmhouse, sleeping a maximum of twelve, empha-
sizes life as it was before World War II. The comfortable rooms
have wonderful expansive views, and the inn has a strong following, so reserve well in advance.

Family-style dining with farm-grown and homemade foods is
the norm. Special diets and vegetarians are gladly accommodated. Vegetables are grown organically; the meat is raised on
the premises; the barn-fresh milk, butter, and eggs are prepared
in traditional Vermont ways. A common room and music room
(with a player piano and pump organ) are for guests' relaxation.

Outdoors, there is gardening, haying, and general farm
chores (if visitors are so inclined, and many are). The inn has its
own 14-foot-deep pond for swimming, rowboating, or ice skating. Many guests get in some ski touring, snowshoeing, or hiking before the ample eight o'clock breakfast.

The classic red barn houses cows, all sorts of horses, a pig, a
flock of chickens, and dogs and cats. A small herd of Scottish
Highland cattle graze nearby. The farm is sometimes geared to
conferences, but individuals are still welcome.

Liberty Hill Farm
Liberty Hill Road
Rochester, Vermont 05767
802-767-3926

Innkeepers: Elizabeth and Robert Kennett
7 rooms (4 baths)
$40 per adult, $20 per child, MAP
No credit cards

Children welcome
No pets
Open year-round

Liberty Hill Farm, run by Bob and Beth Kennett, a couple with two young sons, provides simple but clean rooms in a rambling farmhouse and two hearty meals a day. Farm animals, toys, and acres of backyard make this spot particularly appropriate for families. But anyone seeking primarily a base from which to explore this abundant valley will find the farm well located, friendly, and reasonably priced.

The large white clapboard farmhouse stands alone, under the shadow of the Green Mountains, a few hundred yards off Route 100. From the rocker on the small wood-planked porch you can hear the gurgle of White River, which runs just in front of the house.

The house is comfortably lived in, with pillows on the sofa and chairs, tables stacked with magazines and papers, and toys piled in corners. The spacious guest rooms are adequately furnished. Both the solid doors and walls and the design of the house — one section is separated from another by a few steps or a hall — provide plenty of privacy. Beth places guests thoughtfully, often giving families a suite that includes three bedrooms, a sitting room with a sofa, table, and chairs, and a private bath. Other rooms share large hall baths; one has an old-fashioned porcelain tub.

You won't go to Liberty Hill to stay in your room, however, but to take advantage of Vermont's natural beauty. There's skiing, hiking, biking, and fishing, or you can stroll around the vast, peaceful farm, perhaps discovering a swimming hole by the bridge or collecting fresh eggs.

Meals, served at one sitting in a cheerful kitchen, are old-fashioned American style. Beth bakes everything from scratch using farm produce. Breakfast includes juice, cereals, stacks of pancakes, eggs, bacon or sausage, coffee cake, and fresh coffee. Dinner usually centers on a main dish and could include a roast or lasagna, fresh bread or muffins, corn on the cob, a salad, and blueberry pie for dessert.

Maple Crest Farm

Box 120
Cuttingsville, Vermont 05738
802-492-3367

Innkeepers: The Smiths
2 apartments, 6 rooms (some shared baths)

Apartment $55 per couple, rooms $20-$25 per person,
   including full breakfast
No credit cards
Children welcome in the apartments
No pets
Open March through November for B&B

High on a hill with a commanding view of stone walls and grazing land, this white brick house was built in 1808 and has been in the Smith family for five generations. The view from the entire house is one of the best, and the secluded setting on a typical Vermont back road adds even more to its beauty. This is a gem of a bed-and-breakfast establishment, framed by an old, hilltop village.

Antiques haven't been brought in to create an effect; these have been used by the family since the early 1800s. The living room and downstairs parlor have Oriental and braided rugs, a Victrola and upright piano, old town ledgers to snoop through, and many flowering violets. The house smells pleasantly old and is full of character.

The downstairs guest room is perfect for those who have difficulty with stairs; it has a private half bath. Upstairs is a wonderful sitting area shared by the three bedrooms. The old beds are short, and the antique dresser tops hold little boudoir accessories found in country life magazines. There is also a modern, two-bedroom apartment on the second floor that can be reserved by the week or weekend.

Outdoor flower and vegetable gardens surround the house. In the gardens is a small patio, where guests can sit and watch the world go by. The Smiths are famous for the quality of their maple sugaring, done in their sugar house at the very top of the hill. Breakfast is as hearty and authentic as one would expect on a working farm. Winter offers spectacular cross-country skiing.

Rodgers' Dairy Farm
R.F.D. 3, Box 57
West Glover, Vermont 05875
802-525-6677

Hosts: James and Nancy Rodgers
5 rooms (with shared bath)
$40 per person double occupancy, $25 per child, with all
   meals; weekly, $200 per adult, $125 per child
No credit cards
Children welcome

No pets
Open June through November

Rodgers' Dairy Farm, a working farm with a healthy herd of Jerseys, offers visitors a chance to sample rural Vermont living off the beaten track. Owned and run by the Rogers family, the farm takes just a handful of guests at a time — never more than ten. There is plenty of peace and quiet, bountiful meals, and a friendly atmosphere.

The farm is spectacularly located in the high, rolling dairy country of northeastern Vermont, 6 miles from a hard-topped road. After 5 steep miles that pass a sun-dappled lake and pretty summer cottages, the tar road gives way to one of the rutted dirt lanes that link the neighboring farms. A mile of this forested labyrinth brings you to a fork marked by a sign, Rodgers Farm Vacation.

Five spotless, paneled guest rooms open off a hallway at the top of the stairs and offer a choice of twin or double beds. The beds have crisp sheets, fluffy pillows, and, when needed, stacks of blankets to guard against the cool night air. A night table with a reading lamp, a bureau, and a wardrobe provide plenty of space to unpack. The rooms share two large baths that have wonderfully steamy showers.

Dinner might be succulent baked ham, homemade sweet rolls, scalloped potatoes, carrot salad, broccoli casserole, and tall glasses of iced tea and fresh farm milk. A leisurely hour or so later, the meal may end with sumptuous chocolate pie and coffee. Breakfast is a full-scale spread of fruit, bacon, cereal, juice, pancakes, eggs, and coffee.

The area abounds with freshwater lakes for fishing, boating, swimming, and sailing. Guests also enjoy the walk around the block, a 4-mile circuit of the neighboring farms. For relaxing there is an enclosed porch, comfortably furnished with a sofa, chairs, tables, and a generous selection of magazines. The living room has the family TV. To understand fully where they are, guests should watch or help with the chores, ride a pony, go on a hayride, and relate to the farm animals.

Gilded Cottages

Some of the grandest of New England's turn-of-the-century summer mansions are now outstanding inns.

Maine

Norumbega
61 High Street
Camden, Maine 04843
207-236-4646

Innkeeper: Terri Griffiths
12 rooms (all with private bath)
From $195 for rooms, $350 for the penthouse suite, breakfast and tea included; from $130 off-season; $50 per extra person in room
Major credit cards
Children over 3 welcome but not appropriate
No pets
Open year-round

This is probably the most elegant B&B in New England. An 1880s Victorian castle-by-the-sea, it is a fantasy of stone, fine woods, and glass. After being painstakingly renovated and furnished to take in guests in the mid-1980s, it was sold and again refurbished completely.

You step into a grand foyer, paneled in golden oak. There's a grand dining room with a magnificent mantel and a table with glittering silver and an equally opulent living room and library.

As you start up the stairs, there's an inglenook — an ornately carved and cushioned nook that begs you to sit down — before you ascend the grand staircase. Some of the guest rooms have balconies and four have working fireplaces, but the thing to request here is a water view (which the master bedroom doesn't have). The penthouse suite has a skylight over the bed as well as spectacular views.

Just far enough from Route 1 to minimize the noise, the

mansion overlooks lawns that sweep down to the bay. Depending on the weather, a full breakfast is served in the dining room, conservatory, or outsides. Tea is offered in the afternoon, and wine or sherry is served before you set out to dine at one of Camden's many restaurants.

Massachusetts

The Apple Tree Inn
224 West Street
Lenox, Massachusetts 01240
413-637-1477

Innkeepers: Aurora and Greg Smith
33 rooms in house and lodge (most with private bath)
$85-$260 per couple, EP
Dinner in high season; breakfast and Sunday brunch
  year-round
Major credit cards
Children over 12 welcome in summer
No pets
Open year-round

Built a century ago as the Orchards, this is one of those sumptuous Lenox "cottages" that has had its ups and downs as an inn. Its past owners have included Alice of eponymous restaurant fame, but the place never seemed quite right until now.

Greg and Aurora Smith have lavished time and talent as well as money on the old mansion. Downstairs there are wing chairs, Oriental rugs, a grand piano, and a Victorian clutter of sculptures and paintings.

The circular dining room, removed from the lounging area, has glass walls that offer grand views of October Mountain. The napery and chairs are white, and in the evening hundreds of tiny white lights create an unusual effect. Open to the public, the moderately expensive restaurant features entrées such as veal scaloppine, saltimbocca, Black Angus steak, fresh seafood, and homemade desserts.

The guest rooms upstairs make the inn special. Four have working fireplaces, and many have window seats with pillows. All are furnished in attractive antiques with fresh wallpaper, curtains, and appropriate rugs and prints. Room 11 stands out, with its country furniture and view of Stockbridge Bowl.

The rooms in the modern lodge are about as pleasant as motel units can be. They have the advantage of being set back near the rose gardens, which are Greg's pride and joy. He grows 450 varieties.

This is a hilltop estate and the Smiths have positioned their pool to command an extraordinary view.

In the summer, guests can walk down the road to the Boston Symphony concerts at Tanglewood—a plus when traffic is backed up for miles. But the Apple Tree Inn is a real find in any season.

Blantyre

Lenox, Massachusetts 01240
413-637-3556; 413-298-3086 off-season

Proprietor: Ann Fitzpatrick
Managing director: Roderick Anderson
23 rooms (all with private bath)
$190-$450 per couple, including breakfast
Lunch and dinner also served
Major credit cards
Children not appropriate
No pets
Open May through October

Blantyre is the only Lenox cottage to be called a castle. Built in 1902 to recreate an ancestral home in Scotland, it is as magnificent as any stockbroker Tudor mansion. But Blantyre Castle had degenerated into a rather dark, shabby inn by 1980, when it was bought by the Fitzpatricks, the owners of Country Curtains and the Red Lion Inn in Stockbridge. They spent an entire year refitting it in royal style, but they dropped the "castle" from its name and lowered its profile.

A Private sign now graces the brick entry gates. The drive proceeds through landscaped grounds to the massive, turreted brick facade. Inside, the splendid rooms are nothing less than museum pieces, with furnishings that create a sense of opulence.

In the entrance hall is an ornate hobby horse, created especially for the space—the sole playful touch in an otherwise formal mansion. Guests are welcome to try it. The hall is baronial, with a stone hearth, ornate paneling, and an antelope head hung beside the French doors that open onto the Berkshires. A brighter, graceful music room, with a piano and a harp, has crystal chandeliers, sofas covered in petit point, and velvet chairs. Exquisite flower arrangements have been placed throughout the public rooms.

The main dining room has dark paneling and is hung with portraits and a tapestry. Guests eat at a long, formal table here or à deux in the octagonal Moiré Room, named for the fabric on its walls. Dinner is by reservation only at $65 per person. The bar is on a trolley that is put out in the glass-walled conservatory, which also serves as the breakfast room.

The guest rooms are impeccably furnished with antiques. Some have four-poster beds, fireplaces, and beautifully upholstered sofas and chairs.

The mansion has four tennis courts, a swimming pool (with a hot tub and sauna), and competition croquet courts set on its 85 acres.

Northfield Country House

R.R. 1, Box 79A
School Street
Northfield, Massachusetts 01360
413-498-2692

Innkeeper: Andrea Dale
7 rooms (sharing 3 baths)
$50-$80 per couple, including breakfast
MasterCard, Visa
No children under 10
No pets
Open year-round

This inn is sometimes blessed with massive pink hydrangeas, but no matter the season, it is always alluring. Guests gather around the pool in back or sit on wicker rockers on the porch. The views from both are stunning and solitary. Inside, the cool, richly paneled common rooms are inviting.

Northfield Country House was built in 1901 as a country mansion for a prominent Boston family. The cherry paneling in the dining room dates from 1850, and the feeling downstairs is almost baronial, with a grand piano, Oriental rugs, and luxurious reading nooks. In the guest rooms there are high, brass bedsteads and color-coordinated walls, furniture, and sheets. Three double rooms have working fireplaces. The cheery single is just as inviting. This room can be closed off with a small double to form quarters for a family.

In the evening guests are welcome to congregate by the fireplace, with its inscription, "Love warms the heart as fire the hearth." Two big sofas face the fire, the smell of which fills the air.

Breakfast is a full one and consists of pancakes or eggs along with juice, fruit, and homemade muffins.

Once known for its grand resort hotel, Northfield is a handsome old Connecticut River valley town just south of the New Hampshire border. Today, most visitors are inspecting the prep school (Northfield–Mount Hermon) or enjoying the hiking, riding, and cross-country ski trails at Northfield Mountain. This also is a prime base for biking on the byways of the valley.

Rhode Island

Cliffside Inn
2 Seaview Avenue
Newport, Rhode Island 02840
401-847-1811

Innkeeper: Kay Russell
10 rooms (all with private bath)
$66-$93 including Continental breakfast; add 10% gratuity
MasterCard, Visa
Children over 10 welcome
Nearby kennel for pets
Open February to mid-December

Trees and houses are in the way now, but in 1880, when Governor Swann of Maryland built this Victorian summer cottage with a mansard roof, it must have had a beautiful view of the Atlantic Ocean. Now, as the guest house of Kay Russell, it offers comfortable rooms in a quiet neighborhood within a 5-minute walk of Newport's famed Cliff Walk. The beach, mansions, restaurants, and shops are also an easy walk away.

Mrs. Russell makes this place special. She serves homemade rolls, juice, coffee, and tea in the spacious living room underneath a portrait of Beatrice Pastorius Turner of Philadelphia, a famous self-portrait artist who spent her summers here.

Each bedroom has been decorated according to a theme, such as the flower room or the wicker room. Bay windows fill the house with light and make the floral wallpaper even more pleasant. Many of the bathrooms are so small that the sink is in the bedroom.

Ivy Lodge
12 Clay Street
Newport, Rhode Island 02840
401-849-6865

Innkeepers: Mariann and Ed Moy
9 rooms (5 with private bath), 2 apartments
$90-$110 per couple for rooms, $135-$140 for apartments
MasterCard, Visa
Children welcome
No pets
Open year-round

After touring one or two Newport mansions, you begin imagining kicking off your shoes and sampling mansion life for yourself.

Step into Ivy Lodge, an 1880s Queen Anne Victorian just a block off Bellevue Avenue. You are in an exquisite 33-foot-high, oak-sheathed entry hall designed by Stanford White. Collapse in an upholstered wicker chair in the neighboring pink and white reception room or test the grand piano in the drawing room beyond. Move on to a Jacuzzi in the downstairs guest room, an immense window seat in the master bedroom, and a tasteful apartment or two in the carriage house. Some of the most appealing rooms are actually the least expensive — former maids' quarters with shared baths tucked under the eaves.

A "Continental English" breakfast, which can include fresh bread pudding, strawberry butter, and an egg dish, is served around the dining room table; there is also afternoon tea. Bicycles, beach towels, and chairs are available. The inn is nicely positioned for getting to the beach and mansions in one direction, downtown Newport in the other.

Sanford-Covell Villa Maria
72 Washington Street
Newport, Rhode Island 02840
401-847-0206

Owner: Anne Couvelier
4 rooms, 2 apartments (some shared baths)
$95-$165; off-season: $55-$95
No credit cards

Children welcome
No pets
Open year-round

At the bay end of Newport's Point historic district, the Sanford-Covell Villa Maria is a Victorian mansion that was once open for tours because of its spectacular architecture. You enter a four-story tower entrance hall that is beautifully stenciled and surrounded with little balconies that create a mazelike feeling. Beyond are magnificent common rooms, again with stenciling; one room has a Chickering piano. The windows have simple lace curtains, and the hardwood floors are covered with Oriental rugs. Passing through to a porch that encompasses three sides of the house, one has a view of Narragansett Bay and Newport Harbor. Below is a new swimming pool that's pleasantly shaped and landscaped, but the best thing about it is its heated salt water, making it a delight. A pier stretches out into the harbor, which guests arriving by yacht are welcome to use.

The Kate Field Room is a favorite, with rich paneling and a cushioned bay window that has a breathtaking view of the bay. This room shares a large bath with two other rooms, but it is worth the inconvenience. Another room has a working fireplace.

Don't miss the dollhouse, which closely resembles the big house right down to the porch swing. It is completely electrified, including the Christmas tree. The detailing is superb—note the Christmas dinner on the table.

A Continental breakfast is served in the dining room, which is so grand that you will feel you are one of Newport's Four Hundred while eating your muffins.

Wayside

Bellevue Avenue
Newport, Rhode Island 02840
401-847-0302

Innkeepers: Al, Dorothy, Don, and Debbie Post
7 rooms (6 with private bath), 1 apartment
$95 per couple, $15 per extra person, Continental breakfast
    included; less off-season
No credit cards
Children welcome
No pets
Open year-round

This is the closest you will get to staying in a Newport mansion with the famous Bellevue Avenue address. Built as a summer cottage in 1896 by Elisha Dyer, Wayside is a yellow Georgian brick building with black shutters. A giant copper beech marks the entrance, through a porte cochere. This tree keeps the place cool in the summer months, eliminating the need for air conditioning.

The innkeepers have restored the house to much of its original grandeur, but the rooms are so large that it's difficult to fill them all appropriately. On the plus side, the scale of the guest rooms permits sitting areas and the addition of enough cots to sleep a family of five. It's also nice to have bathrooms and walk-in closets the size of some hotel rooms and immense windows to let in plenty of sunlight. The beds have colorful sheets and spreads, and there is a TV in each room.

The best room is the original library, with high ceilings, a comfortable seating arrangement, and a terrace that offers private access to the swimming pool.

This inn is convenient for visiting the mansions and shopping at the famous Casino shops. The extra-large free parking area can even accommodate boat trailers. This is actually one of the least formal of Newport's mansion guest houses. There's a big ice chest in the foyer, and children are welcome; they can be tucked comfortably into the corners of those big rooms, which also makes this a relatively reasonable place for families.

Vermont

Shelburne House
Shelburne Farms
Shelburne, Vermont 05482
802-985-8498

Director: Marnie Wolcott
24 rooms (all with private bath)
$80-$220 per couple, EP
Breakfast and dinner served
Major credit cards
Children welcome
No pets
Open Memorial Day to mid-October

Many consider this the best place to stay in New England— justifiably so. Imagine staying in the country house of one of the Vanderbilts and being waited on hand and foot. All of this, plus very good food (much of it grown on the premises), astonishing views of Lake Champlain, and total peace and quiet in a beautifully refurbished house, is here.

You approach to the house through 1,000 acres planned with the advice of Frederick Law Olmsted. Shelburne House is part of a working farm whose operations include a Brown Swiss dairy herd, a bread bakery, a market garden, boat and furniture craft shops, and woodlands managed for firewood and lumber.

The house itself is a brick-over-wood Queen Anne mansion with sixty rooms. We recommend the Webb, Overlook, and L.O.W. South bedrooms. All the rooms have been freshly wallpapered, carpeted, and painted. Some are very simple, with stenciling, while others have exquisite Parisian wallpaper, but all of them are tasteful.

On a warm night you might want to be outside on one of the two massive porches. One overlooks the Coach Barn, pastures, Lake Champlain, and a vast stretch of lawn; the other, the formal gardens, with a different view of the lake. There is also a terrace along the front of the house. Inside is a library with the original furnishings, 6,000 volumes, and a pianist who plays in the early evening. On the third floor is a massive children's playroom with antique toys.

Much of the food served is either grown here or on nearby farms. Dinner, at one of two seatings, is sometimes as good as you would find in New York's best restaurants. At breakfast a small buffet is served, although you can order just about anything you want from the kitchen.

You don't have to leave the farm for days to find things to do. There are tours of the farm and many walks through the scenic grounds. There is a tennis court and a small boat and canoe. Order a picnic lunch the day before, and you can go off and have one of the most scenic and private picnics in all of Vermont.

Perhaps what is most remarkable about Shelburne House is the attitude of the people who work there. They go out of their way to make you feel as if you are in your own home.

The Wilburton Inn, Grand Country Estate

River Road
Manchester, Vermont 05254
802-362-2500
800-648-4944

Owner: Albert and Georgette Levis
General manager: Stan Holton
10 rooms in main house (all with private bath), 22 in cottages
May-October: $115-$135 per couple on weekends; $95-$120 midweek; $120-$155 at holidays, foliage season, special events; full breakfast and afternoon tea included

Off-season: $85-$135; special packages available
Dinner also served
Major credit cards
Children welcome
No pets
Open year-round

The Wilburton was built as a private estate for the philanthropist James Wilbur in 1902. It is perched on a knoll, surrounded by 20 acres of stately grounds, and the views of the Battenkill Valley are magnificent.

This is the brick, stockbroker Tudor kind of mansion that tends to be turned into a private school, and for a spell it was. The public spaces are baronial, replete with grand fireplaces cast in solid brass and Oriental rugs on stained hardwood floors.

Albert and Georgette Levis have retained the Wilburton's air of gentility but enlivened the atmosphere with bright, truly innovative, and interesting art (the ground floor now includes a formal gallery) and a number of comfortable reading corners. The Billiard Room, our favorite of the two dining rooms, combines rich paneling and a carved bar with crisp linen-topped tables and crystal to create the effect of an exclusive men's club, and the food — dishes like Atlantic red snapper with artichoke hearts baked in parchment paper and English-style beef Wellington — is winning top reviews. Cocktails and tea are served in the living room.

Upstairs, each bedroom is furnished in the elegant style that gives the house its charm. The rooms have been painted in calm pastels and are lined with stained wood, and here, too, the Levises have brightened things with splashy, interesting paintings. The marvelous old tubs and sinks remain in the bathrooms.

When we visited, the five cottages, built in the 1950s, were still relatively drab, but Georgette had grand plans for redoing them; it would be difficult to improve on their views of the mountains and valley.

Tennis courts and a swimming pool are on the grounds. Ask about the special workshops in conflict analysis offered by Albert Levis, a psychiatrist and pioneer in the field. Originally from Greece, Levis has been living in Manchester for more than fifteen years. Georgette, incidentally, is the innkeeper and is usually on hand to greet visitors.

Gourmet Getaways

All of these inns are best known as places to dine. To avoid disappointment on Saturday night, guests should be sure to book dinner reservations along with their room.

Connecticut

Bee & Thistle Inn
100 Lyme Street
Old Lyme, Connecticut 06371
203-434-1667

Innkeepers: Bob and Penny Nelson
11 doubles (9 with private bath)
$78-$105 per couple, EP
All 3 meals served, except no lunch and dinner Tuesday
Major credit cards
Children over 12 welcome
No pets
Open year-round except 2 weeks in January

The Bee & Thistle offers very good food served gracefully and with good cheer, attractive and restful common rooms, and tastefully decorated guest rooms on the upper floors. Guests can have breakfast brought to their rooms or eat on a sunlit porch or before the fire in the dining room. Breakfast is fresh orange juice, a variety of other fruit, large homemade muffins, and fluffy omelettes. The soups at lunch are excellent, as are the reasonably priced entrées.

The evenings are a wonderful time to enjoy the two common rooms. Each has a fireplace and is furnished with items from the early 1900s. Dinner is served by candlelight, and the freshest fare is made to order. Entrées include seafood, lamb, veal, duckling, and choice steaks, all beautifully prepared. The wine list is good, and wine by the glass comes in a very large glass indeed.

Our favorite rooms are numbers 1 and 2. The former, with a lovely canopy bed and private bath, is large and spacious.

Copper Beech Inn
Main Street
Ivoryton, Connecticut 06442
203-767-0330

Innkeepers: Sally and Eldon Senner
13 rooms (all with private bath)
$85-$145 per couple, including Continental breakfast
Dinner served except Monday
Major credit cards
Children over 8 welcome
No pets
Open year-round

This small white clapboard inn, in lovely and peaceful Ivoryton, is made for those in need of a rest. It is shaded by a huge beech tree and surrounded by gardens and woodland. It also serves fine food — some say the best in Connecticut.

Four of the guest rooms are in the main house and nine in the carriage house. The rooms in the main house are decorated with cheerful flowered wallpaper, wicker and antiques, white ruffled curtains, and comforters. The baths have old fixtures, like clawfoot tubs. The largest and brightest room is the combination bedroom and sitting area upstairs at the front of the house. It has a brass canopy bed, crystal chandelier, a sofa in front of the fireplace, and a huge bay window overlooking the beech tree. The rooms in the carriage house have country furnishings (particularly appealing on the second floor, where the beams are exposed), and each has a Jacuzzi.

The three formal dining rooms are furnished with reproduction Queen Anne, Chippendale, and Empire furniture, with the tables placed a generous distance from one another. Fresh flowers abound, and roses grace the tables. White linen, sterling silver, candles, hand-blown goblets with napkins tightly rolled and folded into them, and fine china are on each table. The atmosphere is elegant yet warm and comfortable. Before dinner on weekends, guests can have a drink in the greenhouse, which is decorated with white wicker furniture. The owners have added an antique gallery that specializes in Oriental porcelain.

It would be foolish to stay here without enjoying the superior food. Ten appetizers and two soups are available; try the chilled lobster tail with lemon mayonnaise or the wild mushrooms in puff pastry. The lobster bisque is excellent. There are always special veal or fresh fish entrées and breast of duck with sauces that change daily. A dozen other choices, including such classics as beef Wellington, present an array of riches. Glorious desserts top off the meal.

The Homestead Inn
420 Field Point Road
Greenwich, Connecticut 06830
203-869-7500

Innkeepers: Lessie Davison and Nancy Smith
23 rooms and suites (all with private bath)
$105-$165 per couple, including breakfast
All 3 meals served except lunch on weekends
Major credit cards
Children welcome
No pets
Open year-round

Less than a mile from Route 95 on a back road, the Homestead is an example of a phenomenal restoration. The main building, an 18th-century home that was turned into an inn in the mid-1800s, was bought in 1979 in a state of collapse by the current innkeepers, who have completely renovated it. A late-19th-century guest house (the Independent House) and a small cottage built in the late 1920s have also been redone. The food is superb and has been given three stars by the *New York Times.*

The bedrooms are all individually decorated and furnished; the wallpapers and fabrics are the best available, and some of the furnishings are priceless antiques. The Robin Suite is so named because, in the process of stripping away six layers of wallpaper, delicate stencils of robins dating from 1860 were found. It was decided to leave them exposed, cracks and all. All of the rooms have such amenities as bathrobes, electric blankets, color televisions, clock radios, and four pillows for each person. The eight rooms next door are lovely if more uniform, with modern baths, carpeting, and an outdoor porch. The private cottage has a suite and two rooms.

While poking about the common rooms, notice the floor in the foyer, and you will begin to understand the innkeepers' incredible attention to detail. The floor has a painted green border with floral motifs in the corner that have been copied from the wallpaper design.

In the backgammon room you can enjoy the fireplace in the winter. You can have a drink in the Chocolate Bar or in the lounge. The sofa in the lounge is original to the house, having been discovered in the barn and restored.

There are two dining areas; one was a porch and is particularly nice on a sunny day for breakfast or lunch, and the other was once a barn (now called Le Grange), which was grafted onto the house. The old beams in the restored barn are splendid. The tables are well spaced. In the evening, crystal oil lamps and soft outdoor lighting add a romantic touch. As you might expect, dinner is served on Wedgwood china and fine crystal.

The Homestead's chef, Jacques Thiebeault, came from two very well known New York restaurants. Although he is famous for his soups, his hors d'oeuvres can include pâté, fresh crabmeat, or American foie gras. Duck with black currant sauce and wild rice, sweetbreads sautéed with wild mushrooms and Madeira, and veal kidneys finished with Dijon mustard, cream, and chives are typical entrées. The pastry chef is famous for triple chocolate cake and fresh fruit tarts.

The Inn at Chester
318 West Main Street
Chester, Connecticut 06412
203-526-4961

Innkeepers: David and Jaye Joslow
47 rooms, 1 executive suite
April-December: rooms, $80-$95, suite, $150
All 3 meals served
Major credit cards
Children welcome
Pets welcome
Open year-round

The Inn at Chester is made up of a magnificently restored farmhouse that was built between 1776 and 1778, a barn, and two new wings. The stunning old barn was moved to the property from down the street and serves as the main dining area. The brand-new wings contain the bedrooms and a luxurious executive suite with a cathedral ceiling in the living room. All the guest rooms are furnished with antiques and Early American reproductions. The public areas are comfortable and spacious.

Meals are a grand affair here, for the food is superb. In the winter, a fire is always blazing in the huge, gray stone fireplace in the lounge. A piano player performs during dinner, with the music reverberating off the cathedral ceiling, which must be 30 feet high. The living room cum hall, which looks down on the lounge, has the best antiques in the inn. The barn is just off the lounge. Both the hayloft and the main floor are used as dining areas. The tables are large and set with white tablecloths, candles, and fine china. There are smaller dining rooms in the old house, and a small, sunny porch is nice for breakfast and lunch in summer. Meals can also be taken on the patio, furnished with wrought iron furniture. The cuisine is classic, but there is usually a game dish, like water buffalo in raspberry marinade, grilled and served with green peppercorn and raspberry compound butter. Be sure to indulge in the homemade pastries and bread.

The inn is surrounded by state forest, with miles of trails for walking or jogging. You can also use an all-weather tennis court, a joggercize trail, and bicycles. Public beaches are a short drive away.

Old Lyme Inn

P.O. Box 787B
85 Lyme Street
Old Lyme, Connecticut 06371
203-434-2600

Innkeeper: Diane Field Atwood
13 rooms (5 in the original house)
$85–$125 per couple, including Continental breakfast
Major credit cards
Children welcome
Pets welcome
Open year-round except the first 2 weeks in January

The Old Lyme Inn is the kind of place Charles Kuralt, Hal Holbrook, and Norman Mailer would select to take special friends to for dinner—and do! It manages to combine the essence of New England with the sophisticated taste buds of Manhattan. The restaurant is even more popular and well regarded than the inn. But with the attention and caring you'll receive here, you'll be hard-pressed to decide which you like better.

Rich colors are used in the dining rooms (one alcove is small enough for a single table, which gentlemen occasionally book when they are planning to get engaged). The menu might include Connecticut rabbit, rainbow trout, scallops with spinach and red peppers, poached salmon, or chicken with apples and hard cider. The most expensive entrée ($22.50) on our last visit was aged Texas hill country black buck antelope: sautéed medallions in a light game stock enhanced with chopped morels and hazelnuts and finished with hazelnut oil. The chef has received three stars from the *New York Times* on three occasions.

Continental breakfast is served in the Rose Room, a delightful, sectioned-off area at the entrance, done up with gathered fabric covering the wall and partitions.

A romantic and clubby bar serves your favorite libation. The bar itself was bought from an antiques dealer in Manayunk, Pennsylvania, who retrieved it from one of the oldest taverns in Pittsburgh. It still has its original beveled glass mirrors and dart holes.

Five rooms are upstairs in the main house; the others are in a handsome addition that blends well with the inn's own architecture. Some of the rooms upstairs have cannonball bedposts, Queen Anne armchairs, or a Victorian couch. The new rooms are more deluxe and modern, though each has a four-poster bed, wingback chairs, quilted comforters, and George Washington spreads. Most beds are queen-size; three are twins. Everything is topnotch.

The Connecticut River valley offers many historic homes to visit. The Florence Griswold Museum across the street is a unique trove of American Impressionist art, and the Lyme Academy of Fine Arts, just up the street, also has exhibitions. Mystic Seaport is a half hour up the highway.

Silvermine Tavern
Silvermine and Perry Avenues
Norwalk, Connecticut 06850
203-847-4558

Innkeeper: Frank Whitman
10 rooms (all with private bath), 1 apartment
$74-$80 per couple, including breakfast
Lunch and dinner also served
Major credit cards
Children welcome
No pets
Open year-round except Tuesdays from September to May

At the corner of two winding back roads, the Silvermine Tavern is a long white Colonial house with pink shutters. Best known for its terrific, traditional New England fare and six dining rooms, it overlooks the Silvermine River, a waterfall, and the quiet Mill Pond, where swans and ducks frequently feed.

The guest rooms are in the Tavern and the Old Mill House.

(There is also an apartment, in the Old Mill House.) The bedrooms, on the small side, have white bedspreads, hooked rugs, and red pine floors and are furnished with some Early American antiques. You might ask for one of the rooms with a four-poster bed or the one with its own porch overlooking the Mill Pond.

The two living rooms in the low-ceilinged Silvermine Tavern have Early American antiques with creaky floors, well-worn Oriental rugs, wingback chairs, and many fireplaces. One has unusual collections of primitive paintings, prints, and early inn and store signs. A remarkable collection of Early American tools, implements, and utensils hangs in the dining rooms.

The dining rooms are the focal point of the inn. New England soups and chowders, lobster prepared in many different ways, baked and stuffed fish, and chicken pot pie—all prepared beautifully—are staples here. In nice weather, you dine on the riverside deck. On Thursday evening and Sunday brunch, a generous buffet is presented.

Across the street and part of the original complex is an old-fashioned country store, complete with cracker barrels, canned fruits and candies, and an antiques museum in the rear.

Stonehenge Inn
P.O. Box 667, Route 7
Ridgefield, Connecticut 06877
203-438-6511

Innkeepers: David Davis and Douglas Seville
16 rooms and suites (all with private bath)
$95-$140 per couple, including breakfast
Dinner and Sunday brunch also served
Major credit cards
Children welcome
No pets
Open year-round

After suffering a tragic fire in the main house in 1988, Stonehenge has been rebuilt and is better than ever. Slightly off busy Route 7, its 11 acres are quite attractive, with rock walls, walking trails, and a peaceful pond filled with ducks, geese, and swans.

The six inn rooms have a new, rich, and elegant feeling. The best is a corner room with a view of the back grounds and pond. Six low, connected units are popular in the summer because they are next to the pool. In the winter, some guests prefer the more private carriage house out back because they can drive right up to it to unload their luggage. Two upstairs suites in this building are enormous and luxurious, and the two on the lower floor have been nicely done; all the suites can sleep four people. All the rooms have been individually and beautifully redone with excellent reproduction furniture and lovely color-coordinated carpets, fabrics, and wallpapers. All the rooms have air conditioning and a TV. A Continental breakfast and newspaper are brought to your room in the morning.

The very formal dining room, seating 110 in the larger and a small room, has two picture windows and French doors exposing the fieldstone patio outside. Place settings are of china, silver, and lead crystal. The hidden stereo system and air conditioning dispense music and coolness evenly and in just the right amount. (After the fire, the innkeepers could at least build things exactly to their demanding specifications.) The service is excellent, much like that in any of the old famous city restaurants.

Appetizers may include a crêpe of wild mushrooms with Gruyère cheese or fresh hearts of palm wrapped in prosciutto. As a main course, try the crisply roasted duckling with wild rice and a black currant sauce or rosettes of lamb with herb croutons in a Madeira truffle sauce. If you still have room, finish your dinner with a wonderfully creamy cheesecake or a hot apple tart with a butter rum sauce.

Maine

The Blue Hill Inn
P.O. Box 403
Union Street
Blue Hill, Maine 04614
207-374-2844

Innkeepers: Mary and Don Hartley
10 rooms (all with private bath)
$140 per couple MAP, $110 B&B, less November-May; add
   15% service charge
MasterCard, Visa
Children over 13 welcome
No pets
No smoking
Open year-round

An 1830s brick-ended double home, this wonderfully worn and welcoming building has been an inn since 1840. It's near the center of one of Maine's most beautiful villages, known for its musicians, craftsmen, and artists.

The guest rooms are surprisingly large. Some have sitting areas with writing desks, and three have fireplaces; all are carefully furnished, with an eye to creating a space for more than sleeping.

The two living rooms have low beams and are furnished with flair and comfort, again spaces where you want to linger. Cocktails are served here or, weather permitting, in the garden before dinner—a six-course, candlelit affair. You might begin with hazelnut and morel soup finished with Marsala, then savor Maine crabmeat garnished with lemon and capers, cleanse your palate with a Cointreau sorbet before the rack of lamb, followed by a salad, topped off by strawberries Romanoff. One large table seats all who wish to gather around it, but you can also dine at individual tables.

Le Domaine Restaurant and Inn

Route 1, Box 496
Hancock, Maine 04604
207-422-3395, 207-422-3916

Innkeeper: Nicole Purslow
7 rooms (all with private bath)
$160 per couple, MAP
Major credit cards
Children over 5 welcome
No pets
Open May to November

This unpretentious house on Route 1 offers some genuine surprises. Hancock is a shade off the tourist trail, beyond the turnoff for Bar Harbor. But this is still beautiful coastal country, its peninsulas studded with old estates and summer homes, where this inn is revered as the special place to eat out.

Le Domaine is a true French *auberge* with comfortable, nicely decorated rooms upstairs, furnished with niceties like books, magazines, fresh fruit, and bath soaps. And there are mountains to climb, sea excursions, and ocean drives to fill the day. But the big draw is the food.

You might begin the day with wild blueberries and raspberries in thick cream and croissants with homemade jam and honey. In the evening, dinner is set out on white linen tablecloths in the intimate dining room, with French maps and pictures and a large fireplace at one end. The menu features nouvelle cuisine, and the traditional French dishes—such as *escalope de saumon à l'oseille, lapin aux pruneaux, choux de Savoie Farcie* and *coquilles St.- Jacques*—are masterfully prepared.

Nicole Purslow came to Maine during World War II with her parents, who had to flee from their inn in Les Baux after it was discovered that they had been hiding Jews in the basement. She worked with her mother at the inn, then attended the Cordon Bleu in Paris and served an apprenticeship in Switzerland before returning to Maine.

The Newcastle Inn
Newcastle, Maine 04553
207-563-5685

Innkeepers: Chris and Ted Sprague
15 rooms (all with private bath)
In season: $60-$70 per person double occupancy, $80-$100 single, MAP
Off-season: $55-$65 per person double occupancy, MAP; B&B rates available
Add 15% service charge; 2-night minimum on weekends, July through Labor Day
Dinner 6 nights a week
MasterCard, Visa
Older, well-behaved children welcome
No pets
Open year-round

The Newcastle Inn sits by the water overlooking one of Maine's most appealing coastal towns. Although Boothbay is a short drive down River Road and Route 1 is less than a half mile away, the inn is cupped in its own quiet hollow.

Chris and Ted Sprague are that rare innkeeping mix: chef and handyman. Chris was raised in the gourmet food business and was a pastry chef and caterer on Cape Cod, where Ted (technically a high school biology teacher) built their four-bedroom house. When they bought the inn in 1987, they immediately started redoing every room and adding bathrooms. Of course, they had to switch the kitchen around and, to maximize the water view, Ted kept adding octagonal, porthole windows. A few rooms have canopy beds and some have sitting areas. Our favorite is number 9, which has cottage country furniture, a water view, a deep closet, and an immense bath.

Downstairs, the public areas are comfortably welcoming. The Stencil Room, with green and red wing chairs and hooked rugs (the elaborate stenciling is on the floor) opens onto a glassed-in sunporch with a view of the Damariscotta River (which looks more like a bay here) and the village's church steeple beyond.

Before dinner, guests gather in the living room for cocktails and hors d'oeuvres. Dinner, served promptly at 7:00 P.M., is in the candlelit dining room and is magnificent. You could begin with shiitake mushrooms served with sun-dried tomatoes and pignoli, move on to a red and yellow pepper bisque, then a delicate salad followed by perfectly poached fresh salmon with orange Madeira sauce, topped off by pear Charlotte with raspberry sauce. The wine list is appropriate.

The inn's sign is a rabbit, and there are rabbits — stuffed, wooden, and china — everywhere. But the inn's mastiff is Destiny, an unusually friendly, well-trained dog who accompanies Chris on her 6:00 A.M. jogs around town. Between 8:00 and 8:45 A.M., guests feast on downright extravagant breakfasts and eventually set off on sightseeing, antiquing, canoeing, or hiking adventures. Waterside nature trails are just down River Road.

The Oxford House Inn
105 Main Street
Fryeburg, Maine 04037
207-935-3442

Innkeepers: Phyllis and John Morris
5 rooms (2 with shared bath)
$60-$75 per room, including full breakfast
Dinner and Sunday brunch served to the public
Major credit cards
Children welcome
No pets
Open year-round

This spacious, turn-of-the-century house is set back from Fryeburg's Main Street. It is yellow, with a large porch and big bay windows and seems to promise something out of the ordinary.

What you notice first are the dining areas: three rooms full of white-clothed tables and the menu, prominently displayed, listing specialties like salmon Pommery (wine-poached fillet of fresh salmon topped with a mild mustard sauce and green peppercorns) and scallops vin blanc (fresh scallops poached in wine and shallots, finished in sweet butter and served in a flaky puff pastry). The appetizers include the pâté of the day and native Maine crab chowder. Dinners average $20 per person.

The inn's fame as a restaurant draws guests from neighboring resort towns in New Hampshire as well as Maine. But this is also a place to stay. There is a downstairs parlor and the Granite Room lounge for guests; upstairs there are five bedrooms, each furnished with the same care with which the meals are prepared.

Request one of the two rooms in the back of the house, away from the street and overlooking the distant White Mountains. All of the rooms have flowery wallpaper and iron bedsteads with quilts.

The price includes a full breakfast, served on the enclosed back porch, overlooking the mountains.

In the summer, the big reason to come to Fryeburg is the Saco River. A smooth, sandy-bottomed passage through unspoiled countryside, the Saco is a favorite with families and neophyte canoeists. There are several canoe outfitters and put-in points right in Fryeburg. This is also rich hiking as well as shopping country. In the winter, there is skiing at Shawnee Peak in Maine and at a choice of major mountains in the nearby Mount Washington Valley.

The Squire Tarbox Inn
R.D. 2, Box 620
Wiscasset, Maine 04578
207-882-7693

Innkeepers: Bill and Karen Mitman
11 rooms (all with private bath)
$116-$130 per couple, MAP
Major credit cards
Children over 14 welcome
No pets
Open mid-May to late October

In the remote Maine woods, this small, quiet inn is a carefully restored farmhouse on a working farm with a barn full of dairy goats. Plenty of parlors and fireplaces invite guests to visit with one another. The big event of the day is the excellent dinner served in the beamed portion of the house, which dates from 1763. This is truly a retreat for adults.

Chèvre cheese made from the farm's own goats' milk is served before dinner. One typical meal includes peach and cantaloupe soup, warm peasant bread, fillet of sole stuffed with chopped spinach and Parmesan cheese and accented with a buttered wine sauce, three different (and creative) vegetables, sin pie (made with chocolate), and coffee or a choice of teas. Seafood, chicken, and lamb are the most common entrées, and the vegetables are always special. The emphasis is always on the freshest ingredients and homemade cheese, bread, and desserts.

The inn has four large, formal bedrooms in the main house and seven cozy, informal rooms in an adjoining converted 1820 barn, which has a wood-burning stove. The rooms, furnished with country antiques, are restful and tastefully decorated. Colorful, handmade quilts grace some of the beds. The living room offers some fine furniture and a fireplace. A music room contains a player piano and another fireplace. The Colonial dining room has plank floors, a low-beamed ceiling, and a brick and beam fireplace.

Massachusetts

The Windflower Inn
Egremont Star Route 65, Box 25
Great Barrington, Massachusetts 01230
413-528-2720

Innkeepers: Barbara and Gerald Liebert, Claudia and John Ryan
13 rooms (all with private bath)
$140-$180 per couple, MAP
No credit cards
Children welcome
No pets
Open year-round

The Windflower is a turn-of-the-century gentleman's retreat in a lovely little resort town. The white clapboard home with gables, black shutters, and a wraparound porch, across from a country club, exudes informal luxury.

Fine food is the draw here. The dining room, with Currier & Ives scenes on the walls, is open to the public by reservation. Barbara Liebert, the former owner of the Tulip Tree Inn in Chittendon, Vermont, and her daughter, Claudia Ryan, are the chefs; John Ryan supplies berries, herbs, and vegetables from his garden. There is a nightly choice of poultry, meat, or fish, and everything—from soup to bread to dessert—is made on the premises.

The bedrooms and baths are large and bright with matching bedspreads and curtains. Room 12 has a huge fireplace and a four-poster bed. Another room has a private entrance and a large fireplace.

There is a gracious living room with a fireplace, and a reading room with books, magazines, games, and a piano. In the summer guests, can enjoy the inn's swimming pool and the golf course and tennis courts at the country club — not to mention the music, dance, and theater festivals for which the Berkshires are famous. In the winter there is skiing, both downhill and cross-country.

■ *See also:* The Bostonian Hotel, Boston, Massachusetts; The Four Seasons, Boston, Massachusetts; Hotel Meridien, Boston, Massachusetts

---

New Hampshire

Home Hill Country Inn
R.R. 2, Box 235
Cornish, New Hampshire 03745
603-675-6165

Innkeeper: Roger Nicolas
5 rooms (all with private bath), 3-room cottage
$105 per couple in summer, $90 in winter, $15 per extra
    person, includes Continental breakfast
Dinner also served
MasterCard, Visa
Children not appropriate
No pets
Open except March and November

This is one of the magnificent, four-square 1820s mansions spaced along the Connecticut River in the Upper Valley. In the 1890s, many of the houses in Plainfield were bought by prominent artists and their wealthy patrons, and the town remains one of the most elegant around.

Home Hill, however, had seen better days by the time Roger Nicholas, a young Frenchman who grew up on a farm in Brittany, discovered it on his first trip to New England. After two years of painstaking restoration, he opened it as a combination French restaurant and country inn.

"Ninety-five percent of my business is dining and five percent is sleeping," admits Roger (pronounced the French way), who has added a long canopy from the door to the driveway, further emphasizing the restaurant and downplaying the country inn. Admittedly, too, the rooms are nothing to write home about: brass beds, country wallpaper, maybe a handmade quilt. There is a two-room suite and a three-room cottage by the pool.

But the location is beautiful: 25 acres by the river are great for walking when they aren't good for cross-country skiing (trails are maintained). There is also a tennis court and pool and, with the exception of the evening dining hours, this setting is supremely peaceful.

Of course, dining is what this place is about. The prix fixe menu is $30, and there is a nightly choice of four or five appetizers and entrées. You might begin with a soufflé of sole and crab with lobster sauce or a Napoleon of fresh fish with a champagne sauce, then proceed to Peking duck with lingonberries or rabbit braised with wine and tarragon, finishing with either a white and dark mousse with raspberry sauce or a homemade pastry. There is an extensive wine list.

Home Hill is nicely sited both for skiing (at Mount Ascutney, just across the river in Vermont) and general prowling. Dartmouth College and its superb art museum are 20 minutes up Route 12A and the Saint-Gaudens National Historic Site is just down the same road.

Vermont

The Arlington Inn
Route 7A
Arlington, Vermont 05250
802-375-6532

Innkeepers: Paul and Madeline Kruzel
13 rooms (all with private bath)
$50-$125 per couple, including breakfast
Lunch served in high season; dinner and brunch, year-round
Major credit cards
Children welcome
No pets
Open year-round

The combination of Greek Revival architecture, creative new American cuisine, and Vermont country hospitality and service is difficult to surpass, and the Arlington Inn has it all. A dining experience here redefines the term.

Soft music piped through Bose speakers fills the house. At dinnertime, an antique brass music stand at the drawing room doors, leading into the dining rooms, displays that night's à la carte menu. The dining rooms are intimate, elegant, and warmly lit; one has a working fireplace.

To start your dinner, try the Maine crab bisque followed by wasabi pasta and smoked scallops in a light cilantro cream sauce or a Vermont pheasant pâté in a Zinfandel and orange sauce. For the main course, try a Cornish game hen grilled with a black walnut and sour cream sauce. Equally creative and artfully presented is the grilled gulf shrimp wrapped in Vermont corncob smoked bacon, with fresh lemon pasta in a whiskey lemon butter. Of the four culinary honors recently awarded to Paul Kruzel, one was for a lemon-thyme and ricotta bread, another for his Cheddar cheese mousse in an almond tart with raspberry and caramel sauces.

On the first floor, with a nicely refurbished wood ceiling, is a solarium with large slabs of marble and a woody tavern with a few bar stools and a couple of tables. Off the very formal parlor is the only guest room on the first floor.

Guest rooms in the main inn are elegant and filled with antiques. Chloe's Room is cozy, with a bed tucked under an eave. If you stay in Mary's Room, bring a robe, since the bathroom is in the hall. Pamela's Suite is formal, ever so blue, and has curtains that pull back to reveal the bedchambers.

The oversize rooms in the carriage house have wall-to-wall carpeting, air conditioning, and marble-topped bureaus. Rebecca's Retreat is French country provincial. There's a casual common room upstairs with a TV, magazines, and a game table.

On the lushly landscaped lawns you can play croquet, tennis, and horseshoes. Breakfast is a hearty but simple Continental affair, and it can be served in your room if you like.

The Country Inn at Williamsville, Vermont

Grimes Hill Road
P.O. Box 166
Williamsville, Vermont 05362
802-348-7148

Innkeepers: Bill and Sandra Cassill
6 rooms (all with private bath)
$76-$116 per room including breakfast, $121-$161 MAP; extra
  person in room: $19 with breakfast, $42 MAP
Major credit cards
Children over 8 welcome
No pets
Open year-round

This farmhouse, built in 1795, overlooks 115 acres that stretch past the red barn across the road and down to the Rock River.
  Sandra and Bill Cassill spent four years restoring the hand-

some old home before opening it to guests. They installed a fabulous kitchen, where Sandra uses the cooking skills she learned in London, Paris, and at the Vermont Culinary Institute in Montpelier.

Five-course dinners are served on Friday and Saturday evenings. The fixed menu features fine French cooking, but individual allergies and dietary needs are accommodated. A full breakfast is served from seven-thirty to nine o'clock every morning.

The guest rooms are carefully furnished with antiques and original art. Our favorite is the corner room with a fireplace and a hand-painted Vermont scene on its walls.

The public rooms include a large, bright living room with a grand piano and fireplace and a small, inviting library with a TV (good reception) and sound system.

In the summer, you can fish in the round trout pond just across the road or swim in a cool, deep swimming hole in the Rock River, also on the property. There are miles of inviting back roads, and mountain bikes can be rented ($10 per day).

This is rewarding country in which to poke around, and on July and August weekends there is the added lure of the Marlboro Music Festival.

In the winter there is cross-country skiing on 4½ miles of marked, groomed trails right on the property. Maple Valley, a small family ski area, is just down the road, and both Stratton and Mount Snow are not far away.

The Four Columns Inn
P.O. Box 278
West Street
Newfane, Vermont 05345
802-365-7713

Innkeeper: Jacques Allembert
15 rooms (all with private bath), 1 cottage
$80-$120 per couple, including breakfast, $25 for extra person in room
2-night minimum on weekends and holidays
Dinner also served except Tuesdays
Major credit cards
Children over 10 welcome
Pets with prior permission
Open year-round except 3 weeks in November and 3 weeks in April

Facing one of Vermont's outstanding commons, the Four Columns combines the facade of an antebellum mansion with the spaciousness of an old barn. The two were put together when a French chef parted ways with the neighboring old Newfane Inn and opened his own competing establishment next door. Now Jacques Allembert presides over the inn, lending it a warmth and informality frequently lacking in famous gourmet retreats.

The restaurant, which is open to the public, is in the beamed barn. It has a huge brick fireplace and appropriately set tables where guests dine by candlelight. The chef, Greg Parks, who has been on the staff since the inn opened, specializes in European and American cuisine.

Most of the guest rooms are in the old mansion and a connecting wing. They are snug, bright, and furnished with antiques.

There is a pool in the back and a hill with a path through its woods. A surprising number of shops are tucked in and around Newfane. Across Route 30, up a road marked Dead End, there is an old cemetery with an obelisk that marks the resting place of Sir Isaac Newton (Newton is a common local name). Winter visitors can ski on nearby thrown up roads (roads in Vermont that are no longer maintained for traffic) or drive the half hour to Stratton Mountain and Mount Snow.

The Governor's Inn
86 Main Street
Ludlow, Vermont 05149
802-228-8830

Innkeepers: Deedy and Charlie Marble
8 rooms (all with private bath)

$170 per couple, MAP
Major credit cards
Children over 14 welcome
No pets
Open year-round

In the center of busy Ludlow, the Governor's Inn has been under the meticulous care of Deedy and Charlie Marble since 1982. They've developed quite a following and a reputation.

The guest rooms have their own individuality, with antique bed and armoire, needlepoint chairs, and other Victorian pieces for balance. Guests will discover a basket in the upstairs hallway that contains items they might have forgotten. The Marbles really outdo themselves in catering to their guests' comfort and relaxation. In the evening, the beds are turned down and the towels changed. And each room has its own diary in which guests can add their thoughts about the room, the service, the food, or anything else.

The Marbles have studied and received diplomas from L'École du Moulin, a world-renowned French cooking school. Deedy handles the dinner chores while Charlie takes care of breakfast. Both meals are sumptuous feasts. Breakfast is a four-course event that will satisfy you until teatime. It features eggs, oatmeal, perhaps rum raisin French toast, a special breakfast puff, or Charlie's favorite, the Cuckoo's Nest.

A splendid tea is served at 3:00 P.M. in season. Ask about the sophisticated picnic lunches they can pack for you.

The candlelit dinners are six-course events, with each course described by the server, who, you will discover, is excellently trained and most personable. Deedy's lobster and crabmeat Chanticleer may be offered or perhaps game hens in Grand Marnier or steak Diane. Regardless of what else is available, you will also be offered the sorbet that was made for Paul Newman and Joanne Woodward when they visited the inn.

Ludlow is the home of Okemo Mountain for downhill skiing. Cross-country skiing trails start right in town. The Black River, at the end of the inn's property, is a fisherman's paradise.

The Inn at Sawmill Farm
P.O. Box 367
Mount Snow Valley and Route 100
West Dover, Vermont 05356
802-464-8131

Innkeepers: Brill, Ione, and Rodney Williams
12 rooms, 10 cottages (all with fireplace and private bath)

$200-$260 per couple, MAP; $65 for extra person in room
No credit cards
Children over 10 welcome
No pets
Open year-round

The Inn at Sawmill Farm is elegant, from the meticulously trimmed lawns to the polished copper plates. Bring tweeds and cashmeres for kicking about the countryside, whites for tennis, a dinner jacket for after six, and a hefty checkbook (no credit cards).

Inside the main house, wide stairs lead up to a lobby, and a grandfather clock stands behind a glistening baby grand piano. There are several sitting areas, ranging from the main living room, where you will have cocktails by the fire, to a small reading loft lined with books. In all the rooms, country touches like healthy plants, raw wooden walls and beams, dried flowers, log fires, and period furniture are artfully blended with elegant interiors.

The spacious guest rooms have canopy beds, wall-to-wall carpeting, roomy closets, and handsome antiques. The suites and rooms in the cottages have their own living rooms and fireplaces.

Two dining rooms open off the main lobby. One, with a sloping glass roof and a profusion of plants, is light and airy, a cheerful place for breakfast. The other — dark, rich, and intimate — is perfect for a romantic dinner. The tables are set with goblets, slender candles, flowers, and china. The restaurant, known for its Continental cuisine, enjoys a reputation that often makes reservations necessary weeks in advance. The wine cellar of 22,000 bottles complements the menu.

In the summer, guests can have drinks by the pool or play a round of tennis on secluded courts; in the winter, there's skating on the pond followed by cocktails in front of the fire; fall offers glorious long walks in the woods surrounding the inn.

The Inn at South Newfane
South Newfane, Vermont 05351
802-348-7191

Innkeepers: Connie, Herbert, and Lisa Borst
6 rooms (all with private bath)
$80-$88 per person, MAP; $90-$98 in foliage and Christmas
  seasons
No credit cards
Children over 12 welcome

No pets except guide dogs
Open year-round except 3 weeks in April and November

An airy summer mansion built by a Philadelphia family, the inn is framed by a picture-perfect Vermont village. A church with green shutters sits across the road, and the general store is not far. Visitors cross the Williamsville covered bridge and drive by a swimming hole to get to the inn.

The Borst family searched for a full five years for the perfect inn. Lisa is a graduate of the Culinary Institute of America, and her father, Herb, is the artist behind the peerless pastries.

Although the dining room caters to nearby second-home owners (neighboring Newfane Hill is one of Vermont's best summer addresses), guests have their own comfortable living room. There is also a congenial Map Room bar and another spacious parlor.

From the Map Room, French doors lead to an expansive porch and lawns and flower beds that stretch back to the pond and beyond. In all, there are more than 100 acres.

The innovative, award-winning cuisine features various specialties from different regions of the United States: Alaskan fish, buffalo, South Dakota boar, and other game dishes are carefully culled from a variety of sources and artfully prepared.

The rooms are large and bright. Some have their old wallpaper, but most of them were redone in 1984, when the Borsts opened the inn.

The Inn at Weathersfield
Route 106, Box 165
Weathersfield, Vermont 05151
802-263-9217

Innkeepers: Mary Louise and Ron Thorburn
10 rooms, 2 suites (all with private bath)
$80 per person double occupancy, MAP, $105 single, $65 for
   extra person in the room; ski packages available
Major credit cards
Children over 8 welcome
Call in advance about pets
Open year-round

The Inn at Weathersfield, at the end of a tree-lined drive off a hilly country road, is an 18th-century mansion with columns surrounded by tall pines. It features rooms furnished with exquisite antiques, well-kept grounds, excellent individually prepared meals, and a friendly atmosphere.

Afternoon tea is served by a blazing fire in the living room or on the porch, depending on the weather. The dining room, with a low, dark, beamed ceiling, has overflowing bookshelves and a stone fireplace. Ron Thorburn often plays the piano and welcomes requests. Round and square tables are set with starched linens, fine china, candles, and fresh flowers. Mary Louise's imaginative meals draw devotees from miles around. A summer meal might feature savory chicken stuffed with wild rice, cranberries, and nuts, served with an orange sauce; crisp green vegetables; and a rich chocolate cream pie. Afterward, you can have a nightcap or coffee in the tavern, which has a picket grate and a few small tables.

The guest rooms each have their own style and mood. There is a Colonial room, for example, with blue walls, wide floorboards, two dormer windows, and a fireplace. All of the rooms have special features, like Colonial rockers, hand-stitched patchwork quilts, and canopy beds. Seven rooms have working fireplaces, and some have private balconies with a view of Hawks Mountain. All the baths have perfumed soaps, dried flowers, and a pile of soft bath towels; some have claw-foot tubs.

There are box stalls and a fenced paddock out back if you bring your own horse, and you can also arrive and depart on horseback (ask about riding from inn to inn). Horse-drawn sleigh and carriage rides are also available.

Millbrook Inn

Route 17, R.F.D. Box 62
Waitsfield, Vermont 05673
802-496-2405

Innkeepers: Joan and Thom Gorman
7 rooms (4 with private bath)
$48-$60 per person, MAP, $210-$260 for 5-day ski week; $35
    per child under 16; surcharge for singles; less in summer;
    add 15% gratuity
Major credit cards
Children over 10 welcome
Pets with approval in summer and fall
Open year-round, but do call first

You don't notice the dining room at first. You enter through the warming room (actually heated by a woodstove in winter); beyond are two attractive living rooms that invite you to sit down.

The first-floor guest room, the Willow Tree Room, has a double maple and a twin bed, floor-to-ceiling bookcases, and a private bath. The other bedrooms are upstairs: the Henry Perkins Room has a slanted ceiling stenciled with American folk art patterns; the Sunburst Room has a stenciled sunburst and bright, handpainted furniture. The Waterfall Room is named for the style of its bed and matching dresser, the Country Star Room, for the quilt pattern on its antique oak bed, the Shell Room, for the shape of the headboard, matching dresser, and mirror. The spacious Wedding Ring Room has antique pine furniture.

But Millbrook's heart is the dining room, well known locally for an extensive, moderately priced menu featuring fresh ingredients grown nearby and Indian dishes, a vestige of Thom Gorman's days in the Peace Corps. It seats just 26 people, but it feels spacious, and French doors open to the garden. Joan plays hostess/waitress; Thom is the chef/baker.

The menu offers a wide selection—Italian dishes like veal Roma and fettuccine Thom, Vermont lamb in some guise, and Indian entrées like chicken Brahmapuri (boneless breast of chicken cooked in a rich, spicy, village-style curry). Desserts are all homemade, and there is always Anadama bread.

A ski lodge since 1948 (Mad River Glen and Sugarbush North are just up the road), Millbrook has become a true country inn under the Gormans' nurturing. In winter there is extensive cross-country as well as alpine skiing, and in summer the Mad River/Sugarbush Valley, a lively resort center, offers theater, horseback riding, gliding, hiking, and much more.

The Three Clock Inn
Middletown Road
South Londonderry, Vermont 05148
802-824-6327

Innkeepers: Heinrich and Frances Tschernitz
4 rooms (all with private bath)
$60 per person, MAP; $35, B&B
No credit cards
Children not appropriate
No pets
Open year-round except for late October until Christmas and
    April until Memorial Day weekend

This white clapboard inn is a little gem, tucked up a hilly back street in the tiny crossroads village of South Londonderry. Chef Heinrich Tschernitz has been here for more than twenty years; his following is so strong that he rarely advertises.

The guest rooms are lovely—one with a canopy bed and a

fireplace, an extra bed in the corner, and plenty of books; another, a two-room suite with small gable windows and a sitting room. There is also an upstairs sitting room just for guests, to ensure privacy during evening dining hours.

Downstairs there is a gracious living room, but the focal points are unquestionably the low-beamed dining rooms, their tables garnished with fresh flowers and candles. In the summer, there are also tables on the flower porch.

You might begin here with pâté maison or escargots, because this is one of those few New England places where you won't be disappointed in these French classics. Entrées include frogs legs Provençal, but there is a wide choice of specialties: veal scaloppine Marsala, duckling à l'orange, filet mignon with sauce au poivre. For dessert, it's a tough choice between the strawberries Romanoff and the chocolate mousse.

Grand New Resorts

Though they are not particularly old, these resorts offer all the basic comforts plus a range of facilities.

Maine

Inn by the Sea
Route 77
Cape Elizabeth, Maine 04107
207-799-3134
800-888-4287
Fax 207-799/4779

General manager: John Helmke III
43 suites and cottages and beach house
$150-$210 per couple in suites, $285 in cottages, $330 in
  beach house, EP; less in winter
All 3 meals served
Major credit cards
Children welcome
No pets
Open year-round; cottages and beach house open April
  through December

The Inn by the Sea pampers its guests with modern, luxurious accommodations without sacrificing Down East hospitality and decor. A 10-minute drive from downtown Portland, the inn is on a rise above Crescent Beach State Park. Before guests even get to the ocean, the soothing sound of flowing water greets them at the fountain in the drive. The marble lobby with waterfowl prints is elegant but not intimidating.

There is a wide range of spacious accommodations: one- and two-bedroom garden and loft suites, cottages, and a beach house. All the suites have reproduction Chippendale furnishings, down comforters, armoire bars, TVs, VCRs, telephones, and kitchens stocked with interesting foods. The fabrics are soft and luxurious; most come from designer collections. The loft units have balconies with lush plants. All of the bathrooms are especially nice, with showers that are separate from the oval tubs.

The cottages, connected in a town house arrangement, are more rustic than the suites. They are furnished in knotty pine and wicker with thick, rich carpets. Like the larger suites, they have two bedrooms; all have full kitchens. Both the suites and the cottages would be ideal for a family or couples on vacation together.

A wonderful two-bedroom beach house with a full ocean view is closer to the water than the other accommodations and is quite roomy—perfect for a family reunion.

The dining room, serving only resort guests, has lovely views of the lawn and water. The Continental menu has many seafood dishes. A library bar has a clubby atmosphere. A small balcony provides more water views.

The staff is quite special at Inn by the Sea—young and eager to please. Some are from the nearby University of Southern Maine.

The landscaping is beautiful, and a nice boardwalk leads to the beach. Summer evenings are especially nice here, with soft lighting throughout the grounds.

The activities include an outdoor heated pool, two lighted tennis courts, croquet, beachcombing, and biking. A shuttle bus takes guests to the airport and the Old Port historical district in Portland.

Vermont

Mountain Top Inn and Resort
Mountain Top Road
Chittenden, Vermont 05737
802-483-2311
800-445-2100
Fax 802-483-6373

Manager: Bill Wolfe
33 rooms, 22 cottage and chalet units
$53-$98 per person double occupancy, MAP
Lunch also served
Major credit cards

Children welcome
No pets
Open year-round

Secluded on a 1,300-acre estate at an elevation of 2,000 feet, this modern inn commands a truly spectacular view of the Green Mountains and a crystal-clear 650-acre lake just below.

Entering the inn, which was rebuilt in 1977 after a fire, guests are welcomed in a spacious lobby of post and beam construction with a most intriguing stone fireplace. There are many country antiques in two large living rooms and a beautiful panoramic vista. Down the curved, glass-enclosed, cherrywood stairs, which look out on the mountains and lake, is a large, candlelit dining area. An outdoor terrace is used for lunch and breakfast. Live entertainment is scheduled regularly.

Indoors there is a sauna and whirlpool. Outdoors is a heated pool, tennis, a five-hole pitch 'n' putt golf course, shuffleboard, boating, fishing, horseback riding, and a white sandy beach—the perfect launching pad for swimming. All activities without instruction are free to guests. Mountain Top is a major ski touring center, with snowmaking on the trails. Killington and Pico are a 15-minute drive away.

All of the accommodations are comfortable. Most of them are spacious, decorated in fine New England tradition, and command a fine view. The cottages and chalet units, tastefully furnished in a decor neither modern nor antique, are within a short walk of the inn; many have a fireplace or woodstove and a spectacular view. Room categories and rates—deluxe, superior, and standard—are based on size, location, and view. Airport and bus pickups are available at no extra charge.

The Sugarbush Inn
Warren, Vermont 05674
802-583-2301
800-451-4320
Fax 802-583-3209

Owner: Sugarbush Ski Resort
45 rooms, 51 condos
$80-$175 per room, EP
All 3 meals served
Major credit cards
Children welcome
No pets
Open year-round

Guests enter the inn under a large portico that opens into a larger, gracious reception area. Tea and cookies are served in the elegant but inviting living room in the winter. Guest rooms have access to an outdoor porch/deck on every floor or the lawn. Decorated in Laura Ashley prints, accommodations in the main inn are standard (with a half bath), superior, or deluxe (with well-appointed sitting rooms; possibly in the gatehouse). Several times an evening, room service makes the rounds, offering to turn down the bed or bringing after-dinner mints.

Condominiums are suites or units with one to three bedrooms. In a landscape of birch, pine, and winding drives, these deluxe town houses have private sundecks, fully equipped kitchens, daily housekeeping, and tasteful decor.

Feasting, dining, snacking, or drinking—any guest's wish can be met with competence and flair. The Onion Patch, decorated in country prints, specializes in steaks and seafood. In the bright and elegant greenhouse setting of the Terrace Room, all meals are available. The diverse menu selections are appetizing and beautifully presented.

The extensive conference facilities are superb. Both golf and tennis packages take advantage of the 12 clay courts and the Robert Trent Jones, Sr., golf course. The indoor pool is handsome. At the outdoor pool, bar service is available and a light lunch is served under a big tent. The Pavilion houses saunas, a Jacuzzi, ice skating, and a ski touring center, with 40 miles of trails.

Topnotch at Stowe Resort and Spa
P.O. Box 1458
Stowe, Vermont 05672
802-253-8585
800-451-8686 in the eastern U.S.
800-228-8686 in Canada
Fax 802-253-9263

Proprietor: Jack Cummings
92 rooms, 14 condos, 6 town houses
$90-$127 per couple, MAP, $150-$400 for condos/town houses
All 3 meals served
Major credit cards
Children welcome
No pets
Open year-round

You know you are in an unusual place from the moment you enter the stone-walled lobby, with its 12-foot-high windows and panoramic view.

Each accommodation (room, suite, town house, or condominium) has been individually decorated with carefully selected furniture, antiques, and art. Most of the views are of Stowe's ski mountains and forests. The extras include a private library, TV, imported perfumed soaps and bath gels, and ice delivered every afternoon. Plush towels, personal sewing kits, an AM-FM radio, and a direct-dial phone complete the picture. At night, your bed is turned down and Vermont chocolate is left on the pillow.

The candlelit, formal dining room has an intimate, rich feel to it. Le Bistro has a more casual tone. Varied and expensive menus, vintage wines, and sumptuous desserts are de rigueur. A spa menu is also available. Breakfast can be served in your room; lunch can be taken on the terrace (enclosed by lush foliage in summertime), where the 17-foot statue *Acrobats* is mounted. Tea is served each afternoon in the living room. The full bar is of rustic wood, with farm kitchen memorabilia as accents. Sofas and chairs are grouped around the fireplace.

The recreational facilities include an outdoor heated pool and indoor and outdoor tennis. A full service spa, including exercise rooms, Jacuzzis, steam and sauna rooms, and a range of spa services (seaweed body wraps, mineral and salt hydrotherapy treatments) opened late in 1989. An equestrian center, cross-country ski touring center, and alpine skiing at Mount Mansfield are nearby. Bicycles cans be rented in the village of Stowe.

Woodstock Inn & Resort
14 The Green
Woodstock, Vermont 05091
802-457-1100
800-448-7900
Fax 802-457-3824

Manager: Chester Williamson
109 rooms
$115-$195 per couple, $113-$193 single occupancy, $225 for
   suites; children 14 and under free in the same room; MAP:
   $44 per person extra; sports center fees included
All 3 meals served
Major credit cards
Children welcome
No pets
Open year-round

The Woodstock Inn is a relatively new (1969) building that
forms the heart of one of New England's most beautiful towns.
It stands just off the handsome, oval green and within walking
distance of its museum and shops. It also offers the facilities of a
complete resort: an 18-hole golf course, 10 tennis courts, paddle tennis courts, an outdoor pool in summer, and both an
alpine ski hill and an extensive ski touring center in winter.

The only Rockresort left (once there were six, ranging in
locale from the Virgin Islands to Arizona), the Woodstock Inn is
owned by Laurance Rockefeller, who lives in the Billings mansion in town. (Frederick Billings, the grandfather of Laurance's
wife, Mary, was the most prominent man in Woodstock history
until Rockefeller came along.) Rockefeller is an extremely professional hotelier, and this inn is the hotel he sees most frequently. Despite residents' mumblings about how the old inn
was knocked down to make way for this less lovable, more
efficient model, the dining room is the most popular meeting
spot in town. Here, the elaborate luncheon buffet is one of
northern New England's standout buys.

The first thing you see as you enter is a huge stone hearth
with inviting places to sit around it. The guest rooms are large
and have TVs, and the beds are covered with handmade quilts
made by local craftspeople. In 1989 Richardson's Tavern was
moved and expanded and the dining room and coffee shop
enlarged.

Golf is important here. The 18-hole course is one of the
country's oldest, with carts, a pro shop, and putting green. Ask
about special golf packages.

You can ski at Suicide Six, one of the country's oldest ski
areas (also owned by Rockefeller). It has a 600-foot vertical
drop, snowmaking, two chairlifts, a J-bar, a modern lodge, and
a reputation for being tough for its size. The cross-country
center uses the golf course pro shop and 50 miles of trails.
Sleigh rides are another winter feature.

A two-story racquet and sports center down the road includes a fitness center, saunas, an indoor pool, a whirlpool, steam room, two indoor tennis courts, two squash courts, two racquetball courts, and a lounge and restaurant.

The inn accommodates small groups but is primarily a place for families and couples. Except during foliage and school vacation periods, it offers a variety of packages, and skiing at Suicide Six is included in the price of a room in winter. It also offers special plane rates from Boston and New York (via Command Airways) to Lebanon airport, a half hour away. A rental car, from $186 per person for two nights, transport included, is also available for guests.

Grand Old Resorts

These grandes dames of New England innkeeping are all rather large and fairly formal — and extremely inviting.

Maine

okay

The Asticou Inn
Route 3
Northeast Harbor, Maine 04662
207/276-3344

Innkeeper: Daniel M. Kimball
51 rooms and suites (most with private bath)
Summer: $198 per couple, MAP
Lunch also served in high season
MasterCard, Visa
Children over 4 welcome
No pets
Open early May to late December; main house, mid-June to
    mid-September

This inn has traditionally catered to a distinguished clientele and continues to serve a loyal group of guests who return year after year. The mood is quiet and dignified, almost Edwardian, with low-key luxury, New England fare, and views of the water.

The main lobby is dominated by a huge Oriental carpet and a large fireplace—where a fire is always burning—with wing chairs on either side. A traditional living room has a fireplace and terrific views down to Northeast Harbor; a bar offers the same view. An enclosed contemporary porch for playing cards and watching TV is especially popular at night. The dining room, with Oriental carpets, has a lovely old chandelier. A huge porch runs the length of the inn and overlooks formal gardens and the harbor, filled with boats.

The guest rooms are not large and are simply furnished. Some rooms in the inn have bay windows overlooking the harbor. The Topsiders, contemporary cottages, offer more privacy. Three other cottages contain a variety of rooms and suites and operate as a bed-and-breakfast in the spring and fall.

The food is well prepared and features standard Down East specialties. A lavish seafood and roast beef buffet—which includes lobster and a huge selection of salads and pastries—is offered every Thursday night, followed by dancing to a live band. At breakfast, anything you could possibly want is available, including fried fish.

The inn's flowers are taken from its own cutting beds. Within an easy stroll is the Asticou azalea garden. Thuya Garden, formal and tucked away, is a delightful walk up the raked gravel paths and gentle granite steps. And it's near some of the most beautiful parts of Acadia National Park.

The Bethel Inn & Country Club
Village Common
Bethel, Maine 04217
207-824-2175
800-654-0125
Fax 207-824-2233

Owner: Dick Rasor
General manager: Ray Moran
65 rooms (all with private bath), 40 2-bedroom town houses
$65-$95 per person double occupancy weekend, MAP, less weekdays, more on holidays, $20 per child under 12; slightly more in foliage season, less off-season; ask about packages
Lunch also served
Major credit cards
Children welcome
Pets welcome with advance notice
Open year-round

The Bethel Inn was built in 1913, when most guests arrived by train from Boston and points south. It has always appealed to golfers, but in the 1980s it thrived on the increasing popularity of nearby Sunday River, which grew from a local ski hill to a big-time resort. There is also Mount Abram Ski Area, just a short drive in the other direction, and the inn has its own ski touring trails, with rental equipment, lessons, and guided tours. The inn's indoor-outdoor pool (the well-heated kind you can swim out into under the stars, even on the frostiest nights) is a welcome addition in the winter.

The inn itself is a rambling, yellow clapboard building in the center of a fine old Maine town on the eastern fringe of the White Mountains. The main parlor looks like a luxurious living room, and the large dining room has a cheery hearth, fresh flowers on the tables, and a view of hills through picture windows. Light suppers are served downstairs in the Mill Brook Tavern, usually a lively gathering place with or without entertainment. Children quickly find their way to the TV and VCR and the table tennis room.

All of the guest rooms have phones, and some have working fireplaces. In the main inn, the larger rooms overlook the golf course, unlike the snug ones, originally intended for chauffeurs and maids. Each annex has its own living room, making ideal quarters for small groups or a few couples who like to get away together.

In the summer there is tennis and golf (now expanded to 18 holes), with canoeing, sailing, and swimming in Songo Pond. Bethel itself is good for strolling and shopping any time of the year.

Black Point Inn

510 Black Point Road
Prouts Neck, Maine 04074
207-883-4126

Innkeeper: Normand Dugas
80 suites and rooms (all with private bath)
$220-$300 per couple, all meals included, July and August;
$220-$240, MAP, other times
Major credit cards
Children over 8 welcome in summer; all welcome other times
No pets
Open early May to late October

Black Point Inn is on a spectacular and isolated peninsula only 20 minutes from Portland. The inn is an 1870s resort, and though the physical plant has been beautifully maintained, an older mood has been retained. The food and service are excellent, and the sporting facilities, those of a first-class resort. The views from inside are admirable, and the peninsula offers wonderful bird-watching and walking opportunities.

The large, airy common rooms set the tone, with ample fireside seating in the dark-beamed living room, a grand piano in the music room, and comfortable leather club chairs in the cocktail lounge. Green wicker rockers on the porch overlook well-tended grounds that slope down to the extensive beach. An inside porch, just to the right of the main door, makes rainy days palatable.

The bedrooms are large and simply furnished with Colonial Beals Rock Maple, much of it refinished. The white crewel bedspreads and Colonial print papers emphasize tradition. All the rooms are air-conditioned and have luxurious baths. Be sure to ask for a room with a view.

Each meal here is a special occasion (you eat at your own, assigned table throughout your stay), and tea is served every afternoon as well. At breakfast, hot and cold cereals, eggs, bread, and special fish and meat dishes are offered along with a daily special (perhaps a lobster omelette). Lunch may be served outside, around the pool, weather permitting. A hot and cold buffet, it may include chowder, chicken pot pie, and lobster as well as hot dogs and hamburgers. Dinner is a more formal affair and gives you a chance to dress (appropriate attire does not include slacks for ladies). Some form of lobster is almost always offered, along with other local staples like steamers and fried clam cakes. The five-course meal can end with an exotic dessert or a simple apple or blueberry pie.

The outdoor activities are legion. The heated saltwater pool overlooks a rocky beach and the ocean. The water is cold up here, so only the hardy will want to swim in the ocean; you can sunbathe and picnic on the two sand beaches. A new indoor freshwater pool and Jacuzzi address the frigid ocean dilemma. Golf and 14 tennis courts are available at the Prouts Neck Country Club, boating at the Prouts Neck Yacht Club. The inn owns its own 48-foot sailing yacht and 27-foot Albin fishing boat. The Cliff Walk around the rocky beach of Prouts Neck is spectacular. To enjoy it fully, allow a couple of hours and perhaps bring a lunch or teatime picnic. The inner part of the peninsula is a bird sanctuary. If you still aren't busy, historic Portland and L. L. Bean are only short drives away.

Call ahead if you plan to come after Labor Day or you may find yourself sharing the common areas with a hundred businesspeople, all talking shop.

The Claremont

Claremont Road
Southwest Harbor, Maine 04679
207-244-5036

Innkeeper: John Madeira, Jr.
11 cottages, 3 suites, 25 doubles, 2 singles (most with private bath)
Cottages: $110-$140 EP in season, $75-$80 EP off-season
Hotel and Phillips House: $130-$155 per room, double occupancy, MAP in season, $55-$75 EP off-season
Lunch also served
No credit cards
Children welcome
No pets
Hotel, open mid-June to September; cottages and guest house, late May to mid-October

The Claremont, established in 1884, is Mount Desert Island's oldest hotel and is on the National Register of Historic Places. While maintaining its 19th-century charm, it has all the facilities of a modern summer resort. The hotel's setting is spectacular, outstripping the location of every other public lodging on Mount Desert Island. From its many sitting areas — the porch with dark green wicker chairs and rockers, the lawn with broad-armed white wooden chairs, or the new boathouse, where you can enjoy lunch or a drink at night — you can look from imposing Cadillac Mountain across Somes Sound to beautiful waterfront estates in Northeast Harbor. If you bring your binoculars, you can clearly see the huge swimming pool at Northeast Harbor's swim club and all the lobster boats, sailboats, and yachts that ply these waters. The view changes by the minute, and one never tires of it. This is one of those rare places where you can spend your entire vacation without leaving the grounds and still have seen some of New England's most beautiful scenery.

The Claremont consists of the old hotel with a new dining room, two guest houses, Phillips House and Clark House, and the cottages. Although the whole complex is certainly larger than a standard inn, the atmosphere is friendly, helpful, and comfortable, with a marvelous sense of privacy. The hotel rooms are decorated with chenille bedspreads, white curtains, and old, comfortable furniture. The floors are a bit creaky, but don't worry—folks here go to bed very early. Phillips House has larger rooms, a shared living room with a fireplace, and a broad, wraparound veranda. Clark House has a suite, and the cottages have bedrooms, living rooms with fireplaces, and sundecks. Be sure to ask for a room with a view when reserving.

The common rooms comprise a reception area, a game room, and the living room. The reception area has a fireplace that is roaring most mornings and evenings. The game room is lined with bookshelves. The living room has a television and comfortably worn furniture. There's also a small porch between the living and dining room where all the island's events are listed.

The dining room was designed so that every table has a view of the water. Jackets and ties are required at dinner, but the atmosphere is relaxed, not stuffy. The food is very good to excellent, with an emphasis on fresh fish. Many of the ten or more entrées offered each night, all cooked to order, have a slightly French twist, though they rarely depart from solid home cooking. On Saturday night, prime rib with Yorkshire pudding is served. Boiled lobster is available any night. At lunch, served right in the boathouse on the water, simple, delicious sandwiches are available.

There is much to do on Mount Desert Island, but guests who wish to stay put will find plenty to keep them busy. There are clay tennis courts, badminton, and water sports as well as rowboats and motorboats. The hotel is the home of the Claremont Croquet Classic, held every August. Guests can participate or sip a drink on the veranda and watch.

The Colony

Ocean Avenue and Kings Road
Kennebunkport, Maine 04046
207-967-3331

Manager: John S. Banta
139 rooms (all with private bath)
$143–$268 per couple, all meals included; $10 less for EP rates

Major credit cards
Children welcome
Pets welcome ($18 per day)
Open mid-June through Labor Day

The Colony, which stands on the site of the first hotel in Kenne-bunkport, is one of the last New England coastal resorts that's still maintained in the grand manner, with three meals a day and a dress code. Built in 1914, the three-story, white clapboard building sits on a rise near the point where the Kennebunk River meets the Atlantic Ocean — the obvious place for a hotel.

Since 1948, the Colony has been owned by the Boughton family and managed by John Banta. Almost all the staff members are related or have been recommended strongly by other people who have worked here. Many of the guests have also been coming for generations.

The hotel has wide halls and airy, nicely furnished rooms. All of the rooms have phones, the motel units have TVs, and most have Maine seascapes painted by Banta himself on the walls.

There is an old, formal check-in desk in the comfortable lobby and a vast, pine-paneled dining room hung with stern portraits and chandeliers. The menu is immense and changes daily. American plan guests can have lobster for breakfast (there's usually a lobster omelette or pancakes with creamed lobster sauce), lunch, and dinner if they wish.

In addition to its own swatch of beach, the hotel maintains a large, heated saltwater pool (where lunch is served) for those who can't bear Maine's ocean temperatures. There is access to tennis courts and golf at nearby clubs; a putting green is on the premises, however.

Guests usually spend some time rocking on the wide veranda and walking along Parsons Way, a path above the wave-splashed rocks. It's a pleasant mile's hike up Ocean Avenue into Dock Square, the busy hub of Kennebunkport, with more than its share of boutiques, art galleries, and restaurants. Guests tend to walk one way and take the trolley-on-wheels the other.

Out on this end of Ocean Avenue, the bustle of the village seems far away and the beauty of the ocean dominates. The resort is its own ordered world of manicured lawns, well-mannered guests, and ample staff. Jackets are, of course, required for dinner, and many guests dress formally on Saturday evening. Dance music and cocktails are offered in the Marine Room. Social events include bridge parties, contests, tournaments, visiting lecturers, and entertainers.

Spruce Point Inn and Lodges
Boothbay Harbor, Maine 04538
207-633-4152
800-553-0289

Innkeepers: James Mackey and Dick Rasor
15 suites, 40 doubles, 15 singles (all with private bath), divided
    between the main inn and cottages; 6 Oceanhouse
    condominiums (each with 2 or 3 bedrooms)
Rooms: $90-$120 per person MAP; *condominiums:* $185-$395
    per night
Lunch also served
Major credit cards
Children welcome
No pets
Open Memorial Day weekend to mid-October

Spruce Point is a small resort on a 100-acre wooded peninsula
at the entrance to Boothbay Harbor. It offers all activities imaginable, clean and spacious rooms with spectacular views, and
good and abundant food. The inn was founded early in this
century, and many of the same families have been coming here
ever since. In 1989 it changed hands, and the new owners added
condominium units, brightened the public rooms with new
paint and fabrics, and relaxed the feeling of the place.

The rooms are in the main inn and in lodges and cottages
throughout the property. The suites have working fireplaces,
kitchenettes, television, and telephones. Almost every room
has an outside porch. The beds are extremely comfortable,
and the closets are stocked with extra blankets for cold nights.
The furniture is Colonial Down East — sturdy, comfortable,
and clean. The two-story Oceanhouse condominiums have
kitchens, living rooms with a fireplace, and porches and decks
overlooking the ocean.

All the common rooms are in the main inn. A large living
room has a view of the ocean and islands; there is also a television room and a study for reading and writing letters. A recreation room is ready for nighttime and rainy days. The dining
room's windows run the entire length of the room and frame a
view of the ocean on one side, flower gardens and spruces on
the other. A bar and lounge overlook the central lawn and
flagpole.

The recreational facilities are terrific. They include a solar-
heated freshwater pool, a saltwater pool on the ocean, two clay
tennis courts, three shuffleboard courts, croquet courts, and a
private pier. A golf course is just a short drive away.

There are wooded trails and a long boardwalk, with benches

spread along the extensive coastline belonging to the inn. All provide views of the outer harbor, the islands, yacht club sailboat races, lobster boats, and the ferries that constantly come to the inn's dock. There is entertainment every evening, including occasional movies and dancing.

You can also take a ferry into Boothbay Harbor, go for hourlong rides, or take all-day cruises for a thorough survey of the area and the islands.

Massachusetts

Chatham Bars Inn
Chatham, Massachusetts 02633
508-945-0096

General manager: Paul Ronty, Jr.
44 inn rooms (all with private bath), 103 rooms in 27 cottages
$250-$360 per couple, MAP
Lunch also served
Major credit cards
Children welcome
No pets
Open year-round

Chatham Bars was built in a grand style in 1914, with its arms curving gently toward the expanse of Pleasant Bay and the Atlantic Ocean. Named for the sand spit that protects this placid water, the shingle inn is a third of a mile from one of Cape Cod's most pleasant villages.

Like all truly grand resorts, Chatham Bars pampers its guests. Fine food, lavish attention (a staff of 150 for 270 guests), a full schedule of daytime sports, nighttime dancing and entertainment, tempting places to relax, and the natural spectacle of the bay and ocean make this a memorable place for a vacation. It offers something that has become increasingly hard to find: luxurious seaside accommodations in a stately setting with personal, caring service and no pressures.

Life here can be very simple indeed, depending on the weather. On fine days there is the private beach and an outdoor heated pool and beach house; the more remote sands of the Outer Bar are easily accessible via the hotel boat launch. There are also five tennis courts, a 9-hole golf course (an 18-hole course is nearby), shuffleboard, croquet, and volleyball. On gray days, Chatham itself offers plenty in the way of shops, and other Cape Cod attractions are not far. Day in and day out, Chatham's fishing boats dock at a pier next to the inn. Guests can watch them unload their daily catch from a special observation deck.

The main dining room offers three delicious meals in an exquisite atmosphere. Several alternatives add just enough variety to dining at Chatham Bars. The new Beach House Grill offers a light lunch, to be eaten inside or on the terrace. The dinner menu offers a fine selection of fresh seafood and selected meats prepared on a grill with complementing salads and vegetables. During the summer, Chatham Bars holds a legendary clambake on Wednesday evenings, serving everything from chowder and steamers to lobster and corn. On Sunday evenings, an overwhelming buffet is served in the main dining room.

The rooms and cottages, all with private baths and phones, are designed to encourage guests to linger indoors, too. Many of the inn rooms have decks, and a number are quite large. Some of the waterside cottages have splendid views; others have a shared living room with a television and fireplace.

Special theme weekends in the fall are offered at half the summer rates.

New Hampshire

The Balsams Grand Resort Hotel
Dixville Notch, New Hampshire 03576
603-255-3400
800-255-0800 in New Hampshire
800-255-0600 elsewhere
Fax 603-255-4221

Innkeepers: Stephen Barba and Warren Pearson
232 rooms
Summer: $240-$316 per couple, all meals included
Winter: $158-$284 per couple, MAP; $670 per 5-day ski week, MAP
Major credit cards
Children welcome
No pets
Open late December through March, late May to mid-October

Everything about the Balsams is astonishing. When approached from the east by car, it suddenly looms out of the forest. Built in the 1870s smack in the middle of nowhere, this rambling wooden hotel is attached to a six-story stucco palace on thousands and thousands of acres. It towers above a small lake against the shoulder of a mountain and is surrounded on all sides by the woods of Dixville Notch. The isolated complex, equidistant (13 miles) from Vermont, Maine, and Canada, is always full, enjoying 80 percent repeat business.

Magnificent views can be enjoyed from the golf courses (both an 18- and a 9-hole course), a lake, putting green, heated swimming pool and adjacent bar, or from one of the many Adirondack chairs on the wraparound porches. Flower beds are everywhere, immaculate and pristine.

The activities are limitless. The Balsams has its own map of eight different hikes as well as a natural history handbook. (Ask about the difficulty of the trails; some are for serious hikers.) There is also tennis on one of six courts (both hard and clay), trout fishing, canoeing, and riding. Children will enjoy the playground, with its elaborate jungle gym and slides. A comprehensive, supervised program for kids from 5 to 12, seven days a week, includes hikes, tours, games, arts and crafts, swimming, and boating. And it's all free.

In the winter, guests can ski downhill at the resort's own Balsams/Wilderness ski area, which has 12 trails, including a 2-mile intermediate run. There is also a 50-kilometer network of cross-country trails.

The common rooms seem endless. There is a large, very formal living room with Victorian antiques, a lovely glassed-in porch (great for early morning coffee or evening games), a TV room that's not too noisy, a library for the more studious; a game room with pinball machines, and an enormous entertainment room/bar with shows nightly. Several cocktail lounges and shops are by the main entrance.

Some rooms are spacious, with big, mirror-faced closets and bathrooms with deep tubs. The best room in the house is number 125. It's circular, huge, and has at least six windows. (The hotel is ingeniously heated, using sawdust from nearby lumber mills.)

But the dining room is the core of the resort. The service is faultless and the food, superb. Breakfast is a combination of buffet and order-anything-you-could-possibly-want. Lunch is a buffet with a massive assortment of goodies, and dinner is a formal, sit-down affair.

From the terrace of the Panorama Golf Course clubhouse, it's possible on a clear day to see far into Canada. If guests tire of the buffet lunch in the main dining room, a simpler repast can be taken here.

What makes the Balsams particularly special is its 450-member staff, most of whom hail from within driving distance and are unusually devoted to this institution—the pride of the area. This is the only place where out-of-staters can meet this many northern New England residents under one roof.

Eagle Mountain House
Jackson, New Hampshire 03846
603-383-9111
800-527-5022 outside New Hampshire
Fax 603-383-0854

Innkeeper: John Sprague
94 rooms and suites
$85-$115 per couple, EP; $113-$143, MAP
Lunch also served
Major credit cards
Children welcome
No pets
Open year-round

Jackson once boasted a number of large old frame hotels, but the number has dwindled over the years. The best among them today is Eagle Mountain House, a rambling, five-story, white clapboard hotel nested high in the valley above Jackson Village, overlooking Carter Notch. Built in 1879, it was totally rebuilt in 1986, but it still feels like a gracious old inn. New carpeting and curtains recall their predecessors, and the same old books still line the reading room shelves.

A striking new fabric portrait of the hotel hangs above the hearth, and the lobby is furnished in glove leather sofas and chairs, with prints and paintings from the late 19th century. The dining room, with large windows overlooking the golf course and mountains, has rich green walls and oak furnishings. It's popular with residents, especially for Sunday brunch. Lighter fare is served in the Eagle Landing Tavern.

Just beneath this old-fashioned lobby is an attractive small spa called Jackson Hole, complete with a Jacuzzi and exercise machines. By the same token, the bedrooms include armoires that conceal TVs. A number of two-room suites have a sofa-bed in the second room. All the furniture was made especially for the hotel, and eiderdown comforters cover the beds.

Recreational opportunities include a heated outdoor pool, tennis courts, a 9-hole golf course, and walking trails that become cross-country trails (part of Jackson's 140-kilometer system) in winter. Alpine skiers can choose from Black Mountain (just up the road), Wildcat Mountain, Attitash, and Mount Cranmore, all within a 15-minute drive.

The Mount Washington Hotel and Resort
Route 302
Bretton Woods, New Hampshire 03575
603-278-1000
800-258-0330
Fax 603-278-5454

174 rooms in hotel; 50 rooms in Lodge at Bretton Woods; 34
  rooms in Bretton Arms Inn; 80 condominium units
Hotel rooms: $80-$275 per person, MAP; *lodge rooms:*
  $60-$95 per couple, EP; *inn rooms:* $79-$114 per couple,
  including breakfast
Summer rates higher; price structure is changing
Lunch also served at hotel
Major credit cards
Children welcome, free under 12
No pets
Hotel open mid-May to mid-October, others open year-round

Your first view of the Mount Washington Hotel is unforget-
table — a mammoth white hotel with a red roof backed by New
England's highest mountains. From the vast veranda, with its
flowers and wicker, you enter a splendid lobby with tall columns and a baronial hearth. The view from the door-size windows in the guest rooms is a sweep of mountains. And the
dining room's menu is immense.

The Mount Washington strives to be grand in manner as well
as size. In its octagonal dining room, designed so that no guest
would be seated in a corner, crystal chandeliers reflect the
colored rays of stained glass.

Recreational opportunities abound. There are twelve red
clay tennis courts and an 18-hole PGA course, a driving range,
and a 27-hole putting green as well as indoor and outdoor pools.
Most people go to Crawford Notch for hiking, and there are
marked trails for jogging. Bicycles may be rented. The only
sports that cost an added fee (besides rental) are golf and horseback riding, but the mounts and trails are worth it. There is a
fully supervised sports program for children.

The rooms vary in size and view. The lowest per-person rates
are in two-bedroom units with a connecting bath, based on
four-person occupancy. Guests who stay at the lodge and condominiums can use all the hotel's facilities.

In the winter the hotel closes, but the lodge, with its own
indoor pool, sauna, Jacuzzi, and restaurant, and the condominiums and cottages represent some of the best ski bargains in
New England. The summertime stables become a ski touring

center in the winter. The adjacent Bretton Arms (which also remains open in the winter) also caters to cross-country skiers. The Bretton Woods ski area offers 26 trails with a vertical drop of 1,500 feet and dependable conditions in addition to a magnificent view of Mount Washington. The 85-kilometer network of cross-country trails here is considered one of the best in the East.

We should note that the hotel has changed management more than once in the past year, and we hope that former standards will be maintained by the new owners. This is the largest and has been one of the grandest of New England's grand hotels.

Spalding Inn and Club
Mountain View Road
Whitefield, New Hampshire 03598
603-837-2572

Manager: William A. Ingram
70 rooms
$170-$250 per couple, all meals included
All 3 meals served
Major credit cards
Children welcome
Well-behaved dogs only
Open mid-June to mid-October

The Spalding Inn and Club is an extremely well run resort that offers all the sports anyone could want either on the premises or nearby, lots of excellent food, and a superb location. The grounds are spacious and well kept.

The common rooms — the sitting rooms, library, card room, terraces, and lounge — are informal and charming. There are many quiet nooks for enjoying a conversation or good book.

The inn can accommodate a hundred people in the simply furnished rooms (most with twin beds) and cottages. All the rooms have telephones. The cottages have a living room with a fireplace, a service bar, and one or more bedrooms. Placed away from the main building, they are very quiet — especially the ones farthest from the road.

The food is outstanding. Breakfast can include juice, fresh berries or cantaloupe, hot or cold cereal, eggs done any way, pancakes, kippers, sausage, creamed salt codfish, or corned beef hash. There are also popovers, doughnuts, and English muffins with all kinds of marmalade. For late risers or those who would prefer dining by their own fireplace, there is room service.

Lunch is available in the main dining room or at an informal poolside buffet. Although the club is generally informal, jackets and dresses are required at dinner, a blend of Continental and New England fare. Fresh seafood and farm produce prevail. The club is famous for its elaborate dinner menu. The service is superior and the wine list good. The occasional lobster bakes and steak roasts around the pool are popular, and every Friday evening there is a lobster boil.

The sporting facilities include a par-3 golf course, four 18-hole courses a few miles away and one just a short walk, four clay tennis courts, a large heated swimming pool, and lawn bowling on two tidy greens. Evening entertainment can mean bridge, bingo, and occasional concerts and performing artists.

This is one of the most beautiful areas of New Hampshire, with ample possibilities for day trips.

Rhode Island

Weekapaug Inn
Weekapaug, Rhode Island 02891
401-322/0301

Owner: Bob Buffum
62 rooms
$250-$260 per couple, all meals included
No credit cards
Children welcome
No pets
Open mid-June to mid-September

This is perhaps one of the least well known inns in New England, yet it's certainly one of the best. Its location is stunning — on a bit of land surrounded by sea water and sheltered by breakwater. It offers all the sporting facilities of a complete resort, including superb food. The rooms are simple, immaculate, and on the small side.

The enchanting common rooms offer enough space so that even if the inn is full, guests do not feel crowded. The paneled Pond Room is an informal gathering area where guest mix their own drinks (BYOB) and relax in front of a fire or overlooking the water. The Sea Room is the large living room, which is used for bridge, bingo, and occasional movies. It is surrounded by a spacious wooded porch that faces the pond, sea, and break-water.

The food is superior. At breakfast, guests can have just about anything imaginable and as much as they want. Lunch is a beautifully presented buffet, and there are excellent choices for dinner. The chef can work with all kinds of meat and fish, and the high standards of this inn culminate in the evening meal.

Activities include tennis, lawn bowling, shuffleboard, sailing, windsurfing, rowing, and fishing. A private golf course, just a short drive away, is open to inn guests. And a splendid, unpopulated beach requires only a short walk. The emphasis here is on total relaxation, healthy sport, and nature. The rooms have no telephones or TV.

Vermont

Basin Harbor Club
Vergennes, Vermont 05491
802-475-2311
800-622-4000
Fax 802-475-2545

Owner: The Beach family
121 cottages and rooms
$180-$300 per couple in cottages, $160-$225 in rooms, all
    meals included
All 3 meals served
Major credit cards
Children welcome
Small pets welcome
Open mid-May to mid-October

This 700-acre retreat is for the wealthy or for those who want to splurge. At the end of a beautiful drive (along an unexpectedly flat road with distant mountain views), a doorman greets the guests. A bellhop then drives them to their cottage to help them get settled. Or, if a guest prefers to fly, the club has its own 3,200-foot airstrip.

Some cottages are tucked away under pine trees. At first glance they seem too close together, but the very private decks and the woods make them feel remarkably secluded. Some are right on the edge of Lake Champlain, and others overlook the golf course, tennis courts, pool, or gardens. Some have screened porches or white picket fences around them; roughly half have fireplaces, with wood replenished daily. The furnishings are intentionally simple to harmonize with the natural surroundings. All the cottages have a private phone for each bedroom and a pantry with a refrigerator and/or a wet bar. The rooms in the main inn have recently been completely redone, but we do not recommend them, particularly when groups are in residence.

The main building houses the formal dining room, where an introductory card announces guests. Boys over 12 and men are required to wear a coat and tie after 6:00 P.M. in the public areas of the resort. While dining on elegant Continental cuisine, guests enjoy a spectacular view of the gardens and lake. The Ranger Room and the Champlain Lounge serve cocktails, while the Red Mill offers snacks and a casual retreat for the younger crowd. Picnics, if the maitre d' is informed the night before, are a snap; a poolside buffet is another casual option.

While adults enjoy the beautiful gardens and many outside sitting areas, children can be supervised at the playground. A variety of activities abound for older youngsters. A sheltered cove with a sandy beach is the base for water sports. The harbormaster has a vast array of water vehicles, including a 40-foot cruiser. Sports gear, the *New York Times* or the *Wall Street Journal,* sundries, books, and unusual gifts all can be found here.

Island Getaways

*Something in everyone craves a periodic escape to an island —
be it a beach-fringed resort island like Martha's Vineyard or
Nantucket or small, unspoiled outposts like Cuttyhunk or Monhegan.*

Isle au Haut, Maine

Accessible by mailboat from Stonington, this heavily wooded,
6-by-2-mile island, half of it preserved — with hiking trails and
limited camping — is part of Acadia National Park.

The Keeper's House
P.O. Box 26
Isle au Haut, Maine 04645
207-367-2261

Innkeepers: Jeffrey and Judi Burke
4 rooms (with shared baths) and cottage
$205 per couple, including 3 meals
2-night minimum in July and August
No credit cards
Children welcome
No pets
No smoking
Open May through October

After a 45-minute mailboat ride from Stonington, you'll be
greeted at the inn's private dock by Jeff or Judi Burke and then
walk the short woodland path — "the road to Oz," Judi calls
it — to this marvelously isolated, very special retreat.

Built for the keeper of the Isle au Haut lighthouse in 1907, this
airy, simply appointed home is pale blue and white inside and
out. Its common rooms and comfortable bedrooms are filled
with antiques, sea chests, and coastal memorabilia. There is no
electricity here: gas lamps illuminate the living room and dining room, and guests carry candles upstairs to bed at evening's
end.

Bedtime usually comes early, for most guests spend the day hiking the island's intricate network of wooded and short paths and then return happy and weary for a memorable homemade dinner. Entrées include haddock with sour cream and dill, stuffed crab over haddock, raspberry chicken, and chicken Isle au Haut (marinated with sour cream, Worcestershire sauce, garlic, and lemon, coated with breadcrumbs, and baked). One entrée is served each night, accompanied by fresh vegetables, bread, and sumptuous desserts like Phoebe's chocolate cake with whipped cream and fresh raspberries, raspberry-peach pie, apple crumb pie, carrot cake, or blueberry pie.

Breakfasts are just as indulgent. An all-time favorite is Finnish pancakes — large, puffy affairs similar to a Yorkshire pudding, topped with fresh fruit and yogurt. Another choice might be potato pancakes or scrambled eggs with Swiss cheese and tarragon or baked apple pancakes. There's always plenty of homemade bread and jam, too.

Guests who plan a day of exploration set off with picnic lunches. Those who prefer to laze about near the inn, perhaps reading on the wide, sun-baked rocks, are served lunch. The Keeper's House does not serve liquor or wine, but guests are welcome to bring a bit along (or they can buy wine at the general store in the tiny village).

The bedrooms — three on the second floor and a fourth, with a sitting area, under the third-floor eaves — have white painted furniture, painted iron and brass beds, and comforters. The two modern baths have hot showers. There is also lodging for two in the Oil House, a tiny, one-room building with a deck overlooking the water. The bed here is a futon, and the outdoor shower and outhouse are up the hill, a situation that guests have been known to complain about, given the price.

Islesboro, Maine

Isleboro is a large, 10-mile-long stringbean of an island accessible by car ferry from Lincolnville Beach, just north of Camden. Many of the same families who built the island's elaborate summer cottages still return every year; just a few are now inns and B&Bs. Biking and boating are both rewarding here.

The Annex

Sabbathday Harbor
Islesboro, Maine 04848
207-734-6470
Winter address: P.O. Box 29
Batesville, Virginia 22924
804/823-4856

Owners: Mr. and Mrs. Frank Ryder
Cottage, Boat House
$65 per couple with full breakfast, $50 single; $450 per week
   for the Boat House
No credit cards
Children not appropriate
No pets
Open June 25 to September 20

The Annex is the only bed-and-breakfast on Islesboro that is
directly on the shore. It consists of one double room in a Victorian building with a fireplace, bath, refrigerator, and antique
furnishings. Also available, by the week only, is the Boat House.
It is completely furnished and has a kitchen and a deck that
overhangs the beach. Often guests have breakfast on the porch
of the main house, overlooking the water, or go directly down to
the beach. The location is spectacular, with views to the shore
of East Penobscot Bay, looking toward Deer Isle. The Ryders are
happy to take their guests sailing, and a canoe is also available.
The Blue Heron serves delicious dinners.

Dark Harbor House

Box 185
Isleboro, Maine 04848
207-734-6669

Innkeeper: Matthew Skinner
7 rooms and suites (all with bath)
$95-$125 per couple with full breakfast
Dinner also served
MasterCard, Visa
Children not appropriate but negotiable
No pets
Open mid-May through late October

This house is one of those wonderfully airy summer mansions
built in the 1890s, with large windows in spacious rooms and a
wide entrance hall graced by a sweeping double staircase.
   Matthew Skinner seems more the master of this house than

an innkeeper. He obviously relished the job of decorating the rooms, filling them with splendid 19th-century antiques, including high four-posters, sleigh, and iron beds. A few of the rooms have working fireplaces, and four have French doors opening onto balconies or an upstairs porch. The corner suite also has a sitting room with a sofa-bed and wet bar. Some of the bathrooms retain their original claw-foot tubs — the deepest, fanciest ones we have ever seen (two are rimmed in fine wood) — and pull-chain johns with marble detailing.

The living room is suitably summery, with a sisal rug and glass door opening onto a porch and large windows overlooking a sloping lawn that's big enough for a good game of touch football.

Guests usually gather in the gracious library for drinks before dinner, which is served at seven o'clock in the oval dining room that holds eight tables. The prix fixe, four-course dinner ($35) offers a choice of two entrées, meat or fish (lobster is always available), soup, salad, and a choice of dessert. The dining room is open to the public every night but Tuesday, and the Jamaican chef (Skinner once owned an inn in Jamaica) has a strong island following. Entrées might be swordfish or quail with grapes or baked stuffed lobster with island spices; desserts usually include baked banana and mango-rum meringue.

While it's hedged from the water by its grounds and tall yews, Dark Harbor House is on a narrow neck between a cove and the protected, pool-like inlet that's Dark Harbor.

"That was the only place north of Portland that I ever had comfortable ocean swimming," Louise Dickinson Rich wrote in her 1950s classic, *The Coast of Maine*. "The pool is separated from the sea by a hinged gate across its narrow entrance, a type of tidal dam, so that it opens on an incoming tide and automatically closes when the tide turns. Thus the water is always at the same level, always calm, and always warmed by the sun. It's a great relief." This ingenious creation is thanks to the large, long-vanished summer hotel that once stood across from Dark Harbor House.

Bicycles may be borrowed from the inn, and there are narrow, seaside roads to explore; day sails on a schooner or picnics on smaller, uninhabited islands can be arranged. On misty or rainy days, the house itself is warmed by fireplaces; it offers an eclectic selection of books, magazines, puzzles, and games.

Monhegan, Maine

Though barely a mile square, this island boasts four hundred years of intriguing history, six hundred species of wildflowers, and steep, oceanside cliffs webbed with hiking paths. It also has no public electricity and more than its share of artists. Served by the mailboat *Laura B* from Port Clyde and excursion boats from Boothbay Harbor and Round Harbor, it tends to get crowded at about midday in the summer. It also offers a wider choice of lodging places than any other Maine island, but they are all relatively small, and guests still experience a sense of adventure, having traveled 10 miles out to sea and found such relatively unspoiled beauty. The one short road is not paved, so this is not a place to bring bikes. But be prepared to walk.

The Island Inn
Ocean View Terrace
Monhegan Island, Maine 04852
207-596-0371

Innkeepers: Marietta and Robert Burton
45 rooms (8 with private bath)
$50.50-$69 per person double occupancy, $62-$69 single, MAP
Lunch also served
No credit cards
Children over 12 welcome
No pets
Open mid-June to mid-September

This classic turn-of-the-century summer hotel has a mansard roof with gables, a long veranda, and a widow's walk. The most luxurious of Monhegan's hotels, this is the only one that offers three meals a day. The inn is very close to the ferry, which makes baggage transfer less of a problem.

The rooms in the inn are rather small and basically furnished. But the views of the small, sheltered harbor are special. The adjacent Pierce House has four rooms and a suite.

The public rooms have low ceilings, dating from the original early-19th-century house around which the hotel has been built. They are comfortable, stocked with games and books for stormy days, and have noteworthy hand-painted murals on the doors.

The Burtons pride themselves on the full, old-fashioned meals served in the big, cheery dining room. The full breakfast always includes English oatmeal, occasionally kippered herring, and there is a choice of five entrées as part of the five-course dinner. Lobster may be ordered in advance. Soups and salads, stews, and lobster rolls are served at lunch, and box lunches are available.

The Island Inn is so popular that it is usually filled for the season by April. Stop by for lunch or dinner and decide whether to book for next year.

Shining Sails
Box 44
Monhegan Island, Maine 04852
207-596-0041

Innkeepers: Amy Melenbaker, Bill Baker
4 efficiencies, 1 double room (all with private bath)
June 15 – September 20: $48-$80 double, $320-$525 per week
Off-season: $45-$70 double, $300-$450 per week
$10 per extra person; 2-night minimum in all Ocean View
   apartments
No meals served
MasterCard, Visa
Children welcome
No pets
Open year-round

Until a few years ago, overnight lodging on Monhegan Island was extremely Spartan and private baths just about unknown. While such basic accommodation appealed to many visitors as part of the Monhegan experience, others wished for a bit more comfort. Shining Sails fills that need.

The flower garden and white picket fence that surround the inn are an indication of the neatness within. The efficiencies here are not particularly spacious, but they provide the basic elements of bed, kitchen, living room, and bathroom. The smallest one combines the bed and living rooms, with a sofa-bed doing double duty. There is also one double room that does not have cooking facilities.

All of these accommodations may be rented by the night or by the week. They are also available in the winter for main-landers seeking some real solitude and quiet inspiration.

The library is across the street, the Island Spa, good for rainy day browsing, is just down the road, and the Monhegan Store, source of all groceries, is a pleasant, level walk. If your menus call for something beyond the basics, however, it might be advisable to bring provisions from the mainland.

Trailing Yew
Monhegan Island, Maine 04852
207-596-0440

Innkeeper: Mrs. Josephine Davis Day
70 guests in 9 buildings (shared baths)
$42 per person MAP, $15-$25 for children under 10, less
  before June 30
Box lunches available
No credit cards
Children welcome
Pets welcome
Open mid-May to mid-October

The Trailing Yew is a holdover from another era. It is the last of
Maine's summer boarding houses (once there were hundreds),
the kind where guests gather at long tables and compare notes
about the food, creature comforts, and the lack thereof.

In her nineties, Josephine Day is less active than she once was
(she has been the proprietor for more than sixty years). She still
cooks both breakfast and dinner, though the codfish can be
rubbery. But the unusual camaraderie among the guests sur-
vives. This continues to be the only place on Monhegan, and
one of the few in New England, where guests mingle easily and
seem to enjoy each other so much.

The main house stands on a rise above the harbor. Before
dinner, guests gather in lawn chairs on the porch, stand around
the flagpole, or play horseshoes. Then someone rings the bell,
and like summer campers, everyone piles into the two dining
rooms and finds a place at the tables, which are set with bright
flowers.

The rooms vary from those with basic twin beds and a
dresser to bright spaces hung with original art. The Mooring
Chain, a cottage apart from the rest of the complex, offers a
common room with a fireplace and piano, six rooms, and a
bath. Guests are asked to bring sleeping bags in the spring and
fall;linens and blankets are supplied, but the buildings have no
heat. This isn't for everyone, but the Trailing Yew has a loyal
following.

Tribler Cottage
Monhegan Island, Maine 04852
207-594-2445

Innkeepers: Martha Yandle and Richard Farrell
4 1-bedroom apartments, 1 room with bath
$50-$85 per day; weekly rates available

No credit cards
Children welcome
No pets
Open May through October; 1 apartment open year-round

Tribler Cottage has been in the same family for three generations, but the furnishings are modern and clean. Doors with
flowers (decoupage) lead to the one-bedroom apartments, with
full kitchens and all linens. One, the Apple Tree apartment, is
available year-round; it is popular with birders who come to
Monhegan to witness the fall and spring migrations.

   Richard Farrell is a photographer, and his works are displayed in a downstairs gallery. The apartments are next to this
gallery/living room.

   A bulletin board by the front door keeps guests apprised of
the goings-on about the island: notices of gallery showings,
talks in the schoolhouse, nature walks, restaurant menus, and
so forth. This is a walker's island. Only a handful of vehicles —
most of them quite aged — are permitted, to haul fishermen's
gear and visitors' luggage.

   Slightly removed from the main footpath, Tribler Cottage sits
beside meadows behind the Island Spa and library. It's a quick
walk up the path to the lighthouse, where a small museum is
complemented by the view of the island and the surrounding
water.

North Haven, Maine

One of the most private of Maine's larger islands, North Haven
is separated from Vinalhaven by the Fox Islands Thorofare, a
harbor filled all summer with a mix of yachts and workboats
moored just off the village of North Haven. Pulpit Harbor, on
the northern end of the island, is, by contrast, very quiet, an
almost circular boat haven; its name derives from the distinctive
rocks, now a rookerie, at its entrance. If you are looking for
action, don't come here.

Pulpit Harbor Inn
Crabtree Point Road
North Haven, Maine 04853
207-867-2219

Innkeepers: Barney and Christie Hallowell
6 doubles (3 with private bath), $55-$90, B&B; winter: 5
   doubles (2 with private bath), $50-$68, B&B; group rates
   available

Full breakfast and dinner also served
MasterCard, Visa
Children welcome
Pets welcome with advance notice
No smoking
Open year-round

Pulpit Harbor is a comfortable and friendly establishment that's quite a walk from the ferry terminal, so those without a car should be sure to request a pickup when booking. The inn is the focal point of a guest's stay, since the island's main attractions are beauty, quiet, and peaceful solitude.

In the summer, activities include biking, sailing, picnicking on the beach, golfing on a 9-hole course, tennis, fishing, bird-watching, going out with a lobsterman for the day, or climbing Ames Knob for a panoramic view of the bay from Monhegan to Mount Desert. In the off-season, there is cross-country skiing, ice skating, and scalloping with a fisherman.

The bedrooms are simply furnished, some with nice quilts. All the common rooms are bright. The living room has a fireplace and a few antiques. The paintings are by well-known island artists, such as Eric Hopkins.

There are three dining areas: the main dining room, a glassed-in porch, and a terrace. At night two entrées are offered. Everything is home-grown or homemade, and fresh fish is quite common. The food is not fancy but very good, very fresh, and very well seasoned—maybe grilled tuna, smoked mussels, or tenderloin of pork. The soup might be a creamy tomato thick with pureed broccoli. Dinner for two, with wine, runs about $65.

■ *See also:* Moonshell Inn, Peaks Island, Maine

Vinalhaven, Maine

A relatively large, 8-mile-long island, Vinalhaven is fairly flat but has some beautiful meadows and coves as well as deep quarry holes that recall its prominence as a granite quarrying center in the 1880s. The roads are paved, good for bicycling, and there are nature conservancy areas in which to watch birds and pick berries. The car ferry from Rockland serves the island.

Tidewater Motel
Main Street
Vinalhaven, Maine 04863
207-863-4618

Innkeepers: Phillip and Elaine Crossman
11 rooms (all with private bath)
June – mid-October: $62-$75 per couple, $49-$65 single
Winter: $49-$65 per couple, $27-$53 single
No meals served
No credit cards
Children welcome
No pets
Open year-round

A part of this very special motel was formerly a blacksmith shop for the island's granite quarries. The eight waterfront rooms command a view from Vinalhaven Harbor—filled with hundreds of lobster boats, a fishing fleet, and sail- and motorboats—all the way to the open sea. Many people come to Maine just to take in such surprisingly elusive views.

The difference between high and low tide is an astonishing 10 feet or more. The motel is built on a granite bridge under which water flows between the main harbor and a large saltwater pond. The tidal change creates an intriguing sight with relaxing sound effects.

All bedrooms and bathrooms have individual thermostats. Reproduction moosehead Colonial maple furniture and cable TV are standard. The most private rooms are numbers 9 and 10. The higher prices are for the housekeeping units.

A number of restaurants—with food ranging from superior cuisine to family style to takeout—are just a few minutes' walk from the inn. Fish and lobster prepared in any manner are an excellent choice on the island.

Cuttyhunk, Massachusetts

Cuttyhunk, a tiny island 14 miles from New Bedford, was discovered in 1602. Originally populated by fishermen and their families, it is still a fisherman's paradise today. It is also a world apart, remaining very much as it was in its early history. It is the westernmost of the sixteen Elizabeth Islands, which trail off in a line from Woods Hole, dividing Buzzards Bay from Vineyard Sound. All but two of them are private. Cuttyhunk is the only one that offers public lodging and, although there were once more inns—primarily for fishermen—the Allen House is the sole survivor. Most of the island's ninety-odd houses are in the harborside village of Gosnold. The island itself is little more than 2 miles long and an irregular ¾ mile wide, most of it good for walking.

The Allen House
Cuttyhunk, Massachusetts 02713
508-996-9292

Innkeeper: Nina and Margo Solod
12 rooms (with shared bath), 2 cottages
$50-$70 per couple in rooms, $85-$175 in cottages, including breakfast
2-night minimum on weekends
MasterCard, Visa
Children welcome
No pets
Open Memorial Day through early October

Cuttyhunk is very much a do-it-yourself island. It has all the wonder and beauty of a natural paradise and none of the organized activity of a resort. If you visit the Allen House, bring books, games, fishing equipment, and walking shoes, but leave your golf clubs and tennis rackets behind. For your convenience, ice is provided along with glasses and setups; wine and liquor are not available on the island. But everything else for a perfect vacation is here in abundance.

Dine on the glassed-in porch overlooking the sea; enjoy the freshest seafood and the most carefully prepared entrées; sleep with the Atlantic breezes drifting through your window. The rooms in the main house share baths; the private cottages have showers. Fairplay has a double and a single bed. Pete's Place comprises the three bedrooms—each with two single beds—

on the lower floor of the house and a living room and bathroom.

Cuttyhunk is an island with limited access; the Allen House is an inn with limited accommodations. In order for the innkeepers to serve you best, you are asked to pay in advance. On weekends there is a two-night minimum, and Monday through Thursday you get three days for the price of two.

Martha's Vineyard, Massachusetts

New England's largest island, blessed with beaches and relatively warm water, can be reached by plane from New York, Boston, New Bedford, and Hyannis, by ferry from Woods Hole and Hyannis, and by hydrofoil from Boston. The island has six towns and an amazing variety of landscapes: the fishing boats at Menemsha, the bleak beauty of Gay Head, the rural look of West Tisbury, the busyness of Vineyard Haven (where the ferry docks), the turn-of-the-century gingerbread cottages of Oak Bluffs, and the Federal mansions of Edgartown. Horseback riding, bicycling, and beach-walking are all easily available.

The Beach Plum Inn
Menemsha, Massachusetts 02552
508-645-9454

Innkeepers: Paul and Janie Darrow
13 rooms (all with private bath)
$130-$250 per couple, including breakfast
Dinner also served
Major credit cards
No children
No pets
Open mid-May to mid-October

In the less inhabited area of the island, away from the crowds, there is a place called the Beach Plum Inn where everything is "just so." Down a narrow drive through the woods, you'll soon come to an oasis of vibrant flower beds, out-of-state Volvos, and velvet plush, comfy chairs. This retreat has overlooks the sea as well.

Formal terraced gardens line the walk to the main inn, the cottages with sea views, and the renovated farmhouse. Languid guests on lawn furniture immediately clue you in to the inn's leisurely lifestyle. The common room is both beautiful and comfortable, as are the well-kept and tastefully furnished guest rooms.

The deservedly renowned restaurant serves fine Continental and nouvelle New England cuisine nightly during high season. Choose in advance from five or six entrées—possibilities include roast duck with honey curry sauce or filet mignon with béarnaise sauce. The prix fixe meal is $35–$45. Ask about the MAP plan, which includes late afternoon cocktails and hors d'oeuvres. Garden views from the light, airy dining room are soothing; the low ceiling is of painted white boards. The atmosphere is unhurried, and you'll probably wish to linger over a scrumptious dessert.

There are plenty of possibilities for more active relaxation. A private pond is stocked with perch and bass; an hour of free tennis is available daily; private beaches offer swimming and sunning. In the area are two public golf courses, horseback riding on trails and beaches, sailing for novices and experts, and biking on a 15-mile path through the woods and along the sea.

The Charlotte Inn
South Summer Street
Edgartown, Massachusetts 02539
508-627-4751

Innkeepers: Gery and Paula Conover
23 rooms and 2 suites
$175–$350 per couple, including breakfast
Lunch, Sunday brunch, and dinner also served
Major credit cards
Children not appropriate
No pets
Open year-round

The most elegant place to stay on Martha's Vineyard is a sea captain's home from the 1860s, complete with a fanlight and widow's walk and impeccably furnished with fine art and antiques. One is taken with the collection of paintings in the gallery that occupies much of the ground floor and with the medley of furnishings and art that makes every guest room special. Fresh flowers within and without scent the air. The Charlotte Inn soothes the senses.

The rooms in the inn itself are a shade more formal than those in the Carriage House (bright, fantastic rooms with cathedral ceilings and French doors) and the Garden and Summer houses. A lovely suite offers a separate living room with a Palladian window and a view of the harbor. There are four-poster beds, fireplaces, down pillows and comforters, and private patios. The Coach House is decorated with English antiques; on a more modern note, it also has air conditioning.

The Continental breakfast consists of fresh muffins and fruit. But a full breakfast is also available year-round, as is Sunday brunch, a popular tradition; reservations are a must. In season, L'Étoile, the dining room, is open nightly, but in winter it's only open on weekends. Its French cuisine is spectacular. Literally nothing on the menu will be a disappointment.

Edgartown's shops are just steps away, and buses to beaches and other island points stop nearby.

The Daggett House
59 North Water Street
Edgartown, Massachusetts 02539
508-627-4600

Owners: James and John Chirgwin
Innkeeper: Sue Cooper-Street
25 rooms (all with private bath)
$110–$190 per couple, including breakfast
Major credit cards
Children welcome
No pets
Main house open year-round

The Daggett House, square and shingled, was built as an inn in 1750. It now sits on one of Edgartown's most handsome downtown streets, with a territorial white picket fence and an acre-deep lawn stretching down to the water. You can swim from the private dock, sun on a small private beach, and watch the comings and goings of the Chappaquiddick ferry *On Time.*

The chimney room, now part of the house, dates from 1660 and looks it. A long pole musket and warming pans hang above the old hearth. Small windows overlook the water; for early risers, the harbor will come alive from this vantage point. Each morning, guests enjoy fresh bread and coffee before the hearth.

The guest rooms have small-patterned paper, muslin curtains, and furnishings that suit the low ceilings and wainscoting. There is a choice of double and king-size beds as well as some suites. The three-bedroom Garden Cottage, a private school in the 1850s, is available as one unit or by the room. It sits on a large lawn right above the harbor. Efficiencies in the Captain Warren House across the street are a good find for families.

The guests here tend to interact a good deal, sharing restaurant finds, stories, and personal histories; repeat clientele is high. While the ocean and beach are the main draw, many other activities are nearby: bicycles, sailboats, tennis, charter fishing boats, a golf course, and shops.

Katama Shores
South Beach
Edgartown, Massachusetts 02539
508-627-4747

Manager: Robert Diduca
64 rooms
$80-$160 per couple, EP
All 3 meals served
Major credit cards
Children under 12 free
No pets
Open mid-May to mid-October

Families and groups will find Katama Shores one of the few places on the island that is both comfortable and affordable. Its biggest drawing card is its location facing South Beach — one of the best on the island. It's safe to let the kids roam; there's no traffic, only dunes to cross. It's also perfect if you want to stay on the beach from sunrise to well past sunset. The great expanse of beach is literally a 2-minute walk — no parking fees, hassles, or traffic.

There is nothing fancy about the place; in fact, it's a converted army barracks. The hall is long, with rooms shooting off it. With a little imagination, you can see that the officers would have had the larger rooms, facing the ocean, and the enlisted men, the smaller rooms across the hall. Prices are determined by facilities and views. You can stay in a two-room duplex or a two- or four-bedroom cottage, both with kitchens and fireplaces. There are also two-room suites overlooking either the ocean or the pool and tennis courts; they have a kitchenette and sometimes a patio. The double rooms, like all the other accommodations, have wall-to-wall carpeting, TVs, telephones, and large refrigerators. The furnishings are comfortable but not remarkable; remember, you're here for the beach.

On the premises, you'll find a barbecue area, bicycle rentals, shuffleboard, volleyball, a recreation room, a sunporch, and a pool. A lounge and restaurant are inside.

Katama Shores is at the opposite end of the island from the ferries, and there isn't much to do within walking distance, so a car is essential for flexibility and exploring the more secluded

areas. There are shuttle buses, though, which periodically connect the beach with the bustle of Edgartown and points beyond.

Lambert's Cove Country Inn

Box 422, R.F.D.
Vineyard Haven, Massachusetts 02568
508-693-2298

Innkeeper: Marie Burnett
15 rooms (all with private bath)
$95-$125 per couple, including breakfast
Dinner and Sunday brunch also served
Major credit cards
No children under 4 in season
No pets
Open year-round

The original 1790s farmhouse here was expanded into a country estate in the 1920s. The inn certainly feels away from it
all—you approach it from a mile-long wooded road. It is set
among a grove of tall pine trees, rambling English gardens, and
spacious lawns. There's plenty of room for adults and children
alike to roam here. At the same time, it's a 20-minute walk to
Lambert's Cove Beach, a gorgeous dune-backed stretch of fine,
white sand.

Half the guest rooms are in the house; the rest are in the
converted barn and carriage house. The carpeted rooms in the
main house share a comfortable second-floor sitting area and
an outdoor porch overlooking the backyard. Many rooms have
decks, and each has its own appeal. The private carriage house
next door, nestled in a secluded grove, has rooms with private
screened porches; the barn has a Scandinavian, exposed-beam
interior. One suite (in the carriage house) has its own greenhouse, converted into a sitting room, and another is furnished
in bright wicker. The Bridal Room has a canopy bed and fireplace, and the Blue Room, a private deck and sliding glass
doors.

The low-beamed, spacious, and inviting library is stocked
with well-worn books and periodicals. Plenty of light streams in
from the French doors, which lead out to the back porch and
more gardens. The library and the smaller TV room are comfortably furnished with writing tables, plush couches, and Oriental carpets on the hardwood floors.

The pastel dining room (BYOB at all times) currently has a
good reputation. Seafood, vegetables picked from the inn's garden, and homemade soups are specialties. A light and cheery

breakfast room offers a Continental buffet. Tables are set out in the grassy orchard behind the house when the weather permits.

Sunday brunch, set in the apple orchard with a talented young flutist playing Mozart, is very special here. Die-hard romantics and relaxed guests are invariably dressed in white or Laura Ashley florals. Marie Burnett floats from table to table, checking on guests and spreading good cheer with her English accent.

You probably won't want to budge any farther than the beach or the shade of the catalpa tree, where vines of wisteria bloom magnificently in the spring. The property's 7 acres contain many unusual plantings. A tennis court is across the field for the energetic. If you must explore, you'll find that the parts of the Vineyard least clogged by tourists are as handy as Vineyard Haven's shops.

The Lothrop Merry House
Owen Park
Box 1939
Vineyard Haven, Massachusetts 02568
508-693-1646

Innkeepers: John and Mary Clarke
7 rooms (4 with private bath)
$85-$135 per couple, including breakfast
MasterCard, Visa
Children welcome
No pets
Open year-round

The Lothrop Merry House has it all — a warm ambience, comfortable and simple furnishings, plentiful, homemade food, a beautiful property in a central location, and welcoming but unobtrusive innkeepers. As a bonus, it's as nice in the off-season as it is in midsummer.

This snug, shingled home was built in 1790 in West Chop. As a wedding present for the owner's daughter, it was moved with the aid of eight yoke of oxen to its present location. A hundred yards down the sloping back lawn is a private patch of sand on the shore of the small harbor — perfect for a quick dip, sunning, or just reflecting on the nature of the tide from the white Adirondack chairs. It is also a mere 3-minute walk along the shore to the ferry dock. A small boathouse borders the shore on the left, low dunes on the right. In the evening, it's an idyllic place to listen to frogs, crickets, gentle winds, and foghorns. In the morning, the sunrise shimmers off the water and warms up the rooms.

The inn is also a fine introduction to sailing. John and Mary Clarke will take you out in their 54-foot Alden ketch, the *Laissez Faire*. For a fee, you can go for a day sail, an evening sail, a harbor cruise, or an overnight cruise to Cuttyhunk or Nantucket. Guests are also welcome to use the complimentary canoe or Sunfish.

Considering the charm of the guest rooms, the house is equally appealing to landlubbers, of course. Five have perfect harbor views. The one that doesn't has a raised, beamed ceiling, can accommodate three people for an extra $12, and opens onto a brick patio. The three rooms upstairs, reached by an outside stairway, are joined by a hall and share a bath; the three rooms on the first floor all have private baths. The best room downstairs has blue wainscoting, a four-poster bed, rocking chair, braided rug, fireplace, and a view of the harbor. All have sloping floors, uneven door frames, latch-lock doors, and braided rugs typical of a house this old.

In good weather, a Continental breakfast—warm sweet breads, juice, tea, and coffee—is served on the brick patio overlooking the harbor. It's easy to pass two or three hours here in the sun or shade without realizing it. In the winter, breakfast moves indoors to the first-floor common room.

Point Way Inn

Box 128
Main Street and Pease's Point Way
Edgartown, Massachusetts 02539
508-627-8633

Innkeepers: Ben and Linda Smith
15 rooms (all with private bath)
$95–$205 per couple, including breakfast
Major credit cards
Children welcome
No pets
Open year-round

Point Way Inn is special because of the warmth, caring, and interest that the Smiths bring to their work. They enjoy sharing what they have created, and they are continuously enhancing it. And what a job they've done.

Although the inn has no view of the water, it's hardly a detriment—situated on a large corner lot, surrounded by high hedges. After coming onto the property through arched trellis-work, you're immediately struck by the flower garden with a vine-covered gazebo and the impressive croquet course. (Ben is an avid player, and the course is regulation American and

English.) Afternoon lemonade is served here, and occasionally Ben, with the help of visitors, will bring back the fruits of his clam-digging labor. This initial impression will set the mood for your entire stay—relax and enjoy.

Entering the inn through the garden, you find a homey, comfortable living room/library with a large fireplace, ongoing jigsaw puzzle, and corner bar where guests can store and cool spirits. In the off-season, when it's more conducive to meeting people, the Smiths often join their guests for cider or cocktails. The reception area is papered with navigational maps and photographs of ships that have been in Ben's whaling family; family pictures line the halls.

Each guest room is special, though some are small. (It is, after all, an old house.) Each has a decanter of sherry, fresh flowers, a fan, and a private bath. Many have working fireplaces, four-poster beds, and wing chairs. There is even a large, two-room suite with a deck and a fireplace. The two rooms on the third floor are away from it all.

A Continental breakfast is served in a sunny garden room at tables for four with high cane chairs. Longer-term guests can use the kitchen or gas grill on occasion; Linda realizes that the cost of dining out night after night can be prohibitive.

Near Edgartown's shops and restaurants, the inn is also a short bike ride from South Beach. Buses circling the rest of the island leave from just up the street. And you can use the inn's towels and shower after checkout time for that last trip to the beach.

The Oak House

Seaview Avenue
Box 299
Oak Bluffs, Massachusetts 02557
508-693-4187

Innkeeper: Betsi Convery-Luce
10 rooms (all with private bath)
$85-$175 per couple, including breakfast
MasterCard, Visa
Children over 10 welcome
No pets
Open mid-May to mid-October

You'll never see more oak under one roof than at the Oak House: superb oak ceilings, oak floors, oak paneling, and oak furniture. This is a wonderfully old guest house in the gingerbread Victorian style for which Oak Bluffs is famous. It was built by Massachusetts Governor Claflin in 1876 to resemble a boat, an illusion that has been lost in subsequent alterations.

Through the house's glass doors Nantucket Sound stretches away to Cape Cod, and there is always a breeze on the large porch. Inside, the parlor and dining room are a shade overdone but hardly uncomfortable. In fact, there are some beautiful but heavy dark antiques, such as the intricately carved thronelike chair at the head of the long table. For a brighter and lighter feel, try the glassed-in sunporch, with white wicker chairs, games, a white raised roof, and indoor-outdoor carpeting.

A Continental breakfast (pastry and juice) is set out each morning. You are free to keep beer, wine, and sandwich supplies in the refrigerator.

All the large rooms upstairs are airy and furnished with fine, old, simple summer cottage furniture. Many rooms have an ocean view, a private balcony, or angled ceilings, while some have tin ceilings. Many of the bathrooms have turn-of-the-century fixtures, marble washbasins, and large, deep, claw-foot tubs.

The Wesleyan Grove Camp Ground—dozens of Victorian cottages dripping Gothic wooden lace—is just a few blocks away, as are the restaurants and shops of crowded Circuit Avenue. The Oak House, overlooking the ocean, is on the thoroughfare that bypasses the town green and heads toward Edgartown. Occasional ferries put right into the slip on Seaview Avenue, and a beach—not one of the Vineyard's best but passable by mainland standards—is right here, too. You can rent a bike or hop on a bus to explore the rest of the island.

Thorncroft

Box 1022
Main Street
Vineyard Haven, Massachusetts 02568
508-693-3333

Innkeepers: Lynn and Karl Buder
18 rooms (all with private bath)
$95-$195 per couple, including breakfast
Major credit cards
Children over 12 welcome
No pets
Open year-round

On 3½ acres a mile from town, the Thorncroft's unassuming exterior belies its elegant interior. Architecturally, it's a classic

Craftsman bungalow with a dominant roof, carved shutters, and neo-Colonial details. Inside, it's romantic and comfortable.

The Victorian reading parlor with a fireplace exudes the era in every detail, down to its rose-colored floral wallpaper. Also downstairs is a little nook of a sunroom, with a TV and wicker furniture. Knowledgeably chosen antiques—such as a spinning wheel, platform rocker, Sonora Victrola, and even vintage clothing—have been placed carefully throughout the house for maximum effect.

Each room has a distinct personality and has been coordinated to achieve either an early-20th-century or a Colonial look. All the rooms have wall-to-wall carpeting, while some have four-poster canopy beds, private entrances, fireplaces, balconies, brass faucets, or original claw-foot bathtubs; no two are alike. Beyond a doubt, the most beautiful room is tucked in the corner next to the sunroom. Its Renaissance Victorian bedroom set is absolutely exquisite. Out back, surrounded by trees and shrubbery, is the Carriage House, with a few large Colonial bedrooms and one suite with a Jacuzzi. Both structures are centrally air-conditioned. The innkeepers recently purchased the Greenwood House, an inn with five rooms, closer to the edge of the village—a better location for bicyclists or carless overnighters.

The elegant breakfast (two seatings) is served primarily at one long formal table that is set with china throughout the day. (You can opt for the smaller, sunny breakfast room if you're a light eater and wish only baked goods and homemade granola.) The menu changes every morning. You may be served buttermilk pancakes and bacon with a strawberry honey sauce, almond French toast, quiche, or croissant sandwiches. Scrambled eggs and sausages are among the fare for the country breakfast served once a week. The lighting is low, much of it brass or frosted glass.

Food and beverages may also be stored in the innkeepers' refrigerator. If you want to take a swim after checking out, you can use blankets, towels, and an extra shower before leaving. If you'd like restaurant recommendations, you'll be given a list of the hosts' favorites with critiques and prices.

Nantucket, Massachusetts

Nantucket is half the size of Martha's Vineyard but takes twice the time to reach, and the town itself—with its whaling museum and mansions, its many shops, restaurants, and galleries

—is so absorbing that relatively few visitors ever explore the sand and heath beyond. If you come for more than a weekend, plan to rent a car for at least a day or two (it's simpler and less expensive than bringing one over on the ferry) and drive out to Siasconset, at least for dinner, to Diones Beach for the best swimming, and to Madaket to watch the sunset.

Anchor Inn
66 Centre Street
Nantucket, Massachusetts 01554
508-228-0072

Innkeepers: Charles and Ann Balas
10 rooms (all with private bath)
Late June to mid-September: $85-$115 per couple
Shoulder seasons: $70-$95 per couple
Off-season: $50-$85 per couple
Special midweek rates Sunday-Thursday outside peak season,
    discounts for extended stays; all rates include breakfast
Children over 12 welcome
No pets
Open March through December

Nantucket town is studded with picturesque B&Bs, most of them designer decorated and all about the same price. What sets the Anchor apart is its warmth. Many B&B owners hire managers, inevitably young people from somewhere else, to greet guests. But Ann and Charles Balas are really here for you, ready to help plan a day's outing or discuss the town's menus or politics.

The house itself is a classic 1806 Nantucket home built by Achaelus Hammond, the captain of the whaleship *Cyrus* and, according to a historic plaque, the first Nantucket man to strike a sperm whale in the Pacific Ocean. The guest rooms, named for whaling ships, range from fairly spacious areas with canopy beds to snug but inviting quarters under the eaves.

The parlor is nicely furnished with comfortable antiques, and it's the kind of place you want to linger, maybe leaf through a copy of *Cheaper by the Dozen* or *Innside Nantucket*, written by the Gildreths, the owners of this guest house in the 1950s.

Charles bakes muffins each morning and serves them on the enclosed breakfast porch, where there is a refrigerator for guests to use as well as a pay phone and TV. Beach towels and bicycles are also available, the better to strike out for Jetties Beach, an easy ride. The restaurants and shops of the town are a short walk the other way.

Harbor House

Nantucket, Massachusetts 02534
508-228-1500

Manager: Mr. Jan Garis
111 rooms
January-March: $40-$60; *April:* $85-$130; *May:* $115-$160;
  July-August: $145-$225; *September:* $115-$160; *October-
  December:* $85-$130
2-night minimum in July and August, 3-night minimum on
  weekends
Major credit cards
Children welcome
No dogs
Handicapped access and some wheelchair-geared baths
Open year-round

The renovated Harbor House, a large complex of buildings
built around an 1880s summer hotel, offers a variety of luxurious rooms. Open all year, it's just a few blocks from the hustle
and bustle of Nantucket town on a very quiet cul-de-sac. In the
summer it is beautifully landscaped with bushes and flowers,
and a large swimming pool with a service bar is tucked in
between some of the units.

Guests can choose rooms in the main inn or in the units
throughout the property which resemble traditional Nantucket
town houses. Ask for a room that has views of one of the many
small gardens.

The main inn has an attractive split-level lobby/living room
decorated with antiques and opening onto the Hearth dining
room. There is also a turn-of-the-century lounge with open
beams that features live entertainment with dancing on summer weekends. The hotel is owned by First Winthrop Corporation, the development firm in Boston that owns much of downtown Nantucket.

Jared Coffin House

29 Broad Street
Nantucket, Massachusetts 02554
508-228-2405

Owner: Philip Whitney Read
56 rooms
In season: $110-$175 per couple; singles: $60-$70; less off-season
All 3 meals served
Major credit cards

Children welcome
Well-behaved pets welcome
Open year-round

The Jared Coffin House is in the heart of Nantucket's Historic District, just a short walk from shops and the boats to the mainland. The complex consists of the main inn with an addition, a building constructed in 1964, and Federal and Greek Revival houses across the street.

The public rooms of the main house are gorgeous, furnished with period antiques that reflect Nantucket's whaling history, but the guest rooms in the Federal Henry Coffin House and the Greek Revival Harrison Gray House are most desirable. The Henry Coffin House contains six rooms, each with a queen-size canopy bed. The Harrison Gray House, built for the owner of the whaleship *Nantucket,* contains twelve rooms, also with queen-size canopy beds. Room 602 has a secluded outside sitting area, a daybed in its own niche, a refrigerator, and a fireplace (not working). Room 605 has high, beamed ceilings and is particularly suitable for families: there is a great loft area for kids.

There are two common rooms in each house, but the two in the Gray House are the best. The parlor is quiet and inviting, with a fireplace and lovely period antiques. Just off the parlor is a bright sunporch with windows on all sides and bamboo furniture covered in pale green; it has a lovely view of a secluded garden. Off-season, when this house is less apt to be full, guests can imagine they're in their own summer house.

The main house has dining rooms and a taproom, and the food is very good New England fare. Many other restaurants just a short walk away offer an incredible variety of food.

The White Elephant Inn and Cottages
P.O. Box 359
Nantucket, Massachusetts 02554
508-228-2500

Innkeeper: Rita Hill
91 rooms, suites, and cottages
June 9 – September 16: rooms $200-$260 per couple, cottages $180-$535; rooms in the Breakers: $325-$485; less in shoulder seasons
All 3 meals served
Major credit cards
Children welcome; special program for those under 12
No pets

Open Memorial Day weekend through Columbus Day
 weekend

The White Elephant combines the convenience of a harborside,
Nantucket town location with the facilities of a resort. The
low-slung complex includes the main inn (which has common
rooms and the Regatta dining room as well as guest rooms),
cottages, and the Breakers, a building that is set off from the
main grounds and offers 24-hour concierge service and other
conveniences.

There are water views from the rooms in all three of these
buildings, so be sure to request one. The panorama can include
both Nantucket Harbor, whose boat traffic is delightful during
the day, and the gardens and extremely well tended grounds.

The common rooms in the main house are all large and airy.
A card room just off the lobby is attractively decorated with
wicker, and the lobby and bar have comfortable, overstuffed
sofas. Both the bar and restaurant overlook the harbor.

Room 216 in the main house commands a view of the open
sea and a little garden as well as the harbor, and most rooms
there have access to a long outside porch, where guests enjoy
breakfast while watching the ferry come and go. Arbutus,
Alouer, and Holly cottages are recommended for their views.
The cottages are particularly nice for a longer stay and for
families.

The Breakers is the elite corner of this enclave. We found the
reproduction furniture a shade heavy, but the niceties include
fresh flowers, complimentary wine and cheese, and champagne and mixers in the refrigerator in the room. Potables are
available from 4:00 to 9:00 P.M. in the subdued private lounge.
A complimentary Continental breakfast is served either here or
in guests' rooms.

Tennis courts are just a short walk from the inn. There are
two 9-hole putting greens and a harborside pool. The hotel has
been refurbished by its new owners, the First Winthrop Corporation, the Boston development firm that now owns much of
the town.

■ *See also:* Cliffside Beach Club, Nantucket, Massachusetts;
Wauwinet, Nantucket, Massachusetts

Block Island, Rhode Island

Quieter, less pretentious, and more relaxed than many other New England islands, Block Island is reached by ferry from Newport, Providence, and Galilee, Rhode Island, as well as from New London, Connecticut, and Montauk Point, Long Island. Easily managed by bicycle, the island is approximately 7 miles long and half that distance wide. Practically all activity is in town, but at the southeastern end of the island is a lighthouse and Monhegan Bluffs. Crescent Beach, on the eastern shore, is also popular.

The Hotel Manisses, The 1661 Inn
Spring Street
Block Island, Rhode Island 02807
401-466-2421, 401-466-2063

Innkeepers: Joan and Justin Abrams, Rita and Steve Draper
Hotel Manisses: 17 rooms (all with private bath)
1661 Inn: 28 rooms (most with private bath)
$65-$215 per couple, including breakfast
Lunch and dinner also served
Major credit cards
Children welcome
No pets
Open year-round

The Hotel Manisses, built in 1870, was once considered one of the best summer hotels in the East. The Abrams family saved this historic landmark when they purchased it in 1972 and began ten years of refurbishing and restoring. The hotel now offers guests tastefully decorated and beautifully furnished bedrooms and common rooms.

The guest rooms, four with Jacuzzis, are all decorated in a special Victorian style. A nice small touch includes brandy and an ice bucket in each room.

The common rooms are magnificent, and the Abramses have been incredibly creative in finding Victorian parts from other houses and buildings to help restore the hotel. The 23-foot-long bar with a mahogany top dates from 1870 and was originally part of a South Boston saloon. The stained glass windows and the 44-inch-diameter ceiling dome belonged to other New England mansions. Many of the hand-grooved arches in the house, including the one in the library, came from the Plimpton House in Norwood, Massachusetts.

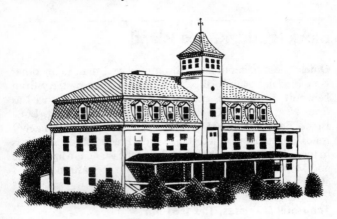

A vast array of complimentary hot and cold hors d'oeuvres with wine are served every afternoon. Dinner begins at 6:00 P.M. The appetizers include escargots in mushroom caps and oysters Augusta (oysters glazed with a curry-flavored Hollandaise). The Manisses clam chowder is excellent. The entrées are remarkably diverse, given that food is difficult to transport to the island. There might be unusual variations on steak, duck, and chicken, and of course a wonderful selection of fish — possibly swordfish, flounder, salmon, scallops, or lobster. The superb desserts and bread are all homemade.

For those who like a slightly less formal atmosphere and would rather have a water view from their rooms, we recommend the 1661 House. The views from about half of the rooms (some in an adjacent guest house) are sweeping. There are vistas of meadows, a pond, and the Block Island harbor. The rooms with the best views also have outside decks.

The breakfast buffet, served in the 1661 Inn (either in the two dining rooms or on an outside terrace overlooking the harbor), is always extensive. It may consist of many kinds of fruit and fruit juice, four or five kinds of muffins, eggs, fish, hash, sausage, ham, baked beans, and homemade jams and jellies.

Lakeside

By and large, these old summer retreats are on the shores of some of New England's most beautiful lakes.

Connecticut

Boulders Inn on Lake Waramaug
Route 45
New Preston, Connecticut 06777
203-868-0541

Innkeepers: Ulla and Kees Adema
2 suites, 9 doubles (all with private bath), 8 cottages
$180-$200 per couple, MAP
Lunch served in summer and October
Major credit cards
Children over 12 welcome
No pets
Open year-round

The Boulders Inn is the best place to stay in the Lake Waramaug area. In a quiet location, it overlooks the scenic lake, offers excellent food, and has a variety of accommodations.

The main house, which was built in 1895 and became an inn in the late 1940s, has six guest rooms. They are furnished with lovely antiques and have the best views of the lake. Those who prefer something more modern, want to feel a little more away from it all, and enjoy a wood-burning stove might prefer one of the cottage rooms. They have slight views of the lake through large picture windows as well as a living room, bathroom, and a small bedroom. Plenty of wood is stocked just outside the door. The cottages also have private decks. (Some have kitchenettes, but the Ademas prefer that guests not use them.) The most recent addition to the inn includes five rooms (air-conditioned and with fireplaces) in the Carriage House next door.

In the living room of the main house, an expanse of windows allows unrestricted views of the lake and the surrounding area. Both this room and an adjoining TV den have fireplaces, and

there is a library nook and stereo system in one corner of the living room. Sunsets are wonderful from any of the three or four groupings of chairs and comfortable couches. Tea is served from a Russian samovar here in the winter. In summer, tea and meals are taken on the three terraces.

An octagonal addition to the dining room has even better views. The menu can be eclectic, and food is taken seriously. (It was rated "very good" in the *New York Times*.) The entrées might include venison, partridge, or quail, veal with lemon and capers, or one of many fine European dishes. Desserts can include brandied orange-nut cake or lemon pie in a meringue crust.

This is a marvelous spot in the warm weather—especially for those climbing Pinnacle Mountain, just behind the inn. Guests may also use the private beach, with its sailboats, canoes, and paddleboats. But it is also a remarkable place to spend a winter weekend, with ice fishing, tobogganing, and skating close at hand.

Maine

Kawanhee Inn Lakeside Resort
Lake Webb
Weld, Maine 04285
207-585-2243
Winter address: 7 Broadway
Farmington, Maine 04938
207-778-4306, 207-778-3809 (evenings)

Innkeepers: Sturges Butler and Marti Strunk
14 rooms, 11 cabins, each accommodating from 2 to 7
Double rooms $50 and up, cabins $360 per week and up
MasterCard, Visa
Children welcome
Pets in shoulder season in one cabin
Inn and cabins open May through mid-October; restaurant,
  June–Labor Day

The Kawanhee Inn is in Maine's Rangeley Lakes district, off a rural road in a pine forest. The inn sits on a precipice overlooking a shimmering lake ringed by mountains. The log cabins dot the lakeshore below. Virgin woods, unpolluted air, freshwater lakes, and a charming timber lodge with a dining room and bar make this a simple yet complete hideaway.

A huge central fireplace is the focal point of the open-beamed and pine-paneled lounge; cushioned rockers and chairs make it a fine place to talk, read, and relax. In one corner, a glass case displays maps of the area and Maine souvenirs.

A doorway off the main lounge leads to a simple dining room, where thoughtfully prepared meals of fresh fish and Maine lobster, crisp salads, and warm breads are served by candlelight. From any of the dozen tables, guests have a spectacular view of the lake and the dusky mountains. The adjacent outdoor veranda is a peaceful place to sip an aperitif while watching the sun slip away or tracing a lone boat plying the lake's calm waters. After dark, a telescope and a brilliant, star-studded sky invite guests to test their knowledge of astronomy.

A narrow wooden staircase in the lounge winds up to the lodge's guest rooms, which are not nearly as desirable as the cabins. Separated by walls of thin paneling and sparsely furnished with a camp bed, night table, lamp, chair, and sink, these rooms are Spartan. Each cabin, by contrast, has a screened porch, camp chairs and tables, a stone fireplace, a roomy bedroom, and a bath.

The inn has a private beach and dock. Fishing, boating, sailing, long walks, all-day hikes to nearby Mount Blue, Tumbledown, or Bald mountains, and panning for gold on the nearby Swift River are all popular.

Lake House
Routes 35 and 37
Waterford, Maine 04088
207-583-4182

Innkeepers: Michael and Suzanne Uhl-Myers
4 rooms (all with private bath)
$65-$89, including breakfast
Major credit cards
Well-behaved children welcome
No pets
Open year-round

This graceful old staging inn has traces of a ballroom under the eaves; it's one of twenty-one buildings in Waterford Flat listed on the National Historic Register.

Waterford is a quiet pocket in Maine's Western Lakes region, a gem of a village on the shore of small Keoka Lake. The general store and the inn are the only commercial ventures in town, and the inn is an eye-stopper: it has a double porch and lacy wooden touches that must date from its early-19th-century days as Dr. Shattuck's Hygienic Institute for Ladies.

The Uhl-Myers have restored the building lovingly, converting the old ballroom into a luxury suite. It retains the curved ceiling and has a canopy bed and sitting area. Another suite has country furnishings and a separate library/reading room. Waterford South, another room, has twin beds, oak furnishings, and access to the upper porch. Waterford North offers a double bed with Empire furnishings and a "Love" couch.

Downstairs there is a comfortable sitting room and two public dining rooms, one reserved for nonsmokers. A full breakfast, available only to guests, is served at 9:00 A.M. The dining room has a strong local following; its specialties include Atlantic salmon with a light sauce of Tequila and lime and shelled lobster in fennel and cream. Most recipes are Suzanne "originals" and use fresh ingredients. All the baking (try the parfait pie) is done at the inn.

In warm weather, you can swim at the beach just across the street; there is also easy access for canoeing and sailing. You can also hike up Mount Tirem, which rises abruptly from the village, or tackle longer trails in the nearby Maine White Mountain National Forest. In the winter, there is informal cross-country skiing right around the inn. Groomed trails and downhill skiing are available either a short drive to the south, in Bridgton, or a reasonable ride north, in Bethel.

■ *See also:* Westways on Kezar Lake, Center Lovell, Maine

New Hampshire

Follansbee Inn

Route 114, P.O. Box 92
North Sutton, New Hampshire 03260
603-927-4221

Innkeepers: Dick and Sandy Reilein
23 rooms (11 with private bath)
$65-$85 per couple, including breakfast
Dinner also served
MasterCard, Visa
Children over 10 welcome
No pets
No smoking
Open year-round, but do call first

This is a distinctive-looking old summer inn, with white clapboard and green trim. Its locale is a good spot for year-round relaxing. Sandy and Dick Reilein, with their son, Matthew, have brought enthusiasm to this landmark—the heart of the early-19th-century village of North Sutton.

The rooms, upstairs, are simply furnished and very clean. Downstairs there are comfortable sitting spaces with fireplaces and plenty of reading material. A big porch with rocking chairs overlooks Kezar Lake. Guests enjoy clean air inside and out, since this is a completely nonsmoking inn.

Breakfast always includes homemade granola, fresh fruit, and a hot dish. Guests help themselves and sit together, so the atmosphere is friendly and relaxing. Dinner is offered only to guests; they need to sign up after seeing the menu at breakfast. Beer and wine are available.

Kezar Lake is a few steps away, and there's a public beach just down the way. The small island on the lake is a nice place for a picnic. The inn has a private pier with a canoe, rowboat, windsurfer, and paddleboat. In the winter there's ice fishing on the lake, downhill skiing at nearby King Ridge and Mount Sunapee, and cross-country skiing from the inn (the trails around the lake are great) or at a touring center in New London.

Mountain Lake Inn

P.O. Box 443
Bradford, New Hampshire 03221
603-938-2136
800-662-6005

Innkeepers: Carol and Phil Fullerton
9 rooms (all with private bath)
$80 per couple, including breakfast
Dinner also served at certain times
Discover, MasterCard, Visa
Children welcome
No pets
Open year-round except parts of November and April

Across the street from Lake Massasecum, amid 165 acres of forest, is a real old-fashioned country inn that welcomes everyone. It's comfortable, with no priceless antiques, and embodies the best of the past. With Currier and Ives wallpaper and the like, it reminds one of a grandmother's house. It's the kind of place where the innkeeper will lead you on a morning snowshoeing expedition after giving you a set of homemade snowshoes.

One living room has a woodstove, knotted area rugs, and comfortable chairs and sofas. It's bright and sunny here in the morning. The screened-in front porch with rockers is also a good place to pass the time; you can look across the street onto the lake.

The guest rooms are furnished comfortably and simply. With a queen-size and two twin beds, Room 5 is the best one for families. For the few rooms that have private baths in the hall, robes have been thoughtfully provided.

The dining room is heated by an old-fashioned potbelly stove from Maine. A full country breakfast is served at lacquered wooden tables and chairs. In addition to a cold buffet, there's always a hot dish like a soufflé or casserole. At dinnertime, a set meal is served to guests only. If you tell the innkeepers ahead of time about special dietary concerns, they're very flexible. When meals are served, the pool table is covered.

Out the back door are trails for hiking and skiing as well as a waterfall and a rushing stream, which lends itself to a leisurely picnic. Across the way are swimming, canoeing, and boating from the private sandy beach. The Fullertons genuinely love welcoming people into their home. Guests' photographs on the walls attest to the family atmosphere that develops here. It's particularly well suited to groups and families.

Pick Point Lodge
P.O. Mirror Lake
Mirror Lake, New Hampshire 03853
603-569-1338

Innkeepers: The Newcomb family
10 cottages, 2 rooms (all with private bath)
$630-$1,700 per week, depending on many factors
All 3 meals served
No credit cards
Children welcome
No pets
Open early May to mid-October

It seems to take forever to reach Pick Point Lodge, at the end of a long road on one of the most beautiful points of land on Lake Winnipesaukee. But once you find it, all your troubles will be over. You can enjoy 112 acres of woods, a wildlife pond, feeding stations for deer, 60 birdhouses, a private sandy beach, a half mile of shorefront, and, of course, the lake itself.

There's a full range of activities at the lodge. Sailboats, rowboats, and canoes are available for all adult guests, while the small rubber rafts and floats are just right for young children. There is also table tennis, a pool, shuffleboard, lawn games, indoor board games, a playground, dock space, gas grills, hiking, indoor and outdoor tennis, and a variety of other summer sports nearby.

For those who want to get to know other guests and their families (as well as the Newcomb family, which skillfully runs the place), there are weekly "get-together" parties, with cocktails for adults and juice for children on the side lawn or in the main lodge. Although most people stay in cottages or "lodges" in the woods, there are a couple of rooms in the main lodge. They are nicely decorated and ideal for those without children.

The dining area and living room of the main lodge have substantial wooden beams running the length of the rooms, large stone fireplaces, and unpretentious but attractive furniture. In front, impressive pines stand before the white clapboard building.

The main lodge is just a short walk from the cottages, which have their share of statuesque pines as well as deciduous trees and scrub maple and oak. The cottages are carefully spaced to give the most privacy possible and the best views of the lake, woods, and mountains. They all have a TV, radio, direct-dial phones, and at least one king- or queen-size bed. The three- and four-bedroom cottages have two baths, and most of them have fireplaces supplied with wood.

One very special feature of Pick Point cottages is that all linens, blankets, and towels are provided. Except for cleaning up in the kitchen after snacks or meals, you don't have to make beds or clean since maid service is included (in season) in the price of your stay. There's a remarkable no tipping policy here.

Pleasant Lake Inn

P.O. Box 1070
Pleasant Street
New London, New Hampshire 03257
603-526-6271

Innkeepers: Grant and Margaret Rich
12 rooms (all with private bath)
$75-$80 per couple, including breakfast
Dinner also served on weekends
MasterCard, Visa
Children over 8 welcome
No pets
Open year-round

This was one of many farms that began taking in boarders in the 1880s. Guests came from New York and Boston, and strangers were expected to bring letters of introduction. Today the inn is a homey haven on 5 acres, slightly off the beaten track. The guest rooms have painted floors, white walls with stenciling, and simple but comfortable furnishings.

Pancakes at breakfast are served with maple syrup that Grant Rich makes from the maples on the property. To encourage guests to mingle, hors d'oeuvres are served in the living room a half hour before dinner. Dinner, at 6:30 P.M., may be served by the fireplace (part of the original homestead) or in the patio room, which has a very special view of Pleasant Lake backed by Mount Kearsarge. The Riches ask that guests bring no food or beverages to the inn.

The lake just across the road offers a place to swim, boat, and fish. The views from the extensive beach are breathtaking. Tennis, golf, and hiking are available down the road. Downhill skiing is at King Ridge (also in New London) or 15 minutes away at Mount Sunapee. There is cross-country skiing on the inn's property or at a nearby touring center.

Vermont

Echo Lake Inn
Box 154
Ludlow, Vermont 05149
802-228-8602

Innkeepers: Kathy and Phil Cocco
27 rooms (13 with private shower)
$116-$160 per couple, MAP
Lunch also served
MasterCard, Visa
Children over 5 welcome
No pets
Open year-round (except April)

Echo Lake Inn has a number of drawing points: its proximity to summertime lake activities across the street; Killington's Northeast Passage Chair, 4 miles north; Okemo Ski Area, 5 miles south; a variety of sleeping arrangements; and fine food.

This four-story hotel has peaked gables and a long white porch with red wicker rocking chairs. The sturdy building dates from 1799, with an 1820 addition. Since 1984, the Coccos have devoted much time and energy to making this large inn (with a capacity of 72) more personal, responding in longhand to every inquiry. Phil serves many guests himself; and Kathy cooks breakfast and makes desserts.

Upon entering the inn, guests are welcomed at the bell desk. To the right is the Basket Case Lounge, an intimate place with baskets hanging from the ceiling; cocktails are served here before dinner. To the left is a large, informal living room with a fireplace and piano. The atmosphere throughout is relaxed and casual. The Stoned Tavern, at ground level (the cellar), provides a cozy rathskeller setting with electronic games, pool, and draft beer. After hanging fresh wallpaper, the Coccos dotted the place with their own antiques. The halls are wide and well lit; the rooms are bright and fresh.

Kathy's specialties are pasta dishes and unusual Italian crepes; otherwise, the cooking is done by a professional chef. The menu changes daily and seasonally. Guests can eat inside or on the front porch.

The lush lawn features a tennis court, a pool, a bath house, and an old gazebo. One of three lakes in a chain is right across the street, behind a long bank of trees that obstruct the view but give privacy to those on the lake. Guests are free to use the inn's rowboats and canoes.

Fox Hall
Willoughby Lake
Barton, Vermont 05822
802-525-6930

Innkeepers: Ken and Sherry Pydens
8 rooms (some with private bath)
$65-$85, with breakfast; less mid-October through June
No credit cards
Children welcome
No pets
Open year-round

This is an expansive turn-of-the-century summer mansion turned girls' camp turned B&B. The last step required tedious, lengthy labor: stripping and restoring all the intricate paneling in the dining room and living room, steadying the foundation, and rebuilding the vast veranda and all the stairs leading down to the lawn. Ken, Sherry, and their children did the whole job.

Still, guests come to Fox Hall for the view. It's the most dramatic lake view in New England, one of the most spectacular in the country: right down Lake Willoughby to the fjordlike cleft between Mounts Pisgah and Hor. It's the kind of romantic scenery that drew tourists by the trainload a century ago, and in the 1890s Lake Willoughby had its share of summer hotels, cottages, and a dance hall. But not so long ago lodging on the lake was limited to rental cottages, and there was no place to eat.

There's a lonely, even haunting, quality to Lake Willoughby, and twin-towered Fox Hall fits right in. The guest rooms are large, some (in the towers) round, some with fireplaces, some with private baths, all with antiques and views of the lake.

The common rooms are comfortable, dotted with small moose in every stuffed form (everyone seems to contribute to the collection). There are always a few live animals around: cats, dogs, and a horse or two. The feeling, despite the grandeur of the place, is homey.

The inn's 76 acres include lake frontage and a dock. Canoes, a paddleboat, and windsurfers are available, and in winter there's ice fishing as well as skiing at nearby Burke Mountain. Weather permitting, the best activity here is porch sitting. The wide old veranda commands that spectacular view down the lake that's just as beautiful in the 1990s as it was in the 1890s.

The Highland Lodge
R.R. 1, Box 1290
Greensboro, Vermont 05841
802-533-2647

Innkeepers: The Smith family
Rooms and 11 cottages, accommodating 60
Rooms $152-$165 per couple, MAP, $20-$45 for children;
  cottages $165-$175, $20-$55 for children
Lunch also served
MasterCard, Visa
Children welcome
No pets
Open December 22 to March 17, May 26 to October 15

The Highland Lodge is a old-fashioned white clapboard inn overlooking Caspian Lake. The main lodge is a classic summer hotel with a homey wooden porch; the cottages sprawl across a hill on a rural road above Greensboro village.

The inn has several public rooms, all furnished comfortably. A living room with a sofa, rocker, and fireplace, a sunny sitting room with a baby grand piano and claw-foot chairs, and a library with desks and armchairs allow guests to mingle with friends or find a quiet corner. Three substantial meals, emphasizing fresh fruits and vegetables and wholesome country dishes, are served in a cheerful dining room. In the summer, lunch and dinner are served outdoors at tables covered with blue-and-white-checked cloths; the Vermont air has just a bit of chill, and the setting is wonderfully relaxing.

Guests have a choice of spacious, comfortably furnished rooms in the main house; all are different and have a private bath. In summer, with open windows and short white curtains blowing in the breeze, these rooms have an airy appeal.

The cottages, each with a porch, living room, bath, and one, two, or three bedrooms, are particularly suited to small groups and families, but there are no housekeeping facilities.

Depending on the season, guests can ski, hike, bicycle, or motor over the knotty back roads to picturesque rural towns or explore the rugged dirt lanes connecting the nearby dairy farms. More than 40 miles of groomed cross-country trails through maple groves and pine forests originate at the lodge's touring center, which provides equipment rentals, instruction, and tours. Splendid scenery and the silence of virgin woods reward anyone making the effort to explore.

The inn's beach house, with a fireplace and grills, is the focal point of summer activities on pristine Caspian Lake. Swimming in the clear waters, sunbathing on the float, sailing, boating, and canoeing are all popular. There is also a clay tennis court, and in June, September, and early October, anglers can find salmon, lake trout, rainbow, and perch. The tall pine forests surrounding the lake present ideal hiking opportunities.

Depending on the season and the demand, the inn organizes activities for children; there's also a play area and swing set. Children will also find a well-equipped playroom, the base for a supervised program. Baby-sitters are available if requested in advance.

Shore Acres Inn and Restaurant
R.R. 1, Box 3
North Hero Island, Vermont 05474
802-372-8722, 802-372-5853 in winter

Managers: Mike and Susan Tranby
23 rooms (all with private bath)
$50-$90 per room, EP
Breakfast and dinner available
MasterCard, Visa
Children welcome
Pets welcome (extra charge)
Open year-round

The sweeping grounds here are beautifully landscaped and tranquil; the white buildings with navy trim give a crisp appearance. In a rural setting with a 350-foot veranda, guests delight in a 40-mile panorama of Lake Champlain with the Green Mountains as a backdrop. While lawn chairs dot the back side of the motel, Shore Acres has a half mile of private shore for swimming, lawn games, and a 300-yard driving range.

All the rooms are in very quiet lakeside structures except for two master bedrooms at the guest house and two rooms in the annex next to it. Most units sleep two people, but all can hold an extra bed; each has a TV but no phone. Rooms are rented by the unit, regardless of the number of people occupying them. Lodging is airy and clean, with an almost homey atmosphere.

The dining room, next to the full bar, overlooks the lake and specializes in charbroiled fish, steaks, and chops. Off-season rates include breakfast.

■ *See also:* Hawk Inn and Mountain Resort, Plymouth, Vermont

Resort Area Finds

These villages are definitely on the tourist map, and their bed-and-breakfasts may just be the best bets in town.

Connecticut

Austin's Stonecroft Inn
17 Main Street
Goodspeed Landing
East Haddam, Connecticut 06423
203-873-1754

Innkeeper: Bonnie Baskin
5 rooms (all with private bath)
$75-$90 per couple, including full breakfast
No credit cards
Children over 12 welcome
No pets
Open year-round

Stonecroft is one of the fancier offerings in East Haddam, a Connecticut River town clustered around the Goodspeed Opera House, unquestionably the most picturesque playhouse in New England and known for the quality of its almost year-round shows. The inn, a short walk uphill from the Opera House, is an eggshell-colored, Federal home that was built in the early 1800s by a blacksmith.

Some folks come here for the romantic rooms. Two have working fireplaces and all have sitting areas. Others come for the hearty breakfasts, served at a long pine table with Colonial-style chairs or on the front porch, with a view of Main Street. A fireplace warms the cool fall mornings and frosty winter days in the dining room.

The Inn at Mystic
Junction Routes 1 and 27
Mystic, Connecticut 06355
203-536-9604

Innkeepers: Jody Dyer, Nancy Gray
67 rooms
$95-$195 per couple; November-April, $65-$95, afternoon tea
   included; packages available
All 3 meals served
Major credit cards
Children welcome
No pets
Open year-round

The Inn at Mystic consists of a 59-unit modern motel facility
and an adjacent 8-acre estate purchased in 1980. The motel is
tidy and well decorated, but those looking for something special should stay in the main inn, with its landscaped gardens, an
orchard, and walking trails. The rooms are furnished with canopy beds, two have working fireplaces, and some have bathrooms with whirlpool soaking tubs. Some of the rooms and
the wide Victorian porches overlook the formal gardens and
Mystic Harbor out to Fisher's Island.

The living room of the old house has beautiful carved paneling and is furnished with a few antiques. The dining room,
done in Chinese wallpaper, has an unusual fireplace with circular painted miniatures. There is a breakfast room and a terrace filled with plants. Oriental rugs are scattered throughout.

The main dining area, the Flood Tide restaurant, is in a
separate building on the premises. Be sure to reserve a room
overlooking the ocean. For dinner, choose from the huge regular menu or a daily special such as fettuccine Alfredo, beef
Wellington, chateaubriand, or roast rack of baby lamb.

This is a great base for visiting the Mystic Seaport Museum or
Mystic Marinelife Aquarium. But at the inn there's much more
to do. Two canoes and two rowboats are available for exploring
the inn's cove. There's a tennis court on the premises (small
extra charge) and a pool for guests only.

Maine

Bass Cottage in the Field
Bar Harbor, Maine 04609
207-288-3705

Innkeeper: Jean Turner
10 rooms (4 with private bath)
$45-$85 per couple, EP
No food served

No credit cards
Babies past crying stage welcome
No pets
Open Memorial Day weekend through Columbus Day

Folks, this is a real find—one of the most reasonably priced and convenient places to stay in Bar Harbor. Bass Cottage is just off Main Street but in a private world of its own, behind a stand of flowering lilacs and bushes.

They don't make them like this anymore. And it's remained that way because it's been in the same family for more than a hundred years. Women through the generations have headed the household or managed it when they began to take in guests. Jean Turner is no exception, and she still presides at the dining room table when family members come for the holidays.

One of Bar Harbor's old gilded cottages, Bass Cottage still has its stained glass and many of the original appointments. The large, glass-enclosed porch is furnished with wicker, stocked with magazines, and brimming with flowers. The stamped ceilings are high, and the guest rooms are airy and clean; some have private baths and an ocean view. Most have old bathroom fixtures; many, simple brass or iron beds. A newly enlarged suite on the first floor can accommodate three people. A few single rooms are available for as little as $30.

Meals are no problem, because there are dozens of restaurants within a short walk. Bar Harbor offers great dining in every price range. The inn is also good for people without a car. It's handy to a variety of boat and bus tours of Acadia National Park as well as to bicycle rental shops.

The Captain's Quarters Inn and Motel
P.O. Box 83
Main Street
Stonington, Maine 04681
207-367-2420

Innkeeper: Bob Dodge
13 units
$35-$90 in summer; less off-season
No meals served
Major credit cards
Children welcome
Pets welcome
Open year-round

p of harborfront buildings isn't for everyone. Reac-
our readers have varied widely. Some love it. Others

The Quarters are in a former barbershop and fish store on the harbor in Stonington, one of the most picturesque working fishing villages in Maine. You enter through a former storefront, which now is an office that includes a foul-weather breakfast nook and gift shop. Beyond is a large deck overlooking the busy harbor. In summer it is brimming with flowers and spotted with tables, where you can eat breakfast or snack (coffee and muffins are available all day).

The rooms, suites, and apartments have no antiques, but they offer comfort, personality, and harbor views. Room 3 has a tin ceiling, and two rooms, 10 and 11, have fireplaces.

Bob Dodge also owns the Bayview restaurant up the street. It's an attractive place with a solid reputation for seafood chowder and serves all meals, including candlelit dinners. Guests at the inn receive a discount (the restaurant is open from May to late October).

Stonington is out of the way, 40 miles south of Route 1 at the tip of the Deer Isle–Blue Hill peninsula. Once known for its pink granite, it is still a busy lobstering port and a favorite stop for Maine windjammers. It offers some exceptional crafts shopping and is also the year-round departure point for the mailboat to Isle au Haut, a part of Acadia National Park (see the Keeper's House).

The Castine Inn

P.O. Box 41
Castine, Maine 04421
207-326-4365

Innkeepers: Margaret and Mark Hodesh
17 rooms and 3 suites (all with private bath)
$70-$85, including full breakfast; suites $125 for 4 people
Dinner also served
MasterCard, Visa
Children welcome
No pets
Open mid-April through September

The Castine Inn is in one of Maine's prettiest coastal towns, a resort since the mid-19th century. It's managed by two people who care very much about what they are doing and who want to ensure their guests' satisfaction. Mark Hodesh is the chef at a well-known Manhattan seafood restaurant in the winter, and Margaret is an established artist, as is her mother.

The three-story inn was built as a summer hotel in 1898, and there's an open, airy feeling to the common rooms. But what you notice most are the pictures: fine, unusual landscapes by Margaret's mother and Margaret's own mural of Castine in the dining room. Actual views of the town and harbor beyond complement the painting.

The inn's original veranda has been replaced and the gardens have now taken shape, enriched with perennials, paths, benches, and arbors. The guest rooms are spotlessly clean, all renovated, with private baths added where needed and views of the water maximized (request a room with a view).

The food, predictably, is excellent. For dinner, you might begin with mussel bisque and crabmeat in bacon; entrées frequently include broiled fish, lobster, crabmeat cakes with mustard sauce, chicken and leek pot pie, and crushed black pepper steak. Desserts feature baked Indian pudding, pies, strawberry shortcake, crisps, and cobblers.

Edgecombe-Coles House

64 High Street
Camden, Maine 04843
207-236-2336

Owners: Terry and Louise Price
6 rooms (all with private bath)
$90-$135, including full breakfast; $70-$95, off-season
Major credit cards
Children over 7 welcome
No pets
Open year-round

It would be a shame if Terry and Louise Price hadn't opened this exceptional B&B near the ocean just north of Camden. Then their guests would never have a chance to admire their beautiful antiques: furniture, prints, Oriental rugs, and delightful stuffed animals and toys. All of these welcome you to the Edgecombe-Coles House and surround you in elegant but very homey comfort. Terry's collections even dictated the naming of the Sheep Room and the Bunny Room because of the large number of whimsical versions of these creatures.

But the pièce de résistance is the front room upstairs, with a brass bed, working fireplace, rope-spring daybed, and glorious view of the bay over the treetops. Several of the baths have such pleasing touches as a marble sink, a claw-foot tub with an eyelet curtain, a flowered cloth wall covering, or an antique white wicker dressing table.

Downstairs, guests gather in the living room, with its handsome grand piano, in the shady backyard, or out on the sunny deck. The dining room, with a collection of decoys marching across the mantelpiece, is an especially popular place at 8:30 A.M. That's when filling breakfasts such as baked beans and steamed brown bread, eggs any way you like them, homemade muffins, or the house specialty, Dutch Babies (sweet popovers made in a big black frying pan and drizzled with maple syrup), make guests' stomachs as big as their eyes.

Set back from the road on a hillock with views across Route 1 down to the water, the Edgecombe-Coles House is one of only a handful of Camden hostelries that have ocean views. Built as a summer home in the 1890s, it now welcomes guests all year.

The Green Heron Inn
Drawer 151
Ocean Avenue
Kennebunkport, Maine 04046
207-967-3315

Innkeepers: Charles and Elizabeth Reid
11 rooms, 1 cottage (all with private bath)
$54-$78 per couple, including breakfast
No credit cards
Children welcome
Pets welcome with advance permission
Open mid-April to mid-December, some off-season weekends

Breakfast at the Green Heron is considered the best in town; outside visitors must make reservations. The extensive menu consists of a daily special, large portions of eggs any style, meat, and homemade breads and muffins.

The breakfast rooms overlook Fairfield Creek, an estuary of the Kennebunk River, and are used for relaxation and recreation during the rest of the day. There's also another lounge, a library with games and puzzles, and TV space.

The guest rooms are simple, comfortable, and very clean. All have cable TV, most have air conditioning, and three have outside sitting areas. A few can accommodate four people.

Ocean Avenue can be trafficked in the summer but it's less than a mile away from the many shops, galleries, and boutiques of picturesque Dock Square.

The Homeport Inn
Route 1
Searsport, Maine 04974
207-548-2259

Innkeepers: Dr. and Mrs. George Johnson
10 rooms, 2-bedroom cottage on the water
$60-$70 per couple, including full breakfast, $37 single, $17
  per extra person in room, $6 for children under 14 in
  room; $450 per week for cottage; off-season rates,
  November-April
Major credit cards
Children welcome
No pets
Open year-round

Back in the days when Searsport sent more men out on the high seas than any other coastal port did, its ship captains made a handsome living in the China trade. Upon their return, they built elegant houses and filled them with objets d'art they had found on their voyages.

The Homeport Inn is a beautifully preserved reminder of those times. Sitting behind a white picket fence right on Route 1 and topped with a distinctive cupola, it was built in the 1860s by a Captain Nichols. Today, George and Edith Johnson have recaptured the opulence of the captain's era in gracious rooms filled with Oriental rugs, antique furniture, and an understated refinement.

A number of old captain's homes in Searsport are now B&Bs, but this remains our favorite; it has continuously expanded and improved under the Johnsons' care, and it is on the water side of Route 1, with grounds sweeping down to the ocean's edge.

Some of the guest rooms are in the front part of the original house; others are in the converted carriage house wing. All are exceptionally lovely. In the wintertime, the Johnsons close off part of the house, but the carriage house rooms, with their southern exposure, are sunny retreats with views of the bay.

Lodging at the Homeport includes a full breakfast. Mrs. Johnson also serves tea from time to time (she puts a sign out by the picket fence when it's available), and there is also an English-style pub, the Mermaid.

Searsport claims to be the antiques capital of the state: the shops lining Route 1 range from flea markets selling junque to elegant homes filled with outstanding antique furniture. It also has a major marine museum. This is a good place to stop if you're taking the scenic route to Bar Harbor. It's also a good place to relax for a few days and simply explore; the inn rents bicycles to its guests.

The Owl and Turtle Harbor View Guest Rooms

8 Bay View Street
Camden, Maine 04843
207-236-4769

Innkeepers: William, Rebecca, Gene, and Susan Conrad
3 doubles (all with private bath)
$65-$75 per couple, $50 single, including Continental
     breakfast; less off-season
MasterCard, Visa
No pets
No smoking
Open year-round

There are only three rooms and they share little common space, but the location and views are unbeatable—smack in the center of this picturesque resort town yet away from the traffic, overlooking the town landing and an inner harbor that teems all summer with windjammer and other boat traffic.

These are excellent motel units, with wall-to-wall carpeting, a TV, air conditioning, electric heat, and full baths. The two harborview rooms also have phones, and all three share a deck.

The guest rooms are above the excellent Owl and Turtle Bookshop, which the Conrads used to own. Longtime Camden residents, they are ready to offer advice about the dozens of shops and restaurants in the surrounding blocks. Parking, incidentally, is provided.

Pentagoet Inn

P.O. Box 4
Main Street
Castine, Maine 04421
207-326-8616

Innkeepers: Lindsey and Virginia Miller
16 rooms, 1 suite (all with private bath)
$73-$93 per person double occupancy, MAP, $120 single
Dinner open to the public by reservation
MasterCard, Visa
Children over 12 welcome
No pets
Open April through November

The street slopes down past the Pentagoet Inn to the harbor, where pleasure boats of every size anchor in the shadow of the

State of Maine, the training ship for the Maine Maritime Academy. You can go aboard for a tour or simply stroll along the beautiful village streets of Castine, admiring the ship captains' white clapboard homes. Some 137 historical markers recount the long, turbulent history of this quiet coastal community.

Like Castine, the Pentagoet Inn offers a respite from the bustle of Camden and Bar Harbor, each an hour's drive away. The original Victorian structure was built as an inn in 1894. Its eleven bedrooms are decorated with braided and Oriental rugs, flowered bedspreads and curtains, and comfortable chairs in sitting alcoves. Ask for Room 1 or 7 if you'd like a slight view of the water as well as a pleasant sitting area. A second building just behind the inn, 10 Perkins Street, predates the inn by about a century and offers five bedrooms and a lovely suite. The suite's cozy living room has a fireplace where a fire is laid, ready to go, each evening. Hooked rugs, painted pine wide board floors, and views of the water add to the charm here. A nice extra touch in all the rooms is a basket brimming with a generous supply of fluffy towels. The beds are also turned down every night.

The common rooms in the main inn consist of a music/library and a living room with a woodstove and a window seat overlooking Main Street. Next to the living room are two dining areas, one on an enclosed porch.

The breakfast menu includes such temptations as blueberry pancakes, coffee cakes and muffins, eggs any style, and an omelette of the day. Fresh fruit is also served. At dinner, the five-course meal begins with soup or chowder and continues with a choice of appetizer, salad, and about four or five entrées. A selection of desserts might feature cream puffs with chocolate sauce, mint chocolate torte, and blueberry pie. Boiled lobster is always available, and the inn's lobster pie topped with breadcrumbs is offered almost every evening. There is a very respectable wine list. A prix fixe dinner is also offered to the public, by reservation only.

At 6:00 P.M., an hour before dinner, cheese and crackers are offered with your choice of cocktails at a reception. Lindsey and Virginia Miller, originally from Arkansas, are most hospitable, introducing guests to one another and encouraging them to sit together at dinner. There are also tables for small parties, who might prefer them to the larger, family-style tables. The Millers have planned several special autumn weekends, including one focusing on cooking with the inn's chef and another for chamber music enthusiasts.

Penury Hall

Box 68
Main Street
Southwest Harbor, Maine 04679
207-244-7102

Innkeepers: Gretchen and Toby Strong
3 rooms (shared bath)
$27-$50 per couple, including breakfast
No credit cards
Mature children welcome
No pets
Open year-round

Penury Hall was the first B&B on Mount Desert, and it's still one of the best because Toby Strong takes his job as host seriously. (Gretchen is a gracious hostess, but she's usually busy with her job as town manager.)

The house is in the middle of a small yachting village. It's nicely decorated with interesting art and has books and magazines in inviting places where guests can sit for a spell.

The modest guest rooms share two baths. This is definitely a place for those who enjoy the sense of being in someone's home. Needless to say, guests are made to feel like one of the family.

Breakfast includes juice, fresh fruit, and a choice of eggs Benedict, blueberry pancakes, or maybe a "penurious" omelette. It's sure to set you up for a day of sightseeing, hiking, biking, or sailing. A canoe, a 21-foot sloop, and a windsurfer are all available for guests.

This is the quiet side of Mount Desert, handy to some great hiking and sailing (lessons are available nearby). But it's still an easy drive from the busier side of Acadia National Park. This is also a good place in the winter. The village has a snug feeling, yet there are plenty of places to walk by the sea and miles of trails for cross-country skiing. The sauna feels good any time of year.

Sign of the Unicorn
Box 99
191 Beauchamp Avenue
Rockport, Maine 04856
207-236-4042

Innkeepers: Winnie Easton
4 rooms and children's loft (some with private bath)
$65 single, $80 double; off-season: $35 single, $54-$70 double
No credit cards
Children welcome
No pets
Open year-round

Winnie Easton clearly loves running her cozy, unpretentious B&B near Rockport Harbor. Her welcome is genuine, and she takes an interest in each of her guests. She delights in recalling anecdotes about past visitors — many of whom return and become friends, too. If someone is feeling low, Winnie has a hug ready; if someone's feeling a little silly, she's ready to join in the fun.

Sharing the duties is Winnie's husband, Howard Jones, a gentle, smiling man who makes Nantucket Lightship baskets as well as prototype models. Together they are also Rockport Realty and will happily provide information on real estate and take guests to see their favorite artists and photo stops.

The three country bedrooms upstairs each have a special appeal: two overlook the water; the third has its own deck above a tiny garden. Downstairs, another bedroom called the White Room has a double bed and a twin, plus a grand piano, Victorian velvet love seats, and full-length bookcases filled with good vacation reading. Additional sleeping accommodations are perched above the living room in a loft just right for kids. Most of the rooms upstairs are modest in size, but the White Room is like a suite; all are comfortably furnished with antiques and collectibles.

But the bedrooms aren't what sets this B&B apart. It's the ambience, the hospitality — and the breakfasts! Winnie gathers her guests around the kitchen table and watches their eyes grow bigger as she serves up such decadent delights as Tipsy French

Toast, with orange zest and rum or brandy, dripping with maple syrup, or stone-ground three-grain pancakes, with blueberries or apple chunks and more maple syrup. There's homemade granola, eggs with onions, cheese, wine, and herbs, and a giant fruit salad and spiced yogurt. On the Fourth of July, guests can celebrate with pancakes topped with strawberries, blueberries, and vanilla ice cream. Guests can also use the kitchen during the day (an extra refrigerator is set aside for them).

After a hearty breakfast, nothing could be better than a long walk, and the Sign of the Unicorn is within a stroll of everything in Rockport, including the Maine Coast Artists Gallery and the Opera House, where chamber concerts are given. A short walk in the other direction takes you to a wildlife refuge with 3 miles of jogging trails and rocks down by the salt water's edge. Warm lake swimming is nearby.

In the off-season, the Winnie takes advantage of her proximity to this nature preserve to offer weekends on mushrooming. Snow permitting, there is cross-country skiing—and even downhill skiing at the Camden Snow Bowl. Other special workshops focus on learning to use tools and special craft techniques.

Massachusetts

Addison Choate Inn
49 Broadway
Rockport, Massachusetts 01966
508-546-7543

Innkeepers: Chris and Peter Kelleher
8 rooms, 1 apartment (all with private bath)
$72-$115 per couple, including breakfast
Major credit cards
Children over 14 welcome
No pets
Open March through Christmas

In the heart of a lively resort village, Addison Choate offers peace, comfort, and charm: a deep garden with a nicely landscaped swimming pool and rooms decorated with antiques, quilts, and flowers.

Approaching the 1850s house from a side porch brimming with flowers all summer, guests enter a country provincial dining room. Through batik-covered doors there's a small living room, where a museum-quality ship model is encased in glass.

The furnishings here are a blend of high Victorian and antiques from various periods.

The house has a few special guest rooms. The first-floor room has curved walls, high ceilings, and a canopy bed. The Chimney Room is light, with a white center chimney coming up through the floor. Directly up the stairs from the side door is a spacious room with a queen-size bed, flowered spread and drapery, and deep green walls. Other rooms are entered from the outside deck or porch. A two-room suite on the third floor (with an ocean view) has a skylit, stained glass ceiling. A greenhouse apartment with a large bay window overlooks a well-landscaped rock garden and fenced-in pool. A terra cotta tile floor, beamed ceiling, and free-standing spiral staircase lend a romantic feel to this cozy place. Since it has cooking facilities (except an oven), breakfast is not included in its rate.

The Continental breakfast includes breads and muffins and is served in the dining room or on the porch at tables for two. Breakfast in the winter is more substantial, with some kind of quiche or egg dish. Since the dining room is small, guests eat in self-imposed shifts, reading the paper in the living room while they wait.

Cape Ann has wonderful rocky shores, hidden beaches, and the old wharves and fishing boats that have long attracted painters. Rockport also offers more than its share of shops and restaurants.

Asheton House
3 Cook Street
Provincetown, Massachusetts 02657
508-487-9966

Host: Jim Bayard
6 rooms (shared bath), 2 suites (with private bath), 1 apartment
$42-$90 per couple, rooms and suites; $665 per week,
    apartment, EP
No credit cards
No children
No pets
Open year-round

In a town of many guest houses, not many stand out like the Asheton House. This elegant home would certainly hold its own outside P-town. Prices are low, considering the quality of the furnishings, but as is customary in true guest houses, there are no common rooms and no breakfast per se. (You will get what Jim Bayard calls an "eye-opener" of juice and coffee or tea, though).

Asheton House consists of two nicely landscaped white houses of early-19th-century architecture on the quieter end of Commercial Street, known as the East End. Built in 1840 by a whaling family, one house is surrounded by a picket fence and has a gracious "open arm" staircase at the main entrance. The other, built in 1806, is of early Cape style. Both interiors boast a harmonious mix of American, French, English, and Oriental antiques, most from Jim's private collection.

The names of the rooms are clues to their special details. The Suite has a separate dressing room with a fully appointed wardrobe, wall-to-wall carpeting, a fireplace, French antiques, and a view of the bay. The Safari Room has natural wicker and bamboo decor as well as two double beds. The Deck Room is light and spacious, with upholstered chairs, Oriental pieces, and a deck overlooking the bay. The Bay Room has the most extensive view and features Chinese Chippendale armchairs and a chaise. All these rooms share baths. There is also a unit that can be rented as a two-room suite or a three-room apartment. As an apartment, it is available in the summer on a weekly basis, at all other times with a four-night minimum.

A stay in Provincetown can be as active or quiet as you like: sipping cappuccino in an outdoor café, swimming at the National Seashore a short drive away, dancing the night away, imbibing in a nearby watering hole, people- or whale-watching. It's all here, most of it just a short walk away. If you fly in, Jim will be happy to pick you up at the airport; if you drive, there's no worry about parking.

Elling's Guest House
R.D. 3, Box 6
Route 23
Great Barrington, Massachusetts 01230
413-528-4103

Innkeepers: Ray and Jo Elling
6 rooms (2 with private bath)
$55-$80 per couple, including breakfast
No credit cards
Children over 12 welcome
No pets
Open year-round

Two things stand out about the Ellings' B&B: the beauty and tranquillity of its surroundings and the friendly atmosphere created by its easygoing hosts. Ray and Jo Elling, in the business since 1971, offer a warm, comfortable hospitality without being intrusive, so that guests can really feel at home here.

The 1746 white clapboard house, beautifully restored and maintained, sits on a knoll above the road, surrounded by large old pines and maples. From the side porch, complete with rockers, guests can enjoy a lovely view of nearby flower gardens and fields and hills in the distance.

The guest wing is entered from the porch. There is a parlor with a fireplace, TV, and reading materials. Upstairs are the guest rooms, four of which share two baths. The rooms are charming, furnished with antiques and family heirlooms.

Jo serves a breakfast buffet of muffins or biscuits, jams, fruit, coffee, and tea. Guests can take their breakfast into the family dining room next to the parlor or out onto the porch.

Both Jo and Ray are pleasant, affable, and helpful, and they pride themselves on maintaining their values of simplicity, informality, and unpretentiousness. This is a wonderful and reasonably priced place to stay, handy to all the activities offered in the Berkshires — the kind of place you look forward to "coming home to."

The Four Chimneys Inn
Route 6A
Dennis, Massachusetts 02638
508-385-6317

Innkeepers: Christina Jervant and Diane Robinson
9 rooms (7 with private bath)
$40-$82 per couple, including breakfast
Major credit cards
Children over 8 welcome
No pets
Open March through December

The Four Chimneys Inn takes you off guard because you're not expecting much from it. It sneaks up from behind two spreading spruce trees as you whiz by on rural Route 6A. However, it's a subtle eyecatcher, both inside and out. The beach is within a 10-minute walk. (Many of Cape Cod's beaches are private and require resident parking stickers, so the location is invaluable.) Since Dennis is the geographical center of Cape Cod, this inn is a convenient and restful place from which to explore the area on day trips (and to outsmart the traffic as well). The price is right, and it's perfect for those of independent spirit.

Colorful flower boxes line the 8-foot windows of this beige

Victorian house. Inside, most of the rooms are spacious and light. An antique spinning wheel graces the entrance; to the right is the simple dining room with a working fireplace. A Continental breakfast is served, and the coffeepot is going all day long. A refrigerator is available for guests. There are two homey living rooms, one with a TV and VCR, the other with a marble fireplace and soft couches. (One doesn't interfere with the other.) A grand stairway leads the way to the guest rooms.

Most of the rooms have private baths; only the two small double rooms share one. The Sundrop Room is indeed very sunny, as is Rose Hip. On the third floor, the beds don't have fancy headboards and the floorboards are glossy, giving the place a fresh, spic-and-span feel. Natural wood prevails on the second floor. Stenciled walls and modest antiques produce an agreeable effect. It's the kind of place where you want to slip off your shoes and lie down on the bed as soon as you've put down your overnight bag.

A large front lawn is always set for lawn games. The summer porch is for less active recreations. Across the street is the freshwater Scargo Lake for fishing, swimming, and sailing. The town of Dennis offers the famous Cape Playhouse, Cape Cinema, and Cape Museum of Fine Arts. Antiquing is also a favorite pastime, along Route 6A.

Garden Gables

141 Main Street
Lenox, Massachusetts 01240
413-637-0193

Innkeepers: Mario and Lynn Mekinda
11 rooms (all with private bath)
$90-$130 per couple, including breakfast
MasterCard, Visa
Children over 12 welcome
No pets
Open year-round

In December 1988, Garden Gables was purchased by the Mekindas, an ambitious Canadian couple with teenagers who were looking for a change in lifestyle. Since then, with gallons of elbow grease, it has been remarkably and capably transformed while retaining its comfortable qualities.

After taking over the many-gabled inn from an elderly woman who had lived there for more than thirty-five years, Mario proceeded to refurbish it. He wallpapered, stripped floors, built arches in the hallways, and replaced the ceiling tiles, all the while enhancing the original beauty and integrity of the inauspicious 1780 house. The two sitting rooms to the left and right of the front door, like the rest of the house, have low ceilings. The larger and brighter room has a piano, TV, and VCR. The other has comfortable old love seats, a working fireplace, and bottles of port and sherry set out for guests.

The guest rooms in the back of the house (6-12), which date from 1908, have been completely remodeled and given sparkling new bathrooms; they have a nice country feel to them.

Breakfast is somewhere between Continental and full. Large boxes of healthful cereal are put out (not those little six-pack boxes). The dining room, with assorted tables and chairs, looks onto gardens.

Well back from the main road, Garden Gables' 5 acres are nicely wooded, with many gardens (some overgrown), flowering trees, and a 72-foot-long pool. The Berkshires are alive with cultural events and outstanding music. For dinner, guests can try Jimmy Demayo's newest restaurant, Lenox 218, just down the road a bit, or the Church Street Café in the center of town.

The Inn at Seven South Street
Rockport, Massachusetts 01966
508-546-6708

Host: Aileen Lamson
6 rooms (3 with private bath), 1 efficiency, 1 cottage
$70 per couple for rooms, including breakfast; $350 per
   week, efficiency; $550 per week, cottage
No credit cards
Children allowed only in cottage and efficiency
No pets
Open May through October, weekends off-season

This low-beamed, vintage 1750 house stands on the southern edge of the village of Rockport. Deceptively small from the street, it has a deep, narrow rock garden that has sprouted an assortment of annexes and cottages over the years. The centerpiece of the garden is a pleasant tile swimming pool, framed with a chain-link fence.

In the summer months, Seven South Street functions as an ordinary inn. But in the spring and fall, it sponsors Cape Ann Workshops, a series of five-day (six-night) sessions in photography, watercolor, oil painting, and sketching. There are twelve workshops each spring, nine in the fall.

A loyal cadre of distinguished artists returns each year to lead these groups, which are limited to sixteen (not counting non-painting companions). Participants arrive for a Sunday party and spend the week working—usually outside—from 9:00 A.M. to 4:00 P.M. During bad weather and in the evening, the downstairs rec room becomes a well-lit studio. The inn provides a Continental breakfast, and all guests have access to a refrigerator. Painters or no, guests tend to linger over muffins around the long dining room table and to gather by the living room fire.

Rockport itself is a lively shopping and dining spot, long beloved by artists. It is accessible from Boston by train and a 5-minute walk from the inn.

The Inn on Cove Hill

37 Mount Pleasant Street
Rockport, Massachusetts 01966
508-546-2701

Innkeepers: John and Marjorie Pratt
11 rooms (9 with private bath)
$42-$83 per couple, including breakfast
No credit cards
Children over 16 welcome
No pets
Open April to mid-October

A classic, square Federal house, the Inn on Cove Hill is very inviting. Years after the Pratts spent their honeymoon here, and after sampling a number of B&Bs on a trip around the world, they returned to buy the inn. John figures he has made more than 20,000 muffins since, serving them in the daisy garden during warm weather or to guests in bed.

The rooms are meticulously appointed, papered in designer prints and furnished with family antiques, comforters, and canopies made by forebears. Most rooms are doubles; two have an extra bed in them. There's also a bright little single on the third floor with an iron bedstead. A third-floor deck commands a sweeping view of the village, Pigeon Cove, and the bay beyond. The old wide-planked floors gleam, and the original doors and dentil molding have been preserved.

Built in 1791, the house has a spiral staircase with thirteen steps, representing the thirteen colonies. According to legend, the house was paid for with pirate gold found at nearby Gully Point.

Rockport is known for its artists; its eminently paintable and sketchable town and seascape; and its shops and restaurants. The fishing port of Gloucester is also part of this rocky promontory known as Cape Ann.

Isaiah Hall B&B Inn
152 Whig Street
Dennis, Massachusetts 02638
508-385-9928

Innkeepers: Marie and Dick Brophy
11 rooms (most with private bath)
$46-$80 per couple, including breakfast
Major credit cards
Children over 7 welcome
No pets
Open mid-March to mid-December

Home-spun country comfortable describes this B&B, a Greek Revival farmhouse built in 1857. If you had wandered off the main road to search for unexpected treasures, you'd eventually find this place (though it's actually right behind the Cape Playhouse). And once you had found it, you'd probably return, for a spell, year after year. There's nothing phony in this quiet rest stop. Actors from the Playhouse often unwind here when they're up from New York doing a play. There are nice presidential rocking chairs on the front porch.

The innkeepers will eagerly tell you about Isaiah, the original builder, who was a barrel-maker and patented the original barrel for shipping cranberries, and Dorothy Gripp, who owned the place from 1948 to 1978. Small but important bits of each of their legacies remain: stenciled walls, a proofing (beehive) oven, and steep, narrow steps.

The living room is just plain homey, with a free-standing coal stove in front of the fireplace. But the dining room is special — with an old-fashioned icebox, a hutch of crystal, a long kitchen table for twelve, and a smaller round table that seats six amid plants in front of a picture window. A generous Continental breakfast is served here.

Wander through the Brophys' blue kitchen to reach the Great Room in the converted barn, with a cathedral ceiling and a grand arched doorway. The decor is that of a new Cape Cod cottage — white wicker, knotty pine, rush mats, a woodstove, games, a TV, a fridge for guests' use, and notebooks with information on nearby activities.

There are six guest rooms in the barn; four have small, private decks overlooking the grassy backyard. All the beds, most with lovely quilts, are handmade: pineapple poster, spindle, and white iron. One room has a fireplace. In the main house, the rooms (two downstairs, three upstairs) are much less uniform.

They may have queen or double mattresses, brass headboards, or hooked rugs. They don't look quite as polished.

Corporation Beach on Cape Cod Bay is a half mile away; an old cranberry bog is practically outside the back door. Bike trails and several golf courses are nearby. There is a nice area where children can play.

Linden Tree Inn
26 King Street
Rockport, Massachusetts 01966
508-546-2494

Innkeepers: Larry and Penny Olson
18 rooms (16 with private bath)
$56-$80 per couple, including breakfast
No credit cards
Children welcome
No pets
Main house open April to mid-November; motel units, year-round

A gregarious innkeeper who loves to laugh, reasonable prices, a quiet location, and no pretension whatsoever all contribute to the success of the Linden Tree Inn. Penny Olson's baking skills are also a big hit. Penny, Larry, and their three cats opened their house to guests in 1980. As quite knowledgeable and helpful hosts, they display brochures for area events and attractions in the hall.

Predictably, the house is named after a massive linden tree in the front yard. The house itself is a stately, square, three-story captain's home. There is a lovely view from the widow's walk; it's especially romantic to sit up here with a glass of wine during a ferocious winter storm.

Though there is an almost formal living room, with local art and a console TV, guests tend to gather in the homey sunroom, furnished in white wicker with a wool carpet. High ceilings predominate on the first floor, which includes the dining room. At the long table or one of the few smaller ones, you'll sample Penny's moist breakfast cakes and sweet breads. Perhaps you'll be served the sour cream chocolate chip cake or the lemon nut bread. No matter, whatever she's in the mood to bake — she makes four different treats a day — will be wonderful.

White eyelet bedspreads lend a familiar feel to the guest rooms; it's like staying at your grandmother's house. All the rooms are furnished very simply, many with twin beds. Room 27 is the smallest and least expensive, with its private bath in the hall. (But it does have a large private outdoor porch.) On the third floor, Room 34 has great views of the ocean and Mill Pond. Many rooms are air-conditioned; most have antique-looking flowered wallpapers and sparkling glass doorknobs; a few have wall-to-wall carpeting. The bathrooms are '60s style, with spic-and-span shiny tubs.

Four modern housekeeping units, each with a double and twin bed, are out back and good for families. There's also an annex to the main house with two connecting rooms.

Rockport is known for its artists' colony; many seminars and classes are given. This tranquil fishing village comes alive with browsers in the high season. It's part of Cape Ann, the less well known and hence less crowded cape in Massachusetts, a lovely rockbound peninsula accessible by regular train (75 minutes) from Boston.

Old Sea Pines Inn
2553 Main Street
Brewster, Massachusetts 02631
508-896-6114

Innkeepers: Michele and Steve Roman
21 rooms and suites (16 with private bath)
$40-$85 per couple, including breakfast
Major credit cards
Children over 8 welcome
No pets
Open year-round

The Old Sea Pines Inn is a converted girls' schoolhouse — large enough for privacy, yet small enough to make you feel you own the place. This gray shingle building has ample space in the common rooms and a variety of porches for everyone. On a warm summer day, with all the doors and windows open, it has a definite feel of a summer resort (without the facilities, of course). It's also one of the best bargains on the Cape.

The large living room isn't anything fancy, but it's inviting. With hardwood floors and plenty of books to choose from, it's a nice place to relax in front of a fire on a chilly evening. Just outside the front double doors is a split-rail porch with green cane rockers. When you arrive, enjoy your complimentary drink here.

A range of typically quaint accommodations should suit just about everyone's needs. Up the wide staircase in the inn are doubles and twins; rooms with a fireplace also have high four-poster beds. Cots can be put in the larger rooms for an additional charge. The least expensive rooms share baths and are on the small side (they were converted from dorm rooms). A two-bedroom suite with a separate entrance is attached to the back of the house and can hold up to four people for a small extra charge. Two rooms in the front have an adjoining porch that looks out to the spacious front lawn. North Cottage has seven new rooms, each with a TV, air conditioning, and a private bath.

A full breakfast is served on the enclosed porch. Yet another porch is on the shadier side of the house, under oak trees; there are potted flowers on each table. Afternoon tea in the winter months and Sunday brunch in the summer are served in the larger, more formal dining room, in the back of the house.

Brewster offers a number of attractions. In the spring, the herring make their annual surge upstream at the Old Grist Mill. The Cape Cod Museum of Natural History, the New England Fire and History Museum, and Sealand are all on Route 6A.

Rookwood

P.O. Box 1717
19 Stockbridge Road
Lenox, Massachusetts 01240
413-637-9750

Innkeepers: Betty and Tom Sherman
17 rooms (all with private bath)
$75-$150 per couple, including breakfast
MasterCard, Visa
Children welcome
No pets
Open year-round

On a quiet street only a half block from the center of town, this inn is deceptively large, almost elegant. With striped window and porch awnings, a turret, and beautiful flower beds outside and American and English antiques inside, Rookwood really stands out. (Its name comes from an eclectic form of Victorian pottery.)

There's a crisp, clean air about the whole house, but it still retains an authentic sense of the period without being starchy and stiff. The sitting room has unusually comfortable Victorian furniture, a working fireplace, and interesting green-striped wallpaper. Hardwood floors with area rugs predominate, with wide chestnut floorboards in some of the rooms upstairs.

The guest rooms are clean as a whistle; some have daybeds for children, and four have working fireplaces. On the second floor, two rooms have small screened-in porches; one, Room 4, has a four-poster bed in the many-windowed part of the turret. At the top of the open staircase is a nice little sitting area. The third-floor rooms are a tad smaller, but they have gables to give them more character. Amazing wallpapering feats have been accomplished in some of these rooms. Room 10 is small and cozy, with a window and love seat in an alcove. Room 11, the best, with a brass and iron bed, has an attached sitting area in the turret. From the daybed and rocking chairs there are 270-degree views of the mountains and surrounding area.

A buffet breakfast is taken at tables of two or four. Typical offerings include boiled eggs or an egg casserole, cheese, yogurt, and juice. Guests then tend to wander out to the front porch (the only place where smoking is permitted) and discuss the day's activity. The Shermans are helpful with restaurant recommendations and information about events in the area. For those who'd rather stay put, there's a comfortable screened-in porch with wicker furniture.

Staveleigh House

P.O. Box 608
South Main Street
Sheffield, Massachusetts 01257
413-229-2129

Hosts: Dorothy Marosy and Marion Whitman
5 rooms (1 with private bath)
$65-$85 per couple, including breakfast
No credit cards
Children over 12 welcome
No pets
Open year-round

Dorothy Marosy and Marion Whitman have created the homiest bed-and-breakfast anyone could hope to find. And "homey" doesn't mean cluttered or shabby. Every wing chair and sofa is brightly, tastefully upholstered, every room furnished with flair.

The guest room with a private bath is a symphony in blues and whites with a wicker chaise longue and rocker, wide pine floors, and a small, exquisite blue and white quilt hung above the bed. Across the hall is a room with tall antique beds and an antique dresser with pull-out shelves instead of drawers which has been known to inspire children to unpack and fold their clothes. All the rooms have reading lights, fresh flowers, pot-pourri made by Dorothy, and quilts, many made by Marion. There are also two attractive downstairs rooms off by themselves, overlooking the garden. Ideal for those who have trouble with stairs, they are also quieter than the two front rooms, which face Route 7.

Breakfasts are special productions, served elegantly at the oak dining room table. Dorothy and Marion actually keep a record of what they prepare every day so that they never repeat the same dish for the same people. Still, guests complain if they don't get what they had on their first visit. Marion's puffed pancakes, topped with brown sugar and apple slivers, are especially memorable.

Dorothy and Marion like to visit with their guests over afternoon tea. Of course, they are full of advice on what not to miss in the area. Wooded paths at Bartholomew's Cobble and dozens of antiques shops in Sheffield are among the attractions. But guests should also consider lingering at the inn, reading and watching Lucy, the black cat, play with Tiffy, a big sandy feline.

The dignified house was built in 1821 for a parson. It stands on spacious grounds that include a delightful sitting area under very old and large trees. The Housatonic, inviting to even the laziest canoeist (canoes can be rented a few doors down), is just across the way. In the winter there are ample ski touring trails, and two alpine ski areas are a short drive away.

The Summer House
158 Main Street
Sandwich, Massachusetts 02563
508-888-4991

Innkeepers: David and Kay Merrell
5 bedrooms (1 with private bath)
$50-$70 per couple, including breakfast
MasterCard, Visa
Children over 10 welcome
No pets
Open year-round

In a village of historic homes and stately grounds, the Summer House is a pure example of Cape Greek Revival architecture. It now has particularly fanciful and carefree common rooms.

The showpiece is the living and dining room combination. Originally a formal parlor, the floor is now one big black and white checkerboard. Chinese red walls contrast sharply with the white interior shutters and moldings. The fireplace is shiny black marble. Vivid green hanging plants add another dimension of solid color. The colors all work, somehow.

The bedrooms are tamer, evoking a soothing, 19th-century spirit with lovely antiques and hand-stitched quilts. The hardwood floors have been painted in that unmistakable Cape Cod fashion: some are spackled, and one has a rug painted on it. Signs of the original woodwork and hardware can be seen everywhere. Two upstairs rooms have pineapple post twin beds. The room with a private bath is on the first floor.

A Continental breakfast of fruit and homemade pastries is served at two round tables in the sunny dining room. As you look around over coffee, you'll see that the brochure is accurate when it says, "The bookcases are laden with those books you always meant to read." The glass-enclosed sunporch is nice for coffee or afternoon tea, and it seems there's always a flower blooming within eyesight.

Most travelers tend to bypass Sandwich as they head out to the Cape. But that's a mistake. The town boasts no less than four major attractions: Heritage Plantation, with American history exhibitions; Yesteryears Doll and Miniature Museum; Dexter Mill, where you can buy bags of fresh meal ground that day; and the Sandwich Glass Museum. There's also a peaceful pond where you can contemplate the hurried world outside Sandwich.

Walker House
74 Walker Street
Lenox, Massachusetts 01240
413-637-1271

Innkeepers: Peggy and Richard Houdek
8 rooms (all with private bath)
$60-$135 per couple, including breakfast
No credit cards
Children over 12 welcome
Pets by prior arrangement
Open year-round

The atmosphere and the decor here reflect the creative vitality and open friendliness of Peggy and Richard Houdek. They left their home in California and careers in the arts (she was the editor of *Performing Arts Magazine* and is a trained opera singer, he was an arts administrator and music critic) to run their own business in a musically rich environment.

The house itself, in the center of Lenox, is a handsome Federal landmark built in 1804. It is minutes from Tanglewood and convenient to all the other cultural and recreational attractions of the Berkshires.

Downstairs, guests can relax in the gracious and eclectic parlor, with its grand piano, antique puzzles, books, fireplace, and plants. The overall decor is a harmonious blend of antiques, contemporary art, personal treasures, and lush greenery, with the sound of music filling the house throughout the day.

Breakfast is served in the dining room or out on the veranda in nice weather. The veranda, long and wide and thoroughly inviting, is filled with comfortable wicker furniture and lush plants and overlooks 3 acres of gorgeously landscaped wooded grounds in the back. Complimentary bicycles are available for guests.

The spacious bedrooms have fireplaces and antique furnishings. Each one honors a different composer and tries to reflect that composer's music and personality. For instance, the Chopin Room has a canopy bed and is decorated in pastels, whereas the Handel Room has an impressive brass canopy bed.

There are also several cats who found their way to Walker House and have become permanent and dearly loved residents. During our last visit, an intriguing colony of ants (in a controlled "farm" enclosure, of course) was the latest addition to the animal population.

In addition to running the inn, Peggy and Richard are very much involved in the community's cultural events, and they produce three or four recitals a year for Walker House guests and the public. These concerts give unknown artists the chance to perform and, of course, keep the Houdeks in touch with the world of music, which is their greatest love.

Robert Wallace, a tapestry designer of the highest order, ably assists in running the inn. It's a harmonious threesome, and they make Walker House one of our favorite places to stay in western New England.

Windsor House
38 Federal Street
Newburyport, Massachusetts 01950
508-465-8769

Innkeepers: Judith Crumb, John Harris, and Jim Lawbaugh
6 rooms (3 with private bath)
$85-$115 per couple including full breakfast, $20 for each extra person in room; midweek, off-season, and other discounts available; add 15% service charge

Dinner also served
No credit cards
Children welcome
Pets by prior approval in one room
Open year-round

Newburyport offers ample shopping along its 1830s brick waterfront and pleasant strolling along streets lined with fine Colonial and Federal homes and in an extensive nature preserve fringed with soft sand.

Windsor House is a handsome brick house that was built as a combination ship's chandlery and home in 1786. Architecture buffs will be intrigued by its combination of Federal, Georgian, and Colonial detailing. The guest rooms are large, with the original windows, Indian shutters, and paneling, and the common rooms are gracious, especially the living room, with its comfortable sofa and chairs, books, organ, and pictures by area artists.

What makes Windsor House special is the original chandlery, now the kitchen. A few steps down from the rest of the house, it's a brick-walled space with a fireplace and 14-foot ceilings. Guests gather around the table for hearty breakfasts, often featuring Jim's homemade sausage (heavily herbed and lean), baked beans, fruit, and much more, keyed to the season. It's not unusual for guests to linger over the excellent coffee for many hours. The special warmth of the room draws guests back at all hours.

Jim Lawbaugh, a former educator who now writes in his spare time, and Judith Crumb have welcomed guests for many years, and they convey that rare sense of knowing their town and business well and still enjoying both immensely. Judith married John Harris, an Englishman, in 1989, and they now share innkeeping duties with Jim. Dinner will be served, we are told, by the time this book appears.

New Hampshire

Wildflowers Guest House
Box 802
Intervale, New Hampshire 03845
603-356-2224

Innkeepers: Eileen Davies and Dean Franke
6 rooms (2 with private bath)
$60-$80 per couple, including breakfast

MasterCard, Visa
Children welcome
No pets
Open year-round, but call first in off-season

North of the retail strip in North Conway on Route 16 in Mount Washington Valley, Wildflowers is a refreshing change from the sterile places to stay that dominate this part of the White Mountains. After more than ten years of restoring their 1878 bed-and-breakfast, Eileen and Dean offer that wonderful combination of old and new.

In the afternoon and evening, guests meet around mulled cider and light snacks. The small, simple living room is quite homey, with lots of plants, a love seat and sofa, and a wood-burning stove.

The wildflower motif is carried throughout the house by the wallpapers. Six-foot windows, with only a simple top curtain to show off the stripped woodwork, are standard, as is wall-to-wall carpeting in the guest rooms. Room 4 has nice views of Mount Washington. Up a narrow staircase on the third floor is a guest room in which tall people might feel confined. A single and double bed are tucked under the angled roofline, and an exposed chimney shoots up through the center of the room.

In the firelit breakfast room, you can take the Continental morning meal of juice, coffee, and a generous slice of coffee cake. Or for a small additional charge you can have a full breakfast, such as smoked bacon and eggs or French toast with cinnamon and seasonal fruit. Whichever you choose, you'll enjoy starting the day in the cheerful room, with tall windows, a painted blue floor, and blue, yellow, and white flowered wallpaper.

Swimming and canoeing on the Saco River "right around the corner," rock climbing on Cathedral Ledge, shopping at L. L. Bean's only outlet store, and many other year-round recreational activities are all within minutes.

Rhode Island

The Melville House
39 Clarke Street
Newport, Rhode Island 02840
401-847-0640

Innkeepers: Rita and Sam Rogers
7 rooms (5 with private bath)

$85 per couple, including breakfast, $10 less on weekdays
MasterCard, Visa
Children over 12 welcome
No pets
Open year-round

If you want to spend the night in Newport and still have money left over to spend on shopping, a stay at the Melville House is a must. For all its country appeal, this 1750 Colonial bed-and-breakfast could well be in rural Vermont or New Hampshire — it's hardly the kind of place you'd expect to find in posh Newport. However, in the Melville House, the Rogerses have created a special, unpretentious space. Abutting the sidewalk in a downtown historic district, the house is literally a 2-minute walk to the shops at the Brick Marketplace.

Upon entering, you'll be offered sherry or some kind of refreshing drink, depending on the time of day and season. The small country living room is quite homey, with a couch and rocking chair flanking the ornamental fireplace filled with a basket of pine cones. There's also a display of antique household appliances, including meat grinders, a toaster, and a dough maker. Sam designed modern versions of these until he retired.

The living room opens onto the sunny breakfast room, where the buffet breakfast of homemade muffins, granola, yogurt, juice, and coffee is set. Individual small tables are set with pineapple placemats, a recurring symbol of hospitality seen throughout Newport. Here you can plan the day, and Sam and Rita are happy to offer suggestions for touring, shopping, or lunching.

There are small modern bathrooms and the original low ceilings (uncomfortably low for tall people in only one room) in this historic house. One bedroom is at the base of the stairway, the others off the halls at the top of the stairs. A long hall, with chests of games and books lining it, leads to the bathroom shared by two of the bedrooms. The furnishings are comfortable — well-worn, solid country furniture, including pineapple-post beds, chests and bureaus restored by Sam, braided rugs, muted flowered wallpapers, and lacy curtains. Small touches like flowers and candy in every room show that Rita and Sam enjoy their work; their enthusiasm certainly spills over.

There couldn't be two nicer hosts in all of Rhode Island, and this is what makes a stay at the Melville House most attractive. It's the kind of place where you might leave Rita and Sam token thank-you gifts. They will suggest that you come back in the off-season, when things are quieter and the streets are more manageable. And if it's your birthday or some other special day and they know about it, don't be surprised if you wake up with balloons on your door or wine at your bedside.

The Richards
144 Gibson Avenue
Narragansett, Rhode Island 02882
401-789-7746

Innkeepers: Nancy and Steven Richard
4 rooms (2 with private bath)
$55-$65 per couple, including breakfast
2-night minimum on weekends; 3 on holiday weekends
No credit cards
Children over 12 welcome
No pets
No smoking
Open year-round

You might not think about stopping in Narragansett, but you should definitely think about staying here; make reservations so you won't be disappointed. On the National Register of Historic Places, this massive stone house was built in 1884 for the prominent Joseph P. Hazard family; you approach it on a circular gravel driveway well guarded with tall, thick trees.

Ten-foot ceilings downstairs and 9-foot ones upstairs create a sense of spaciousness. The dark entrance area opens to a grand hall, from which you can see up to the second-floor guest rooms or walk out onto the grounds. With chintz drapes, French doors, forest green molding, a fireplace, and a large comfortable couch, the living room feels almost like an intimate club.

The guest rooms are decorated with grace, style, and a sure designer's touch. The yellow room has a lace canopy, deep windows, and shares a bathroom that has a free-standing shower and old-fashioned pedestal sink. The blue room has a king-size bed and a door that opens to overlook the yard. Its luxurious, old-fashioned bathroom has a large porcelain tub, a built-in dresser, and peach walls with dark flowered wallpaper. The light lavender Hydrangea Room, with a canopy bed, cotton throw rugs, and a couple of wicker chairs, is lovely. Its large, deep windows are covered with swags and valences. Last, and perhaps Nancy's favorite, is the room with antique twin sleigh beds. Each room has a working fireplace, thick towels, and a down comforter—luxurious on the one hand, simple on the other.

The dining room is formal but not stuffy. Breakfast, served at the long mahogany table at 8:30 A.M., may include baked apples, muffins, grains, a soufflé, or a strudel.

A 10-minute walk down a private way leads to the rocky coast, with plenty of relatively undiscovered beaches nearby. South County Rhode Island has a wealth of resources.

The Victorian Ladies
63 Memorial Boulevard
Newport, Rhode Island 02840
401-849-9960

Innkeepers: Donald and Helene O'Neill
9 rooms (with full baths)
In season: $105-$120, including full breakfast
Off-season: $75-$85, including full breakfast
MasterCard, Visa
Children over 10 welcome
No pets
Open year-round

Even if the Victorian Ladies were not a beautifully restored three-story building with a mansard roof and burgundy awnings, its ideal location would make it a great place to stay. Walk down the hill one way to Newport's beaches and famous Cliff Walk; walk the other direction to the Colonial town, harborfront, and fantastic shopping area.

Because the building was renovated for its present use, the mauve and blue rooms are fresh and crisp and the bathrooms modern and well planned. Tasteful furnishings pick up the Victorian theme. The guest room doors have epergnes full of flowers.

A garden with a brick walk leads to a second, smaller house out back. The rooms here escape some of the noise of Memorial Boulevard. However, both buildings are air-conditioned, so outside noise is not really a problem in the summer. One room in the back house has a summery feeling, with yellow and blue flowered fabrics; another has wicker furniture and dark blue and rose fabrics.

Villa Liberté
22 Liberty Street
Newport, Rhode Island 02840
401-846-7444

Manager: Patrick McGuirleth Hamilton
4 suites and 8 doubles (all with private bath); 1-, 2- and
    3-bedroom apartments in annex
In season: $110-$150
Off-season: mid-October–March, $59-$79; April–mid-May,
    $75-$95
MasterCard, Visa
Children welcome
Dogs welcome with permission; no cats
Open year-round

The three-story Villa Liberté, originally known as the Hof-
Braue House, was built by Mrs. Peterson in 1910. In its earlier
days, it was an elegant house of the evening and a German
restaurant. More recently, it was a popular spot for drink and
good jazz.

Purchased by a group of lawyers in 1986, the Villa has been
remodeled so that it has clean, modern guest rooms and suites
with the decor enhanced by Italianate detailing. The light
rooms with gray walls are decorated in hues of sea-foam green
and peach. Dramatic black and white tile baths feature pedestal
sinks in arched alcoves that open into the bedrooms.

Each floor has a comfortable public space next to the suites.
The second floor has a sunroom with wicker furniture and a
terra cotta tile floor. The windows, with small panes, distinguish the front of the building architecturally. The third floor
has a Palladian window with flowered damask wing chairs.

Air conditioning, phones, and televisions add to the convenience and comfort, making it very much a modern hotel, and
in summer there's a Continental breakfast on the second-floor
deck. While it is neither in the historic waterfront or Bellevue
Avenue section of town, this little gem within walking distance
of both and in a pleasant neighborhood on the fringe of the Hill,
with an eclectic mix of architecture that jumbles the centuries.

Vermont

Hayes House
Bear Hill Road
Grafton, Vermont 05146
802-843-2461

Innkeeper: Margery Heindel
4 rooms (1 with private bath)
$25-$65 per room, including Continental breakfast

No credit cards
Children welcome
Dogs welcome; no cats
No smoking in bedrooms
Open year-round except April

A small bed-and-breakfast, the blue shingle Hayes House is the best bargain in Grafton, a beautifully restored southern Vermont village that's best known for the Old Tavern (see Village Inns).

From the porch's weathered wicker to the aroma of simmering soup, Margery Heindel's home has an inviting, lived-in appeal. Here are both a host and a house with character, a simple environment, and a terrific location on a country lane overlooking a covered bridge.

The front porch of this 1803 home has a profusion of potted plants, a worn wooden floor and railings, and cushioned chairs —it's an ideal place to relax, plan the day's outing, and soak up the country air.

The house is furnished with antiques collected over the years. You'll look forward to returning to the warm living room after a day of sightseeing, stretching out on the sofa in front of the fire, and reading one of the magazines on the coffee table. The living and dining rooms record generations of family history; it's easy to while away an hour just looking at books, pictures, and odds and ends or playing with one of Margery's friendly Chesapeake Bay retrievers.

Each of the guest rooms is spotless and comfortable, but the undisputed jewel is the corner room, which boasts an antique four-poster bed and its own fireplace, an old-fashioned rocker, and a bath. The other rooms have antique bureaus, chairs, and tables and comfortable beds with warm quilts. A small single room with shelves of children's books is ideal for a child.

The Continental breakfast consists of homemade biscuits or muffins, country jams, juice, and tea or coffee. In the winter there's often soup on the stove—guests can help themselves.

Romantic Getaways

These are the places we think of when we want to be completely alone in a beautiful place with someone we like.

Connecticut

The Cotswold Inn
76 Myrtle Avenue
Westport, Connecticut 06880
203-226-3766

Innkeepers: Joanna and Janusz Czaderna
4 doubles (all with private bath)
$175-$225 per couple, including breakfast
Major credit cards
Children over 6 welcome
No pets
Open year-round

The Cotswold Inn, built in 1982, offers unadulterated luxury. In a very quiet part of Westport (with soundproofed bedrooms), it is small, intimate, and beautifully decorated. The rates reflect the fact that the inn is a weekend destination for New Yorkers and a midweek stop for businesspeople.

The inn is decorated in a sophisticated, elegant country style. The wallpapers and fabrics have been brilliantly coordinated, and the furnishings are excellent copies of the kind of furniture found in Connecticut homes more than two hundred years ago. The pieces include reproduction Chippendale and Queen Anne wing chairs, love seats and sofas, highboys, mule chests, schoolmaster's desks, four-poster beds, and butler's tray tables.

The bedrooms come with every luxury imaginable. There's a telephone, cable TV, a clock-radio, and individual climate control. Beautiful flower arrangements appear all over the house.

Small bars of exotic soap and plenty of shampoo are found in the bathrooms, which have European showers, fans, and heat lamps. The towels are large and fluffy. Cotton sheets and enormous, comfortable pillows complete the scene.

Breakfast is served at a time arranged by each guest the night before. It includes orange juice, homemade rolls, and a choice of an excellent herb omelette, waffle, pancakes, or eggs. A complimentary glass of wine and cheese is served on request in the evening.

The dining room window overlooks a very attractively planted small patio. Though the six-year-old house is on a small plot of land, it's beautifully maintained nonetheless. Window boxes sprout geraniums everywhere.

Guests may use the Westport YMCA.

Maine

The Captain Jefferds Inn
Box 691
Pearl Street
Kennebunkport, Maine 04046
207-967-2311

Innkeepers: Warren Fitzsimmons and Don Kelly
12 rooms (all with private bath), 3 apartments
$75-$125 per couple, including breakfast; weekly apartment rates on request
No credit cards
Children over 12 welcome
Pets accepted with prior notice
Open May through October and long weekends in December

The Captain Jefferds is filled to the brim with collectibles, art, and antiques, many left over from the antiques business that the innkeepers ran before they took on this project. The inn itself is a Federal home built in 1804, and the well-traveled innkeepers are two of the most delightful imaginable!

The inn has been meticulously maintained, both inside and out. The bedrooms in the house — all with wonderful proportions — and efficiencies in an 18th-century carriage house are decorated with fine fabrics, wallpapers, and antiques. There is ample country pine and wicker throughout, all arranged to create a comfortable and informal atmosphere. Be sure to see the stunning quilts on the upper hallway walls. Room 12, on the third floor, is country contemporary, with angled ceilings, wicker, and a little porch with chairs, where you can catch a glimpse of the ocean.

Attached to the house are three cozy apartments, with low-beamed ceilings, full kitchens, and one-, two-, and three-bedroom configurations. Daily maid service is included for longer stays; for nightly stays, apartment guests get a luscious breakfast at the inn.

There is plenty of space for relaxing in the common areas. On a brick patio under an awning in the backyard, afternoon tea is sometimes served. On cooler days there is a glassed-in sunporch with wicker and white cushions. The living room, painted a warm yellow, has a magnificent dhurrie rug, sofas and chairs covered in chintz, a Steinway grand piano (music is important to both innkeepers and guests), and a country cupboard filled with majolica. A large collection of majolica—more than 1,000 pieces—is scattered throughout the house.

Breakfast here is an enchanting performance, not simply the first meal of the day. There are two seatings, usually featuring imaginative crêpes. Don serves the meal on fine china and silver, in black tie and a white jacket, with a twinkle in his eye and an unmatched wit.

The Captain Lord Mansion
P.O. Box 800
Kennebunkport, Maine 04046
207-967-3141

Innkeepers: Bev Davis and Rick Litchfield
24 doubles (all with private bath)

In season (*May 24-October*): $89-$249, including breakfast
Off-season (*November-May 23*): $69-$175, including breakfast
MasterCard, Discover, Visa
Children over 12 welcome
No pets
Open year-round

As much museum as lodging, the Captain Lord lives up to every expectation one might have of a country inn. It is so extraordinary that the proprietors have given public tours of the place.

The house, built in 1812, abounds in unusual architectural details, including a four-story spiral staircase, a three-story suspended elliptical staircase, double Indian shutters, blown-glass windows, *trompe l'oeil* painted doors, original pumpkin pine wide floorboards, and 18-foot bay windows with curved sashes, all in pristine condition. In the gathering room, carpeted with Oriental rugs, photograph albums document the incredible restoration of the house. Visitors are welcome to see the house's common areas and may want to pay special attention to the pictures of each bedroom—the easier to choose where to stay on the next visit. The cupola offers magnificent views of Kennebunkport.

The common rooms are attractively decorated and inviting, but the bedrooms are equally well equipped for lounging: at least two chairs, and sometimes a sofa, provide plenty of room to spread out. The second-floor rooms are unusually large. Six rooms in the front of the house overlook a landscaped lawn and provide a glimpse of the Kennebunk River. Each room is meticulously decorated with reproduction period wallpaper, an antique four-poster bed with a firm mattress, and magnificent color-coordinated linens. Seventeen of the rooms have working fireplaces (wood is supplied), and the furniture is arranged to take best advantage of the fire.

Breakfast is served family style in the modern country kitchen. Seven different kinds of muffins and sweet breads are served each week along with French vanilla yogurt with a fruit topping. Sunday morning breakfast is special, with sticky buns, quiche, and English-style porridge.

Harbourside Inn
Northeast Harbor, Maine 04662
207-276-3272

Innkeepers: The Sweet family
15 rooms and suites (all with private bath)
$85-$210 per couple, including breakfast

No credit cards
Children welcome
No pets
Open mid-June to mid-September

If you are searching for absolute peace and quiet, this is the place to find it. If you want a spectacular ocean view, however, don't come here. The inn's brochure clearly states that when the inn was built, all the land between the harbor and the inn was under one ownership. Now, however, the cottages on the water belong to someone else. Even though the inn's water views have been reduced to mere glimpses, you can look forward to a memorable stay.

The inn stands on a hillside overlooking a stand of pine. There are two buildings on the premises, one for the innkeepers and one for their guests. The substantial three-story house was built as an inn in 1888-89 in the popular Shingle Style. All of its rooms remain old-fashioned but are cheerful and meticulously maintained. All except one of the rooms on the first two floors have fireplaces, which you are encouraged to use. Upon arriving, you will find that your fire has been laid, with extra wood piled by the hearth.

All the rooms are large and bright, and thick walls ensure privacy. Four rooms on the first and second floors have small but fully equipped kitchenettes. The suite (Room 2) on the first floor has a living room with the chairs arranged nicely around the fireplace and a kitchen in an alcove. The second-floor suite (Room 7) has a large living room, again with kitchenette and fireplace, with a glassed-in sunporch just off the living room. Room 4 has an outside entrance for greater privacy and an 1870 queen-size brass bed. For local calls at no charge, you may use the telephone in the common room.

Every room has at least two chairs so that guests can visit by the fire. Although all the rooms have private baths, two do not have showers, so be aware of this when you make your reservation if you must have a shower. (Remember that this is just the kind of place where you may want to soak in a tub.) Do send for the brochure, which diagrams all of the rooms.

A Continental breakfast is served every morning in a bright sunporch furnished with attractive, antique white wicker. You may sip your coffee or tea and eat delicious blueberry muffins on the porch, relax in the living room on comfortable furniture near the woodstove, or retreat to your room.

After breakfast, there is ample opportunity for activity. The area around the inn is honeycombed with woodland trails, and there is access to tennis courts and golf. You can walk from the inn's west drive into Acadia National Park.

John Peters Inn
Peters Point
Blue Hill, Maine 04614
207-374-2116

Innkeepers: Rick and Barbara Seeger
9 rooms (all with private baths)
$70-$90 per couple for rooms, including breakfast, $120 for
   honeymoon suite; 2 housekeeping units, in the carriage
   house, at daily and weekly rates
MasterCard, Visa
Children over 12 welcome
No pets
Open May through October

As soon as you drive through the gates to the John Peters Inn, you'll be struck by its setting. Crowning the lawns and meadows that sweep down to the water on three sides, this 1815 white-columned mansion evokes the antebellum South more than the coast of Maine. Try to arrive early enough to walk through the fields down to the rocky shore before dinner.

Another welcoming way to begin a visit is to stretch car-cramped muscles in the inn's small outdoor pool. Or you may simply want to unwind in your room, enjoying the books or magazines that Barbara has determined will be of special interest to you.

The rooms are unusually spacious and several have sofas and tables; five have fireplaces. The suite has a large deck and wet bar. You have a choice of beds: queen- or king-size or twin.

Other special touches include wonderfully fresh-smelling, line-dried linens (changed daily), fresh flowers, and bowls of fruit.

There's a grand piano in the living room, and chamber music groups sometimes perform here or out on the piazza. A beautiful, unusual Oriental rug covers the floor before a well-used fireplace.

Barbara likes to call her meals "fantasy breakfasts," because they seem to include all the wonderful treats people dream of on a visit to Maine. The pièce de résistance is a lobster omelette garnished with lobster claws to make it look like the critter. Other indulgences include eggs Benedict, homemade granola, grilled muffins, waffles with pecans and fruit (blueberries, apples, or bananas, depending on the season), and fresh fruit and juice. Breakfast is served between 8:00 and 10:00 A.M. on the enclosed porch; lovely china, crystal, and silverware are used, and classical music is playing. The Seegers' engaging Welsh terrier, Doc (DisObedient Canine), has been known to show up dressed in his nightshirt, endearing himself and earning a few treats with his antics.

In addition to the shops, potteries, and sightseeing that abound in the Blue Hill area, you may want to paddle about in the inn's canoe or go for a sail in the 16-foot Widgeon.

Manor House Inn

West Street
Bar Harbor, Maine 04609
207-288-3759

Innkeeper: Mac Noyes
14 rooms (all with private bath), 2 cottages
$74-$140 per couple, including breakfast; $500 per week for cottages
Major credit cards
Children over 8 welcome
No pets
Open mid-April through October

The Manor House may lack water views, but it offers more of the feeling of a country inn than many of Bar Harbor's lodgings. In 1980, it was placed on the National Register of Historic Places.

Most of the rooms are large and furnished with Victorian pieces. Four rooms have working fireplaces. Bright reading lights are considerately placed; lace curtains, brass bathroom fittings, and marble-topped night tables are standard. The cottages in the backyard have kitchenettes, but for stays of a week, guests don't have breakfast privileges at the inn. The Chauffeur's Cottage, with two suites and a bedroom, offers all the antiques found in the inn as well as privacy.

The inn's double parlor has been restored in an understated way, with flowered wallpaper and pleasingly coordinated upholstery. Rare and unusual woodwork (such as cherry banister and stair spindles) is found throughout the house. The servants' bells are still in working order — go ahead and ring them! It took the previous innkeepers three and a half years to find the upper part of a fireplace mantel in one of the parlors; it turned out to be in fifty pieces, which have all been reassembled.

Seven pretty gardens on the property have been arranged so that guests can enjoy a view of them from many of the bedrooms and common rooms. Well-placed benches and chairs indicate clearly that the gardens are to be enjoyed. The flowers are planted so that something will always be in bloom between mid-April and mid-November. The wraparound porch is constantly in use.

Don't plan on spending just the night here. The inn's guests have privileges at the Bar Harbor Club, across the street, where they can enjoy a delicious lunch or a drink. For a small daily fee per couple, guests can use the club's five clay tennis courts and an Olympic-size pool. The water views from the clubhouse and its facilities are terrific.

The Pilgrim's Inn
Deer Isle, Maine 04627
207-348-6615

Innkeepers: Dud and Jean Hendrick
13 rooms (8 with private bath), 1-bedroom cottage down the
  street

$65-$75 per person, MAP; cottage, $180 per couple, MAP, $120 EP; add 12% gratuity
Dining room open to public
No credit cards
Children over 10 welcome
No pets
Open mid-May to mid-October

In 1793, Squire Ignatius Haskell built this house for his wife. He owned a successful sawmill and wanted to live near his business. She was used to the comforts of Newburyport and demanded a civilized home. So he had the house built in Newburyport and shipped it up to Deer Isle.

All the guest rooms are cheerful and simply and pristinely decorated. Colonial colors have been chosen throughout. Braided and rag cover the beautifully refinished floors. The curtains, comforters, and quilts have been made with flowered prints that tie the rooms together. Many of the rooms have wood-burning stoves; six have fireplaces. All the rooms have a view of the water, some of a millpond out back, and others look across the road to the harbor.

The inn has four living rooms. One of the upper two, at the main entrance level, is furnished with Colonial and simple Victorian pieces. The other is a large, comfortable library, filled with a collection of books about Maine. The two on a lower level serve as a bar for the adjoining dining room. The focal points of these rooms are the massive Colonial fireplaces with Dutch ovens. Throughout, there is attractive pottery and artwork from the area, all for sale. The cottage, Number 15, sits in the middle of this picturesque village and includes a living room with open beams and a fireplace, a dining area and powder room, and upstairs a bedroom and bath; the deck overlooks Northwest Harbor.

An extension of the inn itself, a rustic barn has been converted into a dining room. At dinner, the small tables are covered with linen tablecloths and lit by oil lamps. Cocktails and hors d'oeuvres are served at 6:00 P.M. and dinner at seven. The chef is obviously most concerned about variety; entrées can include a Spanish dish such as paella, fresh fish, or grilled tenderloin. Lobster is served, to inn guests only, every Thursday night.

There's much to do in this area, and the innkeepers will be glad to point the way to nature trails or craft shops. Deer Isle itself probably represents the greatest concentration of artists and craftspeople per capita in all Maine.

Westways on Kezar Lake
Route 5, Box 175
Center Lovell, Maine 04016
207-928-2663

Host: Nancy Tripp
7 rooms (some with shared bath), 7 cottages
$130-$175 per couple MAP, $80-$125 EP; weekly rates available
Major credit cards
Children welcome
Pets in cottages only
Open May to October, December to March

This silver-shingled house sits in the woods above Kezar Lake, a clear, deep body of water surrounded by mountains. The house, far from any road, was built as a millionaire's retreat in 1920. In the low-beamed living room are Oriental rugs, a massive fireplace, and furnishings that range from plush to baronial. A glassed-in dining room has great views of the lake and mountains.

Westways is rarely crowded, especially in winter, when sometimes only one room is occupied. Each guest room is splendidly furnished, each so different that you may want to inquire about the choices before booking. There is an elegant blue room, a homier maple room, and a master bedroom, which has the best view of the lake.

The game room, with a two-lane bowling alley, is in a neighboring library. Down by the lake is a dock for sunning and swimming and a screened-in porch right over the water with smashing views of the lake and mountains. Furnished comfortably with some wicker pieces, this is the perfect place to spend a quiet afternoon reading or to have cocktails in the evening. There is a lovely lakeshore walk from the house to a boathouse and beach, where swimming, boating, and picnic tables are available. Cross-country ski trails traverse the property; downhill skiers need drive just 13 miles to Shawnee Peak Mountain, 25 miles to Sunday River.

■ *See also:* Inn at Canoe Point, Bar Harbor, Maine

Massachusetts

Augustus Snow House
528 Main Street
Harwich Port, Massachusetts 02646
508-430-0528

Owner: Anne Geuss
5 rooms (all with private bath)
$145-$175 per couple, including breakfast
Major credit cards
No children
No pets
Open year-round

For the ultimate splurge without pretension, the Augustus Snow House has few rivals in all of New England. No expense was spared in restoring this 1901 house to its Victorian elegance. The bathrooms, believe it or not, are the most talked-about feature.

The Queen Anne house has heavy front doors with oval etched glass and a fleur-de-lis motif carved in the oak. The foyer has a dark rose carpet, a heavy oak table with a large flower arrangement, and a wonderful open view up the staircase. The drawing room is formal, with mauve velvet drawing curtains, brocade parlor chairs and couch, and two matching flowered area carpets.

The breakfast room is exquisite, with oak cross beams on the ceiling, five intimate wrought-iron tables, rose-striped satin upholstered chairs, and a sideboard with leaded bay windows and built-in cabinets on either side. A swinging door into the kitchen may give you a view of the modern, professional service area. For breakfast, phone downstairs in the morning and order anything you wish; specialties will be suggested if you're at a loss. You can start with homemade muffins, a fruit compote, coffee, and juice.

Up the staircase (with a window seat in front of a stained glass window) are four bedrooms, all with large closets, private bath (two with Jacuzzis), wall-to-wall carpeting, ceiling fans, telephone, and TV. The one guest room downstairs has a private entrance, Jacuzzi, and king-size bed. Two of the rooms have large sitting areas: one is country French, and one has a tremendously high bed with a canopy.

The bathrooms, though, are indeed the pièce de résistance. Anne believes that bathrooms are the first place people look, so with that in mind, she began there and furnished the rooms to match. They are lavish, each individually styled with classic Victorian elegance. Room 4 has a mahogany sink cabinet with brass fixtures. Room 2 has the house's original and largest bathroom: a claw-foot tub with brass fixtures and a brass towel warmer. Room 3's bathroom is small, with an ornate marble and brass sink and a circular brass water closet. Room 1 has veined brown and gray marble and a mahogany mirror and toilet seat cover. Finally, Room 5 has an oak and brass commode and a refurbished tin washbasin in an oak cabinet.

Complimentary hors d'oeuvres and cocktails (or hot mulled cider or lemonade) are wonderful in the afternoon. Constantly changing, they may include teriyaki and ginger chicken and pineapple skewers, a warm cheese dip, garlic and cilantro scallops, and asparagus tips wrapped in puff pastry. A 3-minute walk across and down the street is the house's private beach, and there's a screened-in gazebo on the porch just for sitting.

Beechwood

2839 Main Street
Barnstable, Massachusetts 02630
508-362-6618

Innkeepers: Anne and Bob Livermore
6 doubles (all with private bath)
$90-$125 per couple, including breakfast
Major credit cards
Children over 12 welcome
No pets
Open year-round

Beechwood is a many-gabled, many-eaved Victorian summer home from the 1850s that has been meticulously restored with a sure decorator's touch. Each guest room has been created rather than merely furnished. For a quiet, thoughtful retreat or a romantic interlude, you won't be disappointed here. The inn is set off the road just far enough, and there's a wonderful wraparound porch shaded by an ancient beech tree (hence its name).

On entering the rather staid Queen Anne parlor, you'll wonder if the guest rooms follow suit. On the contrary. Entered through a doorway on one side of the veranda, they are light and airy. On the first floor, the Rose Room has a high, carved four-poster, a fireplace, and floor-to-ceiling shuttered windows. The Marble Room has a brass bed, lace curtains, a garden view, and a marble fireplace. Both of these rooms have marble night tables and large bathrooms that combine modern conveniences with antique elegance. The Garret Room, on the third floor, is our favorite, with steeply angled paneled walls and a half-moon window overlooking Cape Cod Bay. Its private bath, down a short flight of stairs, has a double sink and a black and white tile floor. In the summer, warm breezes stir the lace curtains, in front of which sit a table and two chairs, perfect for writing.

On the second floor there's Eastlake, with two double spoon-carved beds and colored glass windows. The cottage is furnished with handpainted cottage furniture from the 1860s which is registered with the Smithsonian. The walls here are painted a muted purple, but they complement the colored glass windows (a yellow-purple color) quite well. The Lilac Room is country Victorian, with a king-size and single bed, and has two entrances: one through the dining room and one on the side of the house.

A full country breakfast is served in the very Victorian dining room at small tables. After breakfast, you might play a game of croquet or walk the pleasant half mile into Barnstable Village or to the harbor, where there is a public beach. The traffic and shops of Hyannis or the peace of the dunes at Sandy Neck are other options. The inn's long, lush backyard has lovely gardens and a hammock.

Brook Farm Inn
15 Hawthorne Street
Lenox, Massachusetts 01240
413-637-3013

Innkeepers: Bob and Betty Jacob
12 rooms (all with private bath)
$65-$135 per couple, including breakfast
MasterCard, Visa
Inquire about children
No pets
Open year-round

The tag line for all the information that comes out of the Brook Farm Inn reads, "There is poetry here." And indeed there is, both literally and figuratively. Named after the original Brook Farm, a literary commune-farm that began in West Roxbury, Massachusetts, in 1841, the inn holds poetry and writing seminars with famous literati. On a broader level, guests tend to be interested in "matters above things material," as they were at the original Brook Farm. But by no means is this a snobbish, elitist, or stuffy place. It just encourages reflection.

The living room holds more than 650 volumes of poetry, many of which are coveted first editions; they are organized alphabetically on floor-to-ceiling bookshelves. A good selection of poetry on tape is available (with headphones); you can take them to your room or wander outside to a solitary chair on the shady lawn. A dictionary, as well as a poem of the day, is always set out. You're welcome to listen to Bob's CD collection of classical music, light opera, and Broadway show tunes. In the bright but warm living room are vintage *Life* magazines and a bound collection of *Berkshire Evening Eagle* newspapers from 1931.

Five of the guest rooms have fireplaces and some have canopy beds. Fires are always laid; a guest need only strike a match. Room 9 is entered through a small door, which leads down into a room with skylights and a chimney running up the middle. Room 8 has twin beds, comfortable armchairs, a gabled roof, rich wallpaper, and a skylight.

Guests enjoy their full breakfast at the long table or at one of the few wrought-iron ones in the simple and sunny enclosed porch. Afternoon tea in the library (the focal point of the inn) is served from a cart that holds Bob's mother's collection of china cups. He also serves his own special blend of sherry.

Given the soft-spoken manner of the innkeepers and the comfortable furnishings, this is the kind of place where guests want to take off their shoes, tuck their feet up, and indulge in a few hours of reflecting over a verse, an issue, or an idea.

The Captain's House Inn of Chatham

371 Old Harbor Road
Chatham, Massachusetts 02633
508-945-0127

Innkeepers: Cathy and Dave Eakin
14 rooms (all with private bath)
$85-$145 per couple, including breakfast
Major credit cards
Children over 12 welcome
No pets
Open mid-February to mid-November

The Captain's House is one of the best-run inns in all of New England. Six English girls on a hotel-management exchange program spend the summer under the Eakins' tutelage, overseeing the day-to-day aspects of running the inn. Think about it — six people (not to mention Dave and Cathy) attending to the needs of fourteen guest rooms! This leaves the Eakins free to enjoy other aspects of innkeeping. But they are in no way absent hosts. An indication of the friendly, homey atmosphere is reflected in the fact that you enter through the back door and the kitchen. (There is also a refrigerator here that you can use.)

The Greek Revival house, just a short walk from the shore, was built in 1839. The living room is covered with Oriental rugs and furnished with exquisite Early American pieces. You eat a breakfast of warm homemade muffins and sweet breads in a modern white garden room, walled in glass. The *Boston Globe* (copies are at the reception desk) is a common sight over morning coffee. The individual tables are set with linen.

Each guest room is named for a clipper ship, and a number have canopy beds. The adjoining Captain's Cottage has three rooms. One extraordinarily special (and very large) room has hand-hewn beams, a fireplace that is almost tall enough to stand in, a long sofa, dark paneling, a lacy white canopy bed, and four fluffy pillows on the bed. Another interesting room is almost split in half by a fireplace; it has low, sloping ceilings and plenty of character. The restored Carriage House in back is tastefully done in more modern country furnishings. Everything is first class here, too. Small groups of friends or families would enjoy it.

The Eakins obviously have impeccable taste and an insatiable appetite for scouring the East for four-posters and wing chairs. "Cathy picks it and I hang it," says Dave in response to a compliment on the period wallpapers and swag curtains.

Quintessential Chatham is a fine old fishing and resort town at the elbow of Cape Cod. Watch the boats coming in at the fish pier in the afternoon, check out the lighthouse on Shore Road, or take a trip to Monomoy Island for some bird-watching. The Eakins will give you a complete sheet of sightseeing suggestions in the area. They are also restaurant connoisseurs; trust their recommendations. Particularly noteworthy and pricey is Café

Elizabeth. The Eakins will gladly make dinner reservations for you and give you typed directions.

Charles Capron House
2 Capron Street
Uxbridge, Massachusetts 01569
Major credit cards
508-278-2214

Hosts: Kenneth and Mary Taft
3 rooms (all with private bath)
$65 per couple, including breakfast
No credit cards
Children not appropriate
No pets
Open year-round

This grand old Victorian house has had all the starch taken out and light and air added. Built on a quiet, shady street on the edge of town for local mill owners in 1865, it has been the Tafts' home for more than twenty years. They are unusually genial hosts who enjoy sharing their appreciation of this little-known area of New England.

The rooms throughout are spacious and well decorated with antiques. Two of the guest rooms have queen-size beds, one has twin beds. Marble-top dressers, a campaign chest, and hand-made quilts add to their charm. The red room is a work of art that has a bathroom with a deep, deep tub.

Although guests can use a comfortable living room, most head for the sunporch, with its wicker and greenery. There are two dining rooms, one with a round table, and a fabulous kitchen in which Mary makes guests feel welcome while she whips up muffins, baked apples, and the like.

Uxbridge is known throughout the country for the fine woolens sold at bargain prices at two old mills. This part of the Blackstone Canal, which was built in 1828, has been restored. A nearby segment, including a scenic millpond, became a Heritage State Park in 1986. Bikers will appreciate the flat land and handsome old houses.

Charles Hinckley House
Box 723
Olde King's Highway
Barnstable, Massachusetts 02630
508-362-9924

Innkeepers: Les and Miya Patrick
4 rooms (all with private bath)
$98-$135 per couple, including breakfast
No credit cards
No children
No pets
Open year-round

The Charles Hinckley House boasts no water view, no beach. Neither is it the place to go if you mind creaking floors, stairs, or beds. But do come if you want authentically restored rooms and hospitality that recall a simpler era. Yes, it's on a busy road, but somehow time and the well-cultivated wildflower garden seem to protect you. There are no brochures in the front hall, no wall-to-wall carpeting. But especially if your visit coincides with a special occasion (you are encouraged to tell them ahead of time), there will be a gracious, country-style red carpet rolled out for you.

The Patricks really want you to have a memorable respite. They want you to drink the complimentary sherry, to smell the cut flowers that grace practically every surface, to eat from the baskets of fresh fruit. Les and Miya have been at this since the early 1970s — he, restoring old houses, she in the catering business. Their lifestyle obviously agrees with them, and it will rub off on you.

Their Federal house is very much a part of this quiet, history-proud side of Cape Cod. Two of the guest rooms are upstairs, both with four-poster beds and quilts, one with a sitting room. All have working fireplaces; one has only a tub. The third, in what once was the summer kitchen, has a private entrance at the side of the house. Though a bit smaller and darker than the others, it features a raised ceiling, skylight, white brick walls, a hearth, and two white wicker chairs as well as a tarnished antique brass bed (queen-size). (Honeymoon couples will get breakfast in bed.) If you want to sleep late, choose the room off the living room — it's darker here in the morning and very romantic.

The small country living room contains more magazines than you could read in a year. Blue love seats flank the fireplace; two armchairs are before the front window. Perhaps a Windham Hill selection will be playing quietly in the background.

The full English breakfast (served between 9:00 and 9:30 A.M.) is no ordinary affair here, in the old tavern-like dining room at intimate tables. It's slow and leisurely, course by course — very country-civilized with well-worn heavy silverware. First comes an urn of Colombian coffee or a pot of special tea, then a delicate fruit plate of papaya and unusually sweet raspberries with warm blueberry muffins. At that time, you choose between two breakfasts — perhaps an egg creation or very thin pancakes with strawberry butter.

The house is as attractive off-season as it is in the summer, and their bookings reflect it; reserve early.

Cyrus Kent House Inn
63 Cross Street
Chatham, Massachusetts 02633
508-945-9104

Innkeeper: Richard T. Morris
8 rooms (with private bath)
$98 per couple, including breakfast
Major credit cards
Children over 12 welcome
No pets
Open year-round

Richard Morris has won awards for the immaculate restoration and transformation of this former sea captain's home. The person who brings the place to life on a day-to-day basis, though, is Mary Flaig, who operates the inn with flair and soft-spoken charm. Together they have created a space that subtly and successfully combines the past and present.

Blue and white runners line the hallways, but the hardwood floors are exposed for your appreciation. The spacious living room with high ceilings is done in similar colors, light blue and oatmeal. To enhance the open and light feel, buttery oak antiques and modern couches have been placed sparingly. Elaborate plaster moldings, brass hardware, ceiling rosettes, and etched marble fireplaces in both the common room and dining room across the hall hark back to an earlier time.

The guest rooms are bright and airy, too. Nothing is overdone; simplicity and elegance reign here. Original art and fresh flowers grace each room. One has a small entrance, a brass bed, and a braided rug. Another has twin beds, stenciling, and lovely curtains. Two rooms (one on ground level and one upstairs) are entered through doors off the small back porch, adding an extra dimension of privacy. Number 5 (the only "dark" room) has an exposed brick chimney coming through the painted beige floorboards, a short bank of windows, and cornices. All the rooms have digital clocks and telephones.

Next door, a converted carriage house boasts a massive

arched window, a cathedral ceiling, a fireplace, a sofa-bed, and a sitting room. It's a masterpiece of architectural interior design.

Chatham has enough variety and activity to satisfy anyone. Within a few minutes' walk of this quintessential but crowded Cape Cod village, Cyrus Kent is on a quiet back road among other historical homes. Be sure to visit Horatio Hall (the converted barn), the innkeepers' own art and antiques gallery; Mary is a painter.

Richard and Peggy DeHan, a fellow innkeeper, have recently purchased and renovated the fifteen-room Cranberry Inn, also in town. The rooms here are more contemporary but quite lovely, with individual climate control, phones, and a new feel to them.

Harbor Light

58 Washington Street
Marblehead, Massachusetts 01945
617-631-2186

Manager: Peter Conway
12 rooms and suites (all with private bath)
$75-$175 per couple, including light breakfast
Major credit cards
Children over 10 welcome
No pets
Open year-round

In the prosperous historic area of Marblehead, Harbor Light is a perfect, easy getaway for Bostonians. Only 15 miles from Logan Airport, the town is a haven for sailors, yachtpeople, antiques shoppers, and historians.

This square, 18th-century house abuts the narrow, winding street. (There's plenty of parking in the rear.) The living room is formal and elegant. Matching sofas flank the fireplace, and a chandelier graces the center of the room. Plush carpeting — Orientals, area, and wall-to-wall — creates a hushed tone throughout the house.

The low-ceilinged guest rooms and suites are quite luxurious, with fine artwork on the walls. Some rooms have a whirlpool and Jacuzzi; others have canopy beds. From the rooftop there's a view of the lighthouse and the harbor.

There's plenty to do in and around Marblehead. The famous painting *The Spirit of '76* hangs in the Town Hall. Take a tour of the Jeremiah Lee Mansion or visit bewitching Salem, a short drive north. The House of Seven Gables and the Peabody Museum are both popular places.

The Inn at West Falmouth
P.O. Box 1111
West Falmouth, Massachusetts 02574
508-540-6503

Owner: Lewis Milardo
9 rooms (all with private bath)
$135-$185 per couple, including breakfast
No credit cards
No children
No pets
Open year-round

The three-story Shingle Style Inn at West Falmouth is an exquisitely restored 1900 home set high off the road. Stately and elegant, it has a very private and secluded feeling. Most people learn of the inn through friends who've stayed here, from business associates who've met here, or through people who have seen the inn on a historical home tour.

To the left of the entrance is the regal main living room, with a perfect blend of contemporary and antique English and Chinese furniture. A tasteful sense of style is clear in the bright chintz and overstuffed sofas. The sunroom, large deck, and heated pool spill off from the living and dining rooms. Breakfast, made from ingredients grown nearby, includes fresh cream, eggs, muffins, and pastries. Tables are set for intimate dining; many of them, like the floor, are faux marble.

A collection of Lewis Milardo's antiques from all over Europe fills the guest rooms. It's an eclectic mix of pieces that complement one another well. Most of the rooms have fireplaces and canopy beds (two are set up with twins), some of which have hand-carved headboards produced by Lewis's brother. All of them are unusual, with an oversize Jacuzzi, telephone, and a view of the water. Some of the rooms have private balconies, others, arched windows. All have a sunny feel despite their large furnishings. With lavish amounts of Italian marble, the bathrooms are worth lengthy visits.

An exquisite garden at the side of the house is a nice place to stop and smell the roses; flower gardens surround the rest of the house. In the back is a tennis court and a small heated pool, good for a quick splash on a humid day. The secluded feeling here inspires long walks and bike rides. On a different note, a manicurist, hairdresser, and masseuse are on call should you decide to pamper yourself.

Falmouth is the port of call for ferries to Martha's Vineyard and Nantucket. The New Alchemy Institute, where organic vegetables are grown with solar and wind power, is nearby and definitely worth a visit. Summer theater is offered at the Falmouth Playhouse, too.

Mostly Hall
27 Main Street
Falmouth, Massachusetts 02540
508-548-3786

Innkeepers: Caroline and Jim Lloyd
6 rooms (all with private bath)
$85-$95 per couple, including breakfast
No credit cards
Children over 16 welcome
No pets
Open mid-February through New Year's Day

Mostly Hall is the incarnation of elegance. Its name comes from the distinct impression you get upon entering the house: it really is "mostly" hall—35 feet worth! Upon further exploration, you'll discover that there are, in fact, other rooms that are equally spacious.

This stately house was Falmouth's first summer residence, built in 1849 for the New Orleans bride of a Yankee sea captain. Architecturally known as a Greek Revival raised cottage, it has a history as grand as the house itself. It is set far back from the busy road, bordered by a wrought iron fence. A row of hedges, an acre of land, and a number of old trees keep noise to a minimum and privacy to a maximum.

Both the country and traditional furnishings in the living/dining room are mostly Victorian. Across from the marble fireplace is a collection of antique clocks. Complimentary sherry, large Oriental carpets, and a blue velvet love seat give the room a southern ambiance. Ten-foot-high shuttered windows (the ceiling is 13 feet) and a long oval table, where breakfast is served, dominate the room.

During warm weather, the morning meal is served on the wide wraparound porch that overlooks the gazebo. The menu might include stuffed French toast or an eggs Benedict soufflé. There is always juice, fruit, and muffins.

A grand stairway leads to the second floor. Each of the large corner guest rooms has a sitting area with plenty of light and space for reading. A good breeze always billows through the large windows. All the rooms have a variety of beautiful antiques, four-poster and canopy beds. One room has a semiprivate bath; it is outside the room, but no one else shares it.

The enclosed widow's walk that caps the third floor is a great place to escape to. Here the furniture is wicker or upholstered in a floral print. The walls are bright blue, but the drapes have a dark print to complement the furniture.

Across from the town green in the historic district, Mostly Hall is convenient place from which to explore town. It's a short drive to the beach, and the island ferries are down the road a few miles, in Wood's Hole. The innkeepers will be happy to help you in choosing a restaurant or in planning an itinerary.

Palmer House Inn
81 Palmer Avenue
Falmouth, Massachusetts 02540
508-548-1230

Innkeepers: Phyllis Niemi-Peacock and Bud Peacock
8 rooms (all with private bath)
$75-$91 per couple, including breakfast
MasterCard, Visa
Children over 14 welcome
No pets
Open year-round

Old World elegance and old-fashioned hospitality characterize the Palmer House Inn, a turn-of-the-century Victorian inn in the center of town. It's a romantic place with lots of modern touches as well as attentive innkeepers.

Upon entering, you will undoubtedly be shown the house and informed of the routine. The morning paper is delivered early; bicycles, cable TV, stereo, books, and games are available; a pay phone is on the first-floor landing; menus and brochures are there for your perusal. Coffee is ready by 7:45 A.M., and breakfast is served at 8:30 or 9:45 A.M. Should you need anything else, you can usually find one of your hosts somewhere in the house.

You will notice an impressive rock maple stairway to the right of the entrance and a rather Victorian parlor with stained glass windowpanes to the left. Old photographs line the mantel and sideboard. The brown velvet couch and armchair are draped with lace. All in all, it's a warm and inviting room.

Rich woodwork and hardwood floors run throughout the inn. Each guest room is furnished with appropriate antiques, quilts, lace doilies, and silk flowers. You'll sleep in a four-poster bed, an impressive sleigh bed, or a brass bed.

A full breakfast is served on china and crystal. In addition to seasonal fruits and homemade pastries, you might get a cheese

blintz with blueberry compote or Finnish pancakes and strawberry soup.

With a fire drawn, the inn is equally inviting in the off-season. In the summer, two theaters, fine restaurants and shops,
and many historic buildings are within walking distance. Of
course, there are always the black, red, and white wicker rockers
on the front porch should you just want to watch the sights
around you.

Whalewalk Inn
169 Bridge Road
Eastham, Massachusetts 02642
508-255-0617

Innkeepers: Norman and Ginny de la Chapelle
10 rooms and suites (all with private bath), 1 cottage
$90-$135 per couple, including breakfast
No credit cards
Children over 12 welcome in suites
No pets
Open April through October

With 3½ acres of lawns, gardens, and meadowlands, the Wha-
lewalk Inn is a quiet place off the very busy Orleans rotary
heading to Provincetown. With a harmonious mix of classic
New England architecture, modern facilities, and country
French sophistication, it's perfect for a tranquil, romantic retreat.

An 1830s whaling master's home, it has two small but relaxing common rooms with working fireplaces. Conversations
over complimentary sherry flow easily here. The decor is contemporary, but comfortable. Executives vacationing with their
families and middle-class couples on a splurge will do equally
well here. Hors d'oeuvres and a wet bar keep guests entertained
in the evenings.

An excellent full breakfast is served. Ginny keeps a file on
what she serves to whom and when and vows never to repeat
herself. Needless to say, she's always experimenting on creative
breakfast items. Guests eat on the flagstone patio or in the
sunny dining room.

Four suites with full kitchens are in the converted barn and
guest house. And a classic Cape saltbox with its own fireplace
has been turned into an airy studio. A harmonious blend of
furniture styles, fabrics, and art are found in the guest rooms in
the main house. The deluxe room has a private entrance off the
patio and a queen-size bed. The other rooms, with twin or

double beds, are all individually styled, with complementary wallpaper, drapes, and pillow fabrics.

Guests can rent one of the inn's bicycles and ride the nearby trails. The Salt Pond Visitor Center of the National Seashore is minutes away, offering protected beaches and walking trails. A Audubon bird sanctuary is nearby in Wellfleet, and the French Cable Station is in Orleans. Glacial freshwater ponds (Pilgrim Lake in Orleans among them) offer swimming and other recreational uses. In 1620, at First Encounter Beach in Eastham, the Pilgrims first met the native Indians. For a daily parking fee, you can also use the beach there.

New Hampshire

The Notchland Inn
Harts Location S.R.
Bartlett, New Hampshire 03802
603-374-6131

Innkeepers: John and Pat Bernardin
11 rooms and suites (all with private bath)
$52-$75 per person, MAP; $45, B&B (not always available)
Major credit cards
Well-behaved children welcome
No pets
Open year-round

Crawford Notch is one of the most spectacular spots in the East, walled by high mountains on either side. At its entrance stands a lone stone house, unlike anything else in New Hampshire. Abandoned for many years, it has now been returned to its former grandeur.

The mansion was built of native granite by Samuel Bemis, a Boston dentist and inventor who began summering in Hart's Location (as this lovely and lonely part of the Notch has always been known) in 1852. He completed the English manor house in 1862 and lived there, a bachelor, until his death in 1881. His caretakers inherited the estate, and it remained in their family until 1983, when the Bernardins bought it.

Which is all by way of saying that the building is fascinating and almost unchanged except that it is undoubtedly cozier now than ever before. It took four years of hard work to restore the hardwood floors and paneling, the embossed metal ceilings, and the tiled fireplaces. Each of the guest rooms is different, with incredible views and antique furnishings, designer fabrics, wall coverings, and wing chairs by the fireplace.

Pat, a professional cook, prepares a five-course dinner that is served by candlelight. Her specialties include beef Wellington, Cajun chicken, and baked stuffed haddock. Soups, appetizers, and desserts are all made from scratch.

In warm weather, there is hiking. The Crawford Path, one of the oldest hiking trails in the country, begins on the property and leads all the way to the top of Mount Washington. You can swim or fish in the Saco River right on the inn's 400 acres. In the winter you can strike out on 25 kilometers of cross-country trails on the property, or it's a mere 8 miles to the 100-kilometer cross-country system maintained at Bretton Woods. Alpine skiing can be found at both Bretton Woods and Attitash, 5 miles in the other direction. There is skating on the pond.

The Bernardins maintain a sanctuary for endangered and rare breeds of domestic animals, so don't be surprised if you are greeted by a llama or long horned woolly goat. One way or another, the couple strives to please and welcomes you as a friend into their country home.

Wonderwell

P.O. Box 128
Philbrick Hill
Springfield, New Hampshire 03284
603-763-5065

Innkeepers: Susan and Samuel Alexander
8 rooms (all with private bath)
$115 per couple, including breakfast; $160, MAP
No credit cards
Children over 3 welcome
No pets
Open year-round except April and from Thanksgiving to
    Christmas

At once an English country estate, baronial mansion, and regal lodge, Wonderwell is a delight. Near Lake Sunapee and only 25 minutes south of Hanover, it attracts, as the brochure suggests, "peaceful people with pampered palates." The home of the Alexander family since 1935, it opened as a country bed-and-breakfast in 1989.

Entering the large, spacious living room, you'll see twin granite fireplaces dominating either end of the two-story room. A balcony wraps around the entire room. Guests tend to stroll around up here and look down into the great room, curl up in window seats, and wander out onto the porch. A Steinway concert piano is frequently the focus of recitals throughout the year—the acoustics are magnificent.

One special feature of the house is an outdoor fireplace that warms the side porch on chilly fall evenings. From there—as from all the porches and terraces—you overlook peaceful fields and woods.

The elegant guest rooms, furnished with antiques, are romantic and comfortable—almost luxurious. Geranium, the third-floor suite, has two connecting bedrooms and bathrooms, with colored tile floors and arched windows. The floor-length mirrors are an unusual feature in a country inn.

For breakfast, you'll be given a card to fill out, telling the innkeepers what you'd like and when you'd like to eat. One special dish, such as Scottish kippers and cottages fries or baked buttermilk pancakes with peaches, sour cream, and cinnamon sugar, is offered each day. You can always get fresh fruit and juice, eggs any style, and a choice of cereals.

Dinner, in a grand room, is served to guests and guests of guests by special arrangement. Wonderwell would be perfect for a family reunion—a great place to take over and imagine it's yours for a day.

Vermont

The Darling Family Inn
Route 100
Weston, Vermont 05161
802-824-3223

Innkeepers: Chapin and Joan Darling
5 rooms (all with private bath), 2 cottages
$65-$85 per couple in rooms, $68 in cottages, including full breakfast
Dinner also served by reservation
No credit cards
Children over 10 welcome in rooms, any age in cottages
Open year-round

Everything about this place is redolent of Vermont hospitality, warmth, and attention to the small pleasures of life. And if that is not enough reason for stopping here, the village of Weston should be.

This 1830 building has been the Darlings' house and inn since 1980. Surrounded by a 400-acre dairy farm, it is set back from the road. The swimming pool, though in the front yard, is landscaped for privacy.

The living room, library, and spacious guest rooms are charmingly decorated in English and American country antiques. Quilts made in the area, braided rugs, and white curtains add a special touch. There are wide-planked wooden floors throughout and detailed stenciling, done by Joan, in the hallways. The fully equipped housekeeping cottages sit on the hill behind the inn.

Before guests turn in for the night, they'll find the bed linen has been turned down and cookies and fresh fruit placed by the bed. Hearty country breakfasts are served in the dining rooms by candlelight. Candlelit dinners are available on request. Guests may bring their own liquor.

Weston and the surrounding area offer plenty of good fare. Weston Priory and its singing monks are only 3 miles away. The village offers a marvelous summer theater, antiques and crafts, unusual shops, and art exhibitions. Skiing abounds in nearby mountains, and cross-country skiing is right out the door.

Edson Hill Manor

R.R. 1, Box 2480
Stowe, Vermont 05672
802-253-7371

Owners: The Heath family
27 rooms (21 with private bath)
$55-$99 per room, EP in summer, $73-$89 per person,
    double occupancy in winter; B&B rates available
Major credit cards
Children welcome
No pets
Open year-round

This 300-acre estate holds an unusual brick mansion patterned on an 18th-century New York design and built in 1940 with bricks from a defunct Burlington hotel. The fireplace tiles were imported from Holland, and the brass accents and roof shingles came from Williamsburg, Virginia. The beams in the living room were hand-hewn for Ethan Allen's barn. Oriental rugs, pine-paneled walls and floors, and floor-to-ceiling windows with elegant drapes further enhance the inn. Most exciting for some guests, Edson Hill Manor has its own stables and riding trails.

The best view is from the room at the end of the hall upstairs (it also has a sitting room). Five guest rooms in the Manor have fireplaces. All the rooms are modestly furnished in pine. Cozy brick hearths, wide-planked floors, and beamed ceilings characterize the sixteen newer rooms in the nearby carriage houses.

The dining room has been redone with simple tables. The views are magnificent — three walls are all window. A variety of meals (New England and Continental) are skillfully served. Breakfast is filled with fresh fruit in every form; lunch is taken by the fire or on the patio. During the summer, the Manor has barbecues. The lounge, at ground level, is also inviting.

The swimming pool, below a skillfully terraced hillside, has award-winning landscaping. The property offers all levels of terrain for ski touring; fine rental equipment and complimentary skiing are available. Come winter, the stables are converted into a ski center. Winter riding and sleigh rides are available. In mild weather, English and Western instruction is given on scenic bridle paths. Stocked ponds, a putting green, and lawn sports are right here. Tennis and alpine skiing are in town, and Stowe is down the road.

1811 House

Manchester Village, Vermont 05254
802-362-1811

Innkeepers: Jeremy and Pat David, Jack and Mary Hirst
14 rooms (all with private bath)
$100-$160 per couple, including full breakfast and gratuity
Major credit cards
Children over 15 welcome
No pets
No pipe or cigar smoking
Open year-round

This New England frame house, built in the 1770s, has been an inn since 1811 except for a thirty-year period when it was the home of Mary Lincoln Isham, the granddaughter of President Lincoln. Since the Hirsts have owned it, the inn has been restored in a Federal style. The elegant period appointments include handsome American and English antique furniture, paintings, Oriental rugs, and porcelains. The tavern has been recreated, complete with carriage lamps, pewter mugs, and horse brasses.

All of the bedrooms are named after a famous person of the early 1800s. Six have working fireplaces, a fine Oriental rug, and a canopy or four-poster bed. The Robinson Room has a marble shower and a porch that overlooks 3 acres of English gardens and a golf course. The Jeremiah French Suite, the only guest room downstairs and one of the most expensive, offers an elegant sitting room. The Hidden Room, the smallest and least expensive, is lovely but not recommended for tall people.

A full English-style breakfast is served: fresh juice and fruit precede bacon and eggs with grilled tomatoes, mushrooms, sautéed apple rings, fried bread, and home fries. Chances are, the eggs were laid the day before.

The Hirsts and Davids combine elegance with informality and ease. Above all else, they want the 1811 House to be a place where guests can take their shoes off, wander into the kitchen, make themselves a cup of tea, and relax.

The Juniper Hill Inn

R.R. 1, Box 79
Windsor, Vermont 05089
802-674-5273

Innkeepers: James and Krisha Pennino
15 rooms (all with private bath, 9 with fireplaces)
$65-$100 per couple, including full breakfast
Prix fixe, single entrée dinner served; open to the public on weekends
Major credit cards
Children over 12 welcome
No pets
Limited smoking
Open May through October, December 20 through late March

Juniper Hill is a 28-room mansion that was built in 1901 by Maxwell Evarts, a lawyer and general counsel for the E. H. Harriman Railroad. He was also a personal friend of Theodore Roosevelt's, who visited Juniper Hill in 1902. The house remained in the Evarts family until 1944, when it became an inn and restaurant. It was later purchased by the Catholic Xaverian Brothers and used for retreats. In 1984, it was purchased by Jim and Krisha Pennino, who are furnishing and restoring the inn to its original splendor.

Visitors immediately enter the immense, oak-paneled living room, which measures 30 by 40 feet. A room this size is a challenge to furnish, but the Penninos have succeeded with well-placed antiques, comfortable lounge chairs, and sofas and writing desks. Excellent Oriental rugs help, too.

The elegance continues in the dining room, where one can enjoy dinner, prepared by Krisha, or the full breakfast prepared by Jim. The dining room also houses a 15-by-5-foot solid oak table that was used by the Evarts; it was sold, but Jim found and bought it. This wonderful table is used for breakfast; guests can sit around it or enjoy the privacy of smaller tables.

All the rooms have been individually furnished and have their own charm. Antique beds and accessories prevail. Many rooms have working fireplaces. Five-foot bath towels are another welcome touch. Because the rooms themselves vary so much (a fact reflected in their prices), be sure to ask for some details about the one you book. Our favorite is number 7 because of the blue and white Delft around the fireplace.

Mount Ascutney ski area is nearby; this solitary mountain is center stage in the splendid view from the veranda and rolling lawn. There is also a pool. Hiking, canoeing, cycling, antiquing, or just gazing at the magnificent scenery are yours to enjoy.

Juniper Hill hosts the Yankee Rambler, which is a pedal-and-paddle vacation package. It includes two nights' lodging, daily breakfast and dinner, canoe, paddles, box lunches, 18-speed bicycles, maps, and shuttle service to and from the canoe launch. Further information can be obtained by contacting the Penninos at Juniper Hill.

Stowehof Inn

Box 1108
Edson Hill Road
Stowe, Vermont 05672
802-253-9722
800-422-9722

Owners: Mr. and Mrs. Peter Bartholomew and Billy O'Neil
46 rooms (all with private bath)
Summer: $78-$105 per person double occupancy, MAP;
    winter: $78-$110; *B&B:* $59-$91 per person (not during
    holiday and foliage periods); add 15% gratuity
Meals served on weekends only from mid-April through
    May, November through mid-December
Major credit cards
Children welcome
No pets
Open year-round

Stowehof is unique, almost eccentric. To begin with, the sod-roofed porte cochere is supported by two giant maple trees. Twinkling white lights and a heavy lavender door greet guests before the bellhop does. Inside, hand-planed wide floorboards begin to convey the feeling of an unusual European hotel.

The multilevel living room is divided into three areas: one has a sunken fireplace, one a huge glass pane affording spectacular mountain views, and another is an imaginative alcove. These nooks and corners (with more downstairs in the lounge) are decorated with peculiar antiques and artifacts. Game tables suit every mood, and an almost life-size king, queen, and jack of hearts are painted on the wall. The common room furnishings are modest, but the taproom resembles a Tyrolean bar with barrel chairs, a red rug, and beer steins lining the shelves. A replica of the interior of an old Vermont covered bridge is another imaginative architectural touch.

Upstairs are the distinctive guest rooms, which have been individually designed and furnished. Some have mirrors for walls; some have an extra Murphy bed; some have Chippendale desks or Queen Anne chairs. The rooms classed as superior are spacious, but the deluxe rooms are larger, with private dressing and sitting rooms and mirrored doors. Fireplaces and honeymoon suites are also available. Though it's a bit damp in the summer, one suite incorporates a beautiful greenhouse. All the rooms have an adjoining balcony or patio, but the nicest views are found in the back, toward the birches, fields, and mountains.

The chef creates American cuisine. The elegant dining room is less flamboyantly decorated than the rest of the inn.

There is an attractive heated pool, four tennis courts, a sauna, and sleigh rides in the winter. Golf, tennis, and running packages are available.

The White House of Wilmington
Route 9
Wilmington, Vermont 05363
802-464-2135

Innkeeper: Robert Grinold
12 rooms (all with private bath)
$75-$95 per person double occupancy, $170 per person per weekend, MAP
No credit cards
Children over 10 welcome
No pets
Open year-round

The White House of Wilmington is a stately 1915 mansion crowning a hill above Route 9. Built by a lumber baron, it has wide staircases, French doors, and generous rooms. But it has modern features as well — the porch has been enclosed to make a delightful, sunny cocktail lounge, and the large basement is now a fledgling health spa. The White House is less pretentious and more fun than similarly priced inns in the area, but it is expensive. It's an inn for a variety of moods and activities. Guests can spend the day on the trails (the inn has its own cross-country touring center), meet other guests in the convivial lounge, and end the evening with a romantic dinner in the paneled dining room.

The somber living room has an Old World ambience: dark paneling, a fireplace, a high ceiling, floor-length velvet curtains, and leather armchairs. With lots of hanging plants, a glass wall, a superb valley view, several small tables, and a square central bar, the lounge is well used throughout the day, beginning with breakfast.

The main dining room has chandeliers and silver wall lamps. Fine meals feature such choices as frogs' legs, shrimp scampi, and tender medallions of veal. One special feature of the White House is that guests can have breakfast wherever they want and they can request anything within reason—from last night's quiche to traditional bacon and eggs.

Eight of the guest rooms, handsomely furnished with high double beds (firm mattresses and several soft, bulky pillows), large wardrobes, and night tables with full-size lamps, are spacious and sunny. Polished wood floors, thick drapes framing large windows, solid walls and doors, and white tile bathrooms with old-fashioned tubs (the showers are not terrific) are reminders of their original grandeur. All these rooms have pleasant valley views; two have private terraces, and the suite has a fireplace.

Winter guests can enjoy the ski touring center, which offers rentals, instruction and guided tours. In the summer, guests can relax by the pool or read in the garden. There's also a basement-level pool, a whirlpool, and a sauna.

Seaside

You can see the sea, or at least a harbor, from all these inns.

Maine

Buck's Harbor Inn
South Brooksville, Maine 04617
207-326-8660

Innkeepers: Peter and Ann Ebeling
6 rooms, 1 suite (all shared baths)
$50 per couple, $60 for suite, including full breakfast
MasterCard, Visa
Children welcome
No pets (sometimes off-season)
Open year-round

Buck's Harbor is one of the most beautiful little byways along the Maine coast. Its atmosphere still reminds one of the late 1800s to 1930s, when vacationers arrived by steamer from New York and Boston and settled in for months at one of two large summer hotels.

The present inn was built in 1901 as an annex to one of these more elaborate but long vanished hostelries. It looks more like a Maine farmhouse, the kind with a mansard roof and attached barn in the back. The rooms are simple and sunny, drenched in the light and fresh feel of the sea. The suite, one large room with a queen-size bed and a smaller room with a single bed, is a wonderful deal for a family.

Downstairs there's a double living room, a dining room (open to the public), and a glass-faced breakfast room; there's another sitting room on the third floor.

The nearly circular harbor is now a quiet backwater favored by yachtsmen. There's a small, old shingle yacht club across the street and a good little restaurant and snack bar next door; a crafts store or three are within walking distance. Day sails are usually available from the dock.

The town of South Brooksville isn't far from Blue Hill. The best way to come is still by boat, but if you must drive, it's worth it.

Craignair Inn at Clark Island
Spruce Head, Maine 04859
207-594-7644

Innkeepers: Norman and Terry Smith
9 doubles, 5 twins, 2 singles (shared baths), 6 rooms in annex (private baths)
July and August: $60 per couple, $75 with private bath, including full breakfast
Off-season: $55 per couple, $65 with private bath, including full breakfast
MasterCard, Visa
Children welcome
Pets welcome
Open year-round except February

The inn, surrounded by flower and vegetable gardens, stands on 4 acres of shorefront in the very quiet town of Spruce Head. There are spectacular wide views of the bay, with hundreds of lobster pots being hoisted by lobster boats. Craignair originally housed workers from the nearby quarry. Guests of the inn are allowed to explore nearby Clark Island, accessible by foot across a small causeway that's just a minute's walk from inn's front door. The island is the primary attraction of the inn, so it shouldn't be missed. There, guests can walk the many trails, watch for deer and mink in meadows, sight the birds common to this area, fish for mackerel or shellfish, swim in the quarry's warm water, and admire the beautiful water lilies growing on the smaller quarries. The inn is most attractive to visitors who are fond of simplicity and natural beauty.

The bedrooms are sunny and cheerful and simply furnished, with painted iron beds and painted wooden furniture. Eight baths are shared among all rooms in the main building. In the early evening or morning there can be a wait if the inn is full. Half of the rooms benefit from the great view, so be sure to ask for a room with a view of the bay when you make your reservation.

The common rooms are all full of antiques that have been collected by the proprietors on their many trips abroad. The sitting room/library, with its Franklin stove and overstuffed furniture, can be especially cheery on a foggy day. The dining room, the heartbeat of the inn, is oriented to the view, but if it's foggy you will still enjoy it because of the fine antiques displayed on the walls and in hutches.

Checked tablecloths in the morning and peach linens at night add a nice touch to the dining room. Steve Watts, the chef, is known especially for his homemade pastries and bread. There's a full menu, and many of the vegetables are grown right in the Smiths' garden (if you wake early, you will see Terry picking). A shore dinner is served every night. The inn has a full liquor license.

Dockside Guest Quarters

Box 205
Harris Island Road
York, Maine 03909
207-363-2868

Innkeepers: The Lusty family
5 cottage apartment/suites, 16 doubles (13 with private bath)
Cottage apartment/suites $110.50 for doubles with private
    bath $70-78, doubles with shared bath $46
All 3 meals served
2-day minimum stay July through September, lower spring
    rates and June package
No credit cards
Children welcome
Pets welcome with prior approval
Open Memorial Day to Columbus Day

People often drive hundreds of miles farther up the Maine coast to find what is here at Dockside: peace and quiet and outstanding views of the harbor and coastline. The secluded inn is on what is essentially an island.

The Quarters comprise the Maine House and several multi-unit cottage buildings. The Maine House has five bedrooms with painted pine floors and simple country decor; the rooms on the second floor share a common outside deck that offers spectacular views of the water. The sunny, contemporary cottages stand along the shoreline, offering decks with comfortable chairs for lounging.

The living room in the Maine House is decorated in period antiques. Ship models, paintings of clipper ships, early marine prints and lithographs, scrimshaw, and books on nautical and Maine subjects abound. A telescope on the second floor provides a good view of some of the boats passing by; the innkeepers have printed up their own Boat Watcher's Guide to help identify them.

Dockside Dining Room is a popular restaurant in the area, but it is far enough from the inn not to disturb guests' sense of being on their own private island. Of course, it overlooks the water, too, and the menu is primarily seafood, although roast duckling is a specialty of the house. Cocktails are available.

Breakfast is served buffet style in the Maine House and in fine weather can be enjoyed outside. Seven acres of grounds are meticulously planted with annuals. Old wooden chairs on the lawn are perfect for enjoying great views, north out to the yacht basin and east out to sea.

David Lusty and his son, Eric, frequently take guests on motorboat excursions though York Harbor and nearby waters; both of them hold Coast Guard licenses.

The Driftwood Inn & Cottages
Bailey Island, Maine 04003
207-833-5461

Innkeepers: Mr. and Mrs. Charles Conrad
16 doubles, 9 singles (shared bath), 4 housekeeping cottages
$60 double, $40 single EP, $50 per person MAP, $550 per
  couple per week MAP; housekeeping cottages from $225
  per week for 2, $375 per week for 4 people
Lunch also served
No credit cards
Children welcome
Pets in cottages only
Open June to mid-October

The Driftwood is a weathered shingle complex perched on the edge of the sea — a fading breed of Maine summer inn. Meals are served in an open-timbered dining room, where every table has a view of the water. Sunday lunch often brings roast turkey with all the fixings.

The bedrooms are divided between three houses, each with its own common rooms. The bedrooms themselves are simple, with unfinished wood walls, the way Maine seaside rooms have always been, and in many of them you can hear the sound of waves crashing against the rocks. Some are on the small side, but they are all neat.

There is a saltwater swimming pool down by the rocks that's good for children. And you can walk along the water a ways, up a wonderful old path called the Giant Stairs. There is also a private dock.

The Driftwood sits at the end of a narrow road, near the tip of Bailey's Island — which isn't an island at all anymore, thanks to the series of bridges that link it to a scraggly peninsula, bounding Casco Bay. "Bailey's" is known for its restaurants and boat excursions, which range from deep sea fishing expeditions to the ferry into Portland. Once you are here (it's a relatively short distance up the coast), you need do very little driving.

The East Wind Inn and Meeting House
P.O. Box 149
Tenants Harbor, Maine 04860
207-372-6366

Innkeepers: Tim Watts and Ginnie Wheeler
22 rooms (8 with private bath), 3 suites, 1 apartment
Rooms $64-$82, suites $94, apartment $120 (lower off-season)
Breakfast and dinner served
Major credit cards
Children over 12 welcome
No pets
Open year-round

The East Wind is on beautiful Tenants Harbor — a picture-perfect Maine fishing village. From its wraparound deck, with plenty of chairs and rockers, there's a prime view of the continuous commercial and pleasure activities of the harbor. The food is excellent — lots of good Maine specialties.

The inn has an old building and a new building; the new one can be used as a conference center. The rooms are simple and kept immaculately clean. The older rooms are furnished with oak bureaus, Victorian side chairs, and antique brass beds. Most of them have terrific views of the harbor.

The lobby, which is also used as the living room, has unpretentious, old furniture. Be sure to read the guest book; former guests rave about the food. Besides the standard Maine fare, which is delicious here, the menu at night boasts Penobscot Bay bouillabaisse (a classic stew of mussels, shrimp, scallops, and fish in a broth of wine, leeks, garlic, and fennel) and Cajun-style blackened haddock as well as daily features. All of the breads and desserts are made on the premises.

Eggemoggin Inn
R.F.D. Box 324
Little Deer Isle, Maine 04650
207-348-2540
Winter address: 3681 Seminole Avenue
Fort Myers, Florida 33901
813/694-6417

Innkeepers: Sophie Broadhead and Barbara Allen
8 doubles (1 with private bath)
$45-$65, EP
Breakfast served
No credit cards
Children welcome
No pets
Open Memorial Day to October 21

This very secluded inn has stunning 270-degree water views and is an incredible bargain. The master bedroom, with the one private bath, is huge. It has its own porch overlooking the well-maintained, simple grounds and, in the distance, a view of an island with a lighthouse and the mainland beyond.

The rooms are all simple, clean, and very airy. The living room has an eclectic collection of furniture accented by crocheted coverlets and braided rugs. Both a screened and an open porch have spectacular views.

Breakfast is served at two tables for four. A refrigerator is available for storing perishables for a picnic lunch or dinner.

Five Gables Inn
Murray Hill Road
East Boothbay, Maine 04544
207-633-4551

Innkeepers: Ellen and Paul Morisette
15 rooms (all with private bath)
$80-$120 per room, buffet breakfast included
MasterCard, Visa
Children not appropriate
No pets
Open mid-May to November

The Five Gables was built as the Forest House in 1865, an unpretentious guest house to take the overflow from the stick Gothic cottages that hug this little bay.

East Boothbay, of course, isn't Boothbay. One of Maine's still-active boatbuilding communities, it is now a shade off the tourist track, and the Five Gables sits up a dead-end road, overlooking the water from a small knoll. As the Forest House, the inn snoozed away most of the 20th century. Then Ellen and Paul Morisette, who already owned the Kennistin Inn in Boothbay, spent a year rebuilding it from the bottom up and opened the Five Gables in 1989.

Never was the Forest House this grand. The whole facade is

now smartly painted, and the period detailing has been high-lighted. The long front veranda is now perfectly plumb. A new fireplace warms the large combination living and breakfast room, and spiffy new wing chairs and well-chosen antiques have been carefully mixed.

The Morisettes' daughter-in-law is a decorator in California, and each of the guest rooms attests to her skill. Five have new working fireplaces, and all have new baths and are nicely furnished in reproduction pieces, with interesting art. The least expensive rooms in the house, those in the four smaller gables, are very appealing, too.

The Gosnold Arms

HC 61, Box 161
Northside Road
New Harbor, Maine 04554
207-677-3727

Innkeepers: The Phinney family
12 inn rooms (all with private bath), 11 cottage units
$98-$128 per couple, MAP
MasterCard, Visa
Children welcome
No pets
Open mid-June to November

This inn and cottages are in New Harbor, one of Maine's love-liest fishing and lobstering harbors. The food is good Down East cooking, and the views from the waterfront cottages give guests ample opportunity to watch life in a lobstering village. The overall atmosphere is of tranquillity, though not isolation. The grounds and buildings are well maintained. Small Brothers and the New Harbor Co-op, two of Maine's best known and least expensive lobster restaurants, are a short walk away.

In the main inn, there is an assortment of single and double rooms, most with water views. There are also cottages, some of which have fireplaces. Be sure to ask for one with a good view of the water. Next to the cottages is a large deck where guests can sit and watch all of the activity on the harbor. The view extends from the harbor out to the ocean.

The glassed-in dining porch in the main inn, overlooking the harbor, seats about eighty and is open to the public for breakfast, dinner, and Sunday brunch. Dinner entrées include steak, roast beef, Maine lobster dishes, and fresh fish cooked many ways. Homemade desserts top off the meal.

Grey Havens Inn
Reid Park Road, Box 308
Georgetown, Maine 04548
207-371-2616

Innkeepers: The Hardcastle family
14 doubles (11 with private bath)
$65-$125 per couple, including breakfast
Dinner also served
No credit cards
Well-behaved children welcome by prior arrangement
No pets
Open mid-June to mid-October

On a rugged hillside, this solid and magnificent old inn was built in 1904 as a hotel. It's listed on the National Register of Historic Places as the "last Shingle Style hotel on the Maine coast." Half of the bedrooms, the living and dining rooms, and two porches have stunning views of tiny green islands that seem to go on forever. Upon entering the inn, one gets an immediate

sense of peace and quiet. When guests arrive, Hilda drops everything to greet and settle them in. The innkeepers care a great deal that their guests get the rest they've come here for.

The guest rooms are large enough for a queen-size, double, or two twin beds. Four special rooms in the turrets are larger and very charming and have spectacular 180-degree views of the water. All the rooms have quilts or antique bedspreads, brass and iron beds, and Victorian painted furniture. The halls have been covered with an attractive carpet, so don't expect to hear any creaky floors.

A substantial buffet breakfast with hot blueberry muffins is served from an antique sideboard in the large country dining room. The guests return dishes to the long harvest table because they want to — it's that kind of place. Dinner features native seafood, occasional fresh breads, and southern favorites of the Texas-born owners. The menu is posted on a blackboard and the price includes soup, salad, and an entrée. Dinner, served by a very friendly staff, is open to the public but generally only residents come; it gives the inn a special community feeling.

The huge living room and is dominated by an immense fieldstone fireplace. The pine walls are painted white with blue trim, and comfortable wicker furniture has been strategically placed to provide quiet sitting areas. You can't help but notice the lovely collection of baskets that hang from a huge beam. Enjoy the view from the original 12-foot picture window that was brought down from Rockland on an ice barge in 1904. The rocking chairs on the front porch are perfect for experiencing the tranquillity of a moonlit night or quiet early morning.

It's fun to watch the lobster boats haul their traps just a few feet from the rocky shore. There's an Audubon Society sanctuary just down the road, and guests can row across the tiny harbor to an island nature preserve. Reid State Park, with its spectacular cliffs and some of Maine's best beaches, is only a few minutes away.

Inn at Canoe Point
Box 216
Hulls Cove, Maine 04644
207-288-9511

Innkeeper: Don Johnson
5 rooms and suites (all with private bath)
$95-$160 per couple, including breakfast
No credit cards

Not appropriate for younger children
No pets
Open year-round

Tasteful and romantic, sophisticated but accessible, the Inn at
Canoe Point has a stunning location, a small number of rooms,
and peace and quiet. For those who want a retreat, it pretty
much has it all.

After driving through several acres of woods toward the
water, off the busy road heading into Bar Harbor, you reach this
timber and stone house. The reception area is also a living room
with a large fieldstone fireplace, hardwood floors, and comfortable furniture. You'll probably only use it as an entrance
because as long as there's daylight, your time indoors will be
spent in the Ocean Room.

This room overlooks the rocky coastline, with windows exposing 180 degrees of woods, water, and the elements. Dou-
bling as the breakfast room, it has oatmeal-colored wall-to-wall
carpeting, which muffles conversations and gives the room a
contemporary feel. There's a fieldstone fireplace here as well,
and classical music fills the air.

A light gray carpet runs up the stairs and down the hallway
lined with built-in bookcases, from which you help yourself.
The guest rooms, with down comforters, double pillows, fresh
flowers, and fine port, are in keeping with the contemporary
feeling. The Master Suite, with French doors, and the Anchor
Room have private decks overlooking the water. Up a steep set
of steps, the Garret Suite encompasses the entire third floor.
There's a clear view of the ocean from the bed. Since it also has
a pull-out bed, it's a good choice for a family or couples traveling
together. The Garden Room, once the potting room, is surrounded on three sides by windows that open up onto woods
and ocean.

The delightful full breakfast, served at simple, contemporary
tables for four, might include broiled grapefruit and blueberry
pancakes. On warm summer mornings, you'll eat on the deck
perched over the rocky coast. Watch the sailboats drift by, listen
to water splash on the rocks, and you'll hardly realize you're 2
miles from one of the most popular resort towns in New England. You also won't have a single doubt why you chose the Inn
at Canoe Point.

great

Nannau-Seaside Bed & Breakfast

P.O. Box 710
Lower Main Street
Bar Harbor, Maine 04609
207-288-5575

Innkeepers: Vikki and Ron Evers
4 rooms (1 with private bath)
$55-$85 per couple, including breakfast
MasterCard, Visa
Children "above the age of reason"
No pets
Open May through October

There are many good reasons to come to Bar Harbor, such as views of the powerful Atlantic Ocean and the famous storybook cottages (read "mansions"). Surprisingly, there aren't many places that fit the bill, but Nannau satisfies both those requirements and then some. It's rare to find a place so unpretentious and immediately inviting.

About a mile out of town, surrounded by acres of woods and abutting Acadia National Park, the 1904 Shingle Style summer cottage looks large enough to have at least twice the number of guest rooms. To say that they are spacious is an understatement.

The whole house is done in an eclectic style, with a predominance of English Aesthetic furnishings and period flowered wallpapers. Stacks of magazines are everywhere. Worn Oriental rugs on the wooden floors lend a comfortable, homey feeling. In one room are overstuffed chairs and couches; in another, dark wicker chairs are grouped in front of a large bay window that looks down to the water. Through two sets of French doors is a screened porch with lots of plants and chairs. On chilly summer evenings, a fire is likely to be lit in the fireplace. If you don't mind a slight chill in the air, you can come in the shoulder seasons, when Bar Harbor is quieter and the Atlantic more fierce.

The guest room on the third floor has straw mats on the floor, a sitting area, and a queen-size bed. Two rooms on the second floor have fireplaces, views of the water, and a sitting area. The bathrooms have marble sinks and claw-foot tubs, some with hand-held shower nozzles.

Breakfast is served at one long table in an elegant but inviting dining room, with deep burgundy full-length drapes. There are eight choices, including Belgian waffles with whipped cream and strawberries, and homemade croissants are always available.

Though the Everses would like you to stay a couple of days to fully appreciate the area, a two-night minimum (usually the rule in Bar Harbor) is not required. Be sure to make time for afternoon tea at the Jordon Pond House in Acadia National Park. It's served on a large expanse of lawn, where the mountains rise majestically from the deep lake. With woods all around you, it's easy to feel peaceful and secluded. It's no wonder there are so many repeat visitors here.

Rock Gardens Inn

P.O. Box 178
Sebasco Estates, Maine 04565
207-389-1339

Innkeepers: Neil and Ona Porta
4 doubles (all with private bath), 10 cottages
$120-$126 per couple for rooms, MAP; $120-$164 for cottages
3- to 5-night minimum in cottages, depending on season
No credit cards
Children welcome
No pets
Open June to mid-September

Rock Gardens Inn is perched on a rocky peninsula that extends into Casco Bay. If you like to gaze out at the water, this is the place to come. You can enjoy water views in three different directions, watch the sunset, or enjoy the well-landscaped grounds and flower gardens. Rock Gardens offers the peace and tranquillity of a small country inn, but the services of a large resort are available nearby.

Sebasco Estates, just a short walk from the inn, allows guests to use all of its facilities. The huge swimming pool, with its 180-degree view of Casco Bay, can be used at no charge. All the other activities must be paid for; these include golf, tennis, and lawn bowling. There are also movies, bingo, and dancing at night.

There are rooms in the main inn as well as in cottages that have been strategically built for water views. Point of View, Trail's End, and 20th Hole have the best views. The smallest cottages have two bedrooms, the largest four, and share a common living room. All the cottages have fireplaces, and many have glass porches or sundecks. Some have wall-to-wall carpeting; some still have a "cottagey" feeling to them, whereas others seem more like a modern home. Rock Gardens is the kind of place where guests get to know one another during their stay, and many congregate in the main inn before dinner.

The main inn has a small sitting area with white wicker

furniture. The dining room is small but very pleasantly decorated in blue and white. The food is good Down East cooking and includes chicken pie, roast lamb, fish, lobster, and homemade desserts. Once a week there's a lobster cookout, with free cocktails.

Sparhawk Resort
Box 936
Shore Road
Ogunquit, Maine 03907
207-646-5562

Innkeeper: Blaine Moores
78 suites and doubles, 4 apartments
$120-$140 per couple rooms, including breakfast; $135-$170, apartments
Major credit cards
Children welcome
No pets
Open mid-April through October

Sparhawk is an attractive motel just minutes from Ogunquit's major attractions. The solid buildings are well away from the road and its street noise. The overall feeling here is of peace and quiet — every detail has been attended to.

The rooms are all very large for a motel and attractively decorated with top-of-the-line reproduction furniture. The beds have beautiful white bedspreads, and the fabrics and color schemes are well coordinated. Just about every room has a great ocean and beach view and a private outside deck, and they all have individual climate controls, a TV, and a small refrigerator.

The Ireland House suites are perfect for those who are spending some time here and need to spread out. Each suite has a large sofa that overlooks the beach and ocean. Rooms 79 and 45 are the best.

Breakfast may be taken in the very attractive Sparhawk Hall, where cards, games, magazines, and books are also available. There's always a staff member on duty who is more than happy to answer questions about what to do and where to go. Activities on the well-tended grounds include swimming in the large and clean heated pool, tennis, shuffleboard, and croquet.

Tootsie's Bed and Breakfast
R.F.D. 1, Box 252
Jonesport, Maine 04694
207-497-5414

Innkeeper: Charlotte Beal
3 rooms (shared baths)
$30 per couple, $25 single occupancy, including full breakfast
No credit cards
Children welcome ($5 extra for one or two in same room)
Well-behaved pets welcome
Open year-round

This was the first bed-and-breakfast in Washington County, and it's still one of the best bargains in Maine. Washington County, we should explain, is the large swatch of Maine that lies "down east" from Bar Harbor. It is reminiscent of the way more southerly (or westerly) parts of Maine were twenty to fifty years ago.

Jonesport is a genuine fishing and lobstering village connected to Beals Island, which is linked, in turn, to Great Wass Island, where you can walk for many hours through the pine forest and along the rocky shore. It's connected by a bridge rumored to have been purposely built low enough to exclude sailing yachts.

Charlotte Beal (called Tootsie by her grandchildren) lives down near the water in the kind of Maine house that looks small from the outside but swells when you go inside. It's also so spotless and neat that surfaces shine. "Guests tell us that staying here is like going to Grandma's," Charlotte Beal says, "and I consider that quite a compliment!"

The rooms share a bath. One has a double bed, one twins, and one a double and a twin.

■ *See also:* The Colony, Kennebunkport, Maine; Black Point Inn, Prouts Neck, Maine

---

Massachusetts

Seaward Inn
Marmion Way
Rockport, Massachusetts 01966
508-546-3471

Innkeepers: Anne and Roger Cameron
31 rooms (all with private bath), 7 cottages
$126-$164 per couple, MAP
No credit cards
Children welcome

No pets
Open mid-May to mid-October

With brown shingles and beautiful landscaping, Seaward Inn seems very much a part of the granite ledge from which it overlooks Sandy Bay. The spectacular view follows guests inside, into a glass-walled sunroom that's filled with flowers, greenery, and comfortable chairs.

The gracious living room has Oriental rugs and its share of antiques. There are three homey dining rooms, one with a corner full of more than 5,000 clothespins strung together. Each bears the name of the guest who used it as a napkin holder. Some clothespins have been used every summer for more than thirty years.

Roger and Anne Cameron have been welcoming guests to their inn since 1945. As in all seasons, Roger can be found somewhere on the 5 rocky acres, probably tending one of the gardens that supply the dinner tables with greens, flowers, and herbs. Anne tends to be in the kitchen, elbow deep in preparations for the next meal.

The rooms — sea-bright, crisp, and clean — are scattered about the main house, the nine-unit Breakers (across Marmion Way, right on the bay), and in assorted small cottages. A few have TVs, and eight cottages have fireplaces. All of them have night lights and writing tables.

Behind the inn is a sheltered, spring-fed pond with a small sandy beach. A path winds along the shore and through tall blueberry bushes into small woods. Rustic benches stand along the way.

Rockport, incidentally, is "dry," but the inn will serve your own wine with dinner. Guests can use the Rockport Country Club, and there is a 9-hole putting green on the grounds. Tennis, shore fishing, horseback riding, and bicycle rentals are also available. Old Garden Beach is a 5-minute walk down Marmion Way, and the village of Rockport, thick with shops and galleries, is just a mile away. The Camerons will pick up guests at Boston's Logan Airport or at the Rockport train station.

Windamar House
568 Commercial Street
Provincetown, Massachusetts 02657
508-487-0599

Innkeeper: Bette Adams
6 rooms (share 3 baths), 2 efficiencies

$50-$72 per couple, including breakfast; $535-$550 per week
   for efficiencies
No credit cards
No children
No pets
Open year-round

Windamar House is a charming home dating from the
mid-1800s in the quiet, residential East End of Provincetown.
Overlooking Cape Cod Bay, it is within walking distance of
downtown Provincetown, with its fine restaurants, shops, antiques stores, and galleries.

Bette Adams has been the owner/innkeeper here since 1980
and has tastefully redecorated the guest quarters. Bright, cheery
wallpaper combinations are complemented by antiques and
original artwork. Some rooms have color-coordinated handmade quilts; each room is different. The Studio Room, with a
cathedral ceiling, queen-size bed, antique love seat, armoire,
and wall of glass, is the most spectacular room and does cost a
bit more than the others, but it's well worth the difference.

The two apartments are fully equipped and self-sustaining.
One opens onto a flagstone patio and grape arbor; the other, on
the third floor, offers an excellent view, not only of the gardens
at the back of the house, but of the bay and harbor as well.

The common room in the center of the house allows guests to
watch TV and enjoy the Continental breakfast set out each
morning. A refrigerator and toaster oven are also available to
guests.

Windamar House offers a rarity in a crowded spot like
Provincetown — free parking at the back of the property. In this
yard guests can also barbecue, picnic, and sunbathe.

The relaxation one gains from the dunes, the bay, and the
ocean coupled with the charm and warmth of Bette Adams
cannot be equaled.

■ *See also:* The Inn on Cove Hill, Rockport, Massachusetts;
The Lothrop Merry House, Vineyard Haven, Massachusetts;
The Oak House, Oak Bluffs, Massachusetts

Rhode Island

Bannister's Wharf
Bannister's Wharf
Newport, Rhode Island 02840
401-846-4500

Manager: Jan Buchner
7 rooms and suites (all with private bath)
Rooms $100, suites $140; off-season: rooms $75, suites $100
Major credit cards
Children welcome
No pets
Open year-round

You might have a hard time finding this place even though it's in one of the most popular areas in Newport. Don't search for something that looks like regular lodgings; look instead for some of the most luxurious yachts, elegant restaurants, and smart shops.

Smack dab in the middle of this classy clutter are simple shingled structures with dark green trim built over the wharf. Guests staying here become part of the Newport yachting set — without having to own a yacht. The rooms are air-conditioned so that guests can get relief from the noisy nightlife that roars on till one in the morning.

The rooms are very much like summer cottages, with low ceilings, café curtains, and wicker furniture. Excellent prints of harbor and yachting scenes accent the light yellow walls.

The Clarke Cooke House, part of the Bannister Wharf complex, is one of the best restaurants in town. It has a formal dining room and several other more casual rooms, with lighter fare and dancing. Don't miss the Sunday brunch; it's not elaborate but there's a lot for the price. Many other excellent restaurants and shops are in the immediate vicinity.

Ski Lodges

All of these places cater to skiers in the winter but are open, usually at reduced rates, in the summer as well.

Maine

Sunday River Inn
R.F.D. 2, Box 1688
Bethel, Maine 04217
207-824-2410

Forget it stay at the Summit

Innkeepers: Peggy and Steve Wight
12 rooms, 4 bunk rooms (all with shared bath), also 4 rooms,
    2 baths in a housekeeping chalet, 1 apartment for 4;
    groups by reservation
$32-$48 per person, MAP
Major credit cards
Children welcome
No pets
Open Thanksgiving to mid-April

This is a no-frills, clean, friendly inn, oriented to groups and families. Peggy and Steve Wight obviously enjoy working with families and outdoor enthusiasts. The guest rooms are plain and bright, accommodating one or several persons. The dorms are down in the basement, off the game room. There is a beamed and paneled living room with a large stone fireplace and a cheery dining room where meals are served buffet style.

The inn has its own 25-mile network of cross-country ski trails, which, thanks to the high elevation and constant maintenance, are superb after a snowfall and passable even when it hasn't snowed for weeks. Sunday River Ski Resort, a half mile down the road, is also known for its standout snow conditions.

The inn has an apartment that sleeps four over at the cross-country ski center. A chalet at the side of the property contains four rooms with twin beds, two baths, and a common room with a kitchenette; it is available year-round. Both are available on either a housekeeping or an MAP basis.

Massachusetts

Stump Sprouts
West Hill Road
West Hawley, Massachusetts 01339
413-339-4265

Innkeepers: Lloyd and Suzanne Crawford
Accommodates maximum of 20 guests
$33 per person with 3 meals, $69 per weekend in spring,
  summer, fall; more in winter, less without meals
Conference facilities available
No credit cards
Children welcome
No pets
No smoking
Open year-round

The Crawfords describe Stump Sprouts as a guest lodge and ski touring center. It is really in a class of its own — a modern clapboard building that Lloyd has built almost entirely with his own hands from timbers he found standing on this 450-acre hilltop spread. From inside, with the sun streaming in through stained glass windows, guests see horses grazing immediately outside and tier upon tier of wooded hills spreading to the east.

The lodge itself is well designed, built into the slope of a hill with a variety of rooms and levels. The guest rooms, which sleep from two to eight, are fitted with bunks made by Lloyd — some double, some tiered, some in lofts. There are skylights and pleasing, unexpected corners like the cushioned reading or meditation loft above the skyroom. The skyroom windows maximize the view, but the gathering space is always inviting. There is a free-standing hearth, comfortable chairs, and sofas made by Lloyd as well as lots of games.

Downstairs are two large bathrooms and a cheerful dining area, furnished with Lloyd's tables and benches. The dining area opens onto a combination rock garden and terrace, which is also a place to eat in good weather.

The lodge is spotlessly clean and often decorated with fresh flowers. Special features include a phone, a free-standing wood-heated sauna and outdoor shower, badminton, volleyball, horseshoes, and croquet. The barn has also been nicely renovated as dancing or meeting space with a "Dairy-Aire" room (the back of the barn where the cows used to be) with a cathedral ceiling, exposed timbers, and a balcony in the old silo.

The Crawfords themselves live across the road with their daughter, Katie, in a tidy 1840s farmhouse with a touring center tacked on. In the winter, they groom 25 kilometers of trails that meander through the property. The trail system culminates at 2,000 feet, on the summit of Lone Boulder Hill. Rentals and waxes are offered, along with hot drinks, in the touring center. Instruction is also available. For downhill skiing, Berkshire East is just 7 miles away.

This is one of the least populated, least known corners of Massachusetts, rich in waterfalls, bogs, and hiking trails, all of which Lloyd has carefully mapped for visitors.

Guests are asked to bring sleeping bags, towels, and soap. But this is far from roughing it. Stump Sprouts offers some rare luxuries.

New Hampshire

Moose Mountain Lodge
P.O. Box 272
Moose Mountain Highway
Etna, New Hampshire 03750
603-643-3529

Innkeepers: Kay and Peter Shumway
12 rooms
$65 per person MAP, $70 in winter, all meals included; 10% discount for 3 nights or more
MasterCard, Visa
Children over 5 welcome
No pets
No smoking
Open June through October, December 26 to late March

Moose Mountain Lodge is at the top of a hill so steep that Kay and Peter Shumway sometimes meet guests at the lower parking lot and take them up the rest of the way in a four-wheel-drive vehicle. As one would expect, the views from the lodge are spectacular. Though it is only 7 miles from Hanover and Dartmouth College, the feeling is one of seclusion and robust mountain living. Kay and Peter prepare and serve three hearty meals a day in winter and breakfast and dinner in summer. Skiing enthusiasts, they enjoy having their guests explore the cross-country ski trails on their property and sometimes ski with them. They also have two live-in staff members who give guests expert skiing tips.

Though Moose Mountain is thought of primarily as a ski lodge, it is also a wonderful place in summer, with a pond a few steps from the door in which to swim as well as hiking trails that connect to the Appalachian Trail. A back porch extends the full length of the building and, at an elevation of 1,600 feet, overlooks miles and miles of hills and mountains in New Hampshire and Vermont. Many guests are content to sit here for hours, reading and gazing out at the spectacular scenery.

In fall and winter, the big sitting room just off the porch is inviting. There are lots of windows here, with window seats upholstered in red corduroy. There is, of course, a massive stone fireplace.

Upstairs, the guest rooms are small but attractive, with spruce log bedsteads that Mary made herself, dressed with Martex bedspreads and shams. All the rooms have shared baths, which are immaculate.

The lodge was built from the stones and logs cleared from the hills to create ski trails, and upstairs and down, the walls are dark pine. It is the kind of place where you feel you can put your feet up and not worry about ruining an heirloom. At the same time, the inn is a very clean, attractive place. In short, Moose Mountain epitomizes the rustic mountain lodge we've all dreamed about finding. Kay, we should mention, is justly famed as a cook, and the couple, who have been here for more than fifteen years, still welcome each new guest with enthusiasm and genuine interest. They obviously enjoy their work and sharing the beauty of their special roost with others.

Whitney's Inn at Jackson
Route 16B, P.O. Box W
Jackson, New Hampshire 03846
603-383-6886
800-252-5622

Innkeeper: Terry Tannehill
35 rooms (31 with private bath)
$86-$174 per couple, MAP
Major credit cards
Children welcome
No pets
Open year-round

Whitney's has a solid place in the history of New England skiing. Back in the early 1930s, it was one of the first farmhouses to accommodate skiers and one of the first to install a motorized cable to tug them up the hill. Then, in 1936, Bill Whitney bought the farm and fitted seventy-five long birch shovel handles onto the cable, a big improvement over other existing "lifts." Whitneys' also offered one of the country's first ski schools.

Over the years, both the mountain and farmhouse grew. In the '50s, Bill and Betty Whitney formed a partnership to develop the larger peak out back (the vertical drop is 1,200 feet), now known as Black Mountain. There are now twenty trails and four lifts, including a triple chair.

Betty Whitney still lives next door. Fortunately, Judy and Terry Tannehill want to preserve the unpretentious, gracious atmosphere of the inn and go all out in their effort to welcome families.

This remains one of the few ski inns that caters to children — with a great basement rec room and a separate dinner seating at 6:00 P.M. A movie follows dinner so that parents can dine alone. Black Mountain (now under separate ownership) has a well-equipped nursery, but parents must find daytime babysitters if they want to take advantage of the East's most extensive and scenic cross-country trail system — 150 kilometers of trails that meander over golf courses, through the woods, up and down mountains, and around the picturesque village of Jackson.

The olive green farmhouse extends on and on, surrounded by mountains. The guest rooms, named after trees, are comfortable. Elder is gigantic, with wooden shutters over the bed and a living room. But there are also snug singles on the third floor and roomy doubles with great views. There's a fireplace in the paneled dining room, where the fare includes sumptuous breakfasts and a generous choice of evening feasts, including charbroiled New York sirloin, duck au poivre, salmon bouchard, veal dijonaise, and rack of lamb. There's also a selection of "heart healthy" dinners.

Although the inn is known best for its winter sports, it is inviting in summer, offering swimming in the delicious natural pools of the Wildcat River as well as tennis, golf, and hiking. Mount Washington is just a few peaks away.

Vermont

The Doveberry Inn
Route 100
West Dover, Vermont 05356
802-464-5652

Innkeeper: Pat Rossi
8 rooms, each for 2-4 people (all with private bath)
$100-$120 per couple, including full breakfast; off-season:
$75-$85
Dinner also served
Major credit cards
Children over 8 welcome
No pets
Open December to April, June to late October

The Doveberry Inn sits right on Route 100, just a mile south of Mount Snow. The new owners, Pat Rossi and her sister Cathy, have inherited an unusually shipshape facility and are working hard to inject their own personality. Pat is the innkeeper and breakfast chef and Cathy, the dinner chef. Both are graduates of the New England Culinary Institute in Montpelier, Vermont.

The center of the inn is a comfortable living room with a fireplace. Upstairs, sun streams through dormer windows, creating patches of light on the sloping ceilings in the guest rooms. Soft beds with flowered covers and down pillows, bedside reading lamps, and modern baths, some with skylights and copper vanities, are pleasant features. The largest of the eight rooms can accommodate up to four people, while cozy doubles are also available. One room has its own sundeck.

This is, incidentally, one of the few inns that offers rooms either with or without TVs and VCRs, and there is a small collection of movies (geared to children so that their parents can dine in peace) as well as a selection of books.

Breakfast is one way Pat pampers guests. The country meal often features cream cheese French toast made with raisin bread and served with Vermont maple syrup. A candlelit dinner is served in the two small dining rooms; the Continental cuisine is complimented by an extensive wine list.

Eagle Lodge
Route 242
Jay Peak Road
Montgomery Center, Vermont 05471
802-326-4518

Innkeepers: Carl and Irene Scott, Dean and Carmen Scott
16 rooms
Winter: $35-50 per person double occupancy, MAP
Summer: $20 per person, including breakfast (dinner by
reservation)
No credit cards

Children welcome
No pets
Open year-round

Eagle Lodge is one of the few Vermont inns run by Vermonters: three generations of the Scott family have welcomed visitors since 1960. It's a tidy old house right on Route 242—a road that ended before reaching the house until Grandpa Scott helped convince the state legislature to extend it 4 miles, up to the ski area at Jay Peak.

Eagle Lodge is effortlessly welcoming. Rocking chairs, braided rugs, wood-burning stoves, and bookshelves are all where one expects them. The guest rooms are a bit small; many have sloped ceilings papered with eagles. The dining room is sheathed in wide pine boards, brightened with the view of the pond out back, and filled with trestle tables, worn shiny by use. The fare is Vermont country cooking, laced with maple syrup made in the Scotts' summer house, down the road.

In the summer there's a pool for swimming, a 9-hole golf course, and a trout pond stocked with fish. The 86-mile Missisquoi River, out back, is good for fishing, canoeing, and kayaking.

In the winter there's handy cross-country skiing on a network of trails; guided tours are also available. Downhill at Jay Peak begins in November and lasts through April. In bad weather, there is always a book and a comfortable corner by a woodstove.

Inn at Long Trail

P.O. Box 267
Killington, Vermont 05751
802-775-7181
800-325-2540

Innkeepers: Kyran and Rosemary McGrath
26-34 rooms and suites (all with private bath)
Winter weekend: 2 nights, $136-$181 per person double occupancy, MAP (only 1 dinner)
Summer: $26-$34 per person double occupancy, B&B
Lunch also served in summer
MasterCard, Visa
Children welcome
No pets
Open November to April 12, July to mid-October

This institution has been serving skiers, hikers, and people who love the mountains since 1938. The present inn, right on Route

4, was built as an annex to the original structure, now burned down.

Too comfortable to be called rustic, the inn boasts treelike tables and chairs in the living room as well as a massive stone fireplace and paneling. The McGraths, well-traveled veterans of the Washington political scene, are natural hosts. Hikers on the Appalachian and Long trails can stop for a shower for a small fee. Those who stay on are favored with special rates.

The Irish Pub, with a bar made from a single 22-foot-long polished log, is one of the few places in Vermont that serves Guinness on tap. There is live bluegrass, folk, and Irish music on weekends and holiday weeks. The library is fully stocked, and a redwood hot tub is another way to unwind.

An 18-foot boulder (literally part of Deer Leap Cliff) has been incorporated into the bar and dining room. The floor-to-ceiling rock creates part of a wall that, coupled with the view from the dining room windows, makes for a truly woodsy feeling. Meals are served amid black-and-white photos that depict the inn's history back to 1923. The food is delicious and plentiful, and special diets can be accommodated. Nothing elaborate is offered, but there is a sufficient assortment of Continental fare for dinner and the standard breakfast offerings. The menus change daily in the winter, weekly in the summer.

The staircase to the guest rooms in the main inn is of hand-hewn logs, and the railings are of thick limbs well worn over the years. The rooms themselves are small and simply furnished with an adjoining bath. Suites, added onto the inn, have a fireplace and their own TVs and studio couches.

Johnny Seesaw's
Box 68, Route 11
Peru, Vermont 05152
802-824-5533

Innkeepers: Gary and Nancy Okun
25 rooms and suites (all with private bath)
Summer, fall: $30-$47 per person double occupancy, including breakfast
Winter: $50-$75 per person double occupancy, MAP; midweek packages available
Dinner also served in summer
Major credit cards
Children welcome
Pets welcome with prior approval
Open just after Thanksgiving through March, Memorial Day through October

Johnny Seesaw's was built in the late 1920s as a dance hall by Ivan Sesow, a logger from Russia. It had no water or power, but there was a fine hardwood dance floor, curtained booths in the rear, and "sin cabins" out back. In the '30s, when Bromley Mountain opened right next door, it became one of New England's first ski lodges, and it's one of the few of the originals still going.

The public rooms retain much of their original atmosphere. With dark wood and low lighting, the ambience can be romantic and woodsy or playful and loud. Guests tend to gather around the circular hearth in the middle of the living room, a cozy dark lounge with its own stone fireplace and a separate game room.

The accommodations include private cottages that sleep from four to ten people, with two bedrooms, private baths, and a common living room with a fireplace and a TV. In the lodge are bedrooms as well as bunkrooms for children and young adults.

Meals can be enjoyed leisurely by candlelight. They include homemade soups, breads, and desserts, and the entrées are always imaginative and bountiful. Special dishes will be prepared for vegetarians and those on a restricted diet.

In the winter, Bromley's upper east slopes are right next door. For the cross-country enthusiast, exceptional trails and facilities can be found at the Nordic, Viking, and Wild Wings touring centers. In the quieter summer months, the clay tennis court and an Olympic-size, marble-rimmed swimming pool provide recreation. Nearby are Bromley's Alpine Slide, the famous Battenkill facilities with horseback riding, fishing, and golf.

Logwood Inn and Chalets
Box 2290
Stowe, Vermont 05762
802-253-7354
800-426-6697

Hosts: Len and Ruth Shetler
20 rooms (most with private bath), 2 chalets, 1 apartment
Rooms, $44-$80 per person, MAP, chalets and apartment up to $65; summer: rooms, $60-$80 per couple, B&B; less in spring
Major credit cards
Children welcome
Pets only in summer
Open year-round

This lodge, which opened in late December of 1941—among the first built for skiers at Stowe—is an attractive low building of logs and fieldstone. It is set back from the road on 5 acres of birches and pines, lawns, and woodland. In the summer, flower beds galore surround rustic houses. Gardens surround the clay tennis court and pool amid wooded privacy immediately behind the lodge.

The guest rooms have country print curtains and comforters. The third floor is used as a dorm in the winter. The apartment has a ground-level private entrance, two bedrooms, two baths, a living room, and a kitchenette. The two-story chalets, tucked neatly into the woods in front of the lodge, offer great indoor privacy and sleep six to twelve people. Both are modest and basic.

The main lodge, with barnboard walls and hardwood floors, is wheelchair accessible. The living room is a large, comfortable room with a roaring fireplace. From here, guests can watch the snow falling in front of the outdoor lights. Downstairs, hors d'oeuvres and a BYOB setup are in front of a fire, with table tennis off to the side.

The food is hearty and plentiful; seconds are available. Simple dining at wooden tables includes one seating for dinner and one meat entrée. Saturday nights are synonymous with roast beef, but the Shetlers are very conscious about diet and are happy to accommodate vegetarians. After more than twenty years at the inn, the recipes are their own, tried and true. In the winter, an outside cook works under their direction. A Vermont breakfast, cooked to order, is a delight on the deck out back in the summer.

Mad River Barn

R.R. 1, Box 88
Waitsfield, Vermont 05673
802-496-3310

Innkeeper: Betsy Pratt
15 rooms (all with private bath)
Winter: $58 per person MAP in the Barn, $62 per person MAP in the Annex, $36 per extra person in a room; meal charge only for children 9 and under; 20% off midweek
Off-season: $60 per room in the Barn, B&B, $65 in the Annex on weekends and during foliage season; $10 less midweek; group rates offered
MasterCard, Visa
Children welcome

No pets
Open year-round

Mad River Barn preserves the rich, warm atmosphere of a '40s ski lodge. It opened in 1948, with the opening of Mad River Glen up the road, and it continues under the same ownership as that unusual ski area. Betsy Pratt is the primary owner and manager of both and she's very much here, answering the phone, waiting up for late arrivals, and, in summer, rising early to cook breakfast.

The Barn houses a large game room, a lounge with a fireplace and a full bar, a restaurant, and many comfortable deep chairs. The bar, in particular, is simply wonderful, a room that comes alive with skiers warming themselves by the fire. Furnished in the rustic, historic decor of the Green Mountains, antlers hang over the fireplace and antique skis grace the walls. A huge sundeck off the lounge is good for breakfast and gazing across the expansive back lawn up into the birches. The dining room is yet another special space, filled with mismatched oak tables and original American art of the '30s.

The pine-paneled guest rooms in the Barn are unusually large, permitting an extra cot or two without crowding and making this a real find for families. The rooms are simply but nicely furnished, and the beds have quilts that Betsy has made herself. The Annex is a small farmhouse dating from 1820; it has been remodeled to provide deluxe rooms, each with a sauna, TV, and kitchenette.

Up the slope behind the Barn and past a grove of birches is a swimming pool, secluded in an idyllic meadow. The gardens are unusually nicely landscaped, with white perennials and conifers — making this, incidentally, a great setting for wedding receptions.

In the winter the Barn's food is exceptional. The chefs, young pros from a famous Vermont restaurant (Mary's, in Bristol), prepare delicately spiced soups and entrées that rival the best meals in this resort valley, known for the Sugarbush ski areas. Mad River Glen, however, is favored by many Vermonters and a number of New England's best skiers. It offers little natural snowmaking and a lot of challenge.

There are also 60 kilometers of old logging roads that unfold from the surrounding meadows to make cross-country and hiking trails. One downhill trail from Mad River Glen runs right to the lodge. In the summer, when the lodge is strictly B&B, the valley offers theater and an unusual choice of sports, including gliding and horseback riding.

Misty Mountain Lodge

R.R. 1, Box 114
Stowe Hill Road
Wilmington, Vermont 05363
802-464-3961

Innkeepers: Elizabeth and Lensey (Buzz) Cole
20 people accommodated (shared baths)
$32-$35 per person, $24-$29 children ages 2-12, MAP; other
   plans available
No credit cards
Children welcome
No pets
Open year-round

Misty Mountain offers excellent value and a very homey atmosphere, making it ideal for families, groups of friends, and anyone seeking a reasonably priced and friendly lodge in this area.
Guests always receive a warm welcome, and the house is designed to be lived in, with a comfortably furnished living room,
clean, simple bedrooms, and a coat room for getting dressed for
the cold. If privacy is a top priority, don't come here; bedrooms
are just for sleeping, bountiful meals are served family style,
and after-dinner sing-alongs in the living room are common.

This sprawling Vermont farmhouse has been the Cole family's home for generations, and their photographs decorate the
walls, the piano, and the desk. This is, in fact, one of the few
inns in Vermont run by Vermonters.

"I don't want anyone to be surprised," Buzz cautions. What
he means is that this is a real country home. The living room —
with a roaring fire, an old-fashioned, cushioned rocker, a sofa
and chairs with embroidered pillows, and a piano — is the heart
of this inn. Everyone gathers to play cards, read, sit, and chat.
Magazines cover the coffee table. Guests will also find a good
selection of board games and books as well as a TV.

The guest rooms include doubles, triples, and a large room
with two twin beds and a double bed, well suited to families and
groups. Sloping attic ceilings and plank floors, plenty of blankets and pillows, lots of sunshine and valley views, make these
spacious rooms comfortable. The furniture includes assorted
bureaus, chairs, and tables. Every two rooms share a small bath
with a shower.

The Coles prepare and serve two meals a day: a big country
breakfast of juice, hot and cold cereals, eggs, toast, and pancakes and an equally bountiful dinner, with soup, a main dish
(perhaps roast beef or baked chicken), seasonal vegetables,

bread, potatoes, salad, and dessert. Dishes are prepared with local farm produce; muffins, cakes, and pies are homemade. Meals are taken at several long tables in the large, beamed dining room.

The inn commands an unbroken view of the Mount Snow Valley and the steeples of Wilmington. In this delightful setting the inn has 150 acres of trails and fields, ideal for hiking and skiing. The inn is also near all the activities of the valley. A variety of special rates, including a five-day winter midweek and a weekend package, are available.

The Old Cutter Inn

R.R. 1, Box 62
East Burke, Vermont 05832
802-626-5152

Innkeepers: Fritz and Marti Walther
9 rooms (5 with private bath)
$34-$48 per room double occupancy, EP, $75-$90 per person for 2 days, MAP, $8 for each extra person; 5-day package: $168-$197, MAP; 3- and 4-day packages available
Dinner (except Wednesday) and Sunday brunch served
MasterCard, Visa
Children welcome
Pets welcome with advance notice
Open year-round except November and April

This inn has good food, comfortable rooms, and an unpretentiousness that makes everyone feel at home. Near Burke Mountain Ski Area, it offers views of both the mountains and valley, long walks in the woods, and easy access to both downhill and cross-country skiing. Bring a bicycle to explore the untrafficked country roads, which wind past golden cornfields, rustic old barns, picturesque farmhouses, and New England villages. In the summer, a pool welcomes you home.

Built in 1845, the Old Cutter's main building is a farmhouse with bay windows and a low ceiling. A narrow hall leads to the sunny, beamed dining room, trimmed with cheerful fresh flowers, candles, and pastel linens. Across the way there's a pleasantly rustic tavern with a semicircular bar and several round wood tables. On cold winter afternoons, guests gather around the fire for after-ski cocktails and snacks; in the summer, light meals and cool drinks are popular.

Fritz Walther, a Swiss émigré, is a trained chef who prepares Continental dishes such as coq au vin and beef tournedos and Swiss specialties like Rahmnschnitzel. The Sunday champagne brunch features eggs Benedict, fresh fruit salad, savory and sweet crêpes, and homemade cakes and pies.

Although the dining room and tavern draw outside visitors, guests can easily find privacy, especially by requesting one of the rooms in the separate Carriage House, behind the main inn. But the rooms in the main lodge are equally pleasant. All the guest rooms, papered in colorful floral prints, are spacious and cheerful. Windows let in lots of Vermont sunshine and offer a fine view (request a room overlooking Mounts Hor and Pisgah). Modern baths, firm mattresses, chairs, bureaus, and good lighting make these rooms comfortable.

Special rates are available for bicycle tour groups and groups staying for two or more nights.

Ski Inn
Route 108
Stowe, Vermont 05672
802-253-4050

Innkeepers: Larry and Harriette Heyer
10 rooms (5 with private bath)
$35-$45 per person; summer: $16-$20 per person, B&B
Breakfast and dinner served in winter
No credit cards
Children welcome with prior approval (no babies)
Pets negotiable
Open year-round, but owners occasionally sneak off

This was the first ski lodge in Stowe, and it's one of the few survivors of a breed for which the resort was once known: a comfortable, even gracious, but unpretentious place that doesn't charge an arm and a leg. It's set way back from Route 108 (better known as Mountain Road), up beyond the commercial clutter — one of the handiest places to the lifts. Larry and Harriette Heyer have been welcoming visitors since they opened — on Pearl Harbor Day.

Although the classic white building resembles a traditional Vermont farmhouse, Larry built it specifically as a ski lodge — hence the game room with a Ping-Pong table and the pine-paneled living room with a fireplace, where guests gather (with their own potables) of an evening. There is also an attractive dining room.

The guest rooms all have a double and a single bed, and some are big enough to permit a cot or two besides (there are family rates).

Cross-country skiers will appreciate the waxing room and

the easy access to Stowe's extensive cross-country trail system. In the summer, guests can use the trails to explore the inn's 28 acres. Needless to say, there is plenty else to do — hiking, biking, and fishing, for starters — in the summertime.

Trail's End, A Country Inn

Smith Road
Wilmington, Vermont 05363
802-464-2727

Innkeepers: Mary and Bill Kilburn
18 rooms (all with private bath)
$65-$100 per person, including full breakfast
No credit cards
Children welcome
No pets
Open year-round except early November and late April

Although we have placed this outstanding inn among the other ski lodges, it is equally appealing in the summer. Certainly, it has many advantages over most of the ski lodges in the Mount Snow Valley: handsomely decorated yet practical public rooms, delicious meals, a pool, a trout pond, well-kept gardens, and a tennis court. Nature lovers will particularly enjoy Trail's End. In a secluded corner of the woods, the inn itself — with solar windows, raw wood ceilings and walls, and a profusion of plants — brings nature's best features indoors. The guest rooms come in all sizes, including a family suite with a fireplace.

The main living area has a sloping full-length solar window framed by dozens of hanging plants. There's a beamed cathedral ceiling and an enormous central fieldstone fireplace. Long sofas built into the wall and stuffed magazine racks make it a central gathering place. There's also a recreation room, with board games and bumper pool. A small loft above the living room, with sofas and chairs, is a comfortable place to watch TV. And there's a refrigerator for guests with BYOB setups.

The aroma of baking bread and simmering soup fills the house each afternoon. Three-course dinners and full country breakfasts are served in the festive dining room, which has antique kerosene lamps on each of the round tables. Guests are invited to bring wine to accompany the meal.

In the summer, the English flower gardens around the pool are lovely. Private nooks and arbors, surrounded by acres of open meadows and deep cool woods, are idyllic places where guests can escape for a walk. The wooded trails that start at the lodge lure explorers in every season.

Spas

The spa spectrum in New England runs the gamut from holistic to glitzy, from bargain-priced to top dollar. These are the best.

Connecticut

Norwich Inn, Spa and Villas

607 West Thames Street
Route 32
Norwich, Connecticut 06360
203-886-2401
800-892-5692
Fax 203-886-9483

Innkeeper: Judy Stell
65 units, including 16 suites in the inn and 80 newer Villa units
Suites $160 and up, rooms from $125 single, $140 double, EP;
   some basic packages: a 1-day Revitalizer, $195 plus room
   rate; 2-day Revitalizer, $510-$724 per person, based on
   accommodation; 5-day programs: $1,455-$1,613 plus
   lodging; special packages available; add 17.5% service charge
Major credit cards
No children
No pets
Open year-round

Built in 1929, the Norwich Inn was completely renovated in 1983 to recapture that era by the former owners of the California's Sonoma Mission Inn & Spa. A separate spa building, added in 1987, resembles a Roman bathhouse with an elaborate tile pool at its center, lined with men's and women's locker areas. There are also ample exercise spaces and treatment rooms, and a full spa program is offered. It's the reason one third of the guests tend to be here on weekdays; on weekends, half are using at least some spa services on an à la carte basis.

In the inn, most bedrooms are large and airy, decorated in warm Colonial shades of cinnamon, sand, and Nantucket blue, and more old fashioned (the bathrooms offer all the pluses and minuses of 1920s plumbing) than the new Villa units. These each have a living room with a fireplace, a small balcony, and a fully equipped kitchen. The rooms as well as condominium units have TVs and telephones, and many overlook the garden or parts of an adjacent golf course.

The common rooms in the inn are very bright, decorated in flowered chintz with some splashy touches, like the huge (over 6 feet tall) white wicker cage in the middle of the lobby, housing two white doves. There's a small bar with a glassed-in fireplace just off the lobby and a large hall that's used as a solarium and sitting room—a tranquil spot for a cocktail before dinner. French doors lead to the dining rooms. Nouvelle cuisine is expertly served on fine china and special spa meal plans are available. The *New York Times* has awarded the chef two stars.

The spa is a full-service health facility, offering everything from full-body massages to Thalassotherapy, facials, waxing, and fitness routines. The pool has jets to raise and lower the water level for specified fitness programs; there is also a whirl-pool, sauna, and steam room. Over the past few years, the choice of exercise programs has been expanded and refined. Guests not on the spa plan can use the center for $10.

The inn has two clay tennis courts and an outdoor pool; the PGA-rated 18-hole Norwich Golf Course is next door. Cross-country skiing and ice skating are popular in the winter.

Maine

Northern Pines Health Resort
Route 85, Box 279
Raymond, Maine 04071
207-655-7624

Host: Marlee Turner

4 double rooms in Hillside Cottage (all with private bath), 9
cabins (6 with baths), 1 yurt (3 rooms, 2 baths,
accommodates 5), 2 rooms with private bath in the new
conference center, 4 seasonal rooms in the lodge (shared
bath)

June-August: $638-$842 per week, $115-$149 per day

December to mid-March: $465-650 per week, $83-$114 per day

November, mid-March to mid-May: $65 per person, B&B,
partial program included

Rates include all meals (holistic, vegetarian), exercise, classes,
use of all facilities; extra charge for special services such as
massage

Major credit cards

Children welcome but inappropriate

Extra charge for pets (on approval)

Open year-round

A Northern Pines day begins with a 6:30 A.M. bell clanging
through the pines, the call to meditation, followed by stretching
exercises and a walk down one of the wooded paths on the
resort's 80 acres. Breakfast can be millet and homemade apple-
sauce or, if you're lucky, yogurt pancakes, but never, never coffee. A selection of herbal teas and a snack are found next to the
ever-hot water urn.

A 9:30 class can be on subjects ranging from growing sprouts
to reflexology. Otherwise, the morning is free for guests to take
one of the canoes, the pedalboat, Sunfish, sailboat, or rowboat
out on Crescent Lake, a sizable, undeveloped expanse of sparkling water that connects with even larger Panther Lake. There is
another workout at 11:00, a walk at 2:00 P.M., yoga at 4:30, and
an after-dinner program at 7:30. One day a week, shopping or
sightseeing trips are also offered (a number of guests are here
without cars; Northern Pines picks them up at the Portland
airport).

But the organized program isn't pushed. It's just there — like
the boats, the lake, the sauna, and the glorious wooden hot tub
that overlooks the lake. The push here is a gentle one, toward

relaxation and an appreciation of the natural beauty. The staff numbers 12, and guests are limited to 40 in summer, 20 in winter.

Northern Pines is a complex of rustic log buildings, literally in the pines. The traditional Maine, open-beamed main lodge has a huge double fireplace serving a cheerful dining area on one side and a library and gathering space on the other. Unfortunately, it can be used only six months of the year (May-October), and a new conference center serves as a focal point the rest of the time. The rooms are scattered in a wide assortment of buildings: cabins unheated and heated, the lodge and conference center, Hillside (a winterized lodge with its own living room), even a yurt. Our favorite is Lakeside, one of the most isolated and rustic cabins, with a fireplace and a porch next to the lake.

Built in 1928 as a riding camp for respectable single ladies, Northern Pines became a fitness center only after Marlee had contracted thyroid cancer, adopted a holistic diet, and recovered beautifully. Most guests are not vegetarians. Some are here to lose weight, others to deal with a specific stress. The idea here is simply to learn to feel healthier.

Massachusetts

Canyon Ranch
Bellefontaine
Kemble Street
Lenox, Massachusetts 01240
413-637-4100
800-326-7100
Fax 413-637-0057

Director: Peter Campbell
120 rooms and luxury suites
$240-$425 per person double occupancy; 2-night weekend package; $500-$1,220; also 3-, 4-, 7-, 10-day packages; add 17% service charge
MasterCard, Visa
Children over 14 welcome (ask about special rates)
No pets
Open year-round

Ask spa-goers where Canyon Ranch is and they will quickly reply: Tucson, Arizona. Billing itself as the "first major coed health and fitness resort to open year-round in the Northeast,"

Canyon Ranch has been in business in the Berkshires only since October of 1989.

The centerpiece of this luxurious complex is one of the grandest of the many 1890s "cottages" in Lenox. Bellefontaine was built of marble and brick to resemble Louis XVI's Petit Trianon, and its rooms, which include a dining room and library, are vast and richly detailed. The 121-inn itself is a separate, new clapboard building designed along traditional New England lines, set well behind the mansion but protected by weatherproofed glass-sided hallways. The halls also connect with the spa facilities: exercise rooms, pools, lockers, a gymnasium, suspended track, racquetball and indoor tennis courts, and more. Of course, there are also treatment rooms as well as a wide variety of programs, from Stop Smoking and Arthritis to myriad specially tailored combinations of exercise and nutrition. The staff has honed its skills at Canyon Ranch in Arizona.

Kripalu Center for Yoga and Health
Box 793
Lenox, Massachusetts 01240
413-637-3280

251 rooms (private, semi-private, and dormitory)
$50-$115 per person, includes all meals, facilities, and the
    Rest and Renewal Program (minimal yoga, exercise,
    sharing sessions); rates for other programs vary
MasterCard, Visa
Summer camp for children 4-12
No pets
Open year-round

Kripalu is called a residential yoga community. With a staff of 250, it occupies a graceless former Jesuit novitiate surrounded by 350 unusually beautiful acres. It overlooks Lake Mahkeenac (good for swimming and boating), and is just a half-mile walk from Tanglewood, the summer home of the Boston Symphony Orchestra. A nonprofit community, Kripalu can offer a lot for a relatively small charge.

Guests are encouraged to develop a balanced attitude toward work, food, and play. They can choose whether to rise at 5:00 A.M. to meditate and exercise. Vegetarian meals are taken in silence in the large, airy dining hall. Meals are served buffet-style, the largest at midday. There's no sugar and no caffeine.

Throughout the day there are classes on yoga, aerobics, stress management, acupressure, nutrition, and the like. Special services, for an extra charge, include flotation tanks, massage, facials, and personal counseling. There are special "weekend adventures" in yoga, stress, communication, dance, and so on. Week-long sessions on such subjects as Quest for the Limitless You and Self-Esteem and month-long programs in holistic training are also offered.

Prices vary with the type of accommodation, which ranges from private to an eight-person dorm. Guests can also choose to come on a daily-rate basis for Rest and Renewal, a personal, unstructured program. The center's founder, Yogi Amrit Desai, came to Philadelphia from India in 1960.

Vermont

New Life Spa Program
Liftline Lodge
Stratton Mountain, Vermont 05155
802-297-2534

Host: Jimmy LeSage
30-35 guests per week
Late June through mid-September: Sunday-Saturday: $990 per person double occupancy, $1,090 single occupancy
Late April through June, weekends: $895 per person double occupancy, $995 single; all meals included (800 calories per day in summer, 1,200-1,500 in winter)
Special weekend program, late October through mid-December
Personal check preferred; MasterCard, Visa
Children over 14 welcome
No pets
Open for full weeks in summer; weekends in spring

New Life is housed in an Austrian-style ski lodge, high on Stratton Mountain, at one of the poshest ski resorts in Vermont. Although it welcomes men and women, it primarily attracts professional women willing to invest the time and money in exercise, controlled diet, and lectures on Body Awareness and Body Conditioning. Guests can use Stratton's tennis courts and the indoor pool in the sports center.

The regimen begins with a 7:00 A.M. wake-up call and includes exercises, lunch, more exercise (skiing or swimming), followed by yoga. After dinner, there may be a workshop. Both regular and accelerated (more exercise for those already in good condition) programs are offered. Meals are varied; a choice is offered, but the emphasis is on healthful nutrition. Guests are weighed at check-in (Sunday at 3:30 P.M.) and again at checkout (the following Saturday after lunch). They usually lose five pounds or more. The idea is also to pick up life-serving habits and to become more attuned to oneself.

The Woods at Killington, Resort and Spa

R.R. 1, Box 2210
Killington Road
Killington, Vermont 05751
802-422-3100
800-633-0127
Fax 802-422-4070

Manager: Douglas Marks
144 condominium units (1-bedroom villas to 3-bedroom cluster homes), also available without spa package daily or monthly
Summer spa packages: 2 days, $632-$707 single occupancy, $484-$521 double; 4 days: $1,042-$1,488; 7 days: $1,748-$2,511; includes all meals, spa treatments, facilities, taxes, and gratuities
Winter: $560-$630 per person double occupancy; 4 days: $1,202-$1,336; 7 days: $2,198-$1,491
Major credit cards
Children welcome
No pets
Open year-round

The Woods is ideal for the person who wants to follow a full spa program yet be with their family on vacation. The resort is secluded in its own woods but at the bottom of Killington Road. In the summer, when the rates are unusually reasonable for this caliber of lodging and spa, there is plenty of golf, tennis, theater, horseback riding, and hiking. In the winter, the kids and Dad (or Mom) can climb aboard the free shuttle every morning and head for New England's most extensive network of downhill ski trails, while Mom (or Dad) heads for the pool and exercise and treatment rooms in Terra Median.

Terra Median, an elegant, Mediterranean-style building, is the centerpiece of the Woods. Here you check in and dine, here you swim in the delightful lap pool cum Jacuzzi with a waterfall at one end. There are also state-of-the-art electronic exercise machines, a sauna, a eucalyptus steam room, and a warren of treatment rooms, soothingly paneled and painted. There are a wide range of European treatments: loofah scrubs, seaweed wraps, Thalasso deepwater therapy baths, and even a Parafango treatment, which entails lying in dehydrated muds that deeply heat and relax stiff joints. There is also a full exercise program and a beauty salon.

The lodging at the Woods is, in many ways, the most luxurious at any New England spa. The condominiums all have full kitchens (including microwave ovens), a dining area, a living room with a fireplace, a TV, VCR, stereo, oversize Jacuzzi, washer and dryer, and daily housekeeping service. Some cluster homes also have their own sauna, a whirlpool for two, and room-to-room stereo. These condominium units are ideal for families and are available off-season at bargain prices. For those who come alone, there are one-bedroom town homes in the Village Center.

Puzant's, the restaurant in Terra Median, is an elegant space around a central hearth. The executive chef, a young Dane named Ken Thers, has firm views about fresh, regional ingredients — rabbit, trout, Vermont lamb, fruit, and vegetables. His dishes are flavored with carefully prepared stocks, not butter and cream. Breakfast can be hearty, maybe a whole grain pancake studded with raspberries and nuts.

The setting here is indeed 100 acres of woods, among which the condominium clusters are widely scattered. The facilities include three tennis courts as well as the services in Terra Median. Killington's ski slopes are open from October through May (really, December through March), and its 18-hole golf course can be played from May through October. A variety of restaurants and shops line Killington Road.

■ *See also:* Topnotch at Stowe Resort and Spa, Stowe, Vermont

Sports Lodges

Known as sporting camps or sports lodges, these are North Country institutions: simple but comfortable cottages (without cooking facilities of their own) grouped around a central lodge where guests tend to gather as well as dine. Most of them cater to fishermen, but some are geared to families.

Maine

The Birches
P.O. Box 81
Rockwood, Maine 04478
207-534-7305

Innkeepers: The Willard family
17 cabins
$65 per person, all meals included; weekly and EP rates
  available
Major credit cards
Children welcome
Pets welcome
Open year-round

The Birches, a 50-year-old backwoods lodge in Maine's Moosehead Lake region, is in a thick birch forest on the shore of mammoth Moosehead Lake. Once you've arrived, you won't need (or want) to leave. The nearest settlement is Rockwood, a tiny fishing and hunting outpost, and involves a ride through dense woods over rutted dirt roads.

You stay in hand-hewn log cabins on the lake under tall, slender trees. Besides a porch, ideal in warm weather, each cabin has a Franklin stove or fireplace in a sitting room, a bath with a hot shower, and from one to three bedrooms. Some cabins have kitchens, but full American plan is also available, including three substantial meals and housekeeping service. Do-it-yourselfers should bring groceries and drinks; Rockwood does not have a terrific selection, and it's expensive.

A rustic timber building decorated with sporting souvenirs, the main lodge houses an informal pine-paneled dining room, a game room with a Ping-Pong table, and a central lobby. Maps, guidebooks, mosquito repellent, and other useful items are sold at the desk in the lobby, which is also the place to inquire about boat rentals, rafting trips, and wilderness guides. The lodge is the focal point of social life at the Birches. Here, guests and staff gather for meals or, in the evenings, to socialize, have a game of table tennis or poker, or arrange a rafting or fishing expedition. The hearty meals feature traditional American fare.

In the winter the Birches runs a ski touring center, with rentals, instruction, snowshoes, and guided treks through the wilderness. Guides for ice fishing trips are also available. In the summer Wilderness Expeditions, a whitewater firm operating from the Birches, arranges trips on various rivers and offers private instruction, guide service, and equipment rentals. There are several other, similar companies in the area. Write in advance for information. The Birches rents motorboats, windsurfers, canoes, kayaks, and sailboats, which can be launched from its private dock.

Bosebuck Mountain Camps
Route 16
Wilsons Mills, Maine 03579
207-243-2945; 207-486-3238 in winter

Owners/operators: Tom and Susan Rideout
11 cabins for up to 35 people
$55 per person per night for 3 nights or less; $50 per person for 4 nights or more, including all meals; family and package rates in summer
MasterCard, Visa
Children welcome
Pets welcome
Open May 10 through November

Bosebuck is in the middle of a 200,000-acre tract of land 15 miles from the nearest road. Yes, you must drive 15 miles down a dirt and gravel road to get to the camps or fly in from Rangeley with pilot Steve Bean (call him for his rate at 207-864-5307). With the exception of a few camps that are only accessible by plane, this is one of the most off-the-beaten-track places to stay in all of New England. The surrounding land is owned by the Boise Cascade Paper Company and is closed to the public.

This is not, though, just a place to get away from it all. It's rustic, and although the cabins all have indoor plumbing and showers, they are small and are meant for one thing—sleep. The rest of your time is spent fishing or hunting or chatting in the living room, decorated with masculine oak furniture, in the main lodge. There's also an abundance of food, and they will happily cook your catch of the day for any of the meals. A chambermaid makes the bed every day, and a dockhand helps you with boats and the fish you decide to keep.

Send for Bosebuck's *Fishing at Bosebuck* for an excellent description of what's available. Primarily native brook trout and landlocked salmon are in Aziscohos Lake, and by all accounts the fishing is tremendous. Grouse hunting is available on a limited basis in the fall. Bosebuck has some of the best. In October 1982, four hunters put up eighty-seven grouse in two days of hunting! Although it's possible to sit on the front porch of the lodge and enjoy the totally tranquil view of the dock and lake, most people come here for the excellent fishing and hunting and to enjoy the friendly, energetic, and extremely knowledgeable innkeepers.

It is imperative to make reservations here and to be sure that you arrive when someone is at the gate to let you in.

Chesuncook Lake House and Cottages
Route 76, Box 655
Chesuncook Village
Greenville, Maine 04441
207-695-2821 radio telephone

Innkeepers: Bert and Maggie McBurnie
10-12 rooms, 3 housekeeping cottages
Rooms $58 per person, all meals included; cottages, $18 per person, EP; $12 for dinner only
For 3-day minimum, no charge for collection by boat, $65 shuttle charge one way for others and for one canoe, $75 for two canoes; $100 round-trip via Folsom's Air Service
No credit cards
Children welcome (half price under 12)
Pets welcome
Open year-round

Chesuncook Village is a cluster of houses on an island-like peninsula deep in the North Woods, accessible only by boat, skis, or plane. It's on the National Register because it is one of the very few remnants of a true 19th-century wilderness lumbering community. The original white clapboard inn, built in 1864, still stands proudly above its lawns by the lake, overlooking Mount Katahdin. It caters to canoeists, hikers, fishermen, and anyone who appreciates the beauty of this very special place.

Bert McBurnie was 2 years old when he came to Chesuncook. He went to school in the one-room schoolhouse—which has since closed for lack of students. While in the service in France he met Maggie, Parisian-born and bred, now an enthusiastic Chesuncook resident for more than thirty years.

Maggie is a famous chef, serving three meals a day in the old Lake House during summer months and in her own snug lodge in winter. Both are gas-lit and cheery. The Lake House has high ceilings and airy rooms, some with old, pressed tin walls and ceilings.

In the summer, Bert will meet you by launch at the south end of the lake; that's 18 miles below the village. He can also take you to the West Branch of the Penobscot, launching you in a canoe so that you can camp that night at Lobster Lake and paddle to Chesuncook the next day. There are endless canoeing possibilities. Bert will also rent you a boat and advise you where to fish for landlocked salmon and smelt, lake and brook trout. Hunters come for white-tailed deer, moose, ruffled grouse, ducks, geese, bear, and coyote.

In the winter, you can drive to within 10 miles of the village; the precise distance depends on the skid roads the lumber company has cut that season. Bert meets you on a snowmobile with a sled tacked on for your gear. If you don't want to take the snowmobile, you can ski in.

In both winter and summer you can also fly in, weather permitting, with Folsom's, the air service in Greenville through which you communicate with Chesuncook Lake by radiophone. Connie Judkins, Folsom's radio operator, can also answer any questions you have about the village because she grew up there.

Chesuncook Village is a very special place. In the summer, the green lawns stretch from the Lake House to the shore and beyond to Graveyard Point, where a lone white pine stands, pointing off toward the mountains. There is a small church, a total of some thirty "camps," and a graveyard in the woods with a surprising number of headstones. Winter and summer, there are quiet paths to walk or ski.

Winter guests should know that they must heat water for a bath (an ingenious hookup permits you to take a shower) and that there is an outhouse. The cabins are, however, snug and attractive, and there is always the lodge, Bert and Maggie's winter home, with its rockers and good smells. Meals are always available.

Leen's Lodge
P.O. Box 40 BP
Grand Lake Stream, Maine 04637
207-796-5575; 207-942-2754 in winter

Innkeepers: Stan and Kathy Leen
9 cottages
$67-$78 single occupancy, $55-$67 per person double
   occupancy, MAP; family and weekly rates
Basket lunch upon request
MasterCard, Visa
Children welcome
Pets with approval
Open mid-May to mid-October

Stan Leen likes to call his lodge the Waldorf in the wilderness, a nickname it deserves. On a point that juts into West Grand Lake, the lodge and cabin are scattered among trees. The lodge has exposed rafters, pine sides, gleaming wood rockers, and plenty of lounging space with views of the lake through picture windows. The Tannery Room (Grand Lake Stream claims to have been the biggest tanning town in the world for some decades after 1874) offers books, TV, and a BYOB bar. Most of the cabins stand on the lake; each has a living room, one to three bedrooms, a bath, small refrigerator, gas heater, and a fireplace or well-stocked Franklin stove, but no cooking stove.

The big lure is fishing: landlocked salmon and smallmouth bass in May and June and again in September; togue, lake trout, white perch, and pickerel all summer. Most guests set out right after breakfast in cedar canoes built by hand in town and known as Grand Lakers. Ideally, they take along a guide ($100 for two), who cooks up lunch, which is packed by the lodge. Those who don't fish can laze on Leen's sandy beach, float on the lake, or hike to the fire tower. Besides table tennis and shuffleboard, bumper pool, canoeing, motorboating, and fishing will appeal to children.

Stan Leen is a warm, able host who makes all ages feel at home — and eager to return.

Migis Lodge
P.O. Box 40
South Casco, Maine 04077
207-655-4524; 207-892-5235 in winter and spring

Innkeepers: Timothy and Joan Porta
7 rooms, 25 cottages
$70-$105 per person, all meals included
No credit cards
Children welcome
No pets
Open mid-June to mid-October

Migis Lodge is an old, lakeside resort that is similar to some of the lodges deep in the heart of Maine, but it is only a 2-hour drive from Boston. Most of its guests return year after year — sure proof that it is very well run and maintained.

The lodge is on 100 acres encompassing pine forest and 1,600 feet of shorefront on a quiet section of Sebago Lake, far from the main road. Upon their arrival, a cabin boy escorts guests to their cottage, nestled in the trees and nicely separated from neighboring cottages. All of the cottages have a living room with a fireplace and a view of the lake, a full bath, one or more bedrooms with handmade quilts, and a furnished porch. Maid service, fresh ice, and firewood are provided daily.

A few rooms are available in the main lodge — the focal point of activity. Its cozy living room is nicely decorated and has a game closet and a great selection of books. A flagstone terrace, particularly popular for cocktails, has smashing views over the lake to the mountains and the sunset. Meals are served in the large pine dining room (coat and tie required at dinner), also with spectacular lake and mountain views. Pine green tablecloths and fresh flowers grace the tables. The food is bountiful and excellent; everything is homemade. A particularly nice group of college students serve as waiters and waitresses. There are weekly buffets, complimentary cocktail parties, Sunday breakfast cookouts, and weekly steak roasts on a private island.

Most guests spend their time at the waterfront, which offers two docks and two sand beaches. There's great swimming, sailing, water skiing, canoeing, and fishing. Others, however, do nothing more strenuous than sunning and reading a good book while enjoying the many different views. There are many niches where guests can find privacy. Many of the grass lounging areas are edged with beautiful beds of annuals that provide bright touches of color in the green, woodsy setting.

Migis also has three clay tennis courts, two shuffleboard courts, horseshoes, marked trails for hiking and nature walks, a 35-foot Chris Craft for scenic lake cruises, a recreation center with table tennis and a pool table, and movies. All the activities are particularly pleasant because of the lovely setting. Migis is the perfect small and cozy resort.

Weatherby's, The Fisherman's Resort
Grand Lake Stream, Maine 04637
207-796-5558; 207-246-7391 in winter

Innkeepers: Charlene and Ken Sassi
16 units in 15 cottages
$56 per person double occupancy, MAP, $70 single
   occupancy; $32 per child under 12
All 3 meals served
No credit cards
Children welcome
Pets permitted with advance notice
Open May to October

Weatherby's is right by Grand Lake Stream, the small river that connects West Grand Lake with Big Lake. The rambling white clapboard lodge with green trim contains a spacious living room with a piano, TV, and hearth. The dining room is homey and the meals down home: fish chowder and lobster stew, native turkeys and berries, and plenty of fresh breads, pies, and cookies. Each cottage is slightly different, but most are log with screened porches, a bath, and a Franklin stove or fireplace. There is daily housekeeping, and Ken and Charlene are right there if you need or want anything.

Grand Lake Stream is one of the most famous fishing spots in the country, known for landlocked salmon, smallmouth bass, lake trout, perch, and pickerel. Non-anglers come to swim, bird-watch (there are more than 100 species of birds in the area), hike, and generally unwind in this remote stretch of the Maine woods.

Vacation Villages

These condominium-based resorts have evolved since the 1960s around sports facilities; a number include both skiing and golf.

Maine

Sugarloaf/USA
Carrabassett Valley, Maine 04947
207-237-2000
800-THE LOAF
Fax 207-237-2718

President: Warren Cook
42 inn rooms and 700 condominiums (not all are rented)
$310 MAP per couple for a winter weekend at the inn, from
 $315 in a condominium; less weekdays, much less in
 summer, packages available
All 3 meals served; 13 restaurants
Major credit cards
Children welcome
No pets
Open year-round

Deep in the North Woods, Maine's biggest ski area has evolved into New England's largest resort. Sugarloaf is the second highest mountain (4,237 feet) in Maine and offers a 2,600-foot, continuously skiable vertical drop; it has 70 trails and 15 lifts. It also has an alpine village, complete with restaurants, boutiques, and a posh sports center. The Carrabassett Valley Touring Center, near one base of the access road, offers some 85 kilometers of well-maintained trails.

Until not so long ago, Sugarloaf was dead in the summer. But in 1986 the Sugarloaf Mountain Corporation built an 18-hole golf course, designed by Robert Trent Jones, Jr., and became a major conference center. Hiking and whitewater rafting round out the summer picture.

The condominiums have been built in clusters over the years, some by the corporation, others by the Sugarloaf Inn. By and large, they are unusually attractive units but vary widely in built-in conveniences (laundry facilities, saunas, and Jacuzzis) and in their convenience to lifts, so it pays to ask the reservations clerk to describe your options. One central check-in area (open 24 hours) now serves both the rental condominiums and the inn.

The Sugarloaf Inn is a '60s ski lodge that has been deftly improved. There is a large, comfortable living room with books and a fireplace, a cozy pub, a game room, and the attractive Seasons restaurant by the slopes which features dining by candlelight. The guest rooms range from basic (on the ground floor) to family deals (third-floor lofts).

We should also mention the Sugarloaf Mountain Hotel (57 rooms, 45 suites; call 800-527-9879), a massive, seven-story brick building that was completed in the mid-'80s, right up there at the base of the mountain.

Massachusetts

New Seabury Resort
Red Brook Road
New Seabury, Massachusetts 02649
508-477-9111
800-752-9700 in Massachusetts
800-222-2044 elsewhere
Fax 508-477-9790

Owner: New Seabury Corporation
170 of 1,700 units in rental pool
1-bedroom unit, $190-$210; 2-bedroom unit, $240-$280, EP
All 3 meals served
Major credit cards
Children welcome (youth programs and babysitting available)
No pets
Open year-round

New Seabury is best suited for people who want to dig their heels in and stay awhile, who will stock the refrigerator and dirty some dishes. The complex is nicely laid out on 2,000 acres of a beach-fringed peninsula overlooking Nantucket Sound. It boasts two championship 18-hole golf courses, 16 tennis courts, 3½ miles of beachfront, and two pools and offers a full range of resort facilities from June to Labor Day. Golf holds year-round appeal, since the courses are free of snow most of the year.

Special packages have been designed to lure the off-season visitor—such as quilting, shopping, winter golf, and Harvest Fair.

In 1962, it took a real visionary to plan this forty-year, ongoing project. It has an interesting history: in the beginning, there were hitches with the sale of single-home lots, first because of the native Indians, whose claim to this land dates from 1660, then because of zoning. With ten years of expansion still to come, you can expect an even wider range of facilities. Be sure to take a map with you while exploring; the size of the place can be confusing. While more than 1,700 units have been built in thirteen "villages," most are not rented to weekly visitors. There are plenty of accommodations to go around, though. The three areas that are open have been designed to appeal to different kinds of people.

Tidewatch is a 1960s hotel complex, right on the ocean on a grassy knoll next to the country club (its dining room is open year-round). It has units ranging from studios to two-bedroom suites, many with decks and ocean views.

The Mews is a cluster of about thirty rentals with its own Nautilus center and pool. Its villas and houses are California modern and stylish, with skylights, angled rooms, and bright colors. They range from two-story, two-bedroom "patio villas" to "patio house villas," which include family rooms and private pools (available only by the week).

Maushop Village, on a bluff above the sound, has gray shingles and many angles to resemble Nantucket cottages. Narrow lanes, gooseneck lamps, and white picket fences characterize this area. All 100 or so units have porches. Voices and noise travel easily between units, so you have to listen to your neighbors' favorite sitcom.

Popponessett Inn is a '40s landmark that has been incorporated into the Maushop development but remains open to the public for dining. Smack on the water, there isn't a nicer, more tranquil setting for dinner and dancing. This is the place to dine; the traditional New England fare is renowned, and there's an extensive wine list.

The other dining option, for all three meals, is the New Seabury Restaurant, at the country club.

Also in this compound is the Popponessett Marketplace (closed from Columbus Day to Memorial Day), with rose trellises and crushed seashells, which satisfies a wide range of shopping desires. At night, little lights twinkle, creating a fairy-tale impression. The Café and Raw Bar attract a more casual crowd for all three meals.

In the summer the attractive condo units — overlooking or within walking distance of a long sweep of beach — make New Seabury a natural standout. All guests have access to one pool or another, and there's a jogging path with "stretching stations." A new indoor recreation complex will help fill rainy days. During the summer there is also an all-day sports program for children and organized activities and weekend entertainment for adults. A special cable station will keep you constantly informed of the day's events.

New Hampshire

Waterville Valley Resort
Waterville Valley, New Hampshire 03223
603-236-8371
800-GO-VALLE (468-2553)
Fax 603-236-4174

Owner: Tom Corcoran, Waterville Company, Inc.
6,500 guests housed in rooms and condominium units and
    hotels
Black Bear Lodge: 107 condominium suites; winter,
    $109-$149 per couple, summer, $69
Golden Eagle Lodge: 120 condominium suites; winter,
    $109-$149 per couple, summer, $69
Silver Squirrel Inn: 32 rooms include bunks and sleeping
    lofts; $59-$89 per couple
Snowy Owl Inn: 80 rooms; winter, $79-$119 per couple;
    summer, $59 per room, with hearty Continental breakfast
Valley Inn and Tavern (800-343-0969): 45 suites, town houses,
    special suites; winter, $138-$348 per couple, MAP;
    summer, $158-$268
Condominium clusters include Waterville Valley
    Condominium Vacations, 80 condominium units, winter
    $133, summer $119 per 2-bedroom unit, 2-night minimum;
    2-, 3-, and 4-bedroom units available
Major credit cards
Children welcome, under 12 free in parents' room, day care
    available
No pets
Open year-round

Waterville Valley has been a resort area since the middle of the 19th century. The valley itself is a 10-mile cul-de-sac cut by one of New England's many Mad Rivers and circled by majestic mountains, many of them more than 4,000 feet tall. A summer inn was built here in 1868, and in 1919 it was bought by its loyal clientele, a high-minded group of hikers who donated all but a few hundred of its 26,000 acres to the White Mountain National Forest in 1928. In 1935, the inn began staying open in the winter, catering to some of the country's first skiers.

Tom Corcoran, who first skied the valley's old trails as a student in 1949, went on to the U.S. Olympic ski team and came back to buy the inn and its remaining 508 acres in 1965. Unfortunately, the old inn burned in 1966, and now everything in Waterville Valley, except for a very few 19th-century buildings, is from the late '60s and after.

The winter centerpiece of the valley is 3,800-foot Mount Tecumseh, a ski mountain with 48 slopes and trails and 12 lifts, including a high-speed detachable quad and three triple chair lifts. There are also 105 kilometers of cross-country trails and a small family area with five intermediate slopes and a snowboard center with a halfpipe at Snow's Mountain.

The Town Square, a magnificent restaurant and shopping complex opened in 1989, now forms the center of the valley itself. Within walking distance there is also a sports center with an indoor pool and a covered ice arena as well as a manmade pond good for summer boating and beaching. The Town Square is also the backdrop for a lively music festival all summer.

A large percentage of Waterville Valley's condominium units are in condo hotels, each a distinctive lodging place with its own common areas, most with game areas and indoor pools. The 143-room Golden Eagle Lodge is a 1990s version of an 1890s grand hotel, patterned on an Adirondack lodge. Five and a half stories tall with seven-story towers, inside it's a whimsical combination of old and new. You check in on a polished granite counter and wander into the airy lobby with its two-story sash windows, 19th-century beams and railings and modern lighting. Request one of the many tower suites with 360-degree views of the mountains. But even the least expensive units offer the exquisite design and detailing that characterize the entire building.

The Snowy Owl is another striking building with a three-story fieldstone fireplace and surrounding atrium (supported by single log posts) and a cupola in which you can sit and contemplate the stars or mountains. The garden-level lounge, with a sunken hearth, is removed from the game rooms, which have table tennis and pool as well as electronic games. They adjoin a very pleasant room where a Continental breakfast buffet is offered. Of course there are indoor and outdoor pools.

The Valley Inn and Tavern is also worth special mention. Independently owned, it is a warm, satisfying place with a fine dining room and a superb indoor/outdoor pool, the kind that is hot enough in winter to float out into on a winter night, under the stars.

Waterville Valley caters to families, offering a strong Skiwee program and a supervised children's program in winter, along with some of New England's most reasonably priced condo-ski weeks (and the condos are a shade above the norm). In the summer, there is a supervised day program for children ages 4 to 7 and organized activities for children 8 and older.

Vermont

Bolton Valley Resort
Bolton Valley, Vermont 05477
802-434-2131
800-451-3220
Fax 802-434-2131, ext. 300

President: Ralph DesLauriers
145 rooms (some housekeeping), 108 condominium units
Winter: Rooms $148 per person double occupancy for 2
    nights; condos $161 per person, 4 per condo, for 2 nights;
    both EP, include lift passes)
Summer: Rooms $99 per person double occupancy for 2
    nights; condos $170 per person, 2 per condo, for 2 nights;
    both MAP, include 1 hour of tennis or 18 holes of golf and
    admission to local attractions)
Black Bear Inn (802-434-2126): owned by Phil and Sue
    McKinnis; $59-$119 per room, EP
All 3 meals served; numerous restaurants
Major credit cards
Children welcome (under 6, lodging and skiing free)
Pets welcome in condos
Open year-round

Bolton Valley is actually a 6,000-acre mountaintop village, a cluster of buildings in various sizes and shapes, a blend of stucco, wood, and hand-hewn shingles. The original lodge, built in 1967, serves a major ski area that boasts New England's highest base elevation. Year-round, this is a resort geared to families.

Small enough for parents to keep track of children, it is large enough to offer facilities such as the elegant Sports Club, with a pool, Jacuzzi, indoor tennis courts, and a full year-round program of supervised activities for children.

In the winter, there is enough skiing here to keep most adults satisfied for a week. There are 39 trails, a new quadruple chair lift and a second base lodge. There are also some 100 kilometers of cross-country trails that, thanks to the elevation (up to 3,200 feet), are usually snow-coated. Bolton's cross-country ridge trails tie in with its alpine runs.

Families come in the summer for five to seven days for a program of tennis lessons or vacations that include tennis, golf, hiking, and sightseeing. There is an 18-hole golf course down the road, fishing, and rewarding hiking. Burlington is just 20 miles in one direction and Stowe, 20 miles in the other. As in the winter, there is a nursery for children from 3 months to 6 years old and Camp Bear Paw for children 6 to 12.

Guests who come for a day or two tend to stay at the refurbished lodge, which has standard hotel rooms and some condo-studio units with either a fireplace or kitchenette. The condominiums, with one to four bedrooms, vary in age, locale, and general quality. One of the oldest trailside units offers the convenience of skiing down to the lifts but is a shade shabby. The newer units are nicely decorated and downright posh. Be sure to ask what you are getting. There is also the Black Bear Inn, an independently owned, modern, two-story inn with a fine little dining room and an attractive living room.

Bolton Valley was bought by the DesLauriers family in 1964. Ralph DesLauriers, who has masterminded its development from the beginning, runs a tight ship and is a genial host.

Hawk Inn and Mountain Resort
P.O. Box 64, Route 100
Plymouth, Vermont 05056
802-672-3811
800-451-4109
Fax 802-672-5067

Founder: Dr. Hugh Kopald
50 inn rooms; 99 condominium and home units in rental pool
Inn rooms, $125-$200 per couple, including breakfast;
   condos, $300-$475 for 2-4 bedrooms, EP; homes,
   $350-$550 for 2-4 bedrooms, EP
Breakfast and dinner served; dinner prepared in condos with
   24-hour notice

Major credit cards
Children welcome
No pets
Open year-round

Hawk calls itself "a hotel with the world's longest corridors" and offers hotel services: meals, child care, housekeeping, larder stocking, and other perks.

The homes here are all designed by Robert Williams, the architect who founded Hawk in the 1960s with his college classmate Dr. Hugh Kopald. All the units, built and managed by the company, are architecturally striking, very private, and luxuriously furnished and equipped. Many have their own whirlpools and saunas.

The company's headquarters is now in an old farmhouse called Hawk Inn and Mountain Resort. The accommodations are a mix of country inn rooms, free-standing homes, and condominium units in the town of Plymouth.

A well-organized children's day camp is run in the summer. There is a restaurant (the River Tavern), stables, tennis, boating, a health club, and swimming. In winter, for no additional charge, there are cross-country trails, skating, and horse-drawn sleigh rides. Okemo Mountain and Killington's Northeast Passage chair is just 10 minutes' drive away.

The Villages at Killington
Killington Road
Killington, Vermont 05751
802-422-3101
800-343-0762
Fax 802-422-3283

General manager: John Rohan
500 condo units in 6 complexes plus a motor inn
Winter: studios from $128 to $539 for a 4-bedroom unit with
    sauna and Jacuzzi high on one of Killington's six peaks;
    Villager Motor Inn, $24.50 to $64 per person; all rates
    drop when combined with ski packages; *summer:* 50% less
All 3 meals served; 2 restaurants
Major credit cards
Children welcome
No pets
Open year-round

The condominium units here are all in multistoried clusters or in the massive Mountain Green, which contains a health club, shops, and a restaurant as well as 216 studios.

During ski season — which, for Killington, extends from early November into June — guests hike across vast parking lots to the lifts at Snowshed base lodge. During the summer, tennis and golf programs are held on the village's numerous courts and 18-hole golf course.

Killington is the biggest ski area in the Northeast, with 107 trails on six mountains. There are more luxurious and altogether more attractive places to stay in the area, but the village is unquestionably the most convenient, with easy access to the center of the vast ski system. There are also frequent packages that include the cost of lifts, making this a more affordable week-long vacation.

The summer golf and tennis programs are well respected, featuring the same teaching techniques that first put the ski area on the map. There is also theater in Snowshed Lodge and dining in the restaurant on Killington's 4,241-foot peak (accessible by both chair lift and gondola). The summer rates are a good bargain, too.

Village Inns

Most of these inns are at the heart of their village or town. Many are old stage stops, and all are landmarks in their own right.

Connecticut

Simsbury 1820 House
731 Hopemeadow Street
Simsbury, Connecticut 06070
203-658-7658

Innkeeper: Kelly Hohengarten
34 rooms
$85-$125 per couple, including breakfast
Lunch (except on Saturday), Sunday brunch, and dinner also
    served
Major credit cards
Children welcome
No pets
Open year-round

Simsbury House got its beginnings during the American Revolution when General Noah Phelps, a member of the Continental Congress, left the land to his son Elisha, who began building the present house. Original details include the oak parquet floor and leaded glass windows. Over the generations, the estate grew and was passed down in the family. After the last family member died it was opened as an inn, then closed, then reopened in 1985 to today's glory.

The guest rooms are country elegant with four-poster beds, delicate fabric coverings, fine reproductions, and many English pieces. Luxury appointments dress each room; the baths are excellent. Each room has cable TV concealed in an armoire, a telephone, and the latest fire-protection system. Some have two twin beds; others have love seats; one has views on three sides. The appointments are blue and wine in the main house, predominantly green and tan in the carriage house. The suites in the carriage house have terraces.

The gray brick building houses a clubby library where dinner can be served, a lounge with Colonial furniture and a fireplace, and a sunroom bar. There is also an inviting veranda where drinks are served. The staff here is young and energetic. Simsbury House has a well-respected restaurant in a basement dining room, with formal service and an intimate atmosphere.

A pond is nearby for swimming, and the town operates a pool. There is lots of antiquing, golfing, and skiing in the vicinity. Hartford is only a 20-minute drive away.

Maine

The Greenville Inn
Norris Street, Box 1194
Greenville, Maine 04441
207-695-2206

Innkeepers: The Schnetzers
6 rooms (4 with private bath), 2 cottages
Rooms, $65-$70 per couple; cottages, 3-night minimum,
$165; $275 per week; off-season rates available
Breakfast and dinner served
MasterCard, Visa
Children welcome
Pets allowed only in cottages in the summer
Open year-round

An elegant Victorian mansion, this inn is a welcome surprise in the sporting town of Greenville. Travelers to Maine's North Woods and Baxter State Park will relish its civilized comforts.

Dominating a hill just off Main Street, the inn overlooks Moosehead Lake and the Squaw mountains. Built by a wealthy lumbering family in 1895, it has many handsome features: cherry-, mahogany-, and oak-paneled interiors, fireplaces ornamented with dainty mosaics, and carved mantels. The focal point, both inside and out, is the magnificent spruce tree painted on a leaded-glass window on the stair landing.

Each of the second-floor rooms, with king-size, queen-size, double, or twin beds, is different. Two of the rooms have working fireplaces and four have private baths, one with a nostalgic pull chain. The well-appointed dining rooms offer fine food with an extensive wine list and a bar.

For its charm, character, and spacious rooms, this is one of the best values around.

The Hammons House
P.O. Box 16
Bethel, Maine 04217
207-824-3170

Innkeeper: Sally Rollinson
4 rooms (shared baths)
$40-$65, including breakfast; 50% deposit required; balance
   due on arrival
MasterCard, Visa
Children welcome
No pets
Open year-round

This 1850s mansion, built by a U.S. congressman, is on the National Register of Historic Places. It has recently been converted into a bed-and-breakfast with that extra something.

The downstairs rooms are large and comfortably furnished with antiques, but not too many to destroy the sense of space. The living room has built-in bookcases and a cozy Count Rumford fireplace. There is a sunny morning room with an arched window leading onto a patio, and a rear sunporch has been converted into an unusual two-story, flower-filled atrium where breakfast is served. The upper level provides a quiet hideaway with views of the garden behind and the mountains.

Two of the guest rooms are corner rooms with twin beds; two have double beds. All are carpeted with the braided rugs that Sally makes herself.

Behind the house stands a large barn which, around the turn of the century, was used as a private summer theater. Now Sally has erected a large yellow tent on her back lawn and stages "picnic plays," for both adults and children. Viewers are invited to bring an elegant picnic. The Upson Playhouse, as the barn was known, has been recently restored as a summer antiques shop.

Hammons House sits right on Bethel's handsome common across from the Bethel Inn, with its 18-hole golf course that serves as a cross-country ski network in winter. Sunday River and Mount Abram, both handy, offer alpine skiing, and in the summer this is fine hiking country, well stocked with swimming holes. Bethel itself is a dining and shopping center.

The Herbert Hotel
Box 67
Kingfield, Maine 04947
207-265-2000
800-THE HERB

Innkeeper: Bud Dick
33 rooms
$50-$74 per couple, $46 in summer, Continental breakfast
    included
Dinner served except Tuesday
Major credit cards
Children welcome
Well-behaved pets welcome
Open year-round

Billed as a Palace in the Wilderness when it opened in 1918, the Herbert still fills the bill. This three-story columned edifice in the center of town has been lovingly restored. There is a grand piano in the lobby, a moosehead above the hearth, and an abundance of polished wood. The dining room could be in Boston's Back Bay; it is light, intimate, and hung with sophisticated prints. Fresh flowers grace the table in January. The menu and wine list are extensive and reasonable. Sunday brunch is memorable.

The guest rooms are fresh, well furnished, and have steam baths. In the basement, a Healthworks spa has a steam room, exercise equipment, and a hot tub with the head of a moose depicted in tile above it. Next door is the Woodwork pub, with handcarved stools that must be seen to be believed.

Once a prosperous lumbering center, Kingfield is now a handsome town with more than its share of shops and restaurants. It's a long way from anywhere except Sugarloaf USA (see Vacation Villages).

Massachusetts

The Colonial Inn
48 Monument Square
Concord, Massachusetts 01742
508-369-9200

Innkeeper: Jurgin Demisch
6 apartments, 57 rooms
Apartments $100-$110, rooms $72-$125 per couple plus $5 per
    extra person
All 3 meals served
Major credit cards
Children welcome
No pets
Open year-round

This rambling gray clapboard building—its various parts dating from 1716 to 1961—sits on Concord's green, serving all the functions of a traditional inn. Civic groups and businesspeople meet in the Merchants Row Dining Room, which also takes bus groups in stride. Still, it manages to be an attractive place to dine on fare like roast beef and chicken pie.

The Colonial Inn is a great place to stay for those souls who prefer not to drive into Boston. It's surrounded by Concord's historic and literary sites, and Lexington is just down the road. You can also walk to the train station for good commuter service into Boston.

The guest rooms in the main inn are old-fashioned, in keeping with their low ceilings and wide floorboards. The 34 rooms in the air-conditioned Prescott Wing, the newest section, are good motel-style rooms. The apartments are in the adjoining, early-19th-century John Leyes House. All the units have TVs and phones. Some rooms with fireplaces and all are attractively furnished, with hooked rugs, wing chairs, and other neo-Colonial touches.

Deerfield Inn
The Street
Deerfield, Massachusetts 01342
413-774-5587

Innkeepers: Karl and Jane Sabo
23 rooms
$115 per couple, including breakfast; $170 per couple, MAP
All 3 meals served
Major credit cards
Children welcome
Pets welcome
Open year-round

The Deerfield Inn sits on a broad street lined with 17th- and early-18th-century restored homes, among them a classic brick meeting house and Deerfield Academy, one of the country's oldest prep schools. Deerfield's early homes are impressive, silhouetted starkly against flat, open onion and tobacco fields.

The inn dates substantially from 1884. It was partially destroyed by fire in 1979, but most of its fine antiques were salvaged, and it has been faithfully rebuilt, with the addition of air-conditioning, wheelchair-accessible rooms, and an elevator.

The spacious public rooms are furnished with Chippendale and wing chairs, upholstered sofas, and old portraits. The Beehive Room is so called because of the yellow beehive wallpaper. Very apropos, the beehive was considered a symbol of hospitality before the pineapple symbol came into being.

The large formal dining room contains delicate chandeliers, antique mirrors, and mahogany tables. The food is a big draw here. The chef seems equally proficient with pan-fried venison, baked local brook trout, herbed, roasted game hen, and filet mignon. The lunch offerings are equally substantial and may include a fresh seafood casserole or homemade manicotti. Downstairs is an informal café and cafeteria, serving the many tourists who want a quick bite to eat between house tours.

Eleven of the guest rooms are on the second floor of the inn, a dozen more are in the new south wing, connected by a covered walkway. Most of them have twin or queen-size beds and a few have space for a rollaway. Many are furnished with canopied four-poster beds. The fabrics throughout replicate those used in the Federal era.

The inn caters to small select groups, to parents of students at nearby schools and colleges, and to visitors to Historic Deerfield (twelve house museums along the street), which offers a year-round program of special tours and lectures.

Hotel Barre
On the Common
Barre, Massachusetts 01005
508-355-6501

Innkeepers: Nancy Lee Wright and Douglas Merrifield
38 rooms (3 with private bath)
$54-$125 per couple, EP
All 3 meals served
Major credit cards
Not appropriate for young children
No pets
Open year-round

Because this triple-decker inn is so central to the town — it opened in May 1888 — and because the rooms are each so different, the guest rooms (when not occupied) are left open for tourists and the townspeople to wander through. Each time you visit, you'll notice something new and offbeat; the walls and shelf space are filled to capacity with brick-a-brac, antiques, and art. Whatever mood strikes your fancy, there's a room (and some interesting history) to suit it.

The Empire Room has dark heavy furniture with burgundy drapery; the Music Room is filled with old opera bills and instruments. Three presidents have stayed in the Roosevelt Room, in which everything is shaped like a rose or has a rose on it. It is one of the few rooms with a private bath and a door leading directly to the porch. Room 311, the Tower Suite, with two daybeds, served as an aircraft lookout post during World War II. In the long hall are busts, etched glass mirrors, and miniature furniture. There are large flower arrangements, ceiling fans, and flowered carpets and wallpaper throughout the inn. The first-floor common rooms include a gentleman's parlor. Downstairs is the Side Door, which is quite popular in town and is sometimes boisterous.

Dinner is a set five-course meal with a choice of two or three entrées, such as poached salmon or char-broiled lamb chops. With only one seating on Saturday night (two the rest of the week), dinner lasts a luxurious 2½ hours. A number of packages are offered on weeknights and weekends; they might include champagne in your room on arrival and brunch or breakfast.

Cane rockers on the first- and second-floor porches provide relaxing vantage points for watching the activity on the town green and listening to musicians on the bandstand. The town of Barre, while seemingly in the middle of nowhere, is equidistant to Springfield, Worcester, Boston, Providence, and Hartford. At the turn of the century, Barre had no less than five hotels. The finest of them remains a central meeting place and popular waystation today.

Publick House Historic Inn
Colonel Ebenezer Crafts Inn
Chamberlain House
P.O. Box 187
Sturbridge, Massachusetts 01566
508-347-3313

Innkeeper: Buddy Adler
18 rooms in Publick House; 8 rooms in Crafts Inn; 4 suites, 1
    room in Chamberlain House; all with private bath
$88-$135 per room or suite; only Crafts Inn includes
    breakfast; lowest January-June
All 3 meals served
Deposit in cash or check, major credit cards accepted for
    balance
Children welcome
No pets
Open year-round

The handsome Publick House is one of New England's land-mark lodging places. Built in 1771, it has expanded over the years, with its dining rooms spilling through the stables and on into the barn. Guests can now choose to stay upstairs in the old house or next door at the Chamberlain House. They can also drive for 5 minutes to the top of Fiske Hill, to the peace and solitude of the Colonel Ebenezer Crafts Inn, another 18th-century house named for the founder of the Publick House.

Within a mile of the junction of I-84 and the Mass. Turnpike, the Publick House is a natural stop between Boston and New York. With Old Sturbridge Village just down the road, it has also become a destination, serving as an extension of the atmosphere found at the museum village.

The Publick House has been lucky. Meticulously restored in the '30s, it has been ably managed, first by Treadway and now by Restaurant Associates. Buddy Adler is a real presence and a conscientious host.

While some four hundred patrons can now sit down to dine at once (and usually do on weekends), the gingham-clad waitresses are notably helpful. The fare is prepared with pride — from the morning "Cockscrow" (a $4.50 special of fruit, gooey sweet rolls or memorable muffins, and coffee) to the evening Yankee pot roast or lobster pie. Because the dining rooms are all relatively small and genuinely distinctive — like the Tap Room (with a huge open hearth), the Barn (with tables in the old stalls), or Paige Hall (actually a 1780s barn) — the ambience is surprisingly intimate. If you want to escape the 18th century and moderately high prices, you can walk down to Crabapple's. Yet another part of the complex, it is recognized as the best dining deal in Sturbridge.

But you get no sense of what this amazing complex is about unless you actually stay here. The Colonel Ebenezer Crafts Inn is the standout: an elegant Federal clapboard home with exquisitely paneled rooms and a secret panel behind which runaway slaves were once hidden. The rates include a Continental breakfast, afternoon tea and sherry, and use of the private pool. Guests also can use the tennis court at the Publick House and the local golf course. The high point of the Crafts is its living room, so comfortable and spacious — the one ingredient missing in the Publick House itself.

The rooms at all three of the older buildings are furnished with antiques, including four-poster beds, wing chairs, and canopy beds. Guests can walk out to the pool or rent bicycles at the office.

In all, the Publick House property includes 60 acres, a good percentage of it forested (many lodge rooms overlook woods), much of it grazing land for sheep. At the core of the old village center (as opposed to the middle of the Route 20 motel and shopping strip near the entrance to Old Sturbridge Village), it invites guests to step out and stroll through a slice of genuine New England landscape. It's worth noting that during the bleakest months of the year (January to March), the Publick House offers Yankee Winter Weekends, which include plenty of 18th-century-style feasting and entertainment as well as admission to the museum village.

Red Lion Inn
Stockbridge, Massachusetts 01262
413-298-5545

Innkeeper: Betsy Holtzinger
100 rooms (some with shared bath)
$56-$218 per couple, EP
All 3 meals served
Major credit cards
Children welcome
No pets
Open year-round

This is the most famous inn in the Berkshires, a rambling white clapboard beauty built in 1897, after fire destroyed an expanded version of the tavern that had stood on this spot since 1773.

Staying here is like stepping into a Norman Rockwell painting. The landmark was sagging, and there were rumors of tearing it down and replacing it with a gas station when the present owners, Jack and Jane Fitzpatrick, bought it in 1968. Setting up their Country Curtains business in its ample extremities, they brought the inn back to life, and both businesses have prospered spectacularly.

The curtains have long since been moved (although a nearby shop sells them), and there isn't a musty or dusty corner in the entire place. Even the least expensive rooms are carefully furnished with real and reproduction antiques and bright prints. And there are some splendid rooms, like number 102, with its canopy bed (covered with a Waverly print made expressly for the inn), a marble-topped bureau, and comfortable sitting area with a Victorian sofa. Rooms 442 and 240 have painted country furniture and old-fashioned baths with modern fixtures. The bathrooms in fifteen or so rooms have recently been redone with a slew of marble.

Guests enter the Red Lion from an inviting veranda festooned with flowers and amply furnished with rockers in the warm months. The lobby is formal, usually with an elaborate flower arrangement in the center and a crackling fire in the parlor to one side. A red velvet curtain divides this gathering area from the formal, Victorian dining room, decorated in shades of red. An informal lunch is served in the cozy, paneled Widow Bingham's Tavern. There is a formal check-in area and an old-fashioned cage elevator. The common areas and hallways are a real visual treat.

The restaurant, which specializes in traditional favorites like veal Oscar and baked jumbo shrimp, is a popular dining spot for the region, and all the public rooms serve as a meeting spot for the village. Given the size of the inn, this constant bustle simply adds to its charm. Groups predominate in the off-season.

Summer guests enjoy the pool, walk up the street to theater at the Berkshire Playhouse, or climb the path up Laurel Hill to take in the view from a stone seat designed by Daniel Chester French. Stockbridge is well known for its shops and historic houses. It is also close to the Tanglewood Festival in Lenox, dance events at Jacob's Pillow, and many other Berkshire events. In the winter, when the prices drop, there is nearby cross-country and downhill skiing. This is always a welcoming place, with the same air of quality found in fine city hotels.

The Village Inn
16 Church Street
Lenox, Massachusetts 01240
413-637-0020

Innkeepers: Clifford Rudisill and Ray Wilson
29 rooms (27 with private bath)
$70-$130 per couple, EP
Breakfast and dinner served (no dinner on Monday)
Carte Blanche, Diners Club, MasterCard, Visa
Children over 6 welcome

No pets
Open year-round

A rambling yellow building framed by old trees and colorful plantings, the Village Inn sits on a quiet back street of Lenox, close enough to galleries, boutiques, and restaurants but still keeping its distance.

Guests cross the screened porch, past the rockers, into a friendly foyer with one of those great old full-length antique mirrors and a very dignified grandfather clock. There is usually someone behind the check-in desk, which doubles comfortably as a bar. The inn is open to the public for breakfast, tea, and dinner, so this can be a busy space. But guests can always retreat to the parlor, with its grand piano and Victorian furniture, which Cliff brought with him from his grandmother's home in Texas.

Ray is also from Texas, and the two have transformed this old landmark tastefully but with un-Yankee gusto. The Harvest Room, where meals are taken, is nicely furnished, with small-print wallpaper and crimson tablecloths. The menu is imaginative. The entrées might include shrimp tarragon, pecan-breaded breast of chicken, or veal pommery. Upstairs, the halls meander on and on. Room 23 has a four-poster bed and fireplace.

During the summer, the Boston Symphony Orchestra performs at Tanglewood, just down the road, and nearby are plays, dance, and myriad musical events. Even in the off-season this is a cheery retreat, warmed by the hearths and a sense of being in the middle of a lively community. Ask about the chamber music concerts performed here regularly, followed by an English high tea. Downstairs, in the inn's own Village Tavern, English ales and beers are featured along with a pub menu of lighter fare.

New Hampshire

- *See also:* The Hanover Inn, Hanover, New Hampshire

Vermont

Barrows House
Dorset, Vermont 05251
802-867-4455

Innkeepers: Sally and Tim Brown
29 rooms and suites
$150-$180 per couple, MAP
Bag lunches available in summer and fall
No credit cards
Children welcome
No pets
Open year-round

Dorset is a sleepy old Vermont resort village, with a town ordinance that still requires houses to be painted white with green trim and shutters. Many families have been summering at the Barrows House for the last hundred years. Socializing and having a drink under the awnings of the patio are traditional ways of passing an afternoon. Then, of course, there's golf, summer theater at the Playhouse, the abandoned marble quarry, exhibitions at the Southern Vermont Art Center, and drives on scenic backcountry roads.

Repeat guests always seem to have their favorite rooms. Dating from the 1790s, the oldest rooms are in the front of the main inn; all have bright wallpapers and antiques. These rooms are less spectacular than others around the property, but if you want the feel of a country inn, stay in the main house. Room 17, in the back, is done in a deep green with twin beds and a rocker. The common sitting room, with a working fireplace, is intimate.

Around the property are a variety of accommodations, all in various states of remodeling. The Schubert House has a new feel to it; downstairs is a suite with a Murphy bed and a very private room with a bay window looking out onto the tennis court. The Carriage House is nice for families, with a TV, sitting area, daybed downstairs, and six bunk beds upstairs. The Field House has a small bedroom, but it's been nicely redone as a suite with a TV. The Browns are enthusiastic hosts and are constantly striving to improve and maintain the facilities.

The main dining room is elegant and candlelit, with low ceilings. A full dinner might include sautéed scamorze cheese with marinara sauce, followed by seafood fettuccine with shiitake mushrooms and a homemade dessert. Lighter meals are offered in the Tavern Room, where diners are surrounded by faux bookshelves and books and a beamed ceiling. Offerings here include warm chicken salad and a small steak with gallette potatoes. Most guests choose to take the hearty breakfast in the lovely sunroom, which has a terra cotta tile floor and area carpets. It overlooks the lawn, well-manicured gardens, and robins at play.

On the premises are a swimming pool, two tennis courts, lawn games, and bicycles to borrow. The sauna is great for aprs-ski; downhill skiing is available nearby at Stratton, Magic, and Bromley. The Browns will lend you equipment for cross-country skiing and give you day passes to ski trails at Hildene or Wild Wings Touring Center.

Green Mountain Inn

P.O. Box 60, Route 100
Stowe, Vermont 05672
802-253-7301
800-445-6629
Fax 802-253-9713

Innkeeper/manager: Dean Loukes
48 inn rooms, 15 motel rooms
$68-$115 per couple EP, $26 per person extra for MAP
All 3 meals served
Major credit cards
Children welcome
Pets welcome
Open year-round

At the corner of Route 100 and Mountain Road in the heart of the village sits this landmark, dating from 1833. Today it feels almost like a resort because of the hustle and bustle of the town and the new village athletic club behind the inn. It is complete, large, and ideal for those who want to be in the thick of it during Stowe's skiing and foliage seasons and summer festivals.

Since a complete restoration in 1985, the inn exudes grace. The first floor has many sitting areas, a bar and living room with fireplaces, a library with a chess set, Oriental rugs, and fine antiques reminiscent of old New England. Though there are accommodations on the third floor as well as the second, the second has some nice sitting areas and rambles all around, with more character. Two suites can be converted to triples. The guest rooms are all decorated with reproduction antiques; the queen-size beds have canopies.

Both dining rooms are leased to outside companies. The more formal one, on the first floor, serves hearty dishes. Downstairs, with old black-and-white photographs leading guests toward the bar, lighter dining is available. Wine is displayed in wrought-iron racks, a grand piano waits for a player, and the taproom is festooned with hundreds of antique whips and riding crops. Meals may also be served out on the patio, which leads to the pool. This area leads on to the new athletic club, disguised as an old red barn.

Only some of its facilities are complimentary for guests; they include the whirlpool, sauna, steam room, Nautilus, racquetball and squash courts, rowing machines, treadmills, free weights, Stairmaster, exercise classes, and massage rooms. Behind this barn, next to the large parking lot, are the ordinary motel units, which are accessible to the disabled.

The Inn at Long Last
Box 589
Main Street
Chester, Vermont 05143
802-875-2444

Innkeeper: Jack Coleman
32 rooms
$160 per couple, MAP, $90, single; $110 per couple, B&B,
   $65, single; add 15% gratuity
Breakfast and dinner served except Monday; Sunday brunch
Major credit cards
Children free under 3, half price under 15
No pets
Closed in April

The handsome Inn at Long Last (the former Chester Inn) is literally the center of the gracious old town of Chester, in the middle of the long, thin green. An imposing old double-porched inn with a large lobby, it has been completely redecorated and renamed by Jack Coleman, once president of Haverford College.

Each of the guest rooms has been decorated to illustrate something — an author, personality, place, or idea that appeals to Coleman. This isn't just a case of decor. The Charles Dickens

Room, for instance, has 1870s-style furnishings and colors, but there's also an original print advertising the appearance of a new Dickens volume and ample volumes of Dickens to delve into by the bed. The Brooklyn Bridge Room offers a fine picture of the bridge as well as books that conjure up its mood.

Space permitting, guests are invited to look at each room, deciding whether they would like to spend the night in the Grand Opera, the Connecticut River, or the George Stephens Room (Stephens was a goalie for the English soccer team playing in Addis Ababa in 1876; he let the ball pass between his legs to give the Ethiopians their celebrated 1-0 victory).

The dining room boasts not only excellent food, carefully prepared, but also an ornate 19th-century back bar built for a hotel in Bangor, Maine. Dinner is a relaxing candlelit affair with artfully presented dishes. The soups have become so famous that their recipes have been published and should now be available at the inn.

Coleman is both breakfast cook and genial host. He does not mind discussing his stints as a prisoner, street person, and blue-collar worker, roles he assumed the better to understand and write about. He seems to be approaching innkeeping as seriously and energetically as he did his past roles as college president and foundation head.

On a cool morning, you may wake to find the lobby filled with Gregorian chant, a fire blazing in the hearth, and coffee already set out for early risers. There is space here to linger all day — in comfortable corners of the library, on porch rockers, or in the library. Current best sellers are scattered around tables with the kind of abandon most inns reserve for by-the-yard books. The innkeeper himself is always as ready to discuss a book as the day's possibilities for exploring.

Chester itself is unusually interesting, with its share of art galleries and crafts shops. It includes an unusual stone village and a depot from which (in season) you can take a scenic excursion to Bellows Falls and back. It is also well positioned for striking off in myriad directions. But save time for the inn's lovely garden, its two tennis courts, and a walk back to the suspension footbridge, spanning a trout stream, at the back of the property.

In the winter there is plenty of skiing — nearby cross-country trails as well as formal touring centers not too far away. For downhill skiers, the Magic Mountains, Bromley, Ascutney, and Okemo are all within easy striking distance.

The Old Tavern at Grafton
Grafton, Vermont 05146
802-843-2231

Innkeeper: Richard Ernst
Accommodates 120
Rooms $50-$120 per couple, EP; house rates vary
All 3 meals served
Major credit cards
Children 8 and over welcome, under 8 in 3 houses
Horses welcome (facilities available); pets permitted in 2 houses
Open year-round except Christmas and April

The Old Tavern at Grafton, on the main street of this jewel-like town, is a gracious old stagecoach inn. Built in 1802, it became one of the most popular and distinguished stops between Boston and Montreal, numbering many dignitaries and literary figures — such as Teddy Roosevelt, Kipling, Emerson, and Thoreau — among its guests. A visit to the old barn, now a rustic lounge and bar with a fireplace, brings the inn's history to life. Wonderful old pictures of guests in long dresses and tails, stepping out of horse-drawn coaches and Model Ts, line the upstairs walls.

All of Grafton's houses were up for sale — cheap — in the 1940s and '50s. A New York financier, long a summer resident, thought up the Windham Foundation. Incorporated in 1963, it set about buying up the town, ultimately restoring it to its pre–Civil War glory.

The inn, appropriately elegant, offers spacious and handsomely furnished guest rooms, some with canopy beds. It also has several restored houses, with full kitchens, available for full or partial rental. Some of the houses are in town, but a few are tucked away in the surrounding woods, offering privacy and a spectacular view. The dining room is open for three meals a day; in the summer, lunch on the terrace is a treat. Jackets are required for men after 6:00 P.M.

The pleasures of the inn, and the town, include a lazy afternoon by the swimming pond followed by a round of tennis, long walks, a ski tour through pristine woods, and sitting on the porch under a clear sky. At the Windham Foundation you can see before-and-after photographs of the restored homes and buildings. The inn has its own stables, and there is a cross-country skiing center in town. Golf is nearby, and downhill skiing is a half-hour's drive.

Saxtons River Inn

Saxtons River, Vermont 05154
802-869-2110

Innkeeper: Michael Murphy
21 rooms (11 with private bath)
$40-$85 per couple, including Continental breakfast
Dinner served except on Tuesday
No credit cards
Children welcome
No pets
Open year-round

This is a very Victorian inn with a square, five-story tower and double porches, full of fascinating corners. The guest rooms are divided between this building and a Greek Revival mansion across the street. Obviously it's an interesting street, the only real street in this small southern Vermont town, which also includes an academy, a great general store, a craft shop or two, and a hardware store that rents bikes. This is good biking country, and the inn is a stop on organized bike tours as well as on inn-to-inn horseback riding treks.

The guest rooms are outstanding, having been renovated by Paulette and Bob Lynch. The sunny front room with big windows on the street is now an inviting pub with an ornate mahogany and walnut bar. The upstairs porch has been furnished to make a comfortable summer roost.

Each guest room has its own name and has been individually decorated with flowered wallpaper. There are separate sitting rooms on each floor and art gallery posters that suit the Victorian furniture. In addition, there is a complete tour guide of the area in each guest room, written by the innkeeper.

The dining room is open for guests and travelers from 6:00 to 9:00 P.M. every evening except Tuesday. The moderately priced, à la carte menu offers a wide choice of entrées, from seafood fettuccine and vegetable lasagna to stuffed lobster tails and filet mignon with roasted hazelnuts.

For skiers, Killington and Bromley are nearby and cross-country skiing is everywhere. Excellent fishing is in Saxtons River, tennis can be played at nearby Vermont Academy, and there is summer theater. Murder mystery weekends are also offered.

■ *See also:* The Middlebury Inn, Middlebury, Vermont

Itineraries

These itineraries are outline our favorite things to see and do in or near some of the places where one of the establishments we cite is located.

Connecticut

Connecticut is a curious New England anomaly. For some, it's a bit like New Jersey, a state you drive through on your way somewhere else. For others, it is a treasury of old New England in modern dress, with so much to offer that there's no reason to go farther. For most, it has both a Colonial aura and a maritime mystique that tells the first-time visitor to New England, "You're here."

Steeped in history and tradition (not for nothing is the Constitution State called the Land of Steady Habits), it's also as contemporary and "with it" as today. Nowhere is the ambivalence more pronounced than in Connecticut's western reaches, the New York border areas that for many are the gateway to New England.

You may know that Connecticut leads the country in per-capita income, that Hartford is the insurance capital of the nation, that Fairfield County is the headquarters of more Fortune 500 companies — and their executives — than anyplace outside New York City. But did you know that the state's trendy facade masks back-road byways, lovely lakes, meandering rivers, covered bridges, 17th-century houses, Colonial villages, and historic seaports — all in an area so compact that no point is more than two hours' drive from any other?

If you enter Connecticut from the southwest, as most visitors do, be sure to stray from Interstate 95, else you'll likely think you're in an extension of metropolitan New York rather than the domain of the Connecticut Yankee. The Merritt Parkway, for instance, is far more scenic and conveys a feeling of the rolling, wooded terrain that lies ahead and all around.

Along the Fairfield County "gold coast," pause in Greenwich

to ogle palatial estates both old and new. Shop in the enormous, enclosed Stamford Town Center in the glittering city of Stamford or browse through the galleries and boutiques of South Norwalk, which is gradually living up to its nickname, SoNo. Walk around Southport's harbor, one of Connecticut's first designated historic districts and a stage set from the 18th century. Head inland to the sylvan hills of New Canaan, its lush landscape harboring acres of fancy houses, and on to Ridgefield, as imposing a Colonial Connecticut town as you'll find within an hour's drive of New York City. The 1772 Keeler Tavern, now a house museum, paved the way for contemporary inns and restaurants of distinction, and the avant-garde Aldrich Museum of Contemporary Art blends nicely with the gracious old homes that still line Main Street.

Upcountry from Fairfield County is Connecticut's Northwest Corner—the "hidden corner," as many a travel article has described it. Hidden it is from the world at large, and you'll be surprised that such an area remains so rustic, remote, and unspoiled less than an hour from Hartford and two hours from Manhattan. Here, the Litchfield Hills face the better-known Berkshires and yield more public land and state parks than any other section of southern New England.

In the Northwest Corner, there are dense forests, steep hills, and rushing rivers. Kent and Cornwall are rugged and outdoorsy, the perfect foils for the late Yankee artist-author Eric Sloane and his museum collection of Early Americana; they share the glories of the Housatonic River, which is still crossed by a covered bridge. Sharon and Salisbury are sedate and sophisticated, havens for the good life as lived by noted residents and weekenders. Lake Waramaug, with its alpine setting and hills covered with vineyards, is Brigadoon revisited. All is quaint and quiet in charming Norfolk, the scene of a fine summer chamber music festival, as well as in Riverton, where reproduction Hitchcock chairs are made. The county seat is Litchfield, a National Historic Landmark town that rates as the quintessential 18th-century New England village. On the crest of a long ridge, it shelters a wealth of history (the nation's first law school, the birthplace of Harriet Beecher Stowe) and natural attractions (White Flower Farm and Topsmead).

Southeastern Connecticut presents still another face. Here the Connecticut River cuts beneath tree-covered hillsides before ending at Long Island Sound. Up the coastline are major maritime centers as well as historic seaports.

Heading southeast, meet the Connecticut River south of Middletown, say around the 19th-century hamlet of East Haddam, where the stage of the Victorian Goodspeed Opera House is lighted much of the year for pre-Broadway successes and where theatergoers sip champagne on a riverfront balcony as they relive the past. Actor William Gillette's medieval castle, now a state park open to the public, stands guard atop a hill at Hadlyme. Essex, a noted yachting center from which the first American warship was launched in the Revolution, is a river town of elegance and esteem; the Connecticut River Museum and the venerable Griswold Inn exude the area's heritage. Across the river in Old Lyme, the arts are celebrated as they were when the American Impressionists gathered at the turn of the century under the auspices of Florence Griswold; the artists' pastoral retreat is now a museum of note.

Follow the shoreline eastward to bustling New London and Groton, twin cities straddling the Thames River. This is navy and submarine territory, where the nuclear submarine *Nautilus* is on view along with more recent subs being worked on at Electric Boat Division shipyards. The U.S. Coast Guard Academy is poised on a hilltop across the river from the tight-security U.S. Naval Submarine Base, the nation's largest. This area has a number of museums and historic sites, Fort Griswold State Park, the 1678 Hempsted House, and the Shaw Mansion among them.

The prime attraction, however, is just to the east in Mystic. Mystic Seaport has 17 acres of ships and maritime memorabilia in a recreated 19th-century seafaring village. With the nearby Mystic Marinelife Aquarium and Old Mystick Village shopping complex, it makes Mystic the state's leading tourist destination by far.

On either side of busy Mystic are the waterfront villages of Noank and Stonington, which retain the look and feeling of past centuries. Off the beaten path and bypassed by time, they seem a world removed from their contemporary neighbors — still more evidence of the wonderful anomaly that is Connecticut.

Maine

The very mention of Maine conjures up the image of a "rock-bound coast," and that's what most visitors come to see. Many people try to see too much in their allotted time. While the distance from Kittery (on the New Hampshire border) to Eastport (facing Canada) is just 225 miles as the crow flies, it is more than 3,500 miles as the coastline tacks and jibs its way in and out of coves, inlets, reaches, and bays. It's far better to settle on one particular swatch of shoreline and to explore it thoroughly than to spend your vacation on Route 1.

From the moment you cross the Piscataqua River (its southern border), you are in the real Maine. York, the first exit on I-95 after the Maine Publicity Bureau's information center (don't fail to stop), is one of Maine's earliest settlements and one that still retains its vintage 1719 gaol, billed as the oldest surviving public building of the English colonies. There are a half-dozen beautiful old buildings in the village, all open to the public, as is the shore path from Sewall's Bridge east across the Wiggly Bridge and by the handsome old Victorian houses in York Harbor.

Ogunquit, a dozen miles up Route 1 (of course, there's a longer coastal route), is famed for its splendid, 3-mile-long, dune-backed beach; there's even some relatively warm water in the tidal river, also rimmed by beach. Ogunquit is also known for its ocean path (the Marginal Way), for much-painted Perkins Cove, and for one of the country's oldest summer theaters.

In Kennebunkport, the South Coast's other resort town, summer life revolves around Dock Square, a gathering of old riverside buildings now filled with shops, restaurants, and galleries. Inns trail off down Ocean Avenue, following the river to the rocky shoreline, here rimmed by another path and a spectacular coastal road leading to the fishing community at Cape Porpoise and to smooth Goose Rocks Beach beyond.

Portland, Maine's largest and most sophisticated city, is a livable, likable community with a pervasive sense of the sea, an outstanding museum, and a delightful assortment of shops, galleries, and restaurants packed into a five-block Victorian area known as the Old Port.

In the warm months, no visit to Portland is complete without a sally out into Casco Bay to visit one of the many islands, which include Peak's (just a 15-minute ferry ride from Customs House Wharf) and Chebeague, farther down the bay.

While it's not far across Casco Bay to Bailey Island (Casco Bay Lines offers a summer excursion), it takes a day to get there by land, especially if you stop at L. L. Bean's and the designer outlets in Freeport. Be sure to see the paintings by Winslow Homer (who lived and worked just south of Portland, at Prouts Neck) in the Bowdoin College Museum of Art in Brunswick.

North from Portland, the coast is characterized by long, fingerlike peninsulas that point out to sea. Bailey Island is the name for the southernmost tip of a long skinny land finger composed of islands linked by bridges.

In the days of the steamboats, the tips of these peninsulas

boarded a boat one evening in Boston and debarked the next day at Sebasco (near the tip of the Phippsburg peninsula), at Georgetown (the next peninsula up), at Boothbay Harbor (still a thriving resort, where boat excursions are the big draw), and at New Harbor (a lobstering cove near Penaquid Point).

Today, the mainstream traffic hugs Route 1, leaving the old resort villages to cater contentedly to the relatively small number of enterprising tourists willing to drive the narrow, winding peninsula roads and to the yachtsmen who still sail in.

For those enterprising travelers who lack their own yacht there are the Maine windjammers — more than a dozen two-masted schooners, some of them more than a hundred years old (in part), others recently built replicas of the vessels that once plied this coast by the thousands. Today's commercial windjammers carry between twenty and thirty-eight passengers and are based either in the commercial fishing port of Rockland or in Camden, a lively resort town in which the mountains meet the sea. They cruise the island-studded waters of Penobscot Bay, running "Down East" before the prevailing wind, then working their way back in the course of a week. Each evening they put into beautiful, relatively untouristed ports like Castine and Stonington or into islands.

Of all the Maine islands, Monhegan is, many agree, the most beautiful and certainly the most hospitable. Barely a mile square, it offers paths along its high cliffs as well as through tall pine woods and along stony beaches. Long a summer artists' colony, it also offers many galleries and a few places to stay. You can take a day trip to Monhegan from Boothbay Harbor, but those who want to stay more than a day or two prefer to park in Port Clyde, a small land's end village, from which the mailboat *Laura B* serves Monhegan year-round.

Few other islands offer inns or B&Bs. The exceptions are the old granite-quarrying community of Vinalhaven and the posh old summer havens on North Haven, Isleboro, and Isle au Haut (where the B&B is a former lighthouse keeper's home).

Maine's most famous island is Mount Desert, one conveniently linked to the mainland and webbed with roads for touring by car, others for exploring on horseback, and 120 miles of biking paths.

The summer people of the Gilded Era donated the core of Mount Desert to establish Acadia National Park, now enough of a lure to draw more than three and a half million visitors per year all the way to Bar Harbor. A number of former mansions survive in and around the village as well as in quieter parts of the island, like Northeast and Southwest harbors.

The most dramatic aspect of Mount Desert is its mountains — seventeen high, smoothly rounded, pink granite humps rising from the sea like giant bubbles. While you can circle and climb them, their amazing profiles elude the Mount Desert visitor. They are best viewed either from the west, from the lovely Blue Hill peninsula, or, more spectacularly, from the only truly beautiful stretch of Route 1 — as it continues Down East, by the Hancock peninsula, curving with the coast toward Winter Harbor and the stray scrap of Acadia National Park on Schoodic Point.

Beyond this point you enter Washington County, as Down East as you can get in this country. The harbors are filled with lobster boats and trawlers instead of pleasure craft, and lodging is limited.

Lodging is also limited through much of inland Maine, but there are a dozen old lake resorts that, like the peninsula resort villages, date from the steamboat era, in this case the small lake steamers that met trains. The lakes begin just west of Portland with Sebago, stretching westward in a thin chain to Bridgton, a friendly old village with (relatively) warm water beaches.

Maine's mountains also look down on some beautiful old villages. Bethel is now as much a winter ski resort as a summer golf and hiking mecca, and Rangeley, as much a region as a town, is spotted with large lakes ringed by high mountains.

Much of this mountain and lake region is more remote today than it was in the days of rail. A century ago, New Yorkers could take an overnight train to Greenville, for instance, then board a steamer for the islands and points along the shore of mighty Moosehead Lake, the largest of all Maine's inland waters. In the North Woods, the lure for most urban gentlemen was and remains fishing, a sport they pursued with the help of professional guides (a service still available). Many of the "sports lodges," classic Maine log lodges and log cabins, still survive. The most remote ones are found around Moosehead (one is actually an old clapboard hotel, once part of a remote logging camp) and Rangeley lakes and on Grand Lake in Washington County. Family variations on this theme can be found in the Belgrade Lakes, on Lake Webb, and as far south as Sebago.

Maine's North Woods cover more than six million acres of privately owned timberland bordered on two sides (the sides vary) by Canada. In recent years skiing and, even more recently, white water rafting have enticed many people into this area, the East's last sizable wilderness region. The big ski area here is Sugarloaf, in the steep Carrabassett Valley, once threaded by a narrow-gauge lumber railroad. Kingfield, at the base of this valley, still retains some of the opulence of its old lumber baron mansions and hotel.

Massachusetts

Massachusetts has many faces, each so different that residents think of themselves as coming from Boston, Cape Cod, the Berkshires, or some other region rather than from the state per se.

For many people, Boston is Massachusetts. It is, after all, one of the world's beautiful cities and invites exploration. Visitors amble its Freedom Trail (Revolutionary sites within the Boston National Historical Park), stopping along the way to dine and shop at Faneuil Hall Marketplace, pausing for cappuccino and cannoli in the North End. Although at its best in warm weather —when sidewalk cafés appear and excursion boats circle the harbor—Boston is a city of fine art and science museums, outstanding winter concerts, and the country's original First Night, a celebration of the arts on New Year's Eve.

The T (MBTA), one of the world's oldest public transit systems, links the waterfront museums, shops, and restaurants with Boston Common and the downtown department stores (you can walk right from the train into Filene's Basement). It also connects Back Bay's hotels and shops with the many attractions across the Charles River in Cambridge.

Cambridge is known chiefly as the home of Harvard University and the Massachusetts Institute of Technology (MIT); both offer museums and tours. And no one should miss Harvard Square, a lively shopping, dining, and people-watching scene with an amazing variety of bookstores.

An increasing number of Boston visitors choose, however, to stay north of the city, preferably in small, seaside inns within walking distance of the beach. These can be found both in Rockport, a picturesque art colony, and in neighboring Gloucester, an old fishing port that is now a major departure point for whale-watching expeditions; both towns have commuter rail service to Boston.

The most famous resort area in Massachusetts is, of course, Cape Cod, along with the islands of Nantucket and Martha's Vineyard.

The Cape is known for its 39-mile-long Great Beach and (relatively) warm water swimming and for a beauty that's composed of small, delicate details: a spray of beachgrass snared in shifting sand, a tern nesting in salt marsh, a mosaic of cranberries bobbing on the surface of a flooded bog. The trick, given the two narrow bridges connecting Cape Cod to the rest of southeastern Massachusetts, is to find your way to the Cape's quiet walkways and beaches at off-peak traffic hours. If you plan to come in July and August, do not to arrive on Friday afternoon or evening, when half of Boston seems to have the same idea.

Be aware that there is the Outer Cape, also known as the Lower Cape, which you reach by traversing the Mid Cape, which comes after the Upper Cape. There is also the cold water, relatively uncommercial Bay Side, with historic towns like Sandwich and Barnstable linked by Route 6, and the warm Sound Side, with resort towns like Falmouth and Mashpee served by Route 28. Luckily, there is also a Mid Cape Highway to whisk you to beach towns like Harwich Port and Chatham (a regal old resort village at the Cape's knobby elbow), ending in Orleans near the National Seashore's Salt Pond Visitors Center, the gateway to many miles of superb beach. Provincetown, at the Cape's outer tip, is an old fishing port with a lively summer scene as well as some inns, restaurants, and walks that make it a year-round destination. In the warm weather, a ferry links Provincetown directly with Boston.

The islands are also far livelier in fall, winter, and spring than they were just a few years ago. Most inns, restaurants, and shops now remain open year-round. Both Edgartown and Nantucket town stage early December Christmas celebrations, and Nantucket's spring Daffodil Festival has become a major event.

Nantucket is half the size of Martha's Vineyard, but it takes twice as long to get there. And Nantucket town itself is so absorbing that relatively few visitors ever explore the sand and heath beyond. The town's graceful clapboard and brick buildings date from its 1840s prominence as the world's leading whaling port, a story that's well told in historic houses and museums. Many visitors rent bikes, which, once beyond the town's cobblestones, provide sufficient transport to the beach or to the resort village of Siasconset.

Martha's Vineyard is New England's largest island, 10 miles at its widest and 20 miles long, blessed with fourteen separate beaches. The horseback rider, birder, beachcomber, and bicyclist can find plenty of breathing space. Most ferries put into Vineyard Haven, the island's central shopping center. Most visitors head for Edgartown, the handsome old whaling port with streets lined with former captain's mansions; the vintage 1870s summer village of Oak Bluffs; or maybe for the few inns Up Island, near the fishing village of Menemsha and the multicolored cliffs at Gay Head.

Rural Massachusetts is one of the least visited areas of all New England — in large part because the Mass. Turnpike speeds motorists so efficiently across the state to the Berkshires. The slower but far more scenic way west is Route 2, which draws you out to the historic town of Concord (known for its place in American literature as well as the Revolution), on into the Nashoba Valley and the hills beyond. Off this highway branch country roads like so many veins off the spine of a leaf. They lead to high old resort towns like Princeton and to gracious old Connecticut Valley towns like Northfield and Deerfield (known for its street lined with the dozen museum houses that form Historic Deerfield). As it moves west, Route 2 becomes the Mohawk Trail as it shadows an old Indian path along the Deerfield Valley, threading dramatically humped hills. These hills rise tier on tier and lend themselves, around Charlemont and West Hawley, to both downhill and cross-country skiing.

Williamstown, in the state's northwesternmost corner, is an attractive college town circled by mountains and known for its two fine art museums (the Clark Art Institute and the Williams College Museum of Art) as well as the Williamstown Theater Festival, in the summer. This is North Berkshire, a region of steep, isolated valleys cut by rushing rivers and divided by the massive presence of Mount Greylock, the highest mountain in Massachusetts.

As you drive south on Route 7, the mountains soften into hills and the valleys widen and become spotted with mansions, all built as summer "cottages" before the era of income taxes. (At Naumkeag, a Stockbridge cottage with splendid gardens, you'll learn that its original owner, Joseph Choate, endeared himself locally by managing to reverse an income tax law passed by Congress in 1894.)

Dozens of these cottages survive in Lenox, a number as inns. One estate, named Tanglewood by Nathaniel Hawthorne, is the summer home of the Boston Symphony Orchestra; another, designed and built by Edith Wharton, serves as a backdrop for performances of Shakespeare. A number of other summer concert series, not to mention opera, ballet, and summer theater, are all staged here in Central and South Berkshire. The museums range from the definitive collection of Norman Rockwell canvases and prints to the peaceful Shaker Village at Hancock. The two commercial villages in this area are Lee and Great

Barrington, and, as you move south, the pace slackens. Sheffield is a quietly gracious old antiques center and New Marlborough is a refreshingly sleepy village.

The quick way back to Boston is, of course, the Mass. Pike, but there are other options, notably Route 9, another old east-west high road that follows rivers and ridges, inviting you to pause for a night or two at some of the fine old hill farms in towns like Cummington. Known for its poets past and present, Cummington is also the former summer home of William Cullen Bryant, whose house is now a fascinating museum.

If you do take the Pike, be sure to stop in Sturbridge, where Old Sturbridge Village recreates the life of rural New England in the 1830s.

This South Worcester County area also saw some of America's earliest industrial villages, especially along the Blackstone Canal, completed in 1818 to link Worcester with Providence, Rhode Island. The Stanley Woolen Mill in Uxbridge is the most picturesque of the surviving mills. Under the same management for seven generations, it produces quality woolens, available in its mill store.

New Hampshire

New Hampshire is chiefly known for its White Mountains, the highest peaks in New England. More than half of its lodging places cluster in the few resort villages that pocket the 751,000-acre White Mountain National Forest. Another third are in the Lakes Region, offering water as well as mountain views. There are also a scattering of fine places to stay in the Connecticut River valley and in the Monadnock Region, New Hampshire's southernmost roll of hills.

Any tour of the Granite State should begin in Portsmouth, a gracious old city that has preserved its long history in the form of aristocratic houses, a mid-19th-century market area filled with shops and restaurants, and a 10-acre museum village called Strawbery Banke. In the summer there is free entertainment, including theater, in Prescott Park, on the river, and there is swimming just downriver, along New Hampshire's short but sandy bit of shore.

To reach the mountains, take the Spaulding Turnpike at the Portsmouth Rotary all the way until it peters out into Route 16, a country highway that offers some delightful detours, like the 2-mile run into Tamworth, a beautiful old village with a summer theater and view of Mount Chocorua, or the few miles into Eaton Center, a picturesque village on Crystal Lake.

New Hampshire's biggest resort town is North Conway, a skiing and climbing center that has more than its share of outlet stores. Mount Washington, New England's highest mountain, towers just north of town; you can approach it by continuing north on Route 16, by the lovely mountain village of Jackson (be sure to stop) and through steep-walled Pinkham Notch. You might want to drive the Auto Road (or ride up in one of the vans) all the way to the summit of Mount Washington; it's a memorable experience, whatever the weather. You can also stop at the Appalachian Mountain Club's headquarters and inquire about hiking trails and guided expeditions.

Route 16 meets Route 2 above Pinkham Notch; if you enjoy exploring a ways off the tourist trail, you might turn east along the Androscoggin River and following it through Shelburne and into Maine (see the Bethel section of the Maine itinerary). Or turn down Route 113 through Evans Notch, following this beautiful byway south all the way back to Conway. You can also turn west on Route 2/16, continuing north on Route 16 as it follows the Androscoggin to Errol; it's just a short way east on Route 26 to the Balsams, a grand old resort hotel in Dixville Notch.

From Boston there is another quick way into the White Mountains: Interstate 93. In less than 2 hours you are at Squam Lake (the real Golden Pond) and at the exit for Waterville Valley, one of New Hampshire's largest ski resorts. Waterville Valley stages a summer arts festival and offers all the facilities of a condominium-based summer resort.

A bit farther north on I-93 you can cut over to Conway on the Kancamagus Highway, a 37-mile wilderness road through the National Forest, or you can continue on through Franconia Notch, another spectacular mountain pass offering a number of places to stop the car and walk or hike. Its most famous attraction is the stony-faced profile known as the Old Man of the Mountain. The old resort village of Franconia is squirreled away in a hidden valley beyond the Notch.

Beyond Franconia Notch, I-93 snakes west through the Amonoosuc Valley into Vermont (see the Northeast Kingdom in the Vermont itinerary). We suggest you turn east on Route 3, through the National Forest to Twin Mountain. You might want to continue north on Route 3 to the interesting old resort town of Whitefield, and you will certainly want to turn south on Route 302 into Bretton Woods, a small settlement built around the grand Mount Washington Hotel, set in turn against the western flank of Mount Washington. The cog railway, in business since the 1860s, climbs to the summit (you can also hike). Route 302 continues south through Crawford Notch to North Conway.

South of the White Mountains, I-89 forks off I-93 and cuts across a mountain- and lake-spotted region to the Connecticut River and on into Vermont. In less than 2 hours from Boston you are in the lovely old college town of New London, also known for its ski mountain, King Ridge. The next exit is for Route 11, which plunges downhill for 4 miles to the resort village of Sunapee. In the summer, Lake Sunapee is the centerpiece, and in winter, Mount Sunapee is a popular ski area. Route 11 continues west through interesting old towns to the Connecticut River. Turn north on Route 5 and follow it a few miles to the covered bridge and, just beyond, to the summer home of the 19th-century sculptor Augustus Saint-Gaudens (his house, now a National Historic Site, is the setting for outdoor concerts on summer weekends).

Continue on up Route 5, along the river, to Hanover, the home of Dartmouth College. As we have noted in the Vermont itinerary, this stretch of the Upper Valley—which also includes Lyme and Orford—is distinguished by many handsome 18th-century homes, reminders of the era when residents considered forming a state of their own (it would have been called New Connecticut).

This hilly, southwestern region of New Hampshire is a high, granite island unto itself. The state's recent economic boom region lies just to the east, and I-89 skirts it to the north. Its landmark is the lone mountain that has given its name to all similar monadnocks throughout the world, and it is said to be the most frequently climbed of the world's mountains, right up there after Fuji. Mount Monadnock towers above picture-perfect white clapboard villages like Jaffrey Center and Fitzwilliam, and it's visible from other picturesque villages, such as Hancock and Temple. Little more than an hour from Boston, this is a region of winding roads, wooded hills, and an increasing number of bed-and-breakfasts and small inns.

Rhode Island

Newport, Newport, Newport—that's what most tourists see when they come to Rhode Island, but the Ocean State has much more to offer than the glittering mansions and pricey waterfront boutiques of that venerable seaport. Newport excepted, Rhode Island remains one of the least discovered corners of New England, yet it has many attractions. The South County shoreline has a string of what many consider to be the finest ocean beaches in the country. The capital of Providence is richly endowed with well-preserved 18th- and 19th-century buildings. And lovely Block Island, 12 miles out to sea, is a Victorian jewel, still largely untouched by the commercial world.

Rhode Island's southern seacoast from Narragansett to Westerly is known as South County to natives. Some 20 miles of public and private beach are the prime attraction here. There are barrier beaches, protecting a line of salt ponds that are the home of all kinds of wild waterfowl and fish. Trustom Pond, Kimball Refuge, and the Great Swamp State Management Area are some of the wildlife sanctuaries in the area that are worth visiting. Charter boats are available for deep-sea fishing in Galilee, and many people surf-cast with good success from stone breachways at Matunuck, Charlestown, Quonochontaug, and Weekapaug.

In Narragansett, a modern condominium-shopping complex overlooks Narragansett Beach, a favorite of surfers. South Kingstown has fine, unspoiled beaches, but parking for nonresidents can cost as much as $20. (State beaches charge only $3 for parking, but they tend to be crowded.) A small company called the Theater-by-the-Sea presents a series of performances each summer.

The township of Westerly, on the Connecticut border, includes Watch Hill, a famous society watering hole of the early 1900s that has retained much of its genteel charm, and the less pretentious but even more exclusive cottage colony at Weekapaug. Watch Hill has a charming waterfront arcade of small shops and a historic flying horse carousel; Weekapaug's unspoiled shorefront is entirely private, open only to residents and guests at the inn. Between Watch Hill and Weekapaug lies Misquamicut, a strip of family amusements and a state beach. A waterslide, roller-skating rink, and miniature golf course are among its attractions.

The second largest city in New England, Providence was founded in the 1600s by Roger Williams, a religious refugee from Massachusetts. Many fine 18th-century houses have been preserved in the College Hill and Benefit Street neighborhoods, on the east side, and beautifully restored Victorian houses dot the Broadway and Armory districts on the west side. Although only a few houses are open to the public, walking tours sponsored by the Providence Preservation Society help to recreate the aura of earlier times for tourists.

Providence's small downtown area suffered an economic depression after its heyday in the early 1900s, but today its lovely collection of old public buildings has been joined by some flashy new additions, and the Capitol Center project is pumping new life into the city.

Rhode Island's capital is the home of Brown University and the Rhode Island School of Design as well as the nationally celebrated Trinity Square Repertory Company. The Civic Center has a busy schedule of rock concerts and sports events, and there are fancy shopping areas in the Arcade (an 1828 Greek Revival building that was the country's first enclosed shopping mall), Davol Square Marketplace (a former rubber factory complex), and along South Main Street (the center of Providence's shipping industry in the 17th and 18th centuries).

Nightlife, boutiques, fine restaurants, museums, mansions, yachting, ocean views, and swimming: Newport has them all — to such an extent that traffic and parking are big headaches for residents and tourists alike in summer.

The restored mansions of the Gilded Age robber barons are indisputably the stars of Newport. Tours are offered of nearly a dozen of these carefully restored white elephants, relics of the time before income taxes in America.

Hammersmith Farm, the Auchincloss family estate that was used as a summer retreat by John F. Kennedy during his presidency, is also open for tours; its gardens are particularly lovely in the spring. Newport's Colonial harborfront has been dwarfed by the tourist industry, but there are still fine examples of 17th- and 18th-century architecture. Hunter House Museum and Trinity Church are two of the best. Cliff Walk is a 3½-mile public park that wends its way between the backyards of the Bellevue Avenue mansions and the ocean. The Walk and Ocean Drive, along the south coast, are two of Newport's most scenic public waterfront areas. Middletown — Newport's less ostentatious neighbor to the north — has good ocean beaches (Sachuest is the most popular) and two notable historic restorations: Prescott Farm, the scene of a Revolutionary War skirmish, and Whitehall, the Colonial residence of the British philosopher George Berkeley.

Jamestown, on an island in Narragansett Bay to the west of Newport, is quiet and mostly residential. Linked by bridges to Newport and the Narragansett area, it is popular with boaters. There are beautiful state parks at Beavertail Point and Fort Wetherill on the island's south coast.

Reached by ferry from Galilee, Newport, and Providence or

by air from Westerly, Block Island is less than 20 square miles in size. Largely uncommercial, it attracts people who like the simpler summer pleasures of swimming, sailing, fishing, and bird-watching. Vast, gently aging frane hotels have been island landmarks since the late 1800s, when Block Island had its modest heyday as a beach resort.

Excellent ocean beaches line the island's east coast, where the sand is fine and white, the view endless and the water a clear blue breaking into a moderate surf. A scenic spot is Mohegan Bluffs, 150-foot clay cliffs along the south coast. Extensive conservation areas are open to the public, including Rodman's Hollow and the Maze. Old Harbor, the island's central village, has shops that are mostly of the postcard and T-shirt variety. A single tiny movie theater and a handful of earthy nightclubs are the only nightlife available, but there are several good restaurants.

Vermont

Vermont is one state that defies an attempt to outline itineraries. Every Green Mountain community offers something of interest, and there are any number of beautiful ways of getting from one village to the next. What you do in Vermont is pick a place — ideally places — to stay and then poke around, exploring backroads that go in all directions.

Vermont is also difficult to break into regions. The Champlain Valley is on the west and the Connecticut Valley on the east, but nowhere are you out of sight of mountains, and everywhere you find the steepled white churches, the general stores, the farmland, and the country inns for which Vermont is known.

Interstate highways play little part in Vermont. True, I-91 snakes up the eastern edge, a conduit for visitors from the south, and both I-93 and I-89 usher in flatlanders from the west. But Route 100, a twisty, old, two-lane road that follows the spine of the Green Mountains right up the middle of the state, remains its principal connector.

Having said all this, we'll divide the Green Mountain State into regions and suggest some ways of getting around.

Southern Vermont includes the West River towns of Newfane, West Townshend — both with outstanding village commons — and Jamaica, all strung like pearls along Route 30. Putney, overlooking the Connecticut River, is known for its scholars and craftsmen. A narrow, paved backroad takes you over the hills and down through a covered bridge to Route 30, just south of Newfane. You can dogleg north on Route 30 for less than a mile and then head west (turn at Maple Valley Ski Area) over an exceptional backroad that follows the Rock River through Williamsville and South Newfane (a tiny gem of a village). The road takes you over steep hills and down to Route 100 in the Deerfield Valley, which is dominated by Mount Snow and Haystack, two ski resorts with 18-hole golf courses. You can also reach West Dover (the village here) via Route 9, a major east-west road that passes Marlboro (known for its superb summer music) and meets Route 100 at Wilmington, a picturesque combination of resort town and trading center. While the 9 miles north to Mount Snow are lined with motels, shops, restaurants, and condominiums, the scenery changes abruptly just north of the entrance to the ski area. Here Route 100 becomes a wooded byway for the 8 miles it takes to join Route 30 in East Jamaica.

Route 30 and 100 part ways again a few miles farther north, the former continuing west past Stratton Mountain (one of Vermont's poshest, most sophisticated ski resorts) and on to Manchester, known for its shopping and its fine summer arts center. Manchester Village is one of New England's most elegant summer resorts, complete with marble sidewalks, golf courses, an old hotel with columns and a tower, and a fabulous mansion built by Robert Todd Lincoln, the son of the president.

From Manchester you can head north on Route 7 to the handsome old community of Dorset (known for its summer theater) and continue through this wide valley to Wallingford. Or you can turn east again, quickly climbing into the Green Mountains on Route 11, passing Big Bromley Ski Area (which maintains an Alpine Slide in warm weather). Take Route 11 north at Peru on the Landgrove Road, a scenic byway. This passes the Hapgood Recreation Area (a great summer swimming spot) and continues through the village of Landgrove on the way back to joining Route 100 in Weston (just 12 miles north of where it left Route 30).

Weston is one of Vermont's most famous villages, complete with an oval common, a bandstand, one of the country's oldest summer playhouses, and the state's most famous general store (it has a thick mail-order catalogue). You can take a pleasant road east (maybe detouring a mile to Simonsville) for 11 miles to Chester, a proud old town with a fine Historical Society and Art Guild and excursion trains connecting it with both Bellows Falls and Ludlow. Seven miles south is Grafton, an exquisite village that has been called Vermont's Cinderella. A decaying derelict as late as the early '60s, the entire village—including its inn and cheese company—have been restored by a private foundation. Of course, you can also reach Grafton by driving 9 miles up Route 35 from Townshend.

Drive north from Chester, or from Weston, or west through Cuttingsville from Wallingford and you come to Ludlow, a former mill town (the picturesque mill has been converted to condominiums). It has a major ski resort, Okemo, rising from its heart. East of Ludlow you pass through the former mill village of Proctorsville, on through river valleys that gradually widen into rich farmland around Weathersfield. North from Ludlow, Route 100 follows a chain of lakes all the way to Plymouth, where a small white clapboard village has been preserved, complete with cheese factory.

Central Vermont is effectively divided by the Green Mountains in this region. Route 4 is the sole major east-west road, beginning as a narrow winding way along the Quechee River in the east and passing (to the disgust of its patrician residents) through Woodstock, frequently called the most beautiful and sophisticated town in Vermont. Continuing west along the Ottauquechee River, the road widens, becoming a highway as it crosses Route 100 (just north of Plymouth) and climbs into Sherburne Pass, past Killington, the largest ski resort in the East. It continues on through Mendon to Rutland, bypassing Chittenden, a small village with some splendid views of a large reservoir, backed by mountains.

North from Killington, Route 100 follows the spine of the Green Mountains through valleys that alternately widen, as in Rochester, and narrow, as in Granville Gulch. The resort area here is the Mad River or Sugarbush Valley (it's known as both). Here the old logging villages of Warren and Waitsfield have been transformed in recent decades, evolving a new look and lifestyle spawned by the ski areas just as earlier villages took shape around their greens.

The top of these ski mountains commands a spectacular view west across the Champlain Valley and Lake Champlain. A few high passes cut across from Route 100 to this region: Route 73 runs through the Brandon Gap, and Route 25 climbs up and up through the Middlebury Gap and down into the valley, where the old college town of Middlebury is the principal community. Many visitors continue west through Shoreham and across the narrow, southern reach of Lake Champlain to Fort Ticonderoga or continue to lakeside resorts near Vergennes.

On the opposite side of the state, the Connecticut River Valley is, at this juncture, known as the Upper Valley. A distinct region that includes river towns in both New Hampshire and

Vermont, this rich bottomland was settled early on, and in the late 18th century it looked as though it would be a state all its own, with Hanover, New Hampshire (the site of Dartmouth College), as the capital. Hanover remains the cultural center for this area, which extends north along the Connecticut well beyond picturesque Thetfords and Fairlee, where two lakes, Fairlee and Morey, offer resort facilities.

Northern Vermont contains the state's most famous resort town, its largest city, and its least visited corners.

Stowe is the resort village, a summer haven since the mid-19th century and one of the country's oldest, liveliest ski resorts. Vermont's highest peak, Mount Mansfield, is here, along with its highest pass, Smugglers Notch (which is closed in the winter). Stowe is a wintertime mecca for cross-country as well as downhill skiers; in summer it offers golf, horseback riding, tennis, and mountain biking.

Burlington, with less than 40,000 people, is Vermont's biggest city, a lively college town with grand views across Lake Champlain. Just south of town is the Shelburne Museum, a magnificent collection of Americana amassed by Electra Havemeyer Webb, whose family built New England's grandest lakeside estate. The central mansion is now an inn, and the grounds are used in summer for Mozart concerts.

North from Burlington the highway heads for Montreal, but the byway (Route 2) leads across a long causeway right out into Lake Champlain and onto its largest islands: Grand Isle and North Hero. This is beautiful summer country—rolling farmland with views across the lake to high mountains on both sides. In this corner of the state there are a few isolated resorts, one on the lake at Highgate Springs and two in the mountains. Bolton Valley, between Stowe and Burlington, is a condominium-based resort that began as a ski area but now offers an attractive summer program as well.

The Northeast Kingdom refers to Vermont's three northeasternmost counties, a name coined by the late Senator George Aikin. This is the state's least seen and, some believe, its most beautiful corner. There are a few dramatic mountains—Jay Peak, a ski resort near Montgomery Village, and Burke Mountain in East Burke. Generally, however, it is an open, gently rolling land of humped hills and farmland, spotted with lakes (some with old resort communities like Greensboro) and some beautiful hill towns, among which the most beautiful is Craftsbury Common. There are also some fine old Connecticut River villages—like Lower Waterford and East Barnet—with views extending across the valley to the White Mountains.

Recommended Guidebooks

These books are excellent sources of sightseeing and restaurant suggestions. This chapter was excerpted from Going Places: The Guide to Travel Guides *by Greg Hayes and Joan Wright, Harvard Common Press, 1988.*

New England

American Jewish Landmarks: A Travel Guide and History. I: The East. *Bernard Postal and Lionel Koppman, Fleet Press, 1977, 400 pages, paper, $18.95.*

Part of a scholarly four-volume set, well suited to the interested traveler, with copious amounts of sightseeing material, well researched and always placed in its historical context.

The Art Museums of New England. *463 pages, cloth, $35.*
The Art Museums of New England: Connecticut & Rhode Island. *111 pages, paper, $8.95.*
The Art Museums of New England: New Hampshire, Vermont & Maine. *101 pages, paper, $8.95. S. Lane Faison, Jr., David Godine, 1982.*

Your choices are several: one hardbound edition covering all of New England or one of three paperback editions of different New England regions (the third is listed under Massachusetts). Either way, you'll receive a beautifully done, superbly crafted, comprehensive work—a publishing work of art—that will serve as an authoritative guide to more than 100 museums housing the art treasures of the New England area. The detail and the amount of research involved is astonishing. Though some changes have no doubt occurred since its last revision, Faison's work is clearly the resource to buy. Absolutely superb.

384 • Recommended Guidebooks

The Best of Daytripping & Dining in Southern New England and Nearby New York. Betsy Witteman and Nancy Webster, Wood Pond Press, 1985, 186 pages, paper, $7.95.

These two experienced authors (several of their other books are listed) have a real knack for assembling great itineraries for outings of every sort. This book offers you 25 day trips in Massachusetts, Rhode Island, Connecticut, and nearby areas of New York. They are thoughtfully arranged to include places to see, wonderful spots to eat, plus clear, hand-drawn detail maps. A good resource.

Coastal Daytrips in New England. Harriet Webster, Yankee Books, 1986 (2nd ed.), 192 pages, paper, $9.95.

Yankee Books has another Daytrips book, but this one sticks firmly to the New England coastline. And what a coastline it is! Anyone would be happy combing such a wonderful place, but *Coastal Daytrips* will add to your pleasure and fun by providing lots of interesting, well-researched suggestions.

A Cyclist's Guide: New England Over the Handlebars. Michael Farny, Little, Brown, 1975, 174 pages, paper, $9.95.

Old, but still available by all accounts, this guide will give you some good ideas for cycling trips — thirty-eight in all — from a few hours to four days in length. Includes mileage log and personal observations.

Day Trips and Budget Vacations in New England. Patricia and Robert Foulke, Globe Pequot, 1988 (2nd ed.), 264 pages, paper, $8.95.

Here are fourteen thorough, flexible, dependable itineraries to vacation fun. The Foulkes are excellent at putting all the pieces together — from things the kids might enjoy to ways to stay within your budget. You will find both well-known destinations and those off the beaten path. This is a good choice for help with vacation plans.

Favorite Daytrips in New England. Michael Schuman, Yankee Books, 1987 (4th ed.), 192 pages, paper, $9.95.

A New England favorite, this well-written little guide presents forty interesting trips that should take a day or less. Thorough and well researched, there are trips for the whole family or just the two of you.

Favorite Weekends in New England. Harriet Webster, Yankee Books, 1986, 192 pages, paper, $8.95.

Another good idea book from Yankee, this one presents a diverse, well-organized collection of weekend trips—everything from ski tours to museums, summer theaters, and more—as well as how to get there, helpful phone numbers, and the like.

Festivals of New England. *Kathy Kincade and Carl Landau, Landau Communications, 1989, 218 pages, paper, $9.95.*
A handy listing of the region's most colorful festivals throughout the year.

Getaways for Gourmets in the Northeast. *Nancy Webster and Richard Woodworth, Wood Pond Press, 1984, 306 pages, paper, $10.95.*
While it covers places to stay, this is primarily a guide to good food in out-of-the-way places. The descriptions and evaluations are extensive and, besides lodging choices, there are other treats for each of the eighteen spots selected. The only problem is the clear need for an update. This is a fine book that deserves a new edition.

The Great Weekend Escape Book from Virginia to Vermont. *Michael Spring, Dutton, 1987 (3rd ed.), 417 pages, paper, $10.95.*
Spring is an excellent travel writer, the author of the highly regarded Great European Itineraries. Here he writes "as though you were a close friend who sat me down and said, 'Tell me about twenty-six glorious weekends.'" And glorious they are. Writing in a friendly style, Spring covers the gamut: major attractions, the arts, antiques and crafts, tours, walks, biking, fishing, riding, skiing, golf, things for kids, after-hours options, and, of course, food and lodging. Excellent.

Guide to the National Park Areas: Eastern States. *David and Kay Scott, Globe Pequot, 1987 (2nd ed.), 272 pages, paper, $10.95.*
Covering all the states east of the Mississippi, this volume has a fairly brief but informative rundown on the two hundred park areas run by the National Park Service. Each writeup gives you a map (that includes the visitors' center), notes the available facilities, camping options, if you can fish, the best trails (if any), and where to find additional information. A handy compendium.

Guide to the Restaurants of New England. *New England Monthly, Little, Brown, 1987, 181 pages, paper, $8.95.*

More than three hundred reviews from the *New England Monthly* are brought together here. Each is well written, with good descriptions of food and atmosphere and the occasional complaint. Practical facts are included: price range, hours, credit cards accepted, and location.

A Guide to Writer's Homes in New England. *Miriam Levine, Apple-wood Books, 1984, 186 pages, paper, $10.95.*

Nineteen homes of famous writers are chronicled in this interesting work. A pretty line drawing of the home and a photograph of the writer precedes some history of the house, its relationship to the writer's life, a bibliographic essay, and more. The effort is to "give the traveler and reader a complete picture of what life must have been like in these houses." The writing style is a bit short and matter-of-fact, but this is nonetheless a fine book. Information on visiting (address, phone, hours, fees) is included.

The Handbook for Beach Strollers from Maine to Cape Hatteras. *Donald Zinn, Globe Pequot, 1985 (2nd ed.), 246 pages, paper, $9.95.*

For the thalassopsammonphile (a.k.a. beach lover), this book provides a wonderful compendium of botanical and zoological information to enhance any sojourn to the eastern seaboard by the budding naturalist. The book sounds a little like a textbook, yet Zinn's love of his subject shines through, keeping it readable even for the nonscientist. It is arranged by the types of ocean life you may encounter and even includes the author's sea source recipes.

How New England Happened: A Guide to New England through Its History. *Christina Tree, Little, Brown, 1976, 269 pages, paper, $14.95.*

Still in print, this account of New England's history from the Vikings to the Victorians covers all aspects of life in the region, its crafts and social customs, its architecture and industry, and does it in a particularly entertaining and readable way that's keyed to hundreds of places that are still worth a visit.

Inside Outlets: The Best Bargain Shopping in New England. *Naomi Rosenberg and Marianne Sekulow, Harvard Common Press, 1985, 204 pages, paper, $8.95.*

A comprehensive guide to factory outlets throughout New England, this book offers a vast array of choices in every price range for almost every type of good imaginable that will save you up to 75 percent of retail. The authors have also assembled shopping itineraries for particularly scenic areas of New England. They give you plenty of tips of what to look for, what to avoid, and where the very best "Blue Ribbon" stores are. Grab your wallet! They can get it for you wholesale!

Island Hopping in New England. *Mary Maynard, Yankee Books, 1986, 176 pages, paper, $8.95.*

There are oodles of islands along the New England coast and you can visit quite a few of them. Here is a well-organized guide to dozens of these offshore hideaways with good descriptions, revealing photos, how to get to each island, where to stay, and what to do there. An excellent resource.

Marilyn Wood's Wonderful Weekends. *Marilyn Wood, Prentice Hall Press, 1987, 680 pages, paper, $11.95.*

This is definitely one of the great getaway guides for those in the New York area. It describes twenty-five general destinations in tremendous detail, offering an incredible variety of events, lodging, dining, walking tours, sightseeing, and other activities. Included are knowledgeable, extensive reviews of more than 450 inns and 700 restaurants. Even the maps are clear and well done. This is a truly wonderful resource — and all the places are within 200 miles of the Big Apple. Recommended.

Michelin Green Guide: New England. *Michelin Guides and Maps, 1986 (3rd ed.), 214 pages, paper, $10.95.*

One of the excellent titles in the Michelin Green Guide sightseeing series.

New England Gardens Open to the Public. *Rolce Payne, David Godine, 1979, 230 pages, cloth, $20.*

Excellent descriptions and illustrations of 150 gardens open to the public. Included are the seasons each is open, hours, and charges, if any. Considering the publication date, you would be wise to call ahead and confirm the current hours and charges before you go (phone numbers are provided for those places charging an admission fee). And, of course, there are quite a few locations that do not charge at all. Certainly a first-rate though unfortunately somewhat dated resource.

New England's Special Places: A Daytripper's Guide. *Michael Schuman, Countryman Press, 1986, 192 pages, paper, $10.95.*

Here are short, beautifully crafted essays on forty-four New England destinations that offer a real insight into the New England character. They can be reached from almost anywhere in New England in a day's time (well, sometimes a long day) and are all of a quality that the author feels he could recommend them. His choices cover a wide range: Colonial New England locations, presidents' homes, special historic sites like the New England Maple Museum and the Saugus Iron Works, castles, mansions, even special sports and games museums. A great selection that will delight the whole family.

Secluded Islands of the Atlantic Coast. *David Yeadon, Crown, 1984, 224 pages, paper, $8.95.*

Yeadon directs his considerable talent toward an array of little-known and relatively unspoiled islands along the Atlantic seaboard. Through his illustrations and charming, informative writing, he lets you in on some interesting vacation ideas.

The Sierra Club Guide to the National Parks of the East and Middle West. *Sierra Club Books, 1984, 300 pages, paper, $14.95.*

Part of the Sierra Club National Parks Guide series, which is reviewed in more detail under Series Reviews.

The Sierra Club Naturalist's Guide to the North Atlantic Coast. *Michael and Deborah Berrill, 1981, 512 pages, paper, $12.95.*
The Sierra Club Naturalist's Guide to Southern New England. *Neil Jorgensen, 1978, 448 pages, paper, $12.95.*
The Sierra Club Naturalist's Guide to the Piedmont of Eastern North America. *Michael Godfrey, Sierra Club Books, 1980, 432 pages, paper, $9.95.*

Three titles in this excellent natural history series, Sierra Club Naturalist's Guide, which is reviewed in more detail under Series Reviews.

Smithsonian Guide to Historic America, Northern New England. *Vance Muse, Stewart, Tabori & Chang, 1989, 294 pages, paper, $17.95.*

Lavish photography, historical paintings, engravings, and maps make this an excellent guide to northern New England's towns, historical homes, and politically, militarily, and culturally significant locales. Practical information is given for major sites as well. Readable, interesting history and anecdotes. An excellent series.

Smithsonian Guide to Historic America, Southern New England. Henry Wiencek, Stewart, Tabori & Chang, 1989, 415 pages, paper, $17.95.

The southern New England version of this already classic series.

Special Museums of the Northeast: A Guide to Uncommon Collections from Maine to Washington, D.C. Nancy Frazier, Globe Pequot, 1985, 304 pages, paper, $9.95.

A good overview of 144 small but fascinating museums covering a vast array of subjects, such as locks, soups, computers, antique toys, baseball, photography, dogs, and on and on. Lots of good ideas.

Water Escapes: Great Waterside Vacation Spots in the Northeast. Betsy Wittemann and Nancy Webster, Wood Pond Press, 1987, 418 pages, paper, $12.95.

Two seasoned travel writers present you with thirty-six waterside holiday ideas, including all the information you will need to choose among them—where to stay, where to eat, what to do, camping, boating, shopping, hikes and nature walks, and more. Every selection is given an extensive and informative writeup. A first-class job and an excellent idea.

Watertrips: A Guide to East Coast Cruise Ships, Ferryboats, and Island Excursions. Theodore Scull, International Marine Publishing, 1987, 264 pages, paper, $12.95.

This guide will give you all the data necessary to arrange a trip by water anywhere from Maine to Virginia. Scull provides a well-written background for each of these inspired vacation ideas as well as practical advice, such as where to park the car and costs. Excellent.

Weekending in New England: A Selective Guide to the Most Appealing Destinations for All Seasons. Betsy Wittemann and Nancy Webster, Wood Pond Press, 1986, 242 pages, paper, $8.95.

The authors of the excellent *Water Escapes*, described above, first teamed up in 1979 to compile this durable assemblage of thoughtful ideas for wonderful weekends in New England.

Connecticut

Where to Eat in Connecticut: The Very Best Meals and the Very Best Deals. *Jane and Michael Stern, Globe Pequot, 1985, 190 pages, paper, $8.95.*

Simply wonderful assessments of eighty-four of the best restaurants in the state. And the Sterns do it right—they dine anonymously, they pay for their own meals, and they sample each restaurant at least twice. There are selections for every taste and pocketbook.

Maine

Discovering Acadia National Park and Mount Desert Island, Maine. *Albert and Miriam d'Amato, Professional Education Services, 1984, 141 pages, paper, $5.95.*

A useful rundown of various points of interest in the park plus information on accessibility, facilities, short hikes, parking, and things of particular interest to children.

Katahdin: A Guide to Baxter State Park and Katahdin. *Stephen Clark, Thorndike Press, 1985, 211 pages, paper, $8.95.*

An excellent guide to the trails and campgrounds of this unique state park. Its fascinating history is well described, the myriad trails carefully detailed (including distances and other pertinent data), winter uses discussed, and the park regulations carefully laid out. All the information you will need is here, including a large, separate topographical map.

Maine: An Explorer's Guide. *Christina Tree and Mimi Steadman, Countryman Press, 1987 (3rd ed.), 293 pages, paper, $13.95.*

An excellent volume in the highly regarded Explorer's Guide series, which is reviewed in more detail under Series Reviews. Updated every two years.

The Maine Coast: A Nature Lover's Guide. *Dorcas Miller, Globe Pequot, 1979, 188 pages, $8.95.*

Published in cooperation with the Maine Audubon Society, this is the handbook you need to understand more of the natural forces at work in this dynamic state. Covered are issues of climate, geology, botany, and zoology. An excellent book for the naturalist.

Maine Geographic: Coastal Islands—A Guide to Exploring Maine's Offshore Isles. Bernie Monegain, DeLorme Publishing, 1985, 48 pages, paper, $2.95.

This little guide will give you a good orientation to the Maine islands you might explore: their history, how you can reach them, where you can stay, places to eat, and things to see and do. Only the major islands are included, but it is a good overview.

Maine Geographic: Day Trips with Children. Barbara Feller-Roth, DeLorme Publishing, 1987, paper, $2.95.

Dozens of great ideas for day trips with the kids: a trip to a fish hatchery, panning for gold, the Children's Museum of Maine, a living history center, an oceanarium, and lots more.

Maine Geographic: Historic Sites—A Guide to Maine's Museums, Period Homes and Forts. Bernie Monegain, DeLorme Publishing, 1987, 48 pages, paper, $2.95.

An excellent, compact compendium of historic sites, both well known and out of the way. Each site is described briefly with interesting historical notes. Location, hours, and admission charges are noted.

Maine Geographic: Lighthouses. Barbara Feller-Roth, DeLorme Publishing, 1985, 48 pages, paper, $2.95.

Maine's rugged coastline has many of these famous sentinels to warn away the ships. This interesting booklet describes thirty-nine lighthouses as well as a bit of their history and location.

Maine Itineraries: Discovering the Down East Region. Albert and Miriam d'Amato, Professional Education Services, 1987, 60 pages, paper, $3.50.

Some suggested driving routes along Route 1 between Ellsworth and Calais which concentrate on the scenic, historical, and cultural sites.

Pocket Guide to Maine Outdoors. Eben Thomas, Thorndike Press, 1985, 242 pages, paper, $9.95.

If it happens outdoors, this directory will give you the facts you need—from river trips to cross-country ski resorts, hiking trails to wilderness camps, charter boats to moose watching sites. An amazing amount of practical information.

Tides of Change: A Guide to the Harraseeket District of Freeport, Maine. Bruce Jacobson, Joel Eastman and Anne Bridges, Freeport Historical Society, 1985, 82 pages, paper, $6.95.

A beautifully done guide to this very special area. There is history and other background, walks to take and trails to explore (including nicely drawn maps), facts and figures on populations of old and local flora and fauna. There are even profiles on softshell crab and mackerel as well as some famous local folks. A thoroughly delightful book.

Massachusetts

A.I.A. Guide to Boston. Susan and Michael Southworth, Globe Pequot, 1984, 396 pages, paper, $14.95.

An extensive architectural view of Boston through numerous, well-described tours that bring the city to life. Photographs are extensively used and the maps are clear. This guide is one of the best of its kind.

The Art Museums of New England: Massachusetts. S. Lane Faison, Jr., Godine, 251 pages, paper, $9.95.

One of three superb paperbacks that have been drawn from the single, hardbound *The Art Museums of New England*, which is reviewed under New England.

Beacon Hill: A Walking Tour. A. McVoy McIntyre, Little, Brown, 1975, 118 pages, paper, $8.95.

A well-written architectural and historical guide to this most famous Boston area.

The Berkshire Book: A Complete Guide. Jonathan Sternfield, Countryman Press, 1986, 345 pages, paper, $14.95.

This guidebook focuses on the Berkshires, the popular counties of far western Massachusetts. The coverage is extensive—the restaurant reviews are particularly fine—and includes well-written chapters on all tourists' needs: transportation, lodging, food, culture, recreation, shopping, history, and a very helpful chapter on other practical matters. You won't go wrong with this first-class guide.

Boston Best Guide: An Official Guide to Boston. M. Kennedy Publishing, 1988, 64 pages, paper, $2.50.

A handy quarterly guide to a bit of everything: restaurants, lodging, places of interest, transportation, nightlife, and more.

The Boston Globe Historic Walks in Cambridge (including Harvard, Radcliffe, and M.I.T.). John Harris, Globe Pequot, 1986, 388 pages, paper, $10.95.

The Boston Globe's Historic Walks in Old Boston. John Harris, Globe Pequot, 1982, 352 pages, paper, $9.95.

Two first-class, comprehensive guides to walking tours through the history of old Boston and Cambridge. Clear maps and an excellent narrative make both these books a good choice if you like to stretch your legs and explore.

Boston in Your Pocket. Barron's Educational Series, 1987, 144 pages, paper, $3.95.

One of the small-format In Your Pocket Guides, which is reviewed in more detail under Series Review.

Car-Free in Boston: The Guide to Public Transit in Greater Boston and New England. Association for Public Transportation, 1987 (5th ed.), 160 pages, paper, $3.95.

If you have ever driven in Boston, you will know why this book was written and why you too should be "car free" when you visit. Leave the headaches to someone else; let this comprehensive guide get you there safely and sanely.

The Complete Guide to Boston's Freedom Trail. Charles Bahne, Newtowne Publishing, 1985, 64 pages, paper, $3.95.

A thorough, well-researched, step-by-step guide to this famous walk through history. Following the trail is easy—it's marked with a red line on the sidewalk or red bricks in the pavement—and with this booklet you will also learn a great deal about the origins of an independent America. A clearly drawn map is also included. Excellent.

Exploring Coastal Massachusetts: New Bedford to Salem. Barbara Clayton and Kathleen Whitley, Dodd, Mead, 1983, 437 pages, paper, $14.95.

Historic reviews and well-written guided tours of twenty-one coastal towns and areas. There is plenty of history in places like Plymouth, Salem, Cape Cod, and Boston—you will learn a great deal and have fun doing it. An introductory chapter on architectural styles will help you appreciate more of what you see. Excellent.

Flashmaps Instant Guide to Boston. Random House, 1987, 80 pages, paper, $4.95.

Part of the Flashmaps series, which is reviewed in more detail under Series Reviews.

Greater Boston Park and Recreation Guide. *Mark Primack, Globe Pequot, 1983, 338 pages, paper, $9.95.*

A comprehensive reference book on public parks, beaches, gardens, wildlife refuges, and state parks. There is a lot of information here, but be sure to check the specifics unless a new edition is put out.

Guide to Cape Cod. *Frederick Pratson, 1988, 208 pages, $9.95.*
Guide to Martha's Vineyard. *Polly Burroughs, 1988 (4th ed.), 208 pages, $9.95.*
Guide to Nantucket. *Polly Burroughs, Globe Pequot, 1988 (rev. 4th ed.), 208 pages, paper, $9.95.*

Two superb, sensitively written guides from Polly Burroughs are joined by another excellent and much-needed addition to Globe Pequot's guidebook series on Massachusetts: the *Guide to Cape Cod,* by veteran author Frederick Pratson. All three guides will give you clear, helpful information on how to get there, what to see, where to stay and eat, and activities you can pursue. Burroughs' books include some excellent guided tours and interesting historical notes.

Hassle-free Boston: A Manual for Women. *Mary Maynard and Mary-Lou Dow, Stephen Greene Press, 1984, 212 pages, paper, $7.95.*

Keyed to the woman traveler, there are chapters on hotels and restaurants chosen for their service to women, shopping tips, cultural activities, traveling in the city safely, networking with women's organizations, and more. Definitely a helpful guide if you plan to travel alone. Some specifics may be a little out of date, however.

In and Out of Boston With (or Without) Children. *Bernice Chesler, Globe Pequot, 1982 (4th ed.), 327 pages, paper, $9.95.*

Very popular since its inception in 1966, Chesler's guide is considered by many one of the standards by which others are judged. The focus is on fun and exploration, though there are also sections on food and lodging. There are chapters on animals (zoos, duck feeding, fish), the arts, day trips, tours, exploring on your own, historic sites, museums, and a vast array of recreational opportunities — plus a separate list of 151 things to do and see for free. With this first-class guide, you'll never be at a loss.

Inside Guide to Springfield and the Pioneer Valley. *James O'Connell, Western Mass. Publishers, 1986, 179 pages, paper, $9.95.*

An excellent guide for both visitors and residents, with well-written interpretations of the region's history and culture, a guide to its historic and interesting sites, and an extensive list of restaurants, delis, diners, inns, and ethnic food of every sort.

Irish Pubs of Boston. *Richard Wesson, Boardworks Publishing, 1986, 134 pages, $7.95.*

A good resource guide to fifty pubs—the food they serve, the beers they serve on tap (and there are some good ones!), and when the entertainment begins. There are helpful descriptions and plenty of Irish pub songs so you can join in "When Irish Eyes are Smiling."

The Other Massachusetts—Beyond Boston and Cape Cod: An Explorer's Guide. *Christina Tree, Countryman Press, 1987, 355 pages, paper, $12.95.*

There is more to Massachusetts than Boston and Cape Cod, and Tree leads you there. It is part of the Explorer's Guide series, which is reviewed in more detail under Series Reviews. We anticipate revisions every two to three years.

Uncommon Boston. *Susan Berk and Jill Bloom, Addison-Wesley, 1986, 242 pages, paper, $7.95.*

Berk has made her living leading tours of Boston. In this fine guide, she shares the unexpected pleasures she has found—both off the beaten path and in the travel mainstream. There is history and culture here plus favorite pubs and taverns, "choco-walks" for candy lovers, ice cream dreams, a fine review of "booklover's Boston," and an excellent chapter on children divided into sections for ages 5 to 8 and 9 to 13. A great complement to more standard guides.

Zagat Survey: Boston. *Zagat Survey, 1988, 120 pages, $8.95.*

The new edition is not yet out, so the pages are approximate. Part of the popular Zagat Survey series, which is reviewed in more detail under Series Reviews.

New Hampshire

Roadside Geology of Vermont and New Hampshire. *Bradford Van Diver, Mountain Press, 1987, 230 pages, paper, $9.95.*
Explore the geology passing by! This is a wonderful book for the non-geologist. Part of the Roadside Geology Guide series, which is reviewed in more detail under Series Reviews.

Rhode Island

Exploring Rhode Island: A Visitor's Guide to the Ocean State. *Phyllis Méras, Providence Journal Co,. 1984, 82 pages, paper, $4.95.*
Here are highlights to help you enjoy Rhode Island more— history, sightseeing tips, and walking tours of various towns, including clear directions to each starting point.

Newport: A Tour Guide. *Anne Randall and Robert Foley, Peregrine Press, 1983, 144 pages, paper, $6.95.*
Practical house-to-house walking tours, including photographs and architectural notes on each structure discussed. Very nicely done.

Walks and Rambles in Rhode Island: A Guide to the Natural and Historic Wonders of the Ocean State. *Ken Weber, Backcountry Publications, 1986, 176 pages, paper, $8.95.*
A well-done guide to forty carefully described walks in every corner of the state. Explore the beaches, woods, rocky ravines, and waterfalls hidden from the highway.

Vermont

Famous Vermont Restaurants & Recipes. *Sue Schildge, Schildge Publishing, 1987, 211 pages, paper, $12.95.*
Thirty-four fine Vermont restaurants have contributed some of their best recipes to this guide/recipe book. Each restaurant is nicely reviewed, clear directions are given, and there are even some notes on what to see in the area. If you like to choose your dining spot by its recipes, this is your chance. Nicely done.

Roadside Geology of Vermont and New Hampshire. *Bradford Van Diver, Mountain Press, 1987, 230 pages, paper, $9.95.*

Geology along the highway for the non-geologist. Part of the excellent Roadside Geology Guides series, which is reviewed in more detail under Series Reviews.

Roadside History of Vermont. Peter Jennison, Mountain Press Publishing Co., 1989, 265 pages, paper, $12.95.

A lively, nicely illustrated companion to driving in the Green Mountain State. The only handy, readable, once-over-lightly Vermont history available.

Vermont: An Explorer's Guide. Christina Tree and Peter Jennison, Countryman Press, 1990 (4th ed.), 322 pages, paper, $11.95.

Another superb guide in the excellent Explorer's Guides series, which is reviewed in more detail under Series Reviews. Updated every two to three years.

Vermont Golf Courses: A Player's Guide. Bob Labbance and David Cornwell, New England Press, 1987, 144 pages, paper, $12.95.

Helpful information on all fifty golf courses open to the public in Vermont. Each is given a good overview, including a drawing of the course layout as well as information on fees, each course's season, and driving directions. A handy summary for the golfer looking for a place to tee off.

Vermont on $500 a Day (More or Less). Peter Jennison, Countryman Press, 1987, 119 pages, paper, $10.

Who could resist looking at a guide with such a title? Admittedly, you will have to work pretty hard to spend that kind of money every day, but you can come close if you take advantage of Tennison's compilation of the very best places to stay, dine, play, and shop in the Green Mountain State. (As he says, it will probably be the shopping that gets you to your spending goal.) Seriously though, if you are lucky enough to have a substantial travel budget, why not enjoy these fantastic, wonderfully described hotels, restaurants, and shops? You can't take it with you. Excellent.

Series Reviews

Explorer's Guides

The first thing that strikes you about the three books of the Explorer's Guide series is their friendly tone. There is this little voice behind all the information that keeps saying, "Come on, let's go." This encouragement to head on out and really explore regions is infectious. And once you are there, the guides will point you in the right direction—while still leaving plenty of room for you to pick and choose. You will learn about the possibilities: where to swim or rent a bike or cross-country ski, the friendly lodging spots in town, where to grab a snack or sit down to a real dinner, or buy an antique. The descriptions are informative, and even when the words are few—as, for example, about a particular eating establishment—you trust that the authors have actually eaten there and enjoyed it and that you will too. That seems to be the basic feeling: the authors feel like friends. And if your friends recommend a place, well, you just know it's going to be good.

Flashmaps

Here is another series where a premium is placed on space. Each title, only 80 to 100 pages long, slips easily into a purse or coat pocket yet includes a substantial amount of information on a variety of topics that will be of interest after you have settled into your hotel and are ready to venture out: restaurants, theaters, transportation, libraries, whatever. The "flashmaps" are numerous single-subject maps that plot all the various locations. The style is utilitarian, the data far from comprehensive, but these little guides are nonetheless quite useful. And they are updated annually so the facts should be as current as possible.

In-Your-Pocket Guides

If you put a premium on the size of your guide, one series that packs a considerable amount of information into a small space is the Barron's In Your Pocket series. For a mere $3.95 you get a very handy directory to restaurants, hotels, museums, theaters, stores, nightlife, sightseeing, and important services. Obviously, there isn't as much in one of these small guides as in one ten times its weight, but, for the money, they have a lot to offer.

Roadside Geology Guides

One family member refers to her experience of taking a geology class in college as the time she took Rocks. Obviously she didn't have the pleasure of using one of the volumes in this delightful series. Even if taking Rocks was the epitome of boredom for you as well, there will always be that occasional thought as the car moves through a cut in the highway, "Gee, I wonder what all those colored layers are." This geology series is specifically directed at what you see from your car window (or what you can see if you take the time to pull over and take a look).

These guides are written for the average person, too. No need to know all those multisyllabic words. Each book is regionally organized by highway, and they are totally fascinating. We recommend them highly. We may even give a copy to our rock expert in the family.

Sierra Club National Parks Guides

Since the Sierra Club was founded by John Muir, who fought so hard to create the magnificent Yosemite National Park (among other battles), it should come as no surprise that this series is of a quality that would make him proud. Each book is chock full of information on the National Parks in the region — their history, facilities, points of interest, hiking paths, natural history, geology, trips and tours to take, food, lodging, and much, much more. Plus a slew of beautiful photos. Very well done.

Sierra Club Naturalist's Guides

For those of you who are particularly interested in geology, natural history, and the flora and fauna of a particular region, the Sierra Club series represents a fine way to expand your horizon. The materials presented are well organized, well written, and fascinating to consider. Why not learn something more about the natural things around you on your next trip? These are first-rate guides whether you are serious about your natural history or just like to look up the occasional fact.

Zagat Survey

The Zagat Survey is conceived and executed differently from most restaurant guides. Instead of one person's opinion on a particular restaurant, this survey employs thousands of people —people like you— to provide the factual information by which each establishment is judged. For example, the 1988 New York survey involved 3,500 people dining out an average of 3.6 times a week. That's over 12,000 meals a week and 600,000 meals a year—a whole lot more than any one reviewer could conceivably cover, obviously. And anyone can participate. The guidebook tells you how to get involved. The sum total of all these meals leads to a rating system that grades food, decor, and service on a scale from 0 to 30. A separate cost column estimates the price of one dinner (including one drink and the tip). A short commentary is also provided, and additional charts rate favorite restaurants, best buys, top food, top decor, and top spots by cuisine. Here is the common man's opinion— collectively. A very popular way to choose a restaurant in the major cities the Zagat covers. Well done.

Appendixes

Bargains

Canoeing

State	Place/Page
	Weatherby's, The Fisherman's Resort 338
NH	The Gilman Tavern 60
	Haverhill Inn 61
	Loch Lyme Lodge and Cottages 109
	The Notchland Inn 283
	Pick Point Lodge 220
	Pleasant Lake Inn 222
	Riverside Inn 80
	Rockhouse Mountain Farm Inn 123
	Waterville Valley Resort 342
VT	Eagle Lodge 314
	Echo Lake Inn 222
	Inwood Manor 84
	Mountain Top Inn 165
	Rutledge Inn & Cottages 115
	Shore Acres Inn and Restaurant 226
	Silver Maple Lodge 116
	The Shoreham Inn and Country Store 67

Golf

State	Place/Page
MA	Chatham Bars Inn 179
	New Seabury Resort, Cape Cod 340
ME	Black Point Inn 173
	Rock Gardens Inn 303
	Sugarloaf/USA 339
NH	The Balsams Grand Resort Hotel 180
	The Mount Washington Hotel and Resort 183
VT	Bolton Valley Resort 344
	Mountain Top Inn 165
	The Sugarbush Inn 166
	Topnotch at Stowe 167
	The Villages at Killington 346
	Woodstock Inn & Resort 168

Groups

State	Place/Page
MA	River Bend Farm 57
	Stump Sprouts 310
ME	The Bethel Inn & Country Club 172
	Sunday River Inn 309

State	Place/Page
NH	Wonderwell 284
VT	Mad River Barn 318
	Old Cutter Inn 321
	Tennis Village 117

Horseback Riding

State	Place/Page
ME	Rockhouse Mountain Farm Inn 123
NH	The Mount Washington Hotel and Resort 183
	Waterville Valley Resort 342
VT	Edson Hill Manor 286
	Harvey's Mountain View Inn 125
	The Inn at Weathersfield 160
	Kedron Valley Inn 85
	Mountain Top Inn 165
	Rodgers' Dairy Farm 128
	Saxtons River Inn 364
	Topnotch at Stowe 167
	West River Lodge 94

Pets Welcome with Permission

State	Place/Page
CT	Old Lyme Inn 144
	Tollgate Hill Inn and Restaurant 69
MA	The Charles Hotel at Harvard Square 40
	Deerfield Inn 352
	Hotel Meridien 32
	Point Way Inn 205
	Windsor House 252
ME	The Birches 332
	Bosebuck Mountain Camps 333
	The Captain Jefferds Inn 261
	Chesuncook Lake House and Cottages 334
	The Colony 176
	The Herbert Hotel 350
	Hiram Blake Camp 101
	Londonderry Inn 52
	Tootsie's Bed and Breakfast 304
	Trailing Yew 194
	Weatherby's, The Fisherman's Resort 338
NH	Dexter's Inn and Tennis Club 79

State	Place/Page
	Hanover Inn 45
	Loch Lyme Lodge and Cottages 109
	Philbrook Farm Inn 110
VT	Berkson Farms 124
	Bolton Valley Resort 344
	The Darling Family Inn 285
	Green Mountain Inn 360
	Harvey's Mountain View Inn 125
	Millbrook Inn (summer) 161
	The Old Tavern at Grafton 363
	Shore Acres Inn and Restaurant 226
	Topnotch at Stowe 167

Smoking Not Permitted

State	Place/Page
MA	Addison Choate Inn 238
	Canterbury Farm Bed and Breakfast 55
	Elling's Guest House 240
	Mostly Hall 280
	Windfields Farm 58
ME	Blue Hill Inn 147
	Harbourside Inn 263
	The Keeper's House 188
	The Newcastle Inn 149
	Northern Pines Health Resort 326
	The Owl and Turtle Harborview Rooms 234
NH	Follansbee Inn 219
	Moose Mountain Lodge 311
	Olde Orchard Inn 62
	Partridge Brook Inn 63
VT	Echo Lake Inn 222
	Hickory Ridge House 65
	Knoll Farm Country Inn 126
	The Rabbit Hill Inn 87
	Wildflower Inn 119

Swimming Pool (Indoors)

State	Place/Page
CT	Norwich Inn, Spa and Villas 324
MA	Boston Harbor Hotel at Rowes Wharf 27

Tennis

Index

Best Places Report

We appreciate any information you can supply about the quality of the lodging. Detailed information about the building, furniture, service, food, and setting is most important. Describe as many rooms as you can, including living rooms, dining rooms, other common rooms, and of course bedrooms. A note about activities and nearby sights would be helpful. Tell us what category you think the place belongs in and why. Finally, how did you hear about the place, and how long have you been going there?

We will be happy to send you a free copy of the next edition of the book if we use your suggestion.

To: Chris Paddock
     Best Places to Stay in New England
     The Harvard Common Press
     535 Albany Street
     Boston, Massachusetts 02118

Name of hotel _____

Telephone _____

Address _____

_____ Zip _____

_____

Description _____

_____

_____

_____

_____

_____

_____

Your Name _____

Telephone _____

Address _____

_____ Zip _____

_____

Best Places Report

We appreciate any information you can supply about the quality of the lodging. Detailed information about the building, furniture, service, food, and setting is most important. Describe as many rooms as you can, including living rooms, dining rooms, other common rooms, and of course bedrooms. A note about activities and nearby sights would be helpful. Tell us what category you think the place belongs in and why. Finally, how did you hear about the place, and how long have you been going there?

We will be happy to send you a free copy of the next edition of the book if we use your suggestion.

To: Chris Paddock
      Best Places to Stay in New England
      The Harvard Common Press
      535 Albany Street
      Boston, Massachusetts 02118

Name of hotel _____

Telephone _____

Address _____

_____ Zip _____

_____

Description _____

_____

_____

_____

_____

_____

_____

Your Name _____

Telephone _____

Address _____

_____ Zip _____

_____